NATIONAL GEOGRAPHIC

# OUR WORLD

NATIONAL GEOGRAPHIC LEARNING

CENGAGE Learning®

Australia • Brazil • Japan • Korea • Mexico • Singapore • Spain • United Kingdom • United States

NATIONAL GEOGRAPHIC

# OUR WORLD

## Table of Contents

## Introduction

*Our World*, a six-level primary series from National Geographic Learning, uses real-world content, stunning photographs and video from National Geographic, and a variety of interactive digital resources to fully engage and motivate students as they learn about the world in English. Young learners will be captivated by the beautiful photography and high-interest content relevant to their world as they learn about people and places from across the globe. *Our World* is unique in the way that it brings the real world, with all its beauty and diversity, into the English language classroom.

# STUDENT BOOK
## Walk-through

## UNIT OPENER

The Unit Opener uses high-interest photographs to engage students, present the unit theme, and provide opportunities for speaking and listening.

A goal-setting activity focuses student attention.

A teacher-led warm-up activity provides suggestions for pre-teaching of unit themes and target structures.

Image captions provide useful cultural and geographic information for teachers to discuss with learners.

## RESOURCES

### Lesson Planner with Audio CD and Teacher's Resource CD-ROM

The ***Our World* Lesson Planner,** with Class Audio CD and Teacher's Resource CD-ROM, provides everything needed to successfully plan, teach, and supplement lessons, including:

- a detailed scope and sequence
- explicit instructions on how best to develop students' awareness of vocabulary and grammar, how to use songs in the classroom and how to teach the four skills of listening, speaking, reading and writing
- answer keys and audio scripts for all activities in the Student Book and Workbook
- support for teaching English in English
- teaching tips for teaching vocabulary and grammar and for using the *Our World* Video and the Classroom Presentation Tool
- an **Audio CD** containing recordings of all exercises, activities, and readings in the Student Book

The **Teacher's Resource CD-ROM,** provided with the *Our World* Lesson Planner supplies additional teaching resources including:

- pacing guides for easy lesson planning
- printable worksheets and templates for in-class games and activities
- customizable Home-School Connection Letters

# VOCABULARY 1

Target vocabulary is presented visually, using photographs and photo-realistic art, to create interest and enhance retention.

Mascots model dialogues which help students use target language to communicate.

All target language is recorded on audio CDs to help students with pronunciation and practice.

## *Our World* Video

Each ***Our World* Video** is 20 minutes of fun-filled, fully integrated content that includes:

- vocabulary and language presentation and review
- original songs
- games
- inspiring, real-world video, and
- *Our World* Readers Story Time

Presented in highly manageable 3–5 minute clips, the *Our World* Video can be used before, during, or after instruction to preview, support, and review. *Our World* Videos are available on a Video DVD, and in the Classroom Presentation Tool DVD.

## SONG

A unit song supports the unit theme. Lyrics incorporate unit target vocabulary and grammar. Each easily learned and remembered song models natural rhythm and intonation.

After the first presentation, songs can be reused throughout a unit. Point-of-use suggestions in the Lesson Planner provide opportunities for reuse and recycling.

Follow-up activities provide opportunities to use the song for group and pair work.

## RESOURCES

### Audio CD

The ***Our World* Audio CD** provides the audio content necessary to all Student Book content, including:

- language presentation and review
- original songs
- readings
- games and activities

# GRAMMAR 1

Grammar lessons include natural examples of real-world language.

A variety of tasks allows learners to use the four skills (Reading, Writing, Listening, Speaking) to practice grammar.

## Workbook

The ***Our World* Workbook** contains exercises and activities that reinforce and consolidate Student Book instruction, and include listening, speaking, reading, writing, grammar, and vocabulary activities.

The workbook includes:

- 12 pages of skills practice and activities, as well as additional readings, for each unit
- unit Review sections
- practice with English pronunciation and sound-spelling relationships
- audio for all listening comprehension and Review sections, provided on an Audio CD bound in with the Workbook, or accessed online through myNGconnect

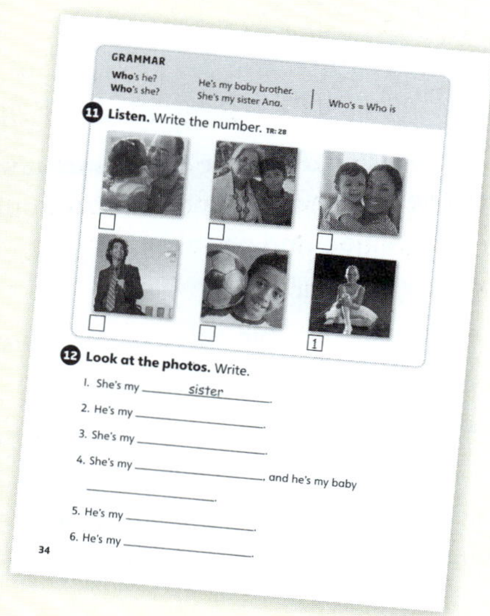

# VOCABULARY 2/GRAMMAR 2

Games and tasks provide independent practice and reinforce target structures.

Additional thematic vocabulary and relevant grammar is presented through photographs and illustrations. Group and pair work gives learners the chance to use structures in conversation as they collaborate with classmates.

Sticker activities in each unit provide reward, motivation, and interactive practice.

## RESOURCES

### *Our World* Picture Cards including the Sounds of English

The ***Our World*** **Picture Cards including the Sounds of English** provide additional support for vocabulary and English pronunciation and phonics.

Picture Cards include:

- full color, double-sided picture cards for target vocabulary.

Sounds of English Cards include:

- individual and contrasted English sounds with related images and spellings.

The cards and audio are also available online through myNGconnect.

# CONTENT READING

Real-world content readings develop language through topics such as science, nature, history, art, culture, music and sport.

Infographics show factual information in fun and sometimes surprising ways.

Graphic organizers help students collect, organize, and visualize information.

## Our World Readers

The ***Our World* Readers** are six levels of original stories, classic folk tales, myths, and non-fiction selections from around the globe. A graded Reader is available to support the theme and language of each unit in the Student Book. Each Reader includes additional fun facts and activities related to the story and unit theme. All Readers are available as "Story Time" in the *Our World* Video or on the **Story Time DVDs.**

# WRITING AND VALUES

Written models provide examples of different types and forms of writing for students to follow.

National Geographic *Our World* pages introduce learners to common values such as fair play, respect for others, caring for our planet, looking after animals, and staying healthy.

## RESOURCES

### Poster Sets

Nine full-color posters bring beautiful photography into the classroom, reinforce the unit theme, and feature National Geographic *Our World* values.

# PROJECT WORK

A variety of projects build 21st century skills through independent research, discussion, presentations, craft, design, and explaining ideas and opinions.

Clear guidance and strong visual support is provided for learners through each project.

Project work is realistic and attainable and instills a sense of achievement in learners. Completed projects serve as tangible evidence of student learning.

'Now I can...' statements refer back to the unit goals. Learners can use the statements to measure and demonstrate their knowledge.

## Assessment Book with Audio CD

The ***Our World*** **Assessment Book** provides teachers with the tools they need to place their learners within the correct level of *Our World*, plan their lessons based on what students already know, and assess students' comprehension of and progress through the content of the Student Book.

Each Assessment Book includes photocopiable Quizzes and Mastery and Final Tests, as well as additional resources, including:

- an *Our World* Placement Test and level Pre-Tests (Diagnostic Tests which help determine students' language ability)
- Listening and Speaking scripts which provide guidance for the listening and speaking portions of the quizzes and tests
- Answer Keys
- an Audio CD, with recorded scripts for all of the quizzes and tests.

## Assessment CD-ROM with Exam*View*©

With the ***Our World*** **Assessment CD-ROM** with Exam*View*©, all of the quizzes and tests found in the Assessment Book can be quickly and easily generated and customized, making it easy to assess whether teaching objectives have been met.

# CLASSROOM PRESENTATION TOOL

A **Classroom Presentation Tool**, provided on DVD, is available for each level of *Our World*. The Classroom Presentation Tool integrates a variety of teaching resources, including video, songs, games, language presentations, and student activities and can easily be used with a computer or Interactive White Board (IWB). For each unit, the DVD includes:

- interactive unit-opening activities that provide the setting for each unit's theme
- presentation of target vocabulary and grammar, through video and animation
- fun classroom activities that practice what has just been presented
- songs presented in two ways: as a video with a singing host, and as a karaoke-style sing-along
- reading activities that support Reading selections
- editing activities that support Writing instruction

# *OUR WORLD* STUDENT ACTIVITIES CD-ROM

*Our World* student activities, provided on a **Student Activities CD-ROM** bound with the Student Book or accessed online through myNGconnect, are fun, engaging, game-like activities that reinforce and expand on Student Book content. Each unit has two Vocabulary and Grammar activities, as well as a Reading activity.

# myNGconnect

Teachers and students can find student activities, as well as Student Book and Workbook audio online at **myNGconnect**.

# PROFESSIONAL DEVELOPMENT

To ensure that instructors are able to improve their classroom practice and get the most out of the *Our World* teaching resources, Dr. Joan Kang Shin, a respected trainer of young learner teachers in over 100 countries and series editor for *Our World*, has developed the ***Our World* Professional Development Program.**

## Professional Development Video

Using short videos of real classrooms and interviews with teachers from around the world, the **Professional Development Video** program, available on DVD, provides useful insights and practical advice on the following topics:

- developmentally-appropriate activities
- managing classrooms for effective learning
- planning successful lessons
- 21st-Century skills

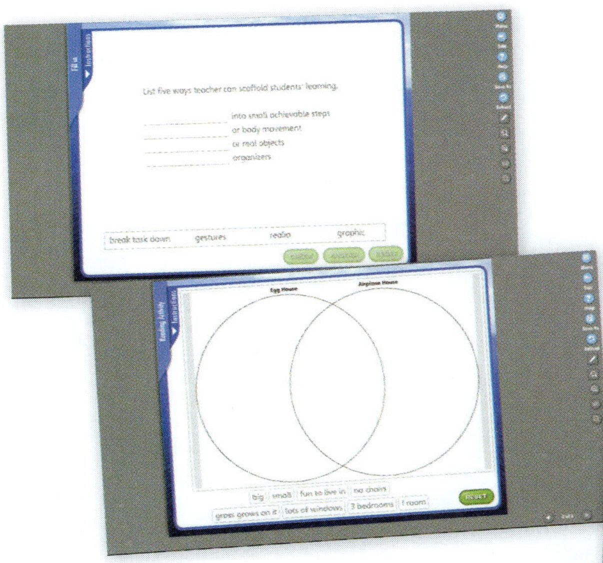


## Professional Development Classroom Presentation Tool

The **Professional Development Classroom Presentation Tool**, available on DVD, can be used to support formal training sessions and presentations on the topics in the Professional Development Video program.

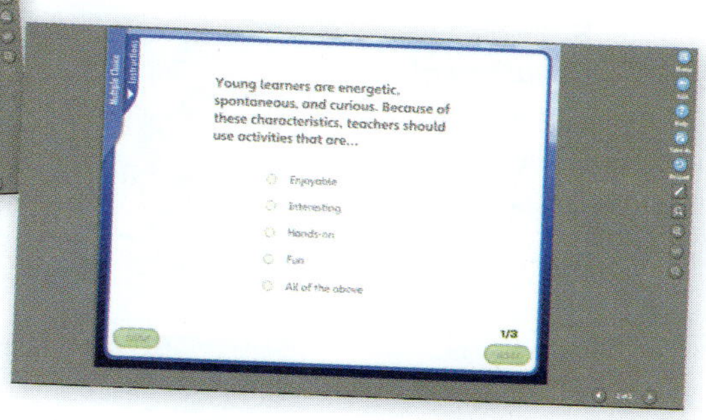

# TEACHING WITH *OUR WORLD*

## *Our World* Philosophy

The *Our World* series reflects key concepts and principles of English language teaching and learning.

• Students learn through a process of constructing meaning. They are active learners who try to make sense of their world through interaction in personal, social, and academic contexts. As they do, they gradually modify their understanding of how both the world and language work.

• Activities designed for young learners must provide multiple opportunities for understanding and construction of meaning at a level appropriate to the emotional and intellectual stages of the students' development.

• Students learn effectively when they are challenged just one step beyond their current stages of cognitive and language development. They most often need support from a knowledgeable person at this time to successfully understand and incorporate new information.

• Goal-oriented learning contributes to young learners' success. In addition to the larger goals of educating children to be responsible global citizens in the 21st century and to be knowledgeable and caring stewards of our planet, providing explicit language-learning goals helps learners understand the purpose of the activities they carry out. Young learners then have the opportunity to compare their outcomes to the original goals, important in judging their own progress.

• Learning about the world through theme-based teaching benefits young learners, as different topics provide informational structure and a meaningful basis for exploration through a variety of language learning tasks. Learning is enriched through activities that expand knowledge of the world and its cultures, people, and places.

• Addressing the needs of the whole child in the language class includes attention to learning styles, learning strategies, critical thinking skills, 21st century skills, and universal cultural values.

• In order to accurately evaluate progress, assessment of young learners must go beyond traditional paper-and-pencil tests. Multiple opportunities for concept checking and performance assessment provide different ways to determine students' depth of learning. Young learners also benefit from peer- and self-assessment.

## *Our World* Content

### Global Citizenship

To empower young learners for the 21st century, teachers of English as a foreign language must understand the global importance of English, as well as what it means to be a global citizen. It is widely recognized that English is the world's *lingua franca*. English is used internationally as the language for science, technology, business, trade, tourism, diplomacy, and global problem solving. Our children will grow up communicating in English with people from countries all around the world. If they are to grow up to become global citizens, able to interact with people from diverse cultures, they must be exposed to real-world content that helps them understand other people and cultures.

*Our World* uses real-world and multicultural content to help young learners grow up to become successful

global citizens. Dramatic photos from around the world spark their curiosity and broaden their perspective by teaching them about the planet and different cultures. Through National Geographic images and content, young learners explore other people, places, and societies and learn to care about our fascinating and ever-changing world. Their increased understanding of the world and their ability to communicate in English across cultures will help them be better prepared to actively and successfully participate in the world of the future.

## Multicultural Materials

When teaching English as a global language, it is important to bring materials that represent different cultures into the classroom. Students are very open to learning about other cultures, and so it makes sense to take advantage of their natural curiosity and openness and expose them to different customs, traditions, and ways of life. Learning about diverse cultures is the first step toward communicating successfully with people around the world using English as a global language. *Our World* incorporates content from other cultures in every unit. For example, in the Book 5 unit called "Arts Lost and Found," students learn about different traditions and art forms from other cultures, including storytelling through dancing in Laos, a jaguar rain dance in Mexico, cloth weaving in Ghana, and the 2000-year-old Chinese tradition of dragon boat racing.

## Cultural Connections

It's also important to connect young learners to their home cultures in the English language classroom. Making connections to the local culture will help young learners relate to the content and build a stronger understanding of themselves and their place in the world. In addition, learning to express aspects of their own culture in English is another step toward effectively using English as a global language. *Our World* helps young learners appreciate their own culture and encourages them to keep their culture strong.

## Global Values

Each unit in *Our World* has a National Geographic values page that connects to the real-world content presented in the unit. These pages promote universally recognized values for students, such as loving your family, being a good sport, and taking care of others. For example, in the Book 2 unit called"Awesome Animals," the National Geographic values page teaches students to respect animals. In upper levels, the National Geographic values page is titled "Mission," and highlights the work and words of a real-life National Geographic explorer. These explorers, like Aparajita Datta in Book 4 and Elizabeth Kapu'uwailani Lindsey in Book 5, are from different parts of the world and contribute to the betterment of our planet. These pages bring more real-world content to the classroom, and inspire young learners to develop their curiosity and to value their own cultural traditions as well as those of others.

## Learning English through "Real-World" Content

The *Our World* series takes into account current research and approaches in teaching language to young learners. Students learn language and content at the same time, so it's natural and authentic to incorporate academic content into the English language classroom. Integrating content from different areas such as Art, Science, and Social Studies makes language learning more interesting and engaging. It will also help prepare young learners who may eventually study these subjects in English.

Contextualizing language instruction by integrating it with other learning provides opportunities to reinforce in English the academic skills and knowledge learned in other classes. A framework for this type of lesson should include four stages:

- ***Processing text***

This includes the use of texts that incorporate visual and text-structure markers such as heading and sub-heading, as well as features like bold or italic text for emphasis.

- ***Identification and organization of knowledge***

This includes the use of graphic organizers such as tree diagrams, timelines, flow charts, and tables.

- ***Language identification***

This includes the use of language features that help students to reproduce core content knowledge in their own words, such as the language of comparison and contrast, cause and effect, and speculation; as well as features such as collocations, subject-specific vocabulary, and academic vocabulary.

- ***Tasks for students***

This includes the use of a variety of learner-appropriate tasks, both receptive and productive. *Our World* uses subject area content as the basis for motivating students to learn English and to support what they are learning in other areas of their curriculum. Each unit has a reading page that integrates real–world content from various subject areas and teaches academic skills. For example, the Book 2 unit "Fun in Class" focuses on language for the classroom. The vocabulary includes various actions for classroom activities, such as reading, writing, counting, coloring, cutting, drawing, and gluing, as well as classroom objects like scissors, markers, glue, and notebooks. The reading content, called "Paper Art," describes the art of paper cutting in China and Mexico. This is cultural content that also integrates art and social studies. In addition, the comprehension activities include a graphic organizer that shows the similarities and differences between paper art in China and Mexico, as well as a counting activity that integrates math.

## 21st Century Skills

Today's students are growing up in an interconnected world. As English language teachers, it is our job to help them become responsible global citizens and leaders of the future. The Framework for 21st Century Learning deals with "the skills, knowledge, and expertise students must master to succeed in work and life; it is a blend of content knowledge, specific skills, expertise, and literacies." These skills can be categorized in four ways:

- ***Ways of working***

Students need to be able to communicate clearly and collaborate effectively. *Our World* helps students use the vocabulary and language structures they are learning to both communicate about real-world content and collaborate on activities and projects that allow them to apply the English they are acquiring in meaningful ways.

- ***Ways of thinking***

Students also need to think creatively and critically. They need opportunities to learn how to make decisions and problem solve. *Our World* challenges them to do so. For example, in Book 5 students create musical instruments from recycled materials and discuss how people in their community can reduce their human footprint. In Book 6, students learn to analyze techniques advertisers use to influence shopping behavior, brainstorm how to conserve water at school, and discuss the importance of local history and how to value it.

**• *Tools for working***

English students today aren't just learning English. They are preparing to enter a competitive global workforce. In order to be ready for the future, they need to be able to navigate technology and to extract information from many forms of media. They also need to acquire technology literacy, information literacy, and visual literacy. All of these needs are addressed in the *Our World* Student Books, comprehensive video program, and interactive technology.

**• *Skills for living in the world***

It's critically important for students to develop awareness of the skills and qualities that will help them achieve success in their future lives and careers. In *Our World*, young learners are introduced in age-appropriate ways to concepts such as openness to new ideas and experiences, adaptability, and initiative. They learn about 21st century professions such as cyborg anthropologist, and National Geographic Explorers are presented as potential role models.

Living in the world also encompasses the idea of personal and social responsibility. On a personal level, younger *Our World* students learn about taking care of themselves and other beings. Older students discuss how they as individuals can make changes or adopt new behaviors for their greater good. On a social level, younger *Our World* students explore ways of linking to their local community, such as exploring where they live and participating in local events. As local citizens, older students interact with their community through activities such as planning and executing events to protect the environment, conducting interviews, and creating a local brochure for tourists.

Personal and social responsibility play a large part in students' preparation for global citizenship as well. Students must commit to developing intercultural competence by building their knowledge of global cultures, by acquiring skills that enhance their interactions, and by refining their attitudes regarding cultural differences and customs. They must be willing to see the world from other points of view, and to understand and respect cultural behaviors.

Throughout the *Our World* series, young learners are introduced to people, places, and cultures from around the world. At the same time students are learning to recognize cultural similarities and appreciate differences, they are also encouraged to express their own culture in English as a first step to building their intercultural awareness and competence. In short, *Our World* prepares students to be curious, engaged, and well-informed citizens of the 21st century.

## Visual Literacy

Visual literacy is a necessary skill for the 21st century, which is increasingly image-, media-, and technology-driven. In the past, the term "literacy" referred to being able to read and write, but today it includes the interpretation of various kinds of texts in print and media. Visual literacy is the ability to construct meaning from images such as photos, illustrations, graphic organizers, signs, symbols, information graphics, and video.

Brain-based research shows that 80-90% of the information we take in is visual. Learning a language, then, is not only reading and writing words; it is also being able to understand visual information and communicate it to others. An additional benefit of learning information simultaneously through text and visuals is that it can dramatically improve retention and recall. *Our World* uses a variety of images to help young learners understand text and organize information; some examples are tables and charts, diagrams, mind maps, T-charts, maps, bar graphs, calendars, timelines, line graphs, Venn diagrams, cause and effect arrows, and pie charts.

National Geographic has the most impressive and highest quality collection of photos and video in the world. These visuals enrich the *Our World* print, video and media components. These materials help young learners become visually literate through imagery that reflects print and media in the real world. This will further help them to succeed as 21st century citizens.

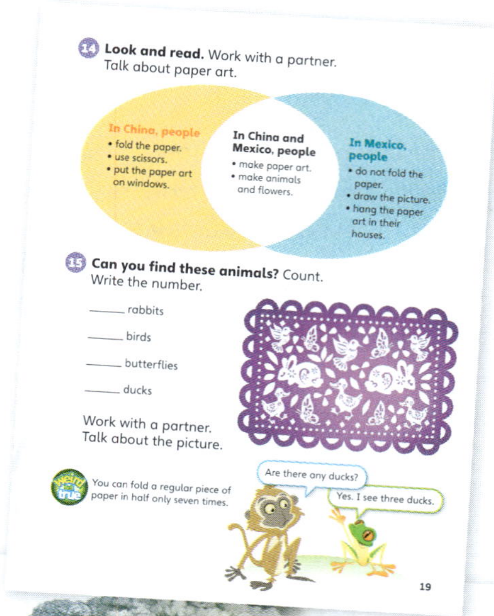
14 Look and read. Work with a partner. Talk about paper art.

| In China, people | In China and Mexico, people | In Mexico, people |
| --- | --- | --- |
| • fold the paper.<br>• use scissors.<br>• put the paper art on windows. | • make paper art.<br>• make animals and flowers. | • do not fold the paper.<br>• draw the picture.<br>• hang the paper art in their houses. |

15 Can you find these animals? Count. Write the number.

____ rabbits

____ birds

____ butterflies

____ ducks

Work with a partner. Talk about the picture.

1 Listen and read. TR: B13

2 Listen and repeat. TR: B14

Go for a walk on a sunny day. The earth seems **calm** under your feet. But **deep** down, it is not. Under the earth's crust, it is so hot that rock is **melted.** This melted rock is called magma.

In some places there are deep **cracks** in the **surface** of the earth. These cracks let magma come to the surface. The magma pushes up the earth's crust. It **creates** a living mountain, a **volcano!**

A volcano **erupts** when magma **explodes** onto the surface. The flow of melted rock is called lava. The lava is thrown into the air and oozes down the volcano. The **heat** of the lava burns everything it touches.

The blast of an eruption throws **steam** into the air. The steam is created from water **inside** the earth. The blast also sends **gases** high into the sky. They make breathing difficult. A volcanic eruption can fill the sky with **ash**. Big eruptions **cover** the land **thick** with ash.

15 Listen and read. TR: A37

### Listening for Life

If extraterrestrials live on other planets, we can't see them. Planets in other solar systems are extremely far away. We can't see the planets, even with our biggest telescopes. But what if the extraterrestrials want to communicate with us? What if they are sending messages? This signal would travel through space. After many years, it might reach our solar system. The signal would be very weak. It would be hidden in the noise from other places in space. We would need special tools to hear it.

Scientists at SETI have made a tool for listening. It uses 42 satellite dishes that are connected together. Scientists plan to have 350 dishes one day. They point all the dishes at the same place in the sky. Then they search for any data they can hear. The dishes can hear very weak signals. For example, they could hear a cell phone on a planet in our solar system. (That's if someone had a cell phone on Jupiter!) The dishes pick up noise from radios on Earth, too. Scientists must be careful to avoid this noise.

We have not heard from an extraterrestrial yet. But is it possible that they are listening to us? If they are, most could not have heard us yet. We have used radios for less than 100 years. That's not much time for the big distances in the universe. In that time, our signal could only reach a small number of stars. Extraterrestrials from nearby solar systems would not hear us for thousands of years.

# Video and Technology

Video is a powerful tool that can bring the world into the classroom and the classroom to life. In learning language, video can be especially valuable because it can provide a real-world context that helps students experience the language in a natural and dynamic way. This will helps them better understand how to use the language and makes learning more fun. The videos in *Our World* are divided into short manageable clips that present the following:

- **vocabulary** through amazing photos
- **grammar** in animated contexts
- **songs** performed by fun hosts
- **video** clips that give examples of real-world communication
- **stories** read by the hosts using images from the *Our World* readers.

***Our World* Video** is flexible. For example, lessons can be presented from the Student Book first and then followed by the corresponding segment in the video to review and check comprehension. Or the video can be used to present the language and then the Student Book can be used to review and practice. Either way, using the video helps contextualize language instruction and engage children in the classroom in fun and meaningful ways.

The **Classroom Presentation Tool** allows the introduction of many types of content, including video, audio, and interactive activities into the classroom using either an interactive white board or a computer with a projector. Learning becomes more active and interactive using this digital classroom tool. For example, young learners love games, and the Classroom Presentation Tool includes games that present and practice the Student Book lessons in new and unique ways. These activities allow for teaching and reteaching that will engage the whole class. With these games, students have opportunities to predict, to think critically, to work in teams, to sing along, and to use English in a safe and motivating environment that sets them up for success.

The computer is an excellent resource for English language learning and teaching. The *Our World* Student Activities, online and on CD-ROMs, encourage language practice through fun game environments that will entertain, inform, and motivate students. For example, they will play soccer against meerkats, puffer fish, polar bears, pigeons, mountain goats, and even alligators. They'll clean up the ocean, feed chameleons, solve puzzles, and explore mysterious mazes, all while practicing and playing with English. Interactive media provide a richer environment for learning and engage young learners in the ways they are used to learning, getting information, and entertaining themselves. More importantly, building students' media and digital literacy skills helps prepare them to use English in the real world in the 21st century.

# Characteristics of Young Learners

In order to teach young learners successfully, it is important to understand how students develop and how they learn. Effective materials reflect gradual growth in ability in the areas of gross and fine motor skills, language, cognition, and socialization. Students of different ages have different levels of development, and it is important that teachers use methods and activities that are appropriate in terms of their students' abilities.

In general, students are very energetic and spontaneous. They do not like to sit still for long periods of time and they have short attention spans. Although they can be easily distracted, they are very curious and will pay attention if the topic is interesting or if the activity is fun and engaging. Although these characteristics can make teaching young learners challenging and even difficult at times, they can also make the young learner classroom joyful and rewarding. *Our World* keeps learners active and engaged by using developmentally appropriate activities that cater to their learning profiles.

## Learning Styles

Young learners tend to process information about the world primarily through their senses. The sensory learning styles are visual, auditory, tactile, and kinesthetic.

- ***Visual learners***

Visual learners notice the details of their surroundings and use color, shape, and position to help them learn and remember information. They understand instructions for activities much better when they are shown what to do rather than told what to do. Visual learners respond well to board work, and to activities involving photos, drawings, flash cards, posters, video, arts and crafts, murals, projects, puzzles, and board games.

- ***Auditory learners***

These students learn and remember information through sound and rhythm. They can memorize information easily and repeat back the text of stories, role plays, and song lyrics after one or two listenings. They understand oral directions for activities and often agree to act them out or repeat them for other students. They do well with listening and pronunciation activities, and enjoy discussions, sound tracks, video and computer games, songs, and chants.

- ***Tactile learners***

As the word *tactile* indicates, these learners use touch and the manipulation of objects to help them process and remember information. They depend on their physical and material surroundings. For example, when they are trying to concentrate, they may flip pencils or play with their hair. To understand instructions, they need to see, hear, and physically carry them out. Tactile learners do well with arts and crafts, flash cards, puzzles, board games, and realia.

- ***Kinesthetic learners***

These students process and remember information through physical movement. Like tactile learners, they also touch and manipulate objects, and they are good at working with their hands. They understand directions for activities much better when they can see, hear, and physically carry them out. They need to release tension through movement, and will look for ways to do so—going to the pencil sharpener or trash basket several times, for example. Kinesthetic learners do well with Total Physical Response (TPR) activities, charades, role plays, puzzles, and board games.

# Skills and Strategies

## Learning Strategies

Strategies are generally defined as behaviors that learners use to understand and complete a task. The use of learning strategies can benefit young learners as well as adults. As described by Ana Chamot and Michael O'Malley, these strategies fall into three categories: metacognitive, cognitive, and social-affective.

- Metacognition is "thinking about thinking." For young learners, this means helping them plan before doing a task. They need to think about the purpose of the task, what information is most important, how they will use the information, what the best way to do the task is, and how much they understand about the task.

- Cognitive strategies include accessing prior knowledge about a topic, seeing how new information connects to the material the student already knows, identifying where more information could be accessed, thinking of good ways to organize the material, and identifying ways to remember the new information.

- Social-affective strategies are especially useful in language classes, as language is social by nature. While using English, young learners can ask for explanations from teachers and classmates, find out how and when they can ask for help, discuss how they can work together with classmates, and how they can get and give feedback.

## Critical Thinking Skills

Critical thinking is a higher order of thought that involves analyzing, evaluating, and synthesizing information. In many young learner classrooms, teachers' questions may be limited to basic comprehension questions (What is the story about? Is it a happy or sad story?) and to display questions (How many planets are there in our solar system? Is the moon hot or cold?). Even though children's analytical abilities are not yet fully developed, teachers can nevertheless design age-appropriate questions that go beyond the surface and require deeper processing on their students' part. Ask questions that bring into play skills such as the following.

| | |
|---|---|
| • ***classifying*** | What are (two) ways you can group together these words? |
| • ***comparing*** | How are (dogs) and (wolves) alike? |
| • ***contrasting*** | How are the (cassowary) and (ostrich) different? |
| • ***getting meaning*** | What clues in this sentence help with the meaning of the word (*ground*)? |
| • ***inferencing*** | Looking at these effects, what do you think is the cause? |
| • ***predicting*** | What will happen when (the volcano erupts)? |
| • ***problem solving*** | What are some ways we can (conserve water at school)? |
| • ***ranking*** | How would you list your (favorite sports) from one to five? |
| • ***sequencing*** | When (planting vegetables), what are the steps in order? |
| • ***using graphic organizers*** | How could you use a graphic organizer to map out the ideas in this reading? |
| • ***visualizing*** | How do you picture (the treasure) in your mind? |

# Creating Successful Lessons

Effective teaching begins with a lesson plan. A lesson is like a long road trip that requires a map: the final destination or goal cannot be reached without carefully planning each stop along the way. These steps help learners reach the lesson objectives successfully, which is the final destination of the trip teachers and students are taking together.

A good lesson plan has many benefits. It helps teachers prepare for class, including gathering or creating the materials needed to make the activities successful. It lays out step-by-step instructions that provide a guide for every moment in class. But most importantly, it requires teachers to define objectives for the lesson, and plan activities in a sequence that will ensure student success.

## Stages of a Lesson

*Our World* uses six steps recognized as the standard for effective language instruction: Warm-up, Presentation, Practice, Application, Extension, and Wrap-up.

- ***Warm-up***

These activities help EFL students switch over from their native language to English, help them remember material from earlier lessons, and help them begin class feeling confident about what they know. Warm-ups create interest and excitement about the topic and prepare learners for the new language input. This new input can be vocabulary, grammar structures, or language functions. Warming up students can involve activating students' prior knowledge of the topic or context, as well as reviewing known language that will be used or recycled in the unit. By helping students see what they already know and connecting the new language to their previous experience, warm-ups prepare them to learn.

- ***Presentation***

After students are warmed up, it is time to present the new language. This means teaching new vocabulary words or new grammatical structures through visuals, realia, examples, or in the context of a song or story. Teachers should take time on this step and provide numerous activities to give lots of meaningful listening and reading input. This will help students gain comprehension of the new language. Use a number of activities that require the four skills to check students' comprehension. For example, use concept checking to see if students know the word *drugstore* by asking quick questions like *Can I buy a bike in a drugstore? What can I buy in a drugstore? Give me an example of a drugstore near here.* Or have students draw a drugstore and write a few lines about what they do and buy in a drugstore. The *Our World* lesson planner suggests multiple activities to present and check comprehension of language to support the activities in the Student Book.

- ***Practice***

An important step in the process of learning, practice focuses on students' first efforts to use the new language. For young learners, especially beginners, the practice is guided, meaning that the students are given the structures and vocabulary needed to produce the language; they are not yet expected to create the language independently. Of course, the goal is to give learners plenty of opportunities to try out the new language in order to prepare them for real communicative contexts. The lesson planner provides suggestions for giving additional support or guidance for the practice stage.

- ***Application***

Applying the new language in a communicative context is a natural step after practice, because it encourages students to act more independently with the language they have practiced previously with more guidance and support. At this stage students should be able to use the new language in a realistic context and to personalize the language with respect to their own lives. Application further develops students' abilities to use language communicatively. The *Our World* Student Books have application activities for each vocabulary and grammar section that encourage students to communicate with each other and apply the language to their lives. The lesson planner provides suggestions to help teachers carry out the application activities successfully.

**• *Extension***

Extension activities are additional communicative activities that help students to use the new language in realistic contexts and to personalize the language. This step is important in that it stretches students' ability to communicate in authentic-like situations. These activities are not in the Student Book, but do provide additional opportunities for real communication among students in the classroom.

For example, if students have just learned expressions of frequency, students can have a conversation with a partner and try to find different things they both do twice a day, three times a week, etc. For further follow-up, they can survey all their classmates and make a class chart.

**• *Wrap-up***

Concluding a lesson or class with a final activity is always important, as students need to leave the class knowing that they have completed an activity and learned something. The Our World lesson planner provides appropriate wrap-up activities for each class. The wrap-up might be a review in the form of a game, song, or chant. It might be a conclusion to a pair work extension activity in which the teacher asks individual students what they learned from their partners. The *Our World* lesson planner provides a wide variety of wrap-up activities for learners of all types.

## Lesson Adjustments

Teachers keep in mind many different elements as they plan their lessons. They identify their objectives and match appropriate activities to them. They plan how they will use their physical space and seating arrangements for individual, pair, and group work. They collect the materials and equipment they will need. They think about time management and pacing. But no matter the plan, teachers know to expect the unexpected as the day's lesson unfolds.

In a classroom full of young learners, there are many factors teachers cannot control. Successful teachers learn to be creative so that they can adapt to unplanned events, whether they be a surprise fire drill, equipment failure, or unexpected student behaviors. This includes adjusting instruction based on students' unique personalities, their mood swings, their varied interests, and their diverse personal, cognitive, and emotional needs.

In mixed-ability classes, for example, teachers spend more time with some students than with others. When this is the case, they have ready a number of other activities for the rest of the class to do. These may include starting homework in class, or choosing something from an activity box that includes worksheets, puzzles, board games, vocabulary cards, comic books in English, and class-produced books. In the *Our World* lesson planner, teachers have many different activities to choose from, including extension activity suggestions that are not in the Student Book. In addition, there are many activities and games in the Classroom Presentation Tool, the CD-ROM, and the video.

## Successful Activities

• ***Activities have meaning and purpose***

Activities for young learners should above all be meaningful and purposeful.

Engaging students in authentic and meaningful contexts helps them recognize and remember language patterns. As Lynn Cameron (2003) wrote, "… children see the foreign language 'from the inside' and try to find meaning in how the language is used in action, in interaction, and with intention, rather than 'from the outside' as a system and form" (p. 107). So instead of presenting language as isolated grammar structures to be analyzed, teachers do well to present language in meaningful contexts. They make sure to provide plenty of opportunities for students to practice the language through both repetition and recycling, and to give students a real purpose to communicate with each other in English.

• ***Activities are supported and scaffolded***

Scaffolding is used to describe the exterior support structure around a building under construction. When the building is finished, the scaffolding is taken away and the building stands on its own. In the same way, teachers have to provide scaffolding to students in order to help them construct knowledge and learn language effectively. *Our World* sets students up for success by supporting and scaffolding the learning process. It is important to break tasks down into small, achievable steps and give students a model to follow. *Our World* teaches language step by step, but the teacher still needs to take the time to make sure students have plenty of ways to show their comprehension of the new language.

• ***Activities are active and hands-on***

*Our World* materials promote the active and hands-on classroom. Because students are kinesthetic learners and like to move their bodies and move around the room, it is important to keep instruction physically active. Students also like to learn by touching and manipulating objects. In other words, students learn by doing. They need to be active and have many hands-on activities that encourage them to interact with objects and visuals. If possible, bring in real objects and incorporate projects that allow students to produce their own creations that further the learning process. Doing artwork, crafts, posters, and projects are great ways for learners to be active and make things with their own two hands.

• ***Activities are enjoyable and interesting***

To teach young learners effectively, language class needs to be enjoyable and interesting. The photographs and artwork in *Our World* will capture students' attention and interest. The units are full of activities that young learners find fun and engaging, such as singing songs, listening to stories, and playing games. There is a song in each unit, as well as games, pair work, and group work that will keep young learners' interest. In addition, the video program and the Classroom Presentation Tool contain a wide variety of motivating and enjoyable activities.

## Repetition and Recycling

Teachers should provide plenty of opportunities to practice the language. Using repetition and recycling is important when working with young learners. Luckily, if there is a fun song, students will ask to sing it again. If there is an interesting story, they will ask to hear it again. Repeating is a natural part of student's learning process. *Our World* provides plenty of opportunities for meaningful repetition, especially if the video program and/or Classroom Presentation Tool is used in conjunction with the Student Book. Students will get the chance to hear, repeat, and use both vocabulary and grammar multiple times.

Recycling is also important to improve young learners' ability to understand the new language structures and use them correctly. Recycling means "to use again." When teachers recycle language, they use it again in another context. Within a unit, the new vocabulary is constantly recycled and used in different contexts in the song, the grammar activities and games, as well as in the reader and storytelling activities.

*Our World* also recycles language from unit to unit and level to level. For example, in one lesson students may learn vocabulary for different clothes. A teacher may recycle this language by teaching about the weather and asking students what to wear when it is hot and sunny or when it is cold and snowy. Recycling helps students increase their proficiency by getting them to use the language in a new context. This makes the learning process more authentic and meaningful.

# Classroom Management

As teachers everywhere know, real learning requires a well-managed classroom. Teachers of young learners need to develop a plan for managing their own classrooms that will keep students engaged and on task, and avoid giving them opportunities to get distracted or out of control. Expectations of proper classroom behavior can vary from culture to culture, but in all cases, effective classroom management goes beyond dealing with misbehavior only.

Many aspects of teaching can affect the behavior of students in the classroom.

- ***Time***

Effective teachers use their class time carefully. They plan the time it takes to greet students and start the class, the duration of each activity, the time spent between activities, the time it takes for student breaks, and the time it takes to assign homework and end the class. They also reserve five minutes or so as extra time to be used as needed during the class. In addition, they keep in mind what is known as "wait time," the amount of time the teacher waits for a student to answer a question. Some teachers count to ten slowly and silently, while others use a watch to allow from three to five seconds. This helps students formulate better quality responses.

- ***Activities and transitions***

It is important to have ready all the materials needed for each activity before class so that young learners don't have time to get restless. Activity instructions are another area that can require advance planning. To keep students' attention, it is a good idea to read all activity instructions before class so that there is time to simplify them and provide a model for learners if necessary.

Moving smoothly from one activity to another requires planning transitions. For the youngest learners, this could be a clapping chant (We are done/That was fun/Now let's do/Another one), visual cues such as a teacher-held stop sign or flipping the light switch on and off three times, or auditory cues such as a whistle or bell. If the previous activity has involved movement, a useful transition to the next activity can be having students close their eyes and rest their heads on their hands for a minute. If the previous activity has been concentrated seat work, a useful transition to the next activity can be having students stand by their desks and "shake out" their hands and legs, or having them jump up and down a few times. For older learners, transitions that link two activities can be language-based. For example, if students have just read about someone's activities last weekend, a teacher may say, "We just read what (David) did last weekend; now we're going to listen to find out what he's doing next weekend."

- ***Classroom rules***

The establishment of rules in the young learner classroom is particularly important because students need rules to function successfully. Teachers need to communicate these rules clearly and simply, and make sure they are consistent in enforcing them, with age-appropriate rewards and sanctions. When possible, allow students to help create the rules and consequences. The teacher and students may come up with rules such as *Be quiet when someone is talking, Raise your hand to talk, Be kind to others, Work hard, Share*, and *Cooperate*. Display the rules on a poster on the classroom wall or provide each student with a copy to keep in their notebooks.

- ***Classroom routines***

Equally important is the establishment of predictable routines. Young learners feel secure when they know what to expect during different stages of the lesson. Routines help them to organize and prepare to learn in English. Common routines include starting the class with a greeting, designating the day's classroom helpers, taking attendance, naming the day and date, establishing objectives, checking homework, dividing the class into pairs or groups, cleaning up the room, assigning homework, and ending the class.

- ***Classroom atmosphere***

Effective teachers take care to build a fair, safe, and supportive classroom climate. As supportive adults rather than friends, they aim for positive relationships with all their students and consciously avoid favoritism. They have high but reasonable expectations and model the values they hope to inspire in their students—kindness, patience, fairness, and respect.

## The 4 Skills: Listening, Speaking, Reading, and Writing

*Our World* provides multiple opportunities for young learners to develop all four skills in a balanced and age-appropriate way.

### Listening

Young learners learn about other people and the world around them primarily through oral interaction. In the classroom they benefit from multiple opportunities to listen to and practice routine language, vocabulary, basic structures, and patterns. And while practicing listening and speaking together is very important, so is a focus on listening-only activities. Some of these activities develop students' discrimination of sounds, words, and sentence boundaries, while others focus on stress, rhythm, and intonation. Songs, chants, and poems are a natural and fun way to practice, too. The Workbook includes a variety of listening activities as well.

In addition, students need practice with basic listening strategies such as listening for the main idea and listening for details. Older learners can listen for sequence (*first, next, then, finally*), for time frames (verb forms signaling present, past, or future time), and for cause and effect (*why, because*), among other strategies.

### Speaking

Listening and speaking interactions are the communicative foundation for language learning. Question and answer exchanges, whether between teacher and student or between student and student, play an important part in the classroom. At first, young learners will rely on modeled language in their exchanges, but it is also important to introduce opportunities for personalized, authentic language use as soon as possible. Gradually move away from display questions (to which students provide already known answers to show their comprehension) such as *What color is your hair?* and *How many students are in our class?* to authentic communication (questions to which the answers are not yet known), such as *Do you have any pets?* and *Did you play soccer today?* Other speaking opportunities include games, group discussions, and project presentations. The more relevant the language is to learners' lives, the more meaningful and memorable it becomes.

*Our World* provides many different speaking models, including work with Basic Interpersonal Communication Skills (BICS) and Cognitive Academic Language Proficiency (CALP) in Books 4–6 on the pages titled *Let's Talk*. In addition, students gain valuable practice with rhythm, stress, and intonation in songs and chants, and with pronunciation and sound discrimination using the Sounds of English cards. The Workbook includes different speaking activities as well.

### Reading

A unique feature of the *Our World* series is the use of engaging content from the world-renowned National Geographic archives. Children are naturally curious about the world around them and will enjoy reading about topics such as copycat animals, chocolate, flesh-eating plants, and pirate shipwrecks. Readings are age-appropriate and provide basic practice in reading strategies such as identifying the main idea, finding details and examples, figuring out meaning from context, and relating texts to graphic organizers.

The Lesson Planner includes a variety of before-, during-, and after-reading tasks that draw students deeper into texts. Before-reading activities help prepare learners for the reading by drawing their attention to titles, headings, photos, and captions; by accessing what they already know about the topic; and by predicting what the reading might include.

During reading, it is useful to train students to ask themselves silent questions such as *Who, When, Where, What, Why,* and *How* and find the answers as they go. They can also underline or highlight information as they read or make brief comments in the margin.

After-reading activities include comprehension questions, but can also include questions that require higher-order thinking, questions that require learners to support their ideas and opinions, summaries, and graphic organizers. Additional readings are found in the Workbook.

In addition, nine *Our World* Readers accompany each of the six levels. These readers are age-appropriate and are designed so that they may be read independently, either in class or at home. Each reader is thematically related to the corresponding Student Book unit, and contains some of the unit target grammar and vocabulary. Texts are an entertaining and informative mix of fiction and non-fiction.

## Writing

Younger learners are systematically introduced to writing beginning in Book 1, where they work at the word level, gradually move into sentence stems, and from there to one to three simple sentences. Students draw and then write about their drawings. In Book 2, young learners are guided to organize and write short paragraphs through answering specific questions. In Book 3, students learn about compound sentences, descriptive words, the parts of a paragraph, complex sentences with *because*, and sequence words. In Levels 1 through 3, a page in each Workbook unit provides additional writing practice.

In Books 4 through 6, older learners are introduced to the concept of paragraph unity, and to different writing genres such as journal entries, blogs, reviews, and paragraphs of opinion, of cause and effect, of contrast, of comparison, of exemplification, of fact and opinion, of persuasion, of classification, and more. Students are guided step by step in the Workbook for each writing assignment in the Student Book. Additional writing tasks are provided in the Workbook as well.

A complete model is provided for each writing task in each unit in Student Books 1 through 6 so that learners have clear, meaningful examples of what they are expected to do. When they are finished, writers read their work to classmates, who listen actively to fill in a chart or take notes. Students are encouraged to give constructive criticism when applicable, pointing out things they liked, found confusing, or wanted to know more about.

Teachers may want students to create individual writing portfolios for evaluation purposes. A writing portfolio is a file or folder of each student's written work, assembled over a period of time. It contains final drafts of assignments, but it may also contain samples of works in other stages of the writing process, such as word maps, outlines, research cards, rough drafts, letters, poems, copies of group-produced work, and inspirational images. The teacher, together with the student, reviews selected work and comments on the student's writing progress.

# Vocabulary

*Our World* helps develop vocabulary through a variety of activities that encourage communication. The target vocabulary items in each unit are presented in thematically related, meaningful contexts, and then recycled several times in different activities and in different components. Active vocabulary consists of words necessary to understand and talk about the unit theme, as well as high-frequency, high-utility items used in real communication relevant to the world of the student.

For younger learners, many items are related to concepts they are exploring in their first language, such as colors, shapes, and numbers. For older learners, vocabulary items are related to their own lives (habits, chores, likes and dislikes), to their relationships (as family members, as friends, as members of the community), and to their studies at school (science, health, language arts, social studies, sports).

Encourage students' active involvement in vocabulary learning through the use of pictures, flashcards, posters, arts and crafts, kinesthetic games, projects, personal dictionaries, word mobiles, and word walls. In addition, when applicable, raise learner awareness of vocabulary strategies such as paraphrase and circumlocution ("the thing you cut paper with," for *scissors*), and familiarize students with the concept of cognates and false cognates.

To clarify meaning, encourage word associations, and teach word collocations such as *have* + noun: *have a good time, have breakfast, have a flat tire, have a toothache, have a quiz.* Have students keep vocabulary notebooks in which they write definitions, use words in sentences, develop word maps, note collocations, and build word groups *(photo, photograph, photographer, photographic, photographically)*. When appropriate, raise awareness of word formation through prefixes and suffixes.

## Grammar

*Our World* presents grammar in age-appropriate, meaning-based ways. Because their analytical skills are not yet fully developed, younger learners gain little from analyzing forms and memorizing rules the way many adults do. They benefit more by seeing many repetitions of a target grammar point in different meaningful contexts, and by using grammar as unanalyzed "chunks" that help them communicate. The Grammar Boxes in the Student Books and Workbooks, then, show target points in meaningful sentences that students can use as models for language production. As learners age and develop cognitively, they are invited to notice certain language features and think about how they function. The oldest learners can keep personal grammar reference notebooks in which they have a page for each grammar point, with examples of form, meaning, and use. They can also record their most frequent errors and write a corrected version of each one in their notebooks.

Grammar practice in the Student Book is supported by additional activities in the Workbook, the Video and the Classroom Presentation Tool.

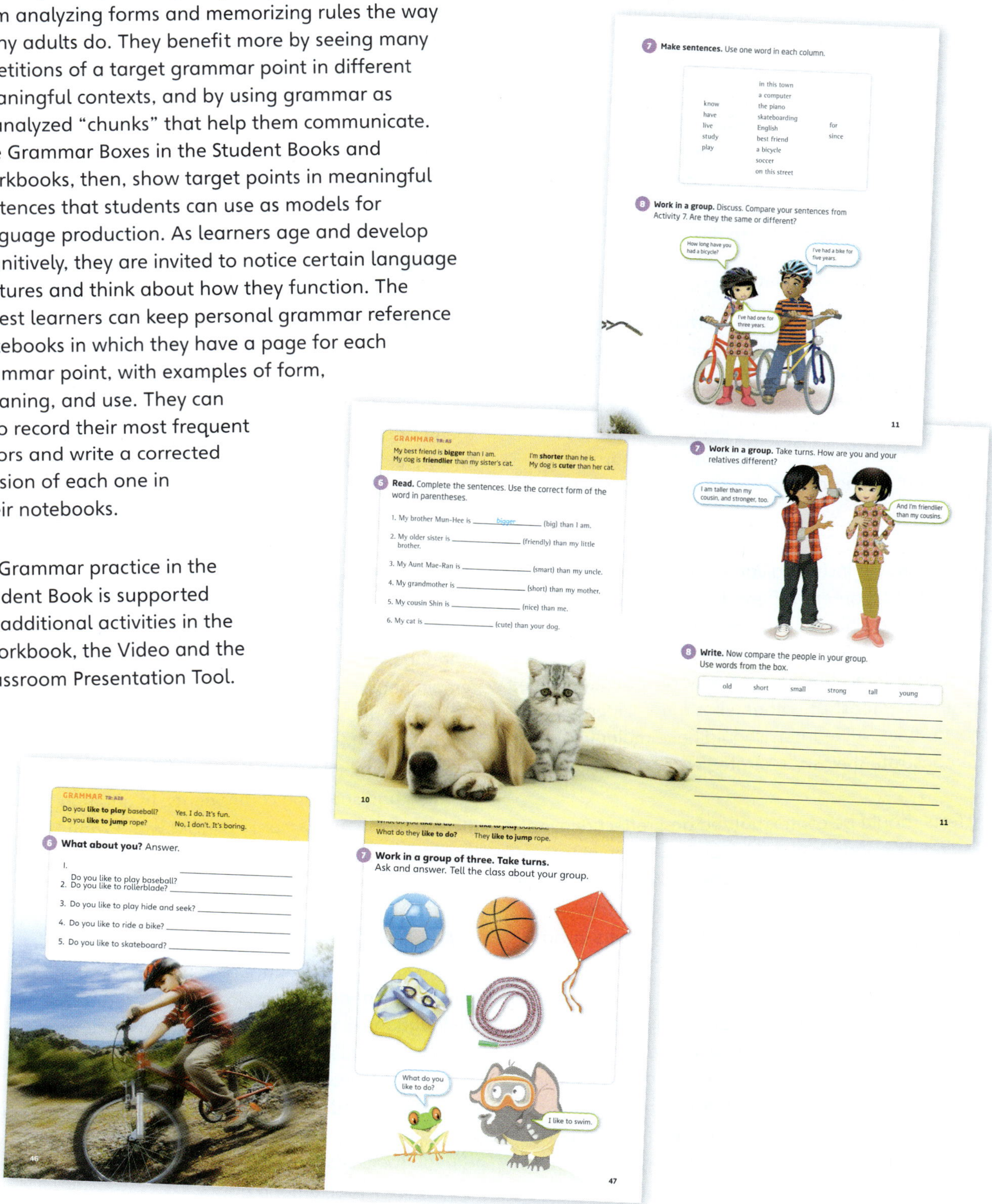

# Assessment

Because of young learners' age, level of maturity, limited range of experience, and cognitive, linguistic, and literacy development, they need appropriately designed assessment tasks, whether traditional or performance-based.

• Tests should mirror learning. The material actually taught in class is what is assessed. Tests should reflect the objectives of the curriculum and provide students with the opportunity to demonstrate what they know and what they can do with the language in tasks and formats that are similar to the ones they have experienced in class.

• Tests should contribute to learning on the teacher's part as well as on the student's part. Test results should provide teachers with information on which to base subsequent instruction, especially modifications that are needed for some or all students. And of course the results should provide information to learners on their current strengths and weaknesses and progress in learning English.

• Tests should include a variety of techniques that correspond to learners' different intelligences and learning styles. That is to say, tests should provide opportunities for learners who are not primarily linguistically, logical-mathematically, or spatially inclined but rather demonstrate other types of intelligences or learning styles. All learners should have multiple chances to demonstrate their skills, strategies, and knowledge.

• Tests should be contextualized and reflect relevant tasks and language for young learners. Assessment items are more authentic when they reflect a previously taught theme or body of content, and when the language tested is that used by young learners in class and in their real lives.

• Tests should allow all learners to experience success, while providing both lower than average learners and advanced learners opportunities to demonstrate their knowledge. Just as teachers deal with mixed-ability learners in class through differentiated instruction, so should they provide opportunities for mixed-ability learners on tests.

• Tests should motivate learners and build learner confidence. Teachers work hard to include a variety of motivating and fun activities in their lessons, and they are conscientious about providing praise and constructive feedback to their students in class. Students should have the same opportunities for fun, engagement, and motivating feedback in their assessments.

• Tests should take place over time in order to collect evidence of growth. Assessment should not be approached as an occasional but necessary, fear-inducing evil. Indeed, the more frequently students are assessed through a variety of ways, the less test anxiety they may have and the more practiced and confident they may feel.

The *Our World* series ensures that students engage in a wide variety of communicative activities in each thematic unit, and many of these themes and activity types are correspondingly reflected in the assessment process. *Our World* provides many opportunities for both formal and informal assessment of different types.

The typical paper-and-pencil test with formats such as multiple-choice, true/false, matching, and fill-in-the-blank is one example of formal assessment. In many language curricula around the world, these task types remain popular. The *Our World* assessment program includes various kinds of written tests: placement tests and level pre-tests, nine unit quizzes, three mastery tests, and final tests, together with an Audio CD for the listening and speaking components. In addition, with the use of the Assessment CD-ROM with Exam*View*©, all of the quizzes and tests are easily generated and customizable to the needs of each teacher's students.

Accurate assessment reflects not only what students can recognize and produce on a written test, but also what they can perform or do as they actually use the language in real or realistic contexts. *Our World* therefore provides a wealth of opportunities for informal assessment. These include many different Expansion activities as listed in each unit of the Lesson Planner, pair and group work, Review pages and Project pages in the Student Book, Workbook activities, and the Classroom Presentation Tool, among others.

# Generic Pacing Guide

## 2–3 hours per week

|  |  |
|---|---|
| Week 1 | **Unit Opener**<br>**Vocabulary 1:** Warm Up; Present; Practice; Wrap Up |
| Week 1 | **Vocabulary 1** *(continued)*: Recap; Apply; Extend; Wrap Up<br>**Song** *(optional)* |
| Week 2 | **Grammar 1:** Warm Up; Present; Practice; Apply; Wrap Up<br>**Song** *(optional)* |
| Week 2 | **Vocabulary 2:** Warm Up; Present; Practice; Apply; Wrap Up |
| Week 3 | **Grammar 2:** Warm Up; Present; Practice; Apply; Wrap Up |
| Week 3 | **Reading:** Warm Up; Present; Practice; Apply; Wrap Up |
| Week 4 | **Writing:** Warm Up; Present; Read the Model; Plan; Write<br>**Mission** |
| Week 4 | **Project:** Prepare; Share<br>**Assessment**<br>**Song** *(optional)* |

## 3–4 hours per week

|  |  |
|---|---|
| Week 1 | **Unit Opener** |
| Week 1 | **Vocabulary 1:** Warm Up; Present; Practice; Wrap Up<br>**Song** *(optional)* |
| Week 1 | **Vocabulary 1** *(continued)*: Recap; Apply; Extend; Wrap Up |
| Week 2 | **Grammar 1:** Warm Up; Present; Practice; Wrap Up<br>**Song** *(optional)* |
| Week 2 | **Grammar 1** *(continued)*: Recap; Apply; Extend; Wrap Up |
| Week 2 | **Vocabulary 2:** Warm Up; Present; Practice; Apply; Extend; Wrap Up |
| Week 3 | **Grammar 2:** Warm Up; Present; Practice; Apply; Extend; Wrap Up |
| Week 3 | **Reading:** Warm Up; Present; Practice; Wrap Up |
| Week 3 | **Reading** *(continued)*: Recap; Apply; Extend; Wrap Up |
| Week 4 | **Writing:** Warm Up; Present; Read the Model; Plan; Write |
| Week 4 | **Writing** *(continued)*: Edit; Share<br>**Mission** |
| Week 4 | **Project:** Prepare; Share<br>**Assessment**<br>**Song** *(optional)* |

## 4–6 hours per week

|  |  |
|---|---|
| Week 1 | **Unit Opener** |
| Week 1 | **Vocabulary 1:** Warm Up; Present; Practice; Wrap Up<br>**Song** *(optional)* |
| Week 1 | **Vocabulary 1** *(continued)*: Recap; Apply; Extend; Wrap Up |
| Week 1 | **Review** |
| Week 2 | **Song**<br>**Grammar 1:** Warm Up; Present; Practice; Wrap Up |
| Week 2 | **Grammar 1** *(continued)*: Recap; Apply; Extend; Wrap Up<br>**Song** *(optional)* |
| Week 2 | **Vocabulary 2:** Warm Up; Present; Practice; Apply; Extend; Wrap Up |
| Week 2 | **Review** |
| Week 3 | **Grammar 2:** Warm Up; Present; Practice; Apply; Extend; Wrap Up |
| Week 3 | **Review** |
| Week 3 | **Reading:** Warm Up; Present; Practice; Wrap Up |
| Week 3 | **Reading** *(continued)*: Recap; Apply; Extend; Wrap Up |
| Week 4 | **Writing:** Warm Up; Present; Read the Model; Plan; Write |
| Week 4 | **Writing** *(continued)*: Edit; Share<br>**Mission** |
| Week 4 | **Review**<br>**Assessment**<br>**Project Prep** |
| Week 4 | **Project**<br>**Song** *(optional)* |

# *Our World* Level 1 Scope and Sequence

## Units 1-9

| | | | | |
|---|---|---|---|---|
| **Unit 0**<br>Welcome to Our World! | **Meet the mascots:**<br>Eddie the elephant<br>Polly the parrot<br>Mia the monkey<br>Freddy the frog | **Greetings; Talking about your birthday:**<br>Hello, I'm ... What's your name?<br>Hi. My name's ...<br>How old are you?<br>I'm ...<br>It's my birthday!<br>Happy Birthday! | **Colors:**<br>black<br>blue<br>green<br>orange<br>purple<br>red<br>white<br>yellow | **The Alphabet:**<br>A-Z |

| Unit | Theme | Goals | Vocabulary 1 | Grammar 1 | Vocabulary 2 |
|---|---|---|---|---|---|
| **1** My Classroom | • classroom objects | • name classroom objects<br>• count classroom objects<br>• name colors of objects | board<br>classroom<br>clock<br>computer<br>crayon<br>map<br>paper<br>pen<br>pencil<br>table | Simple present of *to be*, third person singular<br>***Is it** a pencil? Yes, **it is**.*<br>***It's** a pencil.*<br>***Is it** a crayon?*<br>*No, **it isn't**.*<br>***It's** a pen.* | book<br>chair<br>desk<br>eraser<br>picture |
| **2** My World | • nature<br>• animals<br>• plants | • name objects in nature<br>• name colors in nature<br>• talk about nature | bird<br>butterfly<br>grass<br>mountain<br>ocean<br>river<br>rock<br>sky<br>sun<br>tree | Simple present of *to be*, third person singular and plural<br>*What **is it?***<br>***It's** a bird.*<br>*What **are they?***<br>***They're** birds.* | bush<br>cloud<br>flower<br>moon<br>star |
| **3** My Family | • family members | • name family members<br>• talk about family members<br>• use numbers | baby<br>brother<br>father<br>grandfather<br>grandmother<br>mother<br>my family<br>parents<br>photo<br>sister | Simple present of *to have*, first and second person singular<br>*How many brothers **do** you **have?***<br>*I **have** two brothers.* | big<br>old<br>short<br>small<br>tall<br>young |
| **4** My House | • rooms in a house<br>• furniture<br>• at-home activities | • name rooms in a house<br>• name furniture<br>• talk about actions | bathroom<br>bed<br>bedroom<br>dining room<br>kitchen<br>lamp<br>living room<br>mirror<br>sofa<br>TV | *Is there?/there is*<br>***Is there** a table in the kitchen? Yes, **there is**.* | cleaning<br>cooking<br>eating<br>sleeping<br>taking a bath<br>watching TV |

| | | |
|---|---|---|
| **Shapes:**<br>circle<br>rectangle<br>square<br>star<br>triangle | **Numbers:**<br>1–10 | **Classroom language:**<br>draw<br>listen<br>point<br>read<br>say<br>sing<br>sit down<br>stand up<br>walk<br>write |

| Grammar 2 | Reading | Writing | Value | Project |
|---|---|---|---|---|
| Question words: *what, what color, how many*<br>***What*** *is it? It's a table.*<br>***What color*** *is it? It's yellow.*<br>***How many*** *pencils? Three.* | Drawing and Writing | Make a name tag. | **Value:** Work hard in school.<br>**Caption:** I listen. I talk. I read. I write. | A counting book |
| Question words: *where*<br>***Where*** *is the butterfly? It's* ***on*** *the flower.* | Rainbows | Draw and write about colors. | **Value:** Enjoy nature.<br>**Caption:** Stop and look. Enjoy. | A mural about nature |
| Question word: *who*<br>***Who's*** *she? She's my sister.* | Families Are Different | Draw and write about your family. | **Value:** Love your family.<br>**Caption:** Work and play together. | A family photo poster |
| Present progressive, third person singular<br>*Where's your mother? She's in the kitchen. She's* ***cooking.*** | Houses are Different | Write about your bedroom. | **Value:** Be neat.<br>**Caption:** Be neat. Clean your room. | A plan of rooms in a house. |

| Unit | Theme | Goals | Vocabulary 1 | Grammar 1 | Vocabulary 2 |
|---|---|---|---|---|---|
| **5** Cool Clothes | • clothes<br>• colors | • name clothes<br>• name colors<br>• say what people are wearing | dress<br>gloves<br>hat<br>jacket<br>pants<br>shirt<br>shoes<br>skirt<br>socks<br>T-shirt | Present progressive, first, second, and third person singular<br>What **are** you **wearing?**<br>**I'm wearing** a red dress. | brown<br>closet<br>pink<br>purple<br>shelf |
| **6** My Toys | • toys | • name and describe toys<br>• talk about wants<br>• talk about possession | ball<br>bike<br>car<br>drum<br>game<br>kite<br>puppet<br>top<br>train<br>truck | Simple present of *to want*, first, second, and third person singular<br>***Do** you **want** a puppet?*<br>*Yes, I **do**.*<br>***Does** he **want** a ball?*<br>*No, he **doesn't**. He **wants** a truck.* | board game<br>doll<br>puzzle<br>robot<br>teddy bear |
| **7** My Body | • parts of the body<br>• physical activities | • name parts of the body<br>• talk about parts of the body<br>• talk about actions | arm<br>ear<br>eye<br>feet<br>foot<br>hair<br>hand<br>head<br>leg<br>mouth<br>neck<br>nose | Singular possessive adjectives<br>***My** hair is brown.*<br>***Your** hair is brown.*<br>***Her** eyes are brown.*<br>***His** hair is brown.* | jump<br>long<br>run<br>strong<br>walk |
| **8** Good Food | • food<br>• drinks | • name food<br>• talk about likes and dislikes<br>• talk about my favorite food | apple<br>banana<br>cheese pizza<br>chicken<br>cookie<br>egg<br>fish<br>orange<br>rice<br>salad<br>sandwich<br>soup | Simple present with *like*, first and second person singular<br>***Do** you **like** bananas?*<br>*Yes, I **do**. I **like** bananas.* | lemonade<br>milk<br>orange juice<br>tea<br>water |
| **9** Animal Friends | • animals<br>• animal actions | • name animals<br>• talk about what animals can do<br>• describe a favorite animal | cat<br>chicken<br>cow<br>dog<br>donkey<br>duck<br>frog<br>goat<br>horse<br>rabbit<br>sheep<br>turtle | Present progressive, third person plural<br>*What **are** the horses **doing?***<br>*They**'re running**.*<br>***Are** they **sleeping?***<br>*No, they **aren't**.* | climb<br>crawl<br>fly<br>see<br>swim |

| Grammar 2 | Reading | Writing | Value | Project |
| --- | --- | --- | --- | --- |
| *That/those*<br>*What's* ***that?***<br>***That's*** *my orange t-shirt.*<br>*What* ***are those?***<br>***Those are*** *my purple shoes.* | Clothes Are Fun! | Write sentences about clothes. | **Value:** Take care of your clothes.<br>**Caption:** Put away your clean clothes. | A stick puppet. |
| *This/these*<br>***Is this*** *your teddy bear?*<br>*No,* ***it*** *isn't. It's Sonia's teddy bear.*<br>*Are* ***these*** *our puppets?*<br>*No,* ***they*** *aren't. They're Mark's puppets.* | We ♥ Teddy Bears (We Love Teddy Bears) | Write about a favorite toy. | **Value:** Share your toys.<br>**Caption:** Share your toys with your friends. | A cup-and-ball toy |
| Ability with *can*<br>*I* ***can*** *walk.*<br>*She* ***can*** *jump.*<br>***Can*** *you run? Yes, I* ***can.*** | Sculptures Are Fun | Write about a costume. | **Value:** Be clean.<br>**Caption:** Wash your hands. Wash your body. Brush your teeth. | Make a robot. |
| The indefinite article: *a, an*<br>***an*** *apple*<br>***an*** *orange*<br>***a*** *banana*<br>***a*** *cookie* | Fun Food | Write about favorite foods. | **Value:** Eat good food.<br>**Caption:** Eat fruits and vegetables. Drink water and juice. | Make a placemat. |
| *Want* + infinitive; first, second, and third person singular<br>***Do*** *you* ***want to ride*** *the donkey?*<br>*No, I don't.*<br>*What* ***does*** *Anna* ***want to do?***<br>*She* ***wants to see*** *the ducks.* | Animal Babies | Write about a favorite animal. | **Value:** Be good to animals.<br>**Caption:** Give your pet food and water. | A class book about animals |

# Reviewers

**Marcela Acevedo**, English Coordinator, Colegio St. Charles/Director, Directora Instituto Hilton, Buenos Aires, Argentina, **Joanna Adkin**, Senior Teacher Young Learners, British Council, Ho Chi Minh City, Vietnam, **Vadick Alain Gonzales**, La Salle Colegio, Cusco, Peru, **Andrew Archer**, Nellie's English Books, Tokyo, Japan, **Rasha Ashraf Zaki**, Teacher, Oman, **Raedel Bagley**, AIS, Vietnam, **Maria Barberis**, English Department Director, Colegio Marin, Buenos Aires, Argentina, **Tom Bartley**, ILA Vietnam, Ho Chi Minh City, Vietnam, **Sylvia Borges P. Mendonça**, IEBEU Franquias, Rio de Janeiro, Brazil, **Anne Louise Butterfield**, Korea University, Seoul, South Korea, **Irma Canales**, Coordinator, Colegio Oviedo de Schontal, Mexico City, Mexico, **Grace Cardenas**, La Salle Colegio, Cusco, Peru, **Maritza Castillo**, Colegio Superior Americano, Bogotá, Colombia, **Karla Magdalena Суceña Flores**, Coordinator, PISI - Universidad Autónoma de Sinaloa, Sinaloa, Mexico, **Marcela Cedra Simão**, Supervisor Juniors, Rua Umberto Caputi, São Paulo, Brazil, **Mao Chantha**, General Manager, Modern International School, Cambodia, **Charlie Chen**, Longshine English, China, **Long Chhay**, New York International School, Phnom Penh, Cambodia, **Connie Chien**, Outlook English, Beijing, China, **Gloria Combariza**, ColegioTecnológico del Sur, Colombia, **Yury Cruz**, Colegio Superior Americano, Bogotá, Colombia, **Monica Cruz**, Colegio Agustiniano Suba, Bogotá, Colombia, **Helena Curtain**, University of Washington, USA, **Gabriela Cuscione**, ARIANCA (Rosario), Argentina, **William Cusek**, Mirdif Private School, Dubai, UAE, **Selma de Assis Moura**, Director, Oak School, São Paulo, Brazil, **Jonee de Leon**, Universal English Center, Vietnam, **Ana Lucia del M.L. Carriel**, Coordinator for Elementary-Intermediate Classes, CNA Administracao National, São Paulo, Brazil, **María del Pilar Bravo**, Centro Colombo Americano, Bogotá, Colombia, **Betty Deng**, Taiwan, **Sabrina Devitt**, Apollo Education and Training, Ho Chi Minh City, Vietnam, **Rosane Di Genova**, Private Teacher, São Paulo, Brazil, **Mateus Díaz**, Rio de Janeiro, Brazil, **María Isabel Díaz Ruiz**, ICPNA, Lima, Peru, **Riaz Donaldson**, Nellie's English Books, Tokyo, Japan, **Linda Dos**, Italy, **Maria Tereza dos Reis Gomes**, Casa Thomas Jefferson, Brasília, Brazil, **Anna Sofia Downey**, Teacher, Colegio Santo Americo, São Paulo, Brazil, **Demi Du**, MaxEn Education, China, **Christopher Dundon**, ILA Vietnam, Ho Chi Minh City, Vietnam, **Lalaine Dy**, Sky High English Studio, Tokyo, Japan, **Ayadan Ersoz**, Professor, Head of INGED, Gazi University, Ankara, Turkey, **Thael Escalante**, La Salle Colegio, Cusco, Peru, **Shona Evans**, Oxford, UK, **Maria Constanza Ezcurra**, English Department Coordinator, Colegio San Jose, Buenos Aires, Argentina, **Sondos Fakhr El Deen**, Saudi British Centre, Saudi Arabia, **Maria Amparo Garcia Pena**, Academic Director, ICPNA, Cusco, Peru, **Rosario Giraldez**, Alianza, Uruguay, **Cristina González**, General Coordinator, Liceo Naval Almirante Guise, Lima, Peru, **Nefertiti González Valdez**, Instituto Mexicano Madero Campus Zavaleta, Puebla, Mexico, **Guillermina Grondona**, English Department Coordinator, Colegio Los Robles, Buenos Aires, Argentina, **Hyun Jin Gu**, TESOL, Korea, **Walter Guevara**, Cali, Colombia, **Gimena Guillen**, La Salle Colegio, Cusco, Peru, **Juli Harrington**, International Academic Consultants, Tokyo, Japan, **Lee Harvey**, Academic Director, Ethos Language Institute, Ho Chi Minh City, Vietnam, **Mônica Hermini de Camargo**, Supervisor, Colegio Santo Américo, São Paulo, Brazil, **Kim Horne**, Japan, **Jania Iñiguez Durán**, Assistente, Secretaría de Educación Pública D.F., Mexico City, Mexico, **Lesley Ito**, Teacher/writer, Big Bow English Lab, Nagoya, Japan, **Ángela Jaimes**, Colegio Agustiniano Suba, Bogotá, Colombia, **Andrea James**, Apollo, Vietnam, **Trevor Joseph**, Kings Road English School, Tokyo, Japan, **Eric Kane**, ELF Academy, Japan, **Kenny Khanh Tan Le**, VASchools, Ho Chi Minh City, Vietnam, **Yuco Kikuchi**, English Pier, Tokyo, Japan, **Min Kyoung Koo**, Woong Jin Plus Academy, Seoul, South Korea, **Eduardo Lagos Flores**, English Coordinator, Colegio San Benito, Santiago, Chile, **Nguyen Lan Thanh**, The International School, Ho Chi Minh City, Vietnam, **Mike Lay**, Associate Vice Provost for Academics, American Intercon Institute, Cambodia, **Margarita Leal**, Alianza, Uruguay, **John Lee**, British Council, Ho Chi Minh City, Vietnam, **Sophie Lewis**, British Council, Ho Chi Minh City, Vietnam, **Luz Libia Rey**, Academic Director, Centro Colombo Americano de Bogotá, Colombia, **Susana Liruso**, TT professor at Facultad de Lenguas, Universidad Nacional de Córdoba, Córdoba, Argentina, **Mabel Liu Liu**, Chaoyang Foreign Language School, China, **Chen Long**, Midi International Learning Center, China, **Pisey Long**, Head Teacher, American Intercon Institute, Cambodia, **Yolanda López Avila**, Colegio Anglo Americano, Bogotá, Colombia, **Catarina M. B. Pontes Kruppa**, Cultura Inglesa, São Paulo, Brazil, **Vũ Mai Trang**, Vietnam National University, Hanoi, Vietnam, **Patricia Manrique Galiano**, YSP Head, ICPNA, Lima, Peru, **Maria Amelia Marcus**, School Solutions Coordinator - Young Learner Courses, Associacao Alumni, Sao Paulo, Brazil, **Cynthia Leticia Marquez Paz**, Instituto Guatemalteco Americano IGA, Guatemala, **Ady Marreo**, Alianza, Uruguay, **Silvia Martinez**, Academic Director, Alianza Colonia, Uruguay, **Gabriela Montejano**, Euroamerican School, Nuevo León, Mexico, **Seong-Hye Moon**, Gaewon Elementary School, Korea, **Atsuko Morimoto**, Tezukayama Elementary School, Japan, **Jhulyana Mujica**, La Salle Colegio, Cusco, Peru, **Kerry Murphy**, Apollo Vietnam, Ho Chi Minh City, Vietnam, **Alicia Nasta**, English Coordinator at Colegio Laureles, Uruguay, **Monica Navarro**, Coordinadora, Instituto Cultural, Mexico City, Mexico, **Müzeyyen Nazlı Demirbaş**, Faculty of Education, ELT Department, Gazi University, Gazi, Turkey, **Andrew Nguyen**, Apollo English, Ho Chi Minh City, Vietnam, **Vinicius Nobre**, Director of English Programs/President of BrasTESOL, Cultura Inglesa, São Paulo, Brazil, **Alessandra Noronha de Nascimiento**, Teacher, Colegio Santo Américo, São Paulo, Brazil, **Ji-Hyun Oh**, Dongsung Elementary School, Korea, **Hee-Suk Oh**, Banan Elementary School, Korea, **Yuko Ontani**, Keisen Women's University, Tokyo, Japan, **Higinio Ordonez**, State English Coordinator, Secretaria de Educación del Estado de México, Mexico, **Erika Oya**, Casa Thomas Jefferson, Brasília, Brazil, **Jill Pagels**, KAUST Schools, Saudi Arabia, **Audrey Pan**, Global Kids Education, China, **Mae-Ran Park**, Professor, Pukyong National University, Republic of Korea, **Ji hoon Park**, Gaewon Elementary School, Korea, **Silvia Pasinato**, Professor, Aricana-Rosario Binational Center, Buenos Aires, Argentina, **Guillermina de la Peña**, Cengage Learning, **Cristiane Perone**, Cultura Inglesa, São Paulo, Brazil, **Jeanne Perrett**, Greece, **Loc Pham**, American Preparation Institute, Ho Chi Minh City, Vietnam, **Jose Luis Pimentel**, La Salle Colegio, Cusco, Peru, **Charchit Pradhan**, ILA Vietnam, Ho Chi Minh City, Vietnam, **Yonatan Puon Castro**, Coordinator of Continuing Education, Benemerita Universidad Autonoma de Puebla, Mexico, **Thomas Pyecroft**, Continuing Education Centre, Chulalongkorn University Bangkok, Thailand, **Silvia Helena R. D. Corrêa**, Educational Director, Rua Umberto Caputi, São Paulo, Brazil, **Maria Righini**, Cultura Inglesa, São Paulo, Brazil, **Suzanne Robare**, Freelancer, China, **Philip Roeland**, inlingua, Bangkok, Thailand, **Monica Rueda Cervantes**, ICPNA, Lima, Peru, **Marcos Frasson Ruiz**, Coordinator for Advanced Classes, CAN Administracao National, São Paulo, Brazil, **Eleonora Salas**, English Department Director, IICANA, Córdoba, Argentina, **Irene Salazar Sugizaki**, Irene's Home English School, Tokyo, Japan, **César Sanabria Flórez**, Tecnológico del Sur, Bogotá, Colombia, **Mariel Santarelli**, English Coordinator, Colegio Pestalozzi, Buenos Aires, Argentina, **Kate Sato**, Kitopia, Japan, **Ana Maria Scandiuzzi**, Casa Thomas Jefferson, Brazil, **Nausheen Shafiq**, MAG, Ministry of Education, Dubai, UAE, **Grace Shi**, Leyang Education, China, **Eunjeong Shim**, Shinki Elementary School, Korea, **Mei Li Sierra**, Coordinator, Colegio Vermont, Mexico City, Mexico, **Marcela Cedra Simao**, São Paulo, Brazil, **Peter Smart**, Berlitz, Japan, **Alicia Sotelo Roman**, Coordinator, Colegio Simón Bolívar, Mexico City, Mexico, **Alicia Suarez P.**, Tecnológico del Sur, Bogotá, Colombia, **Lucila Suarez Pinilla**, Tecnológico del Sur, Bogotá, Colombia, **Sunny Sun**, Peizheng School, Beijing, China, **Phillip Sweeney**, Bangkok, Thailand, **Jenny Taboada Coblentz**, Coordinator, Secretaría de Educación Pública D.F., Mexico City, Mexico, **Mayumi Tabuchi**, Ristumeikan Elementary School, Japan, **Roxana Tenano Guimet**, Head of Studies, Asociación Educativa Trifre, Peru, **Huynh Thi Ai Nguyen**, VUS, Vietnam, **Pham Thi Tua Ha**, University of Languages and International Studies, Hanoi, Vietnam, **David Thompson**, ILA Vietnam, Ho Chi Minh City, Vietnam, **Isa Tirado Rodríguez**, Proulex – Universidad de Guadaljara, Guadalajara, Mexico, **María Eugenia Tizzi**, ARICANA, Argentina, **Phiev Tong Him**, Deputy English Academic Manager, New York Institute, Cambodia, **Agustina Torquinst**, Director, St. Trinneans College, Buenos Aires, Argentina, **Carolina Tripodi**, Proulex - Universidad de Gauadalajara, Jalisco, Mexico, **Bui Truong Thien Trang**, AMA, Vietnam, **D. Turner**, inlingua, Bangkok, Thailand, **Isabel Urrutia**, ICPNA, Cusco, Peru, **Le Van Khan**, Griggs University, Hanoi, Vietnam, **Duong Van Loc**, VAS, Vietnam, **Claudia Varela Quiroga**, Colegio Superior Americano, Bogotá, Colombia, **Kong Veasna**, Principal & Training Coordinator, Sovannaphumi School, Cambodia, **Patricia Vecino**, English Department Coordinator, ICANA, Buenos Aires, Argentina, **Cecilia Vivanco**, ARIANCA (Rosario), Argentina, **Jordan Wang**, Teachall Education, Beijing, China, **Audrey Wang**, Global Kids, Beijing, China, **Erik Wennermark**, ILA Vietnam, Ho Chi Minh City, Vietnam, **Rodrigo Whipple**, Executive Director, Gestion Educacional, Chile, **MaryAnn Wilson**, France, **Diana Valeria Zamarripa**, Instituto Simón Bolívar, Mexico City, Mexico.

## Notes

# Unit 0

*Our World* Mascots

Greetings

Colors

**Resources** Audio CD TR: A2–A5; Picture Cards 1–8

## *Our World* Mascots

- Display the front cover of the book. Give students a moment to look at the image and text. Point to the title and say *Our World.* Have students repeat after you. Next, have students open their books to p. 2. Point to and read the dialogue bubble at the top of the page. Say *Welcome to Our World.* Walk around the room and shake hands with several students. As you shake hands, say *Welcome to Our World!*

- Next, point to the first mascot as you introduce it to students. Say *Eddie. This is Eddie the elephant.* Have students point to Eddie and repeat the name. Introduce the other three mascots, one at a time. Have students repeat each mascot's name as they point to its picture.

## Greetings 1

- **Act it out** Write *Hello. I'm* __________. on the board. Then model introducing yourself to students. Walk around the classroom saying *Hello. I'm (Mr. Ramos).* After students have heard you model the introduction several times, call on a student to introduce himself to the class. Say *Hello. I'm (Roberto).* Have the student repeat the introduction. Then have other students introduce themselves.

- 1 Have students look at the first dialogue on p. 2 (Eddie and Mia). Play **TR: A2**. Pause after "My name's Mia." Say *I'm (Mr. Ramos).* or *My name is (Mr. Ramos).* Then read the first dialogue aloud, and have students repeat after you.

# Colors

**2** **Look and listen.** Say. TR: A3

**3** **Listen.** Point and say. TR: A4

**4** **Work with a partner.** Point. Ask and answer. TR: A5

3

## Be the Expert

### About the Photo

The animal in the photo is called a nudibranch. Nudibranchs are marine animals related to snails. They live in shallow tropical ocean water and can grow to be 30 cm (12 in) long and weigh as much as 1.5 kg (3.3 lb). Some nudibranchs, like the one in the photo, are very colorful to match their surroundings.

### Our World in Context

The mascots in *Our World* are an elephant, a macaw (or parrot), a monkey, and a frog.

- Eddie is an African elephant. African elephants are the largest land mammals on Earth.
- Polly is a macaw, or type of parrot. Macaws are found in Mexico and Central and South America.
- Mia is a monkey. Monkeys are found in many parts of the world, including South America, Africa, and Asia.
- Freddy is a red-eyed tree frog. Red-eyed tree frogs are found in Central and South America.

- Have students introduce themselves to a partner. Have partners take turns asking and answering the question *What's your name?*
- Play the rest of **TR: A2**. Say *Freddy is five. Polly is seven.* Walk up to a student and ask *How old are you, (Maria)?* Explain that students should answer by saying *I'm (six).*

## Colors 2 3 4

- **2** Display Picture Cards for the colors *red, purple, yellow, orange, white, blue, black,* and *green.* Hold up the cards one at a time. As you say the name of each color, point to or touch one or two classroom objects of the same color. Say *(Red. Red.)* Play **TR: A3.** Pause the audio for students to repeat each word.
- **3** Point to each Picture Card in turn and ask the name of the color. For example, point to the red card and ask *Red?* Nod your head and say *Yes, red.* Have students repeat after you. Then play **TR: A4**. Have students open their books to p. 3. Have them point to and say each color in the photo.
- **4** Hold up an object from the classroom. Ask *What color is it?* Have a student answer. Repeat with a different object. Play **TR: A5.** Have two students role-play Mia and Polly's dialogue on p. 3. Then, in pairs, have students take turns pointing to objects in the room, asking and answering the question, *What color is it?*
- **Extend** To extend the activity, point to a (green) card and ask *Red?* Say *No, green. It's green.* Repeat with other colors, as well as classroom objects.

**The Alphabet**

**Academic Language** *letter*

**Resources** Workbook p. I; Audio CD TR: A6

**Materials** note cards (optional)

## The Alphabet 5

- Have students open their books to pp. 4–5. Give students a moment to look at the letters and photos. Say *Look.* Point to letter *A*. Move your finger across both pages from *A* to *F*. Do the same for the next rows to model the order of the alphabet.
- **Read together** Point to the letter *A* and say *This is the letter A.* Have students repeat *A*. Then say *A, apple* and point to the apple. Have students repeat after you.
- Point to each letter in order. Say *This is the letter (B).(B).* Have students repeat. Then say *(B, baby)* and point to the photo. Have students repeat and point.
- 5 After you review each letter, return to the letter *A*. Ask the class to repeat each letter as you play **TR: A6**. Have students point to each letter as they hear it.

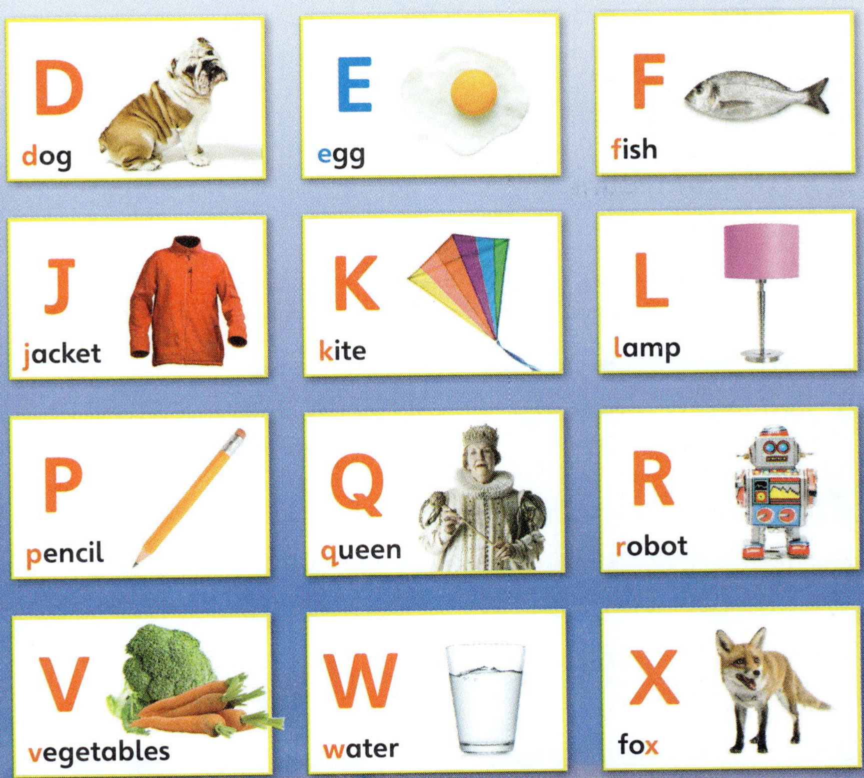


5 **Look and listen.** Say. TR: A6

5

## Be the Expert

### Teaching Tip

Repetition helps students learn new words. Each time you introduce a word, have students repeat it several times. Have students repeat as a class, and then call on students to repeat individually. You might also have students create flash cards and quiz one another in pairs. Provide as many opportunities as possible for exposure to new words. If you have extra time at the end of a lesson, have students review and repeat vocabulary.

- Next, point to a letter. Say *This is the letter* ______ and pause. Call on a student to respond. Have the class repeat. Then say the word that begins with the letter. Have the class repeat. Continue with other letters of the alphabet.

- **Extend** Have students create their own alphabet cards with note cards or sheets of paper. Assign each student a letter. Have students write their letter on a card. Then, students should write a word and draw a picture to go with the letter. Students may use the same words and pictures as on the Student Book pages. Or, challenge students to write a different word they know that begins with the letter. When the cards are complete, have students post them on a wall, in order. Have students present their cards to the class.

# Unit 0

**Shapes**

**Numbers**

**Classroom Language**

**Academic Language** *point, number, shape*

**Resources** Workbook pp. 2–3; Audio CD TR: A7–A14; Picture Cards 5, 9–19

**Materials** ten small objects such as pencils or blocks

**6** **Look and listen.** Say. TR: A7

a square | a triangle | a circle | a rectangle | a star

**7** **Listen.** Point and say. TR: A8

**8** **Look and listen.** Say. TR: A9

| | | | | |
|---|---|---|---|---|
| 1 one | 2 two | 3 three | 4 four | 5 five |
| 6 six | 7 seven | 8 eight | 9 nine | 10 ten |

**9** **Listen.** Point and say. TR: A10

**10** **Ask and answer.** TR: A11

6

## Shapes 6 7

- **6** Have students open their books to p. 6. Say *Shapes. These are shapes.* Have students repeat *shapes*. Point to the square at the top of the page. Say *Square. This shape is a square.* Write the word *square* on the board. Underline *s*. Ask *What letter is this?* (*s*) Hold up Picture Card 9 and point to the square. Ask *What shape is this?* (square) Repeat with the next four shapes in Activity 6. Then play **TR: A7.** Have students repeat each word after they hear it.

- **7** Play **TR: A8**. Pause the audio after each shape. Have students point to the shape on the page. Then call on a few students to repeat the word aloud. Have the class repeat each time.

## Numbers 8 9 10

- **8** Direct students' attention to Activity 8. Point and say *Numbers. These are numbers.* Have students repeat *numbers*. Gather ten small objects, such as pens or pencils. Hold them in your hand. Play **TR: A9.** Each time you hear a number, pause the audio. Place an object on the desk. Point and say *(one)*. Have the class repeat after you. Repeat up to the number *10*, adding objects and counting.

- **9** Write the numbers *1–10* on the board. Play **TR: A10.** Point to each number on the board as you hear it. Pause the audio. Have students point in their books. Then have students repeat the number.

- **10** Have students look at the shapes in the box. Say *Listen. Point to the shape. Square.* Have students point to a square. Say *Circle.* Have

11 **Look and listen.** Say. TR: A12

12 **Listen.** Point and say. TR: A13

13 **Listen and do.** TR: A14



## Be the Expert

### Teaching Tip

When you teach a new vocabulary word, first say the word by itself. Then put the word into context in a simple sentence. This process helps students recognize the word they're expected to repeat and become familiar with context and conversational language.

students point to a circle. Repeat for *rectangle*, *triangle*, and *star*. Walk around the room to check students' answers. Then play **TR: A11** and pause after the question "How many blue squares?" Hold up Picture Card 5 (blue) and have students repeat *blue*. Then ask *How many blue squares?* (three) Point to the mascots at the bottom of the page. Call on two students to role-play the dialogue. Then point to each square on the page and count aloud. Say *One, two, three.* Have students repeat.

## Classroom Language 11 12 13

- 11 Have students open their books to p. 7. Play **TR: A12.** Pause after the word *draw*. Point to the photo. Say *Draw. Draw.* Act out drawing, and have students repeat. Play the audio and pause after *listen*. Point to the photo. Say *Listen. Listen.* Have the class repeat. Continue for the other words.
- 12 Give out Picture Cards 10–19 to different students. Play **TR: A13.** Pause after *draw*. Hold up Picture Card 10 (draw) and say *Draw* aloud. Have the class point to the photo in their books. Have students with Picture Cards use this model when they hear their word. Continue playing **TR: A13.** Pause after each word. Wait for a student to hold up a card. Have the class find and point to the photo in their books. Then, have the class repeat the word aloud.
- 13 **Act it out** Play **TR: A14** and pause after *draw*. Draw a simple picture on the board. Repeat the word aloud as you draw. Have students act out drawing on paper. Play the audio again, pausing after the next word. Hold your hand to your ear and say *Listen. Listen.* Have students repeat. Continue for each word on the page. Act out the word and have students copy your motions.

## In This Unit

**Theme** This unit is about things we use and do in the classroom.

**Content Objective**

Students will

- identify and discuss school routines.

**Language Objectives**

Students will

- identify and name classroom objects.
- count classroom objects.
- name colors of objects.

**Vocabulary**

**Vocabulary 1** *a board, a classroom, a clock, a computer, a crayon, a map, paper, a pen, a pencil, a table*

**Vocabulary 2** *a book, a chair, a desk, an eraser, a picture*

**Grammar**

**Grammar 1** use simple present of *to be*

**Grammar 2** ask questions using *what, what color* and *how many*

**Pacing Guides** LIU1

**Writing** Make a name tag.

**Value** Work hard in school.

**Project** Make a counting book.

## Unit Opener

**Objectives**

Students will

- identify objects in a photo
- name and count classroom objects.
- name colors.

**Resources** Video: Sc. 1—Introduction; Classroom Presentation Tool: Unit Opener; Unit Opener Poster; World Map Poster; Teacher's Resource CD-ROM: Home-School Connection

Unit 1

# My Classroom

In this unit, I will . . .
- name classroom objects.
- count classroom objects.
- name colors of objects.

**Look and check.**

I see a
- ◯ book.
- ◯ globe.
- ◯ pen.

School in Guilin, China

8

## Introduce

- **Activate prior knowledge** Point to the photo on Student Book pp. 8–9. Ask *What do you see?* (a classroom) Point to the girl in the red sweater and ask *What color is it?* Then point to the girl in the yellow sweater and ask *What color is it?* Point to an ocean on the globe and ask *What color is it?* (blue)
- **Build background** Point to the photo and say *This is a classroom.* Look around your classroom and say *This is a classroom, too.* Point to yourself and say *This is my classroom.* Point to a student and say *This is your classroom.* Indicate all of the students in the room and say *This is our classroom.*
- Point to a world map and say *This is a map.* Point to China on the map and say *This is China. The classroom in the photo is in China.* Point to the globe in the photo and say *This is a globe.*

# Be the Expert

## About the Photo

The classroom in the photo is in Guilin, China. Guilin is a city in the southern part of China, in the province of Guangxi. Guilin is known for its beautiful rock formations. The Li River flows through the city of Guilin.

## Teaching Tip

**Classroom Management** Help students learn to be good listeners. Don't try to teach while students are talking. Wait until students are quiet before you speak. Hold one hand in the air to quiet the class and get their attention. Make eye contact with students. Have students raise their hands along with you, until all hands are up and the room is quiet. Then lower your hand and begin speaking.

## Related Vocabulary

*student*

- Discuss the photo with students by asking questions such as the following:

  *What do you see?* (a classroom, a globe, students)
  *What color?* (red, yellow, blue)
  *How many (students, globes)?* (six students, one globe)

- Help students complete the activity on p. 8. Read the sentence stem (*I see a* _________.) and each option aloud. Have students repeat after you. Have them say *yes* or *no* after each option.

- Confirm the correct answer and read it aloud. Have students repeat after you. Have them take turns reading the completed sentence aloud. (I see a globe.)

# Vocabulary 1

**Objective**

Students will

- identify and use words for classroom objects.

**Vocabulary** *a computer, a table, a pen, paper, a map, a classroom, a clock, a crayon, a pencil, a board*

**Resources** Workbook pp. 4–5; Picture Cards 11, 12, 14, 20–29; Audio CD TR: A15–17; Video: Sc. 2—Vocabulary 1a; Video: Sc. 3—Vocabulary 1b; Classroom Presentation Tool: Vocabulary 1a; Minimal Pair Card 66; Teacher's Resource CD-ROM: Activity Worksheet 1.1

**Materials** a small bag; tape

1 **Listen and say.** TR: A15

2 **Listen.** Point and say. TR: A16

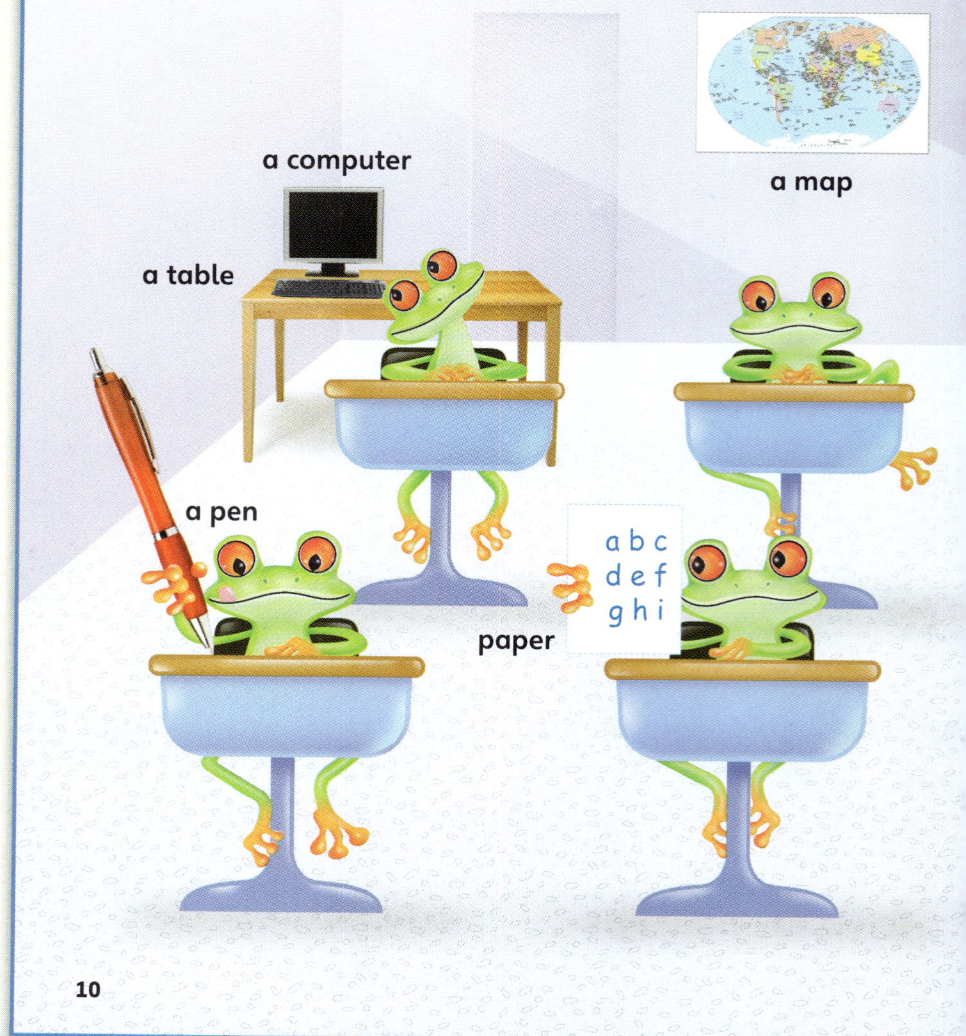


10

## Warm Up

- **Recycle** Review the Unit 0 words *listen* and *point*. First, hold up Picture Card 11 (listen). Say *Listen.* Then point to students and say *You say* listen. If necessary, repeat the word. Next hold up Picture Card 12 (point) and say *Point.* Then point to students and say *You say* point.

- Say each word again, this time acting it out.

  Say *Listen.* Put your hand to your ear as though you're listening to something.

  Say *Point.* Point to a few objects around the room.

- Now have students act out the words themselves. Say *You listen.* Hold up your hand to your ear. Have students do the action with you. Next say *You point.* Point at objects around the room and have students do the action with you. Now say the words again a few times, but have students do the actions on their own, without your help.

## Be the Expert

### Vocabulary Strategy

**Alphabetical Order** Have students review the alphabet on pp. 4–5. Have them match the first letter of target words such as *pencil* to the corresponding letter of the alphabet (*p*). Then have them put the target words in alphabetical order, according to the first letter of each word. Point out that students should ignore the articles *a*, *an* and *the* when alphabetizing words.

### Teaching Tip

Each time students do the right action or answer a question correctly, say *Yes! Very good!* This type of feedback makes students feel more comfortable in the classroom and builds trust between students and the teacher.

### Related Vocabulary

*desk, door, elephant, frog, parrot*

## Present

- Hold up the book, showing the picture of the classroom on pp. 10–11. Point to the picture and say *Look.*
- Point to and say each word. Stop after each word and try to find the same object in the classroom. For example, after saying *a board*, point to the board in the classroom. After saying *a pencil*, hold up a pencil.
- Say each word again. Ask students to point to or hold up each object.
- Give each student a pen, a pencil, and a crayon. Say *a pen*. Have students hold up their pens. Say *a pencil*. Have students hold up their pencils. Say *a crayon*. Have students hold up their crayons. The first time you say each word, hold up the object with students. Then say the words again in a different order, without holding up the objects yourself. If students are ready for more of a challenge, say the words again more quickly.

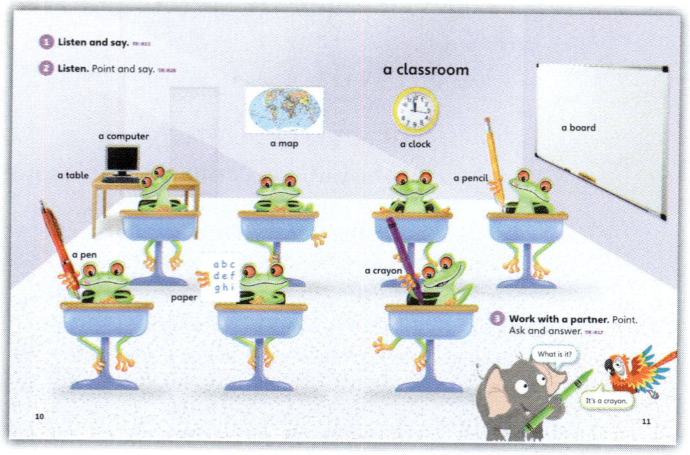


## Practice 1 2

- **1** Hold up the book, showing students the picture on pp. 10–11. Say *Listen.* Play **TR: A15**. Point to the object in the picture as you hear each word. Then say *Now listen and say.* Play **TR: A15** again. After students hear each word, have them repeat it. Listen to make sure students are pronouncing each word correctly.
- **2** Help students follow the order of the words on **TR: A16** by pointing to the first two or three objects named. Then have students point to the rest of the words without your help. Say *Listen. Then point and say.* Play **TR: A16**. ✓ Walk around the room saying words to individual students. Have them point to the words in the book.
- Have students work with partners. Have partners open to pp. 10–11. One student will say a vocabulary word on the page, and the other will point to the picture of the word. Then students will change roles. Model with a student, if necessary.

## Wrap Up

- Put a crayon, a pencil, a pen, and a piece of paper in a bag. Invite a student to come to the front of the class. Have the student close his eyes and pull an object out of the bag. Ask *What is it?* Have students pull out each of the remaining objects. If more students want to have a turn, put the objects back in the bag and repeat the activity.

- Give each student a piece of paper and a pencil, pen, or crayon. Say *I say a word. You draw a picture.* Model the activity for students. Say *clock*. Repeat *clock*. Then draw a simple picture of a clock on the board. Make sure your picture is very simple.

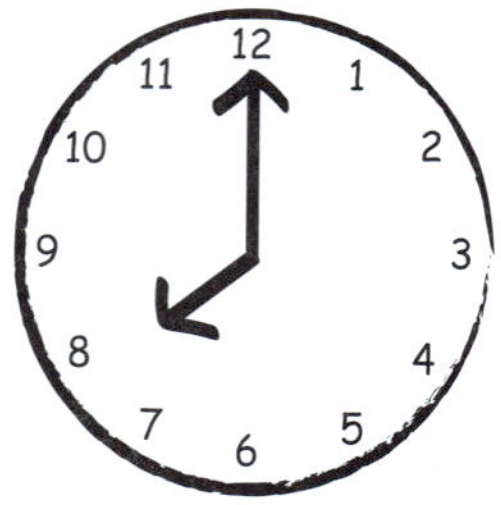


- Say *Now you listen and draw. Table. Table.* Have students draw a picture of a table. Give them two minutes to draw their pictures.
- Repeat this activity with two or three more words, having students draw each picture on a new piece of paper.
- Have several students come to the front of the room, one at a time, and hold up one of their pictures. As each student holds up a picture, ask *What is it?* The class guesses the word for each picture.

## Recap

- Hold up Picture Cards 20–29 one at a time, asking students to call out the things they see.

## Apply 3

- **3** Point to the speech bubbles on p. 11. Play **TR: A17** or read the question and answer out loud. Then have a few students model the dialogue with you. First ask the question and have students give the answer. Then have students ask you the question.
- Explain that the contraction *It's* has the same meaning as *It is*. Write *It's* on the board with the words *It is* underneath.
- Point to another object on pp. 10–11 and ask *What is it?* Have a student answer the question.
- Place students in pairs. Have them ask and answer questions about the vocabulary words, using the dialogue on p. 11 as a model.

## Extend

- Review shapes with students. Hold up p. 6 of the Student Book. Point to each shape, one at a time. For each shape, ask *What is it?* (a star, a square) Each time students answer correctly, say *Good! Yes! That's right.*
- Review colors with students this same way, holding up p. 3 of the Student Book.
- Now prepare students to play a game of 20 Questions. Ask questions about the shape of the board. Say *Look at the board. Is it a circle?* (no) *Is it a square?* (no) *Is it a rectangle?* (yes) Then ask students questions about the color of the board in your classroom. Say *Is it red?* (no) *Is it yellow?* (no) *Is it (white)?* (yes)
- Write some of the questions you asked on the board:

| |
|---|
| Is it a circle? |
| Is it a square? |
| Is it yellow? |

- Put students in small groups. Give one student in each group a Picture Card from this lesson. Make sure each student understands that they should not let the other students see their card. Show students how to cover the card so that other students can't see it.
- Point to one student's card. Ask *What is it?* Say to the other students *Ask questions.* Point to the questions on the board. Then model asking the first student a question such as *Is it purple?* Have the student answer *Yes* or *No*. Have other students in each group guess until they guess the right answer.

## Wrap Up

- Hold up a Picture Card and ask *What is it?* Ask the student who says the correct word first to come to the front of the class. Give that student the next Picture Card and prompt him to ask *What is it?* Continue this game until all of the Picture Cards 20–29 have been reviewed.

## Be the Expert

### Sounds of English

**Comparing Sounds: /p/ and /b/** The sounds /p/ (pen) and /b/ (book) are very similar. To pronounce the /p/ sound, close your mouth and breathe some air into your mouth. Then open your lips to release the air. To pronounce /b/, do the same, but add your voice.

Practice using Minimal Pair Card 66 (push, bush). Have students gently touch their throats to feel their vocal cords vibrate for /b/.

Example words: paper, pen; board, book

### Teaching Tip

When learning vocabulary, it's helpful for students to see a real example of the thing they're learning the word for. For example, when teaching the word *crayon*, show a photograph of a crayon. It's even better to show students an actual crayon and, when possible, to let students hold the crayon.

### Formative Assessment

Can students

- Identify and use words for classroom objects?

  Have students tape the names of classroom objects onto objects in the classroom and then answer the question *What is this?* as you point to the objects around the classroom.

**Review** For additional practice, direct students to Activity Worksheet 1.1.

## Song

**Vocabulary in the song**

**Vocabulary 2** *book, eraser*

**Grammar in the song**

**Grammar 1** use simple present of *to be*

**Resources** Audio CD TR: A18; Video: Sc. 9—Song; Workbook p. 6; Classroom Presentation Tool: Song, Picture Cards 1–3, 5, 7–8, 30, 33

4 **Listen.** Read and sing. TR: A18

# My School

*This is my school.*
*This is your school.*
*This is my school.*
*I like my school.*

*I have my eraser,*
*and I have my book.*
*I have my eraser.*
*Come and look!*

**CHORUS**

12

## Use the Song 4

- 4 **Explain** Hold up a book and ask *What is it?* Say *It's a book. It's my book.* Point to a book on a student's desk. Say *This is your book.* Hold up your book again and point to the student's book. Say *This is my book. This is your book.* Then say *Now it's your turn.* Have the student hold up a book and say *This is my book.*

- Look around the classroom and say *This is my classroom. This is your classroom. This is my school. This is your school.* Point to yourself when you say *my*. Point to students when you say *your*. Repeat, pausing after each sentence. Have students repeat after you.

- Play **TR: A18** once, with books closed, so students can listen. Then have students open their books to pp. 12–13. Play the song a second time. Have students hold up an eraser and a book, or point to the eraser and the book in the picture, as they hear those objects named in the song.

- Play the song again. Have students sing along and gesture when they hear *This is my school. This is your school.* Have them point to themselves when they hear *my*, and to classmates when they hear *your*.

*We can count from one to ten.*
*Just like this, just like this.*

*Is everybody ready?*
*Here we go!*
*1-2-3-4-5-6-7-8-9-10*
*Yay!*

**CHORUS**

*I know my colors.*
*Red and blue,*
*purple, too.*
*Orange, green, and yellow!*

**CHORUS**

*I like my school!*

5 **Sing again.** Hold up pictures.

13

## Be the Expert

### Teaching Tip

Students sometimes confuse shouting or using their voices loudly with singing. Help them experience different ways of using their voices. Have students whisper, speak, shout, and then sing a word or phrase. Remind students when they sing to use a singing voice. Ask *Are you using your singing voice?*

## Use It Again 5

- 5 **Vocabulary 2** Give out Picture Cards 1–3, 5, 7–8, 30, and 33 for *red, orange, yellow, blue, purple, green, a book,* and *an eraser.* Say each word once and have students hold up the correct card. Change the order, and repeat several times. Then have students take turns holding up their cards and naming them.

- Have students open their books to pp. 12–13. Say *Listen to the song. Listen for the words* eraser, book, red, blue, orange, green, yellow, *and* purple. *When you hear one of those words, hold up your card. Are you ready?* Play **TR: A18**. Point at students holding cards. Have students hold up their cards when they hear the words and see you point.

- Have students fill in the blank. Write *I have my* _________. on the board. Play the song and pause at *eraser*. Point to the student holding an eraser card, and have her say *eraser*. Repeat for the next line of the song: *and I have my book*.

- **Project** While reviewing numbers for the counting book, listen to **TR: A18**. Have students point to the numbers 1–10 on p. 13 as they sing.

- **Value** Have students open their books to p. 21. Play **TR: A18**. Pause at *This is your school.* Ask *What do we do in school?* (We listen. We talk. We read. We write.)

## Grammar 1

**Objectives**

Students will

- ask questions with *Is it?*
- answer questions with *Yes, it is* and *No, it isn't.*
- describe objects with *It's a.*

**Grammar** use simple present of *to be*

**Academic Language** *circle*

**Resources** Workbook pp. 7–8; Audio CD TR: A19–20; Video Sc. 6—Grammar 1; Classroom Presentation Tool: Grammar 1; Picture Cards 23, 25, 27, 29, 31

**Materials** paper bag

**GRAMMAR** TR: A19

| | | |
|---|---|---|
| **Is it** a pencil? | Yes, **it is.** | **It's** a pencil. |
| **Is it** a crayon? | No, **it isn't.** | **It's** a pen. |

6 **Look.** Listen and circle. TR: A20

1

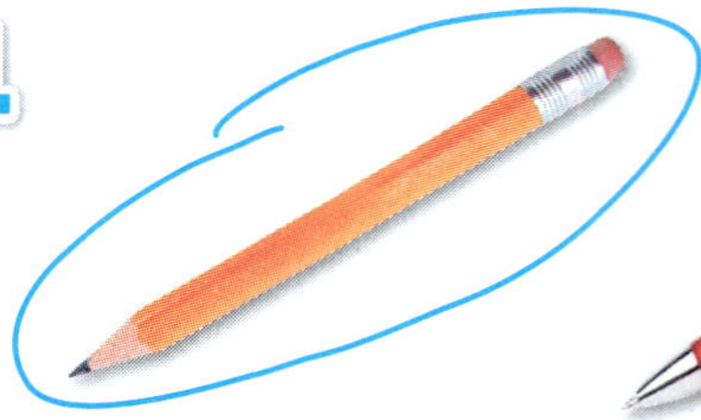

2

3

14

## Warm Up

- **Activate prior knowledge** Place a pen, a crayon, a pencil, and a piece of paper in a bag or container. Reach into the bag four times, each time pulling out an object and saying *Look! It's a (pencil). It's a (pen). It's a piece of (paper). It's a (crayon).*
- Put the objects back in the bag. Take out one object and say *Look! It's a* ________. Have students orally fill in the blank.
- Place the object back in the bag. Have students take turns reaching into the bag and saying *Look! It's a (crayon.)*
- Now place all of the objects on a desk or table. Point to one object at a time and ask *Is it a (pencil)? Is it a (pen)?*

**4**

**5**

**6**

15

## Be the Expert

### Our World in Context

- More than 14 billion pencils are produced in the world each year.
- One pencil can draw a line 112 km (70 mi.) long!

### Grammar in Depth

Write *it is* on the board. Cross out the *i* in *is* and replace with an apostrophe. Explain that *it's* is formed from the words *it* and *is*. Model how to join the two words to form the contraction. Have children practice using *It's (a, an)* plus the names of familiar classroom objects to form sentences. (*It's a desk.*)

## Present

- Write the following on the board:

| | |
|---|---|
| Yes, it is. | It's a pen. |
| | It's a pencil. |
| No, It isn't. | It's a crayon. |
| | It's a desk. |

- Point to or display a pencil. Ask *Is it a pencil?* Say *Yes, it is. It's a pencil.* Then point to or display a crayon. Ask *Is it a pencil?* Say *No, it isn't. It's a crayon.*
- Model with a student. Ask the question and have the student answer. As the student answers, point to and connect the sentence parts on the board.
- Finally, have students answer together. Point to an object and ask *Is it a (pencil)?* Point to or have a student point to the words on the board as the class responds.

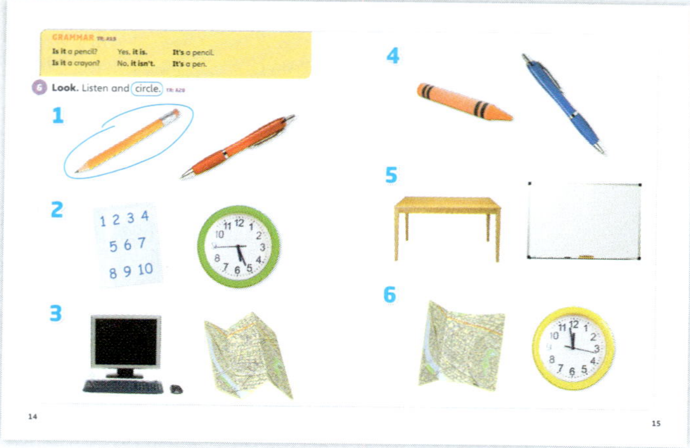


## Practice 6

- Read aloud the sentences in the grammar box or play **TR: A19**. Explain that students will listen to questions and answers like these in order to complete the activity. Then read the directions with students. Explain that they will circle the word they hear in the audio. Say *circle* and practice circling in the air.

- 6 Review the names of the object pictured on pp. 14–15. Then play **TR: A20**. Point out that item 1 has been completed as an example. Have students draw a circle around each correct response as they hear it. ✓ Point to pictures on pp. 14–15. Ask *What is this?*

## Wrap Up

- Walk around the room pointing to classroom objects. Ask questions such as *Is it a map? Is it a globe?*

## Recap

- Remind students that they can use *is it, it is, it isn't,* and *it's* to talk about things inside and outside of the classroom. Hold up a crayon and ask *Is it a pencil?* (No, it isn't.) *Is it a crayon?* (Yes, it is.)

## Apply

- Walk around the room asking about the color of objects. For example, ask *Is it a clock?* (Yes, it is.) *Is it yellow?* (No, it isn't.) *Is it red?* (Yes, it is.) Use objects such as a clock, a crayon, a pen, a map, and a desk to give students practice asking and answering questions with *Is it? Yes, it is. No, it isn't.* and *It's.*

- Have students play a guessing game. Place Picture Cards 23, 25, 27, 29 and 31 (a crayon, a computer, a pen, a table, a chair) in a bag. Pair students. Have each partner take a card, look at it, and place it face down. Partners should not see each other's cards.

- Have partners take turns asking questions until they guess the object. Model with a student. Ask *Is it a crayon?* Have the student answer *Yes, it is* or *No, it isn't.* Continue asking and answering questions until both objects have been named.

- **Expand** Have students ask and answer questions about the objects using the name of an object as well as a color. For example, *Is it an orange crayon?*

## Extend

- Draw a red square, a yellow triangle, a blue star and a green rectangle on the board. Point to the blue star. Ask *Is it a star? Is it a (red) star?* Continue with additional examples. Be sure to ask questions that can be answered with *Yes, it is* and *No, it isn't.*

## Wrap Up

- Have students make their own picture cards. On one side of a sheet of paper, have them draw a classroom object such as a clock, a desk, or a crayon. Have them label the picture. Have students take turns holding up cards and asking *Is this a (chair)?* Have other students answer *Yes, it is*, or *No it isn't. It's a (desk).*

## Be the Expert

### Teaching Tip

Tone of voice goes up or down at the end of a sentence. If a sentence ends in rising intonation, the voice tone goes up at the end of that sentence. Questions can end in either rising or falling intonation. Questions that begin with *who, what, when, where, why*, and *how* usually end in falling intonation.

### Formative Assessment

Can students

- ask questions with *Is it?*

  Display an object such as a pencil or a crayon. Have students repeat after you. Call on students to ask questions about the object.

- answer questions with *Yes, it is* and *No, it isn't.*

  Display an object such as a pencil or crayon. Ask *Is it a (crayon)?* Be sure to have students use gestures to indicate *yes* or *no*.

- describe objects with *It's a.*

  Point to an object pictured on Student Book pp. 14–15. Have students say *It's a (map).*

## Vocabulary 2

**Objective**

Students will

- identify and use words for classroom objects.

**Vocabulary** *a book, a chair, an eraser, a desk, a picture*

**Resources** Workbook p. 9; Audio CD TR: A21–22; Video: Sc. 4—Vocabulary 2; Classroom Presentation Tool: Vocabulary 2; Picture Cards 20–34; Teacher's Resource CD-ROM: Activity Worksheet 1.2

**7 Listen and say.** TR: A21

**8 Work with a partner.** Point and say.

**9 Work with a partner.** Guess and stick. TR: A22

16

## Warm Up

- **Recycle** Review words for classroom objects that students learned earlier in the unit. Point to a table or a desk and ask *What is it?* When students answer correctly, point and ask about other objects in the classroom, for example, a computer, a pen, paper, a clock, a map, a pencil, or a crayon.

## Present

- Hold up your book and ask *Is it a map?* (no) Encourage students to answer *no* or *No, it isn't.* Then ask *Is it a clock?* (no) *Is it a table?* (no) Act as though you are thinking hard and say *What is it?* Then open the book to p. 16 and point to the picture of the book. Say *a book* twice. Have students repeat. Point to the book and ask *What is it?* (a book)
- Have students open their books to p. 16. Point to each of the other vocabulary words one by one. Repeat each word twice and then have students say the word.
- Touch a chair and ask *What is it?* When students give the correct answer, say *That's right. It's a chair.* One by one, touch examples of the remaining target words (an eraser, a desk, a picture). Ask students to use each word. ✓ Say *Point to a book. Point to a chair.*

## Practice 7 8

- 7 Play track **TR: A21** or read the words as students listen and repeat them.
- Say *Listen and say.* Point to the picture of the eraser on page 16. Say *An eraser. An eraser.* Then say each of the remaining vocabulary words twice, giving students a chance to point to and say each word in the book.
- 8 Put students in pairs. One student points to a word and the other student says the word. Model the activity with a student. Point to one of the pictures until the student says the word. Make sure students take turns pointing and saying the words.

## Apply 9

- 9 Place students in pairs. Hold up the book, pointing to Activity 9 on page p. 16. Play **TR: A22**. Model the dialogue with a student. Then have the pairs practice the dialogue together.
- Say *Look at the Unit 1 stickers in the back of your book.* Point to the stickers one at a time and ask *What is it?*
- Model the activity with a student. Have your partner peel off a sticker and not show it to you. Ask questions such as *Is it a (clock)?* Have your partner answer *Yes, it is* or *No, it isn't*. Once you guess correctly, both you and the student should place the sticker in the first box of the activity.
- Put students in pairs. Walk around the room as students place their stickers, offering help as needed.

## Extend

- Have a student come to the front of the room, close his eyes, and choose one of the Unit 1 Picture Cards. Have him face the class. Hold up the student's card for the class to see. The student facing the class should not be able to see the card.
- Have the student ask the class *Yes/No* questions about the word. Give the class examples aloud, such as *Is it a chair? Is it a map?* Once the volunteer student guesses the word correctly, repeat the activity with a different student.

## Wrap Up

- Touch, hold up, or point to real classroom objects, such as a desk, one by one. For each, say *What is it?* Let students call out the answer together.

## Be the Expert

### Teaching Tip

If you do more than one activity in pairs during a lesson, try to pair different students for each activity. Having the opportunity to work with different partners helps keep activities interesting for students.

### Formative Assessment

Can students

- identify and use words for classroom objects?

  Hold up Picture Cards 30–34 one at a time and ask students *Is it a (picture)?* Students should answer *Yes, it is.* or *No, it isn't. It's a (book).*

**Review** For additional practice, direct students to Activity Worksheet 1.2.

# Grammar 2

**Objectives**

Students will

- ask questions using *what, what color,* and *how many.*
- identify, describe, and count classroom objects.

**Grammar** ask questions using *what, what color,* and *how many*

**Resources** Workbook pp. 10–11; Audio CD TR: A23–24; Video: Sc. 7—Grammar 2; Classroom Presentation Tool: Grammar 2; Teacher's Resource CD-ROM: Activity Worksheet 1.3

**Materials** red, blue, and yellow crayons; erasers

**GRAMMAR** TR: A23

| | |
|---|---|
| **What** is it? | It's a table. |
| **What color** is it? | It's yellow. |
| **How many** pencils? | Three. |

**10** **Work in groups.** Look and point. Ask and answer. TR: A24

**11** **Look at the picture.** Write.

1. How many crayons? ________________
2. What color is the frog? ________________
3. How many clocks? ________________



## Warm Up

- **Preteach** Hold up a crayon and say *It's a crayon.* Then hold up two crayons and say *Two crayons.*
- Hold up three crayons and say *Count with me. One, two, three crayons.* Hold up a pencil and say *It's a pencil.* Then hold up three pencils and say *Count with me. One, two, three pencils.* Repeat with books and erasers.

## Present

- Hold up a yellow crayon and ask *What is it?* Model the response for students. Say *It's a crayon.* Ask *What color is it?* Say *It's yellow.* Repeat with blue and red crayons.
- On the board, write the sentence frame *It's a* __________. Hold up a pencil, an eraser, a crayon, and a book, one by one. As you hold up each object, move your finger under the words on the board and say *It's a (pencil).* Have students repeat after you.
- Direct students' attention to the grammar box at the top of p. 17. Play **TR: A23**. Have students listen to the recording once, and then play it again. As they listen, point to a table, the yellow crayon, and the three pencils.

## Practice 10

- Place students in small groups. Say *Look at the photo.* Point to the yellow paper on the right-hand side. Ask *What color is it?* Say *It's yellow.* Point to the red square at the bottom of the photo. Ask *What color is it?* (It's red.)
- 10 Say *Now it's your turn.* Point to one student. Say *Hold up your book. Point to the number eight. Ask What color is it?* Point to another student. Say *Answer. Say the color.* (green)
- Ask *What colors do we already know?* (black, white, red, blue, green, orange, purple, yellow) Once students have successfully named the colors, have them get in groups and complete the activity. ✓ If students need more practice with color names, have them review the photo on p. 3.

## Apply 11

- Write the numbers one through ten on the board.

| | | | | |
|---|---|---|---|---|
| one | two | three | four | five |
| six | seven | eight | nine | ten |

- Have students read them aloud, holding up the correct number of fingers as they read and count. Say *Look carefully at the photo. Read the questions. Then write your answers on the lines. Let's practice together.* Read item 1 aloud. Have students find the crayons in the photo, then say *Three. Three crayons.*
- 11 Have students complete the activity. When they have finished, have students read the questions and their answers aloud.

## Extend

- Place several crayons, pencils, books, and erasers on a table. Have students come up to the table and take turns asking and answering questions.
- Add or remove objects from each group. For example, point to a group of three erasers and ask *How many erasers?* Then add or remove an eraser and ask *How many erasers?*

## Wrap Up

- Hold up a pencil or crayon. Ask *What is it? How many (pencils)? What color is it?* Repeat with classroom objects such as books, pencils, shapes, and letters of the alphabet.

## Be the Expert

### Grammar in Depth

Question words in English usually begin with the letters *wh*, as in the word *what*. The word *how* is an exception. Although it begins with the letter *h*, the word *how* is a question word in English. Question words include *what, where, when, why, who,* and *how*.

### Formative Assessment

Can students

- ask questions using *what, what color,* and *how many*?

  Hold up a pencil, a crayon, and a book. For each object, ask *What is it? What color is it? How many?*
- identify, describe, and count classroom objects?

  Revisit Unit 0, pp. 3 and 6 with students. Ask students to identify objects around the classroom by asking questions like *What is it? What color is it?* and *How many crayons?*

**Review** For additional practice, direct students to Activity Worksheet 1.3.

## Reading

**Objectives**

Students will

- compare drawing and writing in the past and now.
- talk about the past and now.

**Reading Strategy** Compare and Contrast

**Academic Language** *draw, write, check, count*

**Content Vocabulary** *a canvas, a hand, now, paint, in the past, a stick, a tablet, a wall*

**Resources** Workbook pp. 12–13; Audio CD TR: A25; Classroom Presentation Tool: Reading; Teacher's Resource CD-ROM; Graphic Organizers (T-chart)

**Materials** poster board; photos of old and new objects (typewriter, computer, dial phone, smartphone, horse and carriage, modern automobile, etc.)

## Warm Up

- **Build background** Point to the picture of the electronic tablet on p. 18. Say *This is a tablet. What do we use a tablet like this for?* (to write, to read) If necessary, prompt responses with gestures for writing and reading. Point to the photo of the clay tablet. Say *This is a tablet, too. This tablet is from a long time ago. It's from the past. In the past, people used tablets like this one to write.*
- Point to the stick on p. 18. Say *This is a stick. In the past, people used sticks like this one to write. Do we use sticks to write now? What do we use to write?* Pause to get student responses, which may include pencils, pens, or crayons.

## Present 12 13

- 12 Direct students to p. 18. Point to and read the title aloud. Have students repeat after you. Pretend to write in a notebook. Ask *What am I doing?* (writing) Then pretend to sketch or draw. Ask *What am I doing now?* (drawing) Say *Show me what it looks like when you write.*
- **Read together** Play **TR: A25** once and have students read along as they listen. Play **TR: A25** again. Pause the audio at *In the past*. Say *Listen to the words. When you hear a word, point to the photo on the page.* Have students point to the pictures of a hand, a wall, a tablet, and a stick as they hear those objects named.

**13** **What about you?** Circle.

1. I draw on **a wall** **paper.** (circled)
2. I draw with **a crayon** **a stick.**
3. I write with **a hand** **a pencil.**

**14** **Work with a partner.** Look and read. Check. ✓

| | Past | Now |
|---|---|---|
| crayon | | ✓ |
| hand | | |
| paint | | |
| tablet | | |
| stick | | |

**15** **Look in your desk.** Read. Count and write.

1. How many frogs? 0
2. How many pencils? ______
3. How many crayons? ______
4. How many sticks? ______
5. How many pens? ______

19

## Be the Expert

### About the Photo

The Cueva de las Manos is in Santa Cruz, Argentina. The paintings in the cave were made between 13,000 and 9,500 years ago. The cave takes its name (Cave of the Hands) from the outlines of human hands inside. In addition to the images of hands, the cave has many images of animals still found in the area, as well as of hunting scenes.

### Our World in Context

The type of writing shown on the clay tablet is called cuneiform. Cuneiform writing was probably invented in southern Mesopotamia (modern Iraq) about 3400–3300 BCE. Cuneiform was invented as a way to keep records of goods and services.

### Teaching Tip

Make a Word Wall for your classroom. A Word Wall is a collection of words displayed in the classroom. Word Walls can help students identify patterns and make important connections between words. Place Word Walls where students can easily see them. Add new words to your Word Wall regularly.

- Pause the audio at *Now*. Say *Listen for the names of things people use now.* Repeat the process with *Now* and the words *a canvas*, *paint*, and *a tablet*. After students have listened to the audio, say *Point to two tablets on the page. Point to something people used in the past to write. Point to something people use now to write.*
- **13** Say *make a circle* and have students draw circles in the air. Mime the action for students. Say *Look at Activity 13. When you pick an answer, circle the words.* Read item 1. Explain that the answer has been given as an example. Say *The answer to number one is paper. I draw on paper.*
- Write *a crayon*, *a stick*, *a hand*, and *a pencil* on the board. Make a simple drawing of each object next to the word.

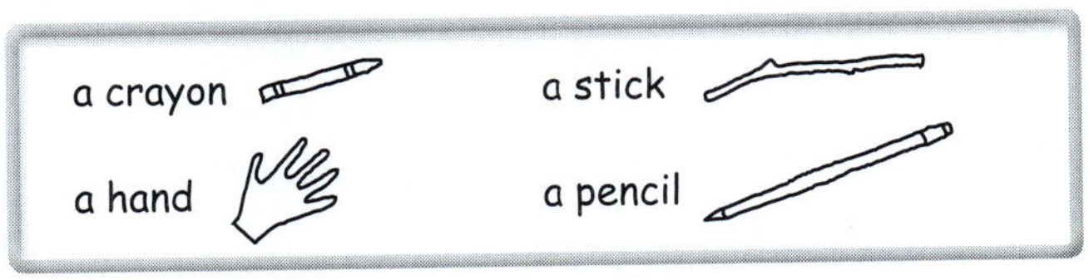


- Read each word aloud, and have students repeat. Say *Now do numbers 2 and 3 on your own.* Have students complete the activity independently. ✓ Walk around the room and ask *Do you draw with a crayon or a stick? Do you write with a hand or a pencil?*
- **Expand** Have students trace their hands on white or colored paper. Have them write the following sentences on different fingers: *I draw. I write. I read. I talk. I listen.* Then have them write *My name is* ________. on the other side of the paper.

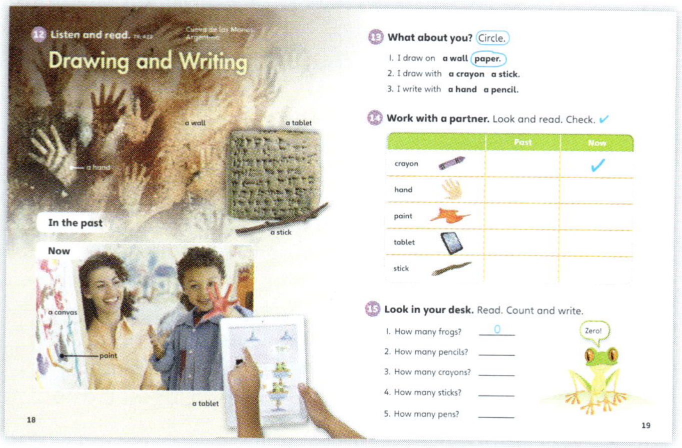
12 Listen and read.

Drawing and Writing

a wall

a tablet

a hand

In the past

a stick

Now

a canvas

paint

a tablet

18

13 What about you? Circle.

1. I draw on **a wall** **paper.**
2. I draw with **a crayon** **a stick.**
3. I write with **a hand** **a pencil.**

14 **Work with a partner.** Look and read. Check. ✓

| | Past | Now |
|---|---|---|
| crayon | | ✓ |
| hand | | |
| paint | | |
| tablet | | |
| stick | | |

15 **Look in your desk.** Read. Count and write.

1. How many frogs? 0
2. How many pencils? ____
3. How many crayons? ____
4. How many sticks? ____
5. How many pens? ____

Zero!

19

## Practice 14

- Have students open their books to p. 19. Have them point to the images in the first column of the three-column chart. Help them read and say *crayon, hand, paint, tablet,* and *stick*. Then have them read the words again. Tell students that they are going to act out the words. Say *Draw with a crayon. Hold up your hand. Paint. Write on a tablet. Use a stick. Have students act out the words.*

- 14 Say *Look at Activity 14.* Say *check* and have students draw checks in the air. Say *When you pick an answer, make a check.* Trace your finger under the first row and say *Crayon. Draw with crayons. There's a check under* Now. *We draw with crayons now. That's right.*

- Say *Now, do the next four on your own. Remember that you can check both* Past *and* Now *for some things.* ✓ As you walk around the room, stop and ask questions such as *Do we use tablets like this now? Where should you put the check?*

- **Expand** Collect photos and pictures of things from the past as well as their modern versions, for example, a typewriter and a computer, or an old-fashioned phone and a modern smartphone. Draw a T-chart on poster board and have students sort the pictures under the headings **Past** and **Now**.

## Wrap Up

- Hold up a sheet of paper. Say *paper.* Then say *I draw on paper.* Repeat with a crayon and a pencil. Say *A pencil. I write with a pencil. A crayon. I draw with a crayon.* Then hold up one object at a time and have students name the object and tell whether they use it to draw or write. Accept short answers such as *draw*, or *I draw*.

## Recap

- Write **Past** and **Now** on the board. Say *I'm going to say some words. Listen carefully. When you hear a word, say* past *or* now. *You can also say* past *and* now *if something is from the past and we still use it now.*

- Say *draw with crayons,* (now) *tablet,* (past and now) *write with sticks.* (past) As students respond, list the terms under **Past** or **Now**.

| Past | Now |
|---|---|
| write with sticks | draw with crayons |
| tablet | tablet |

## Apply 15

- Hold up three crayons and two pencils. Ask *How many crayons?* (three) *How many pencils?* (two) Hold up both hands and have two students hold up their hands. Ask *How many hands?* (six)

- 15 Say *Look at Activity 15. Let's do number one together.* Point to a student and say *Look in your desk. How many frogs?* Wait for the student to respond. Say *Zero. Number one says zero. Freddy says zero, too. There are zero frogs in your desk. That's correct. Now do the rest on your own.*

- When students have completed the activity, have them share their answers. Have them read both the question and their answer aloud.

## Extend

- Write the following words on separate index cards or pieces of paper: *I*, *draw with*, *write with*, *draw on*, *a crayon*, *paper*, *a pencil*, *a pen*, *a tablet*. Sort the words into three groups. In one group, place several cards with the word *I*. In a second group, place cards for *draw with*, *write with*, and *draw on*. In the third group place *a crayon*, *paper*, *a pencil*, *a pen*, and *a tablet*.
- Have students use cards from each group to make complete sentences.

## Wrap Up

- Model how to use the chart on p. 19 to summarize the reading on page 18. For example, point to the hand on p. 19 and to a hand at the top of p. 18. Say *People used to paint with their hands.* Point to the boy with the red hand and say *People paint with their hands now.*

## Be the Expert

### Reading Strategy

**Compare and Contrast** Group several items by color. For example, place a red crayon, a red book, and a red pencil next to a similar group of blue objects. As you name the objects in each group, point out that they are the same color. Repeat with the blue objects.

Then take one red and one blue object and explain that they are not the same because they are different colors. Repeat with combinations of different objects and colors.

### Fluency

To help students develop oral reading skills, echo read the text on p. 18 with them. Read the title aloud. Have students repeat after you as they track the print with their fingers. Repeat with the remaining words and phrases. Guide students to imitate the stress and intonation of each word or phrase.

### Formative Assessment

Can students

- compare drawing and writing in the past and now?

  Revisit the photos and captions on p. 18. Help students rephrase the information on the page.
- talk about the past and now?

  Review the chart on p. 19. Ask students to use short phrases to compare the past and now.

## Writing

**Writing** Make a name tag.

**Objectives**

Students will

- view writing models.
- use capital letters in their writing.
- introduce themselves to classmates using their name tags.

**Academic Language** *cut, put on*

**Resources** Workbook p. 14; Classroom Presentation Tool: Writing; Audio CD TR: A26

**Materials** scissors; colored pencils, crayons or markers

### Formative Assessment

Can students

- use capital letters in their writing?

  Review the name tags in the photo on p. 20. Explain that capital, or big, letters are used at the beginning of a sentence and with the first letter of a name.
- introduce themselves to classmates, using their name tags?

  Have students practice asking and answering *What's your name?* with you.

**16 Make a name tag.**

1. Cut out the name tag on page 159.
2. Write ***Hello*** with a crayon.
3. Write ***My name is*** with a pencil.
4. Write your name in a different color.

**17 Put on your name tag.**

Walk and talk. TR: A26

20

## Present

- Walk around the room and introduce yourself to several students, one by one. Say *My name is (Mr. Ramos).* Ask *What's your name?* Ask students to answer in complete sentences (My name is Dan.), but accept shorter answers. (Dan)
- Next, have students stand in a circle. Have them turn to the person on their left and right side and say *Hello. My name is ________.* Be sure to have all students introduce themselves. Model for students if necessary.
- Have students remain in the circle. Have them introduce themselves and their classmates to the group. Have each student say *Hello. My name is (Chun). This is (Fa). This is (Lin).*

## Write 16

- 16 Have students return to their seats and open their books to p. 20. Point to one of the tags at the top of the page. Say *This is a name tag.* Ask *What's (her name)?* (Marta) Read step 1 aloud and then help students find the name tag in the back of the Student Book. Have them cut out the name tag.
- Say *Let's read together.* Read step 2 together and then say *Choose a crayon. Write* Hello *at the top of your name tag. Write with the crayon.*
- Read step 3 aloud. Say *Write* My name is *under* Hello. *Write with a pencil.*
- Read step 4 aloud. Say *Now choose a different color crayon or pencil. Write your name.*

NATIONAL GEOGRAPHIC

# Our World

## Work hard in school.

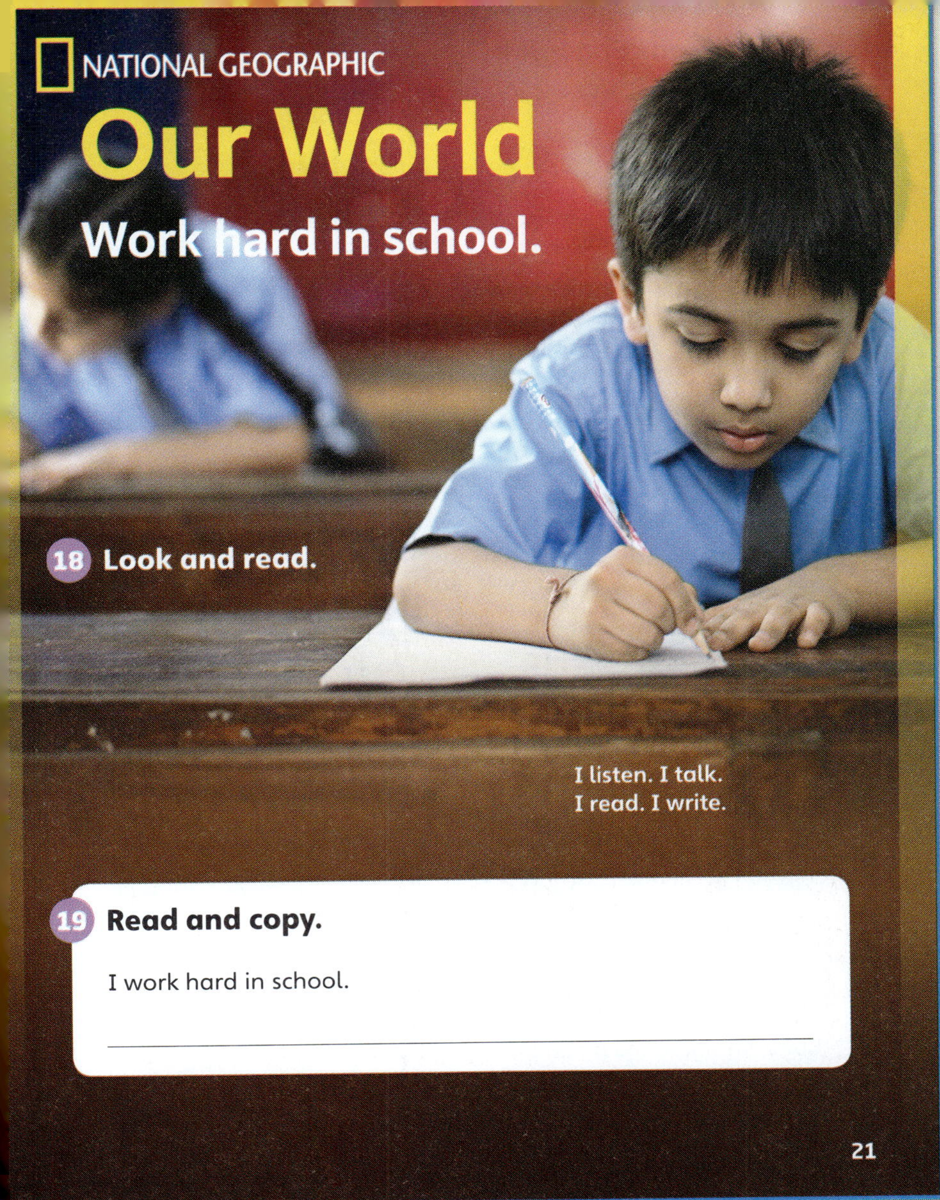

**18** **Look and read.**

I listen. I talk.
I read. I write.

**19** **Read and copy.**

I work hard in school.

___________________________



## Value

**Value** Work hard in school.

**Objectives**

Students will

- read about school-related values and activities.
- read and copy a complete sentence.

**Academic Language** *copy*

**Resources** Values Poster

## Be the Expert

### Teaching Tip

Develop routines to help writing activities run smoothly. Be sure students know:

- when and how to sharpen their pencils.
- where paper and other writing tools are kept.
- where to look for information, or how to ask for help when needed.

### Related Vocabulary

*boy, girl, children*

- Remind students to use capital letters when they write the first letter of their names. ✔ Walk around the room and ask *Where do you put the big letter?*

## Share 17

- **17** Have students look at Activity 17. Have a student read the direction line aloud. Play **TR: A26** and have students listen.
- Then have students put on their name tags. Have them walk around the room and talk to one another, using the speech bubbles as a model. Have them use their own names for *Mia* and *Freddy*. Say *Now let's all walk and talk. Walk around the classroom. Talk. Say hello. Say your name.* If students need additional support, play **TR: A26** again, and have them listen until they feel comfortable with the language.

## Value 18 19

- Point to the photo on p. 21. Say *This is a classroom.* Point to the pencil. Ask *What is it?* (a pencil) *What is the boy doing?* (writing) Say *That's right. It's a pencil. He's using a pencil to write.*
- Read the title and the first sentence on p. 21 aloud. Explain that *work hard* means to do the best you can. Say *The boy in the photo works hard. Do you work hard in school?*
- **18** Say *Read number 18.* Then call on a student to read the text under the photo of the boy. Ask *What are four things you do in school?*
- **19** Say *Now let's read and copy.* Have students read silently and then copy the sentence.

## Project

**Objectives**

Students will

- think and write about objects and numbers.
- create a counting book.
- complete the Unit 1 Quiz.

**Academic Language** *decide*

**Resources** Assessment: Unit 1 Quiz; Picture Cards 20–34; Teacher's Resource CD-ROM: Activity Worksheet 1.4

**Materials** scissors; glue; crayons; ten pieces of colored construction paper per student

### 20 Make a counting book.

Cut out the pictures on page 159.

Decide how many.

Color and glue the pictures.

Draw more pictures and write the number.

22

## Prepare

- Review the vocabulary words students learned in this unit. Hold up the Unit 1 Picture Cards one by one, giving students a chance to call out the name of each object. As you show each Picture Card ask *What is it?* Encourage students to answer It's a ________.
- Say *Point to a chair.* Repeat this activity with as many of the Unit 1 words as can be found in your classroom.
- Open a Student Book to pp. 22–23. Hold it up. Point to the counting book in the photo. Say *This is a counting book. Let's make our own counting books!*
- Help students find the pictures of classroom objects on p. 159. Point to the pictures one by one, calling on different students to name them.
- Next, write these steps on the board:

1. Cut.
2. Decide how many.
3. Color and glue.
4. Draw and write the number.

- Hold up a pair of scissors. Say *Cut out the pictures.* Point out the dotted lines around each of the pictures. Show how to cut out the pictures along these lines, and then have students cut out their pictures.

# Be the Expert

## Project Rubric

✓ Did students cut out the pictures along the lines?

✓ Did students color each of the pictures on the paper?

✓ Did students write the correct number of pictures on the paper?

- Model choosing a picture. Say *How many (maps)? One (map).* Model coloring and gluing the map cutout to the paper. Write *I map* at the bottom of the paper. Then model choosing and copying another picture. Say *How many (chairs)? Two (chairs).* Model coloring and gluing it to the paper. Draw and color one more chair on the paper. Then write *2 chairs* at the bottom of the paper. Say *Now make ten pages for your book for numbers one to ten.*

## Share

- Model sharing a page from a counting book. Stand in front of the class, holding up the page of chairs you made. Count the chairs, then say the number of chairs: *One, two. Two.*
- Have a student share her book with the class. Have her count the objects on each page and say the number of objects.
- **Modify** If less time is available, have students work in small groups and create a counting book together.

## Now I Can

Ask questions such as the following:

- *What's something we use in the classroom?*
- Hold up several (crayons) and ask *How many?*
- Hold up a (red) crayon and ask *What color is it?*

**Review** For additional practice, direct students to Activity Worksheet I.4.

## Unit Assessment

Give the Unit I Quiz. Hand out the quiz and go over the instructions with students. The quiz should take 15–20 minutes.

## Video

**Vocabulary 1a** *a classroom, a board, a clock, a pencil*

**Vocabulary 1b** *a crayon, a map, a table, a computer*

**Vocabulary 2** *a desk, a chair, an eraser, a picture*

**Grammar 1** use simple present of *to be*

**Grammar 2** ask questions using *what, what color* and *how many*

**Song** *My School*

**Viewing** classrooms and classroom objects

**Story Time** *What's in My Classroom?*

**Resources** Student Book, pp. 8–17

## Before You Watch

- Play the opening credits to the episode. Pause when Anna and Freddy are introduced. Say *This is Anna. This is Freddy.* Ask *Where else can we see Freddy?* (in our book)

- Next, play the introduction to the video. Say *This video is about classrooms. It's also about things in a classroom.* Ask *What do we do in the classroom? What do we write with? What do we draw with?*

## While You Watch

- As they watch the video, have students look and listen for target words that tell about things in the classroom.

- Say *Listen carefully. Listen to how Freddy and Anna say the words.*

## After You Watch

- Play parts of the video with the sound off. Have students talk about what's happening on screen.

## Zoom In

### Vocabulary

- Pause the video during the vocabulary reviews, just before Freddy names an object. Have students name each object. Press *Play* to hear Freddy's answer.

### Grammar

- Play the first half of Scene 7: Grammar 2 without pausing. Pause when Anna says *Now it's your turn.* Have students try to answer the questions before the clock stops ticking. If students need additional time, pause the video.

### Song

- Play *My School* once and have students listen. Play it again, and have students sing along as Anna counts from one to ten and names colors.

### Viewing

- Play a few seconds of Scene 10: Viewing without audio. Have students tell what they think the segment is about. Ask *What do you see?*

### Story Time

- View Scene 11: Story Time once with students. Pause the video every time Anna asks *What is it?*

- View it again. Play all the way through without pausing. After students have viewed *What's in My Classroom* twice, pause at still images and ask questions such as *What is it? What color is it?*

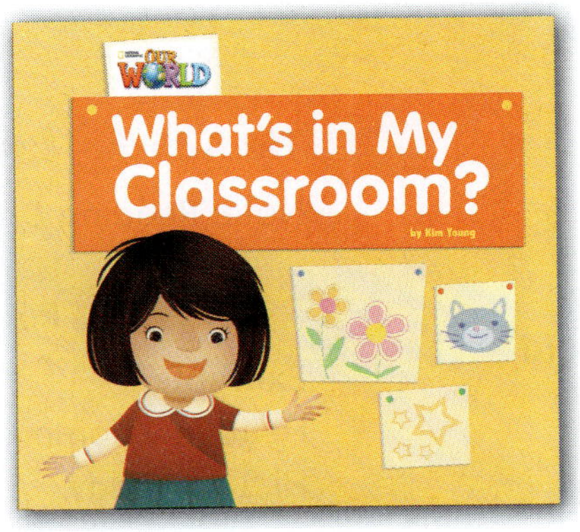


## *What's in My Classroom?*

A teacher and her students give clues about objects in their classroom. Readers guess each object and then turn the page to find the answer.

# Before You Read

- **Activate Prior Knowledge** Hold up the reader. Point to the title. Say *The name of the book is "What's in My Classroom?"* Help students think about what's in their own classroom by pointing to objects in the class and asking *What is it?*
- **Introduce the Strategy** Show Picture Cards 20–34 one at a time, giving students a chance to name each object. Say *Good! You know what's in a classroom!*
- Draw a two-column chart on the board. Label one column **Colors and shapes** and the other column **What is it?** Say *Look and listen for colors and shapes in the book.* Point to the first column and say *Write the colors and shapes.* Point to the second column and say *Write what's in the classroom.*

# While You Read

- Read the book aloud to students. Stop after every few pages and ask questions to help students think about what they already know. Help them use this information to figure out each answer.

  p. 3: What is a circle? Draw a circle.
  p. 5: What is yellow? Point to something yellow in the classroom.
  p. 7: What is a rectangle? Draw a rectangle.

- As you read, stop at the shapes and colors students know and write them in the **Colors and shapes** column of the chart. Have students guess the object. When students see and say the answer, say *Good! Yes! It is a (board).* After each object is revealed, write the answer in the **What is it?** column.

# After You Read

- Have students choose a different classroom object and write their own clues about the object. Give each student a chance to read his or her clues. Give the class time to guess the object.

## Unit 2 Reader

**Text Type** informational text

**Vocabulary** *board, classroom, clock, pencil*

**Grammar** use simple present of *to be;* ask questions using *what, what color,* and *how many*

**Reading Strategy** Connect Text to Prior Knowledge

**Resources** Picture Cards 20–34; Classroom Presentation Tool: Story Time; Teacher's Resource CD-ROM: Graphic Organizers (Two-column chart)

## Be the Expert

### Reading Strategy

**Connect Text to Prior Knowledge** Most readings will include words and ideas with which students are already familiar. This is called *prior knowledge.* Before students read, help them think of the things they know about the subject of the reading. While they read, point out words and ideas in the text that they are already familiar with. Applying prior knowledge helps students understand what they read.

### Teaching Tip

Teach students basic literacy ideas, such as:

- Every book has a title and an author. Point out the title and the author on the cover of the reader.
- Books are read from top to bottom, and books in English are read from left to right. Move your finger along the words of the reader as you read it so that students can see the left to right and top to bottom direction of your reading.
- The pages of a book are numbered. Point out the numbers at the bottom of each page of the reader.

## Student Book

**TR: A15** (1) **Listen and say.**

a computer, a table, a pen, paper, a map, a classroom, a clock, a crayon, a pencil, a board

**TR: A16** (2) **Listen. Point and say.**

table, crayon, pencil, pen, computer, map, classroom, clock, board, paper

**TR: A17** (3) **Work with a partner. Point. Ask and answer.**

Example
What is it?
It's a crayon.

**TR: A18** (4) **Listen. Read and sing.**

Note: Lyrics for the song *My School* are on pp. 48–49.

**TR: A19** **Grammar**

Note: Grammar 1 is on p. 50.

**TR: A20** (6) **Look. Listen and circle.**

1. Is it a pen?
No, it isn't. It's a pencil.
2. Is it a clock?
Yes, it is. It's a clock.
3. Is it a computer?
No, it isn't. It's a map.
4. Is it a crayon?
Yes, it is. It's a crayon.
5. Is it a table?
Yes, it is. It's a table.
6. Is it a clock?
No, it isn't. It's a map.

**TR: A21** (7) **Listen and say.**

a book, a chair, an eraser, a desk, a picture

**TR: A22** (9) **Work with a partner. Guess and stick.**

**Example**
Is it a desk?
No, it isn't.
Is it a book?
Yes, it is. It's a book.

**TR: A23** **Grammar**

Note: Grammar 2 is on p. 56.

**TR: A24** (10) **Work in groups. Look and point. Ask and answer.**

Example
What color is it?
It's yellow.

**TR: A25** (12) **Listen and read.**

Note: Reading *Drawing and Writing* is on p. 58.

**TR: A26** (17) **Put on your nametag. Walk and talk.**

**Example**
Hello, my name is Mia. What's your name?
Hi. I'm Freddy.

## Workbook

**TR: 5** (1) **Listen. Look and match. Draw lines.**

1. a board, 2. a classroom, 3. a clock, 4. a computer, 5. a crayon, 6. a map, 7. paper, 8. a pen, 9. a pencil, 10. a table

**TR: 6** (3) **Listen to the song. Circle.**

I have my eraser,
and I have my book.
I have my eraser.
Come and look!

**TR: 7** (4) **Listen. Write.**

Is everybody ready?
Here we go!
1-2-3-4-5-6-7-8-9-10
Yay!

**TR: 8** (5) **Listen. Color.**

I know my colors.
Red and blue,
purple, too.
Orange, green, and yellow!
CHORUS
I like my school!

**TR: 9** (6) **Listen. Circle.**

1. Is it a clock?
Yes, it is.
2. Is it a pen?
No, it isn't. It's a pencil.
3. Is it a table?
Yes, it is.
4. Is it a computer?
Yes, it is.
5. Is it a map?
No, it isn't. It's paper.

**TR: 10** (9) **Listen. Look and read. Write.**

1. Is it a pencil?
Yes, it is.
2. Is it a table?
Yes, it is.
3. Is it a map?
No, it isn't.

**TR: 11** (11) **Listen and find. Color. Write.**

1. Color the picture gray.
2. Color the book blue.
3. Color the eraser green.
4. Color the chair yellow.
5. Color the table orange.

**TR: 12** (12) **Listen and write. Draw lines.**

1. What is it?
   It's a chair.
2. What color is the clock?
   White. It's a white clock.
3. How many pencils?
   Five pencils.
4. What is it?
   It's a desk.
5. How many books?
   Two books.

**TR: 13** (14) **Listen and draw a line.**

1. What is it?
   It's a computer.
2. How many books?
   Two books.
3. What color is the desk?
   It's white.
4. What is it?
   It's an eraser.
5. How many pens?
   Six pens.

**TR: 14** (16) **Listen and read.**

The English Alphabet
In the past
A B C D E F G H I K L M N O P Q R S T V X Y Z; 23 letters.
Now
A B C D E F G H I J K L M N O P Q R S T U V W X Y Z; 26 letters. Alphabet letters represent sounds.

**TR: 15** (20) **Listen and find. Color.**

C, M, T, F, O, Z, B, X, L, A, N, D, W, P, E, G, I, Q, J, R, U, K, S, V, H, Y

**TR: 16** (23) **Listen and circle. Color.**

1. What is it?
   It's a crayon.
2. Is it a map?
   Yes, it is. It's a map.
3. What is it?
   It's a desk.
4. Is it a computer?
   No, it isn't. It's a book.
5. How many pens?
   Seven pens.
6. How many chairs?
   One chair.

# Answer Key

## Student Book

### Unit Opener SB p. 8

globe

(6) SB pp. 14–15

1. pencil, 2. clock, 3. map, 4. crayon, 5. table, 6. map

(11) SB p. 17

1. three, 2. green, 3. one

(13) SB p. 19

1. paper, 2. a crayon, 3. a pencil

(14) SB p. 19

| | Past | Now |
|---|---|---|
| crayon | | ✓ |
| hand | ✓ | ✓ |
| paint | | ✓ |
| tablet | ✓ | ✓ |
| stick | ✓ | |

## Workbook

Go to pp. 303–306 for the Workbook Answer Key for this unit.

## In This Unit

**Theme** This unit is about animals, plants, and other things in nature.

**Content Objectives**

Students will

- identify objects and colors in nature.
- talk about nature.

**Language Objectives**

Students will

- identify and name objects in nature.
- identify colors in nature.
- tell where things are in nature.

**Vocabulary**

**Vocabulary 1** *a bird, a butterfly, grass, a mountain, the ocean, a river, a rock, the sky, the sun, a tree*

**Vocabulary 2** *a bush, a cloud, a flower, the moon, a star*

**Grammar**

**Grammar 1** use *to be* to talk about the present

**Grammar 2** ask questions with *where*

**Pacing Guides** LIU2

**Related Vocabulary** *our, world, nature, water, beautiful, in, on*

**Writing** Draw and write about colors.

**Value** Enjoy nature.

**Project** Make a mural about nature.

## Unit Opener

**Objectives**

Students will

- analyze a photo for information.
- complete a sentence to describe a photo.

**Resources** Video: Sc. 1— Introduction; Classroom Presentation Tool: Unit Opener; Teacher's Resource CD-ROM: Home-School Connection Letter; Unit Opener Poster; World Map Poster

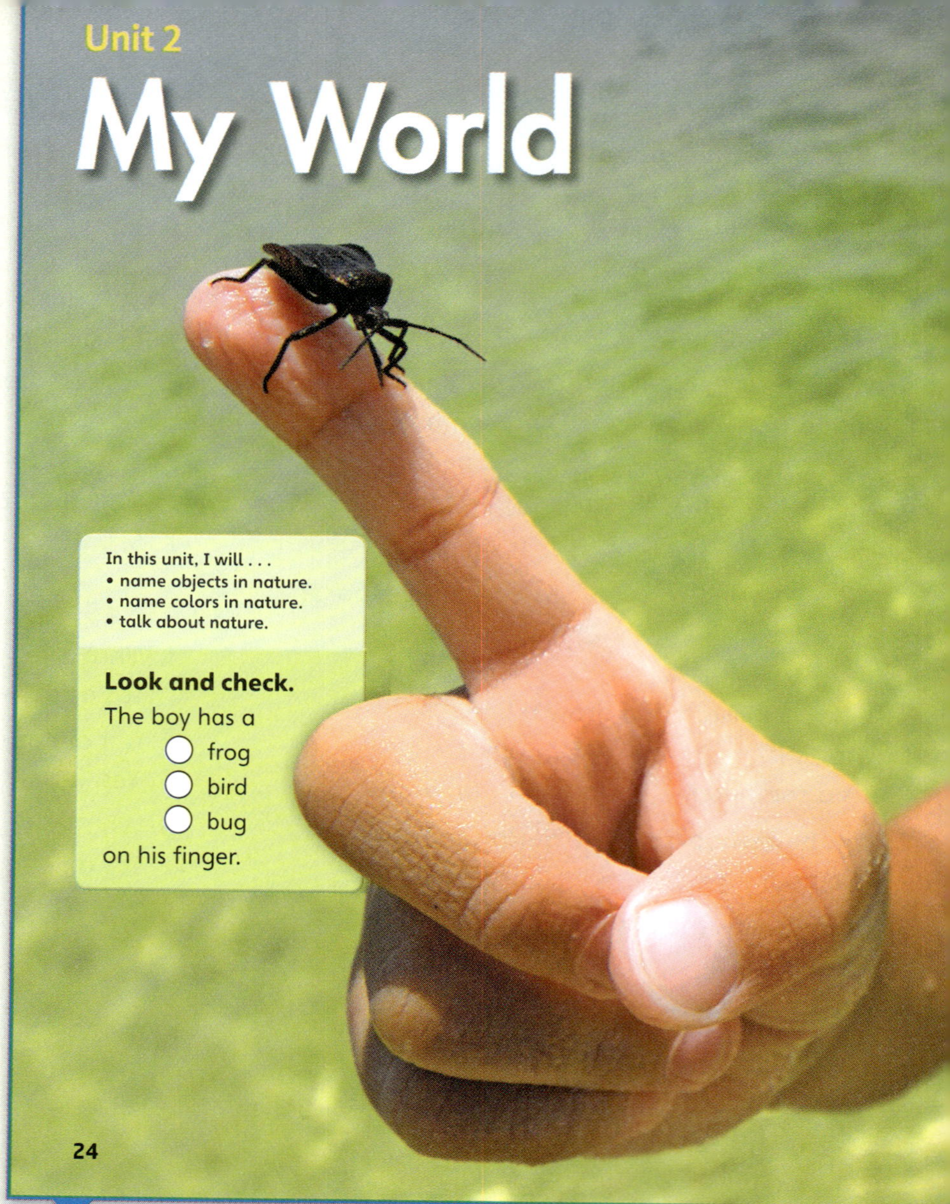


## Introduce

- **Build background** Say *Our new unit is called "My World."* Point to your country on the world map. Say *We are here.* Then slide your hand across the map. *This is the world. Our world is big!* Open your arms wide to express *big*.
- **Recycle** Say *Our classroom is part of our world. Our school is part of our world.* Point to yourself and the class and say *We are in our world.* Say *Look!* Point out the classroom window. Say *That's outside. That's our world, too.*
- Point to the boy in the photo on pp. 24–25. Ask *What do you see?* (a boy) Point to the boy's goggles and ask *What color are these?* (blue) Point to the boy's finger and say *This is a finger.* Show your finger and say *This is my finger. Show me your finger.* Then point to the bug on the boy's finger. Say *It's a bug!* Draw a simple bug on the board. Say and write *a bug* above your drawing. Point to the bug in the photo. Ask *What color is it?* (black)

- Help students complete the activity on p. 24. Read the sentence stem aloud. Say *The boy has a __________. Is it a frog?* (no) Point to the picture of the frog on p. 27 to show students what a frog is, if necessary. Ask *Is it a bird?* (no) Point to the picture of the bird on p. 26, if necessary. Point to the picture you drew of a bug. Ask *Is it a bug?* (yes) Have students say *bug*, and then say *Yes, It's a bug!* Read aloud the completed sentence *The boy has a bug on his finger.* Have students repeat the sentence.

## Be the Expert

### About the Photo

This photo shows a boy in Doral, Florida. Point out Florida on the world map. Explain that Florida is part of the United States.

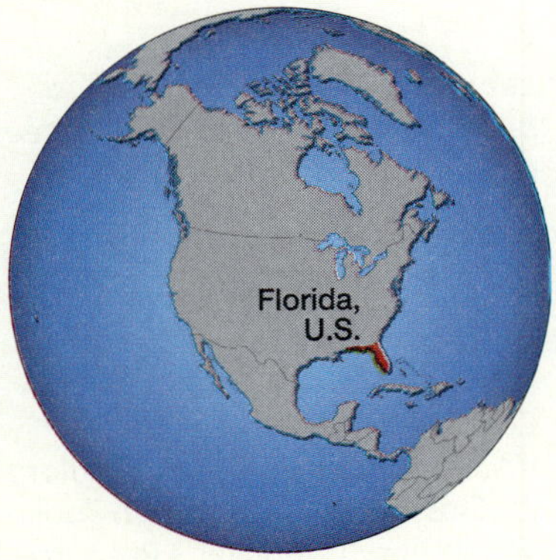


### Teaching Tip

When students are asked a question, they should be given enough time to form an answer. Wait time is an important element of classroom discourse. Students are thinking in a new language, and some may need as long as a minute to form an answer before speaking.

### Related Vocabulary

*bug, goggles, outside, swimming*

# Vocabulary 1

**Objectives**

Students will

- identify and name objects in nature.
- identify and name colors in nature.

**Vocabulary** *the sky, the ocean, a bird, the sun, grass, a rock, a tree, a mountain, a butterfly, a river*

**Academic Language** *answer, ask, listen, point, say*

**Resources** Workbook pp. 16–17; Picture Cards 1–8, 35–44; Audio CD TR: A27–29; Video: Sc. 2—Vocabulary 1a; Sc. 3—Vocabulary 1b; Classroom Presentation Tool: Vocabulary 1; Teacher's Resource CD-ROM: Graphic Organizer (Word web), Activity Worksheet 2.1

**Materials** note cards; crayons or colored pencils

1 **Listen and say.** TR: A27

2 **Listen.** Point and say. TR: A28

26

## Warm Up

- **Recycle** Tell students to take out paper and crayons or colored pencils. Draw a square, a triangle, a circle, a rectangle, and a star on the board. Then put Picture Cards 1, 3–5, and 8 face down Ask a student to choose one of the cards. Show the card and say the color. Then point to the square on the board and say *Draw a (green) square.* Repeat with the remaining colors and shapes.
- Draw or display a large green square, a blue circle, a red rectangle, a yellow star, and a black triangle on the board or on pieces of paper. Then play a guessing game with students. Say *It's yellow. What is it?* Model the answer. Say *It's a star. It's yellow.* Then say *It's red. What is it?* (It's a rectangle.) Continue with the remaining shapes and colors.

## Present

- Have students open their books to pp. 26–27. Say *Look.*
- Say *Point and say.* Point to the ocean. Say *the ocean.* Have students point to the picture of the ocean. Ask *What color is the ocean?* (blue)
- Point to the bird and say *A bird. Point to a bird.* Have students point to the picture of the bird. Ask *What color is the bird?* (yellow and black) Continue for all the labeled pictures.
- Ask *What colors do you see?* Connect each color students name to the vocabulary words in the picture. For example, say *The ocean is blue.*
- **Preteach** Draw a word web with ten outer circles. In each circle, write a word from pp. 26–27. Say each word as you write it. Then say *One word names all these words. It's nature.* Write *Nature* in the center of the web. Point to and say the word. Have students repeat it. Ask *What's in nature?* Model an answer. Point to the word *trees* in the web and say *Trees. Trees are in nature.*

## Be the Expert

### Vocabulary Strategy

**Ending -s** A plural of a noun is used when there is more than one of something. For most nouns in English, you simply add -s to the end to make a plural. Here are some examples:

*bird* → *birds*
*tree* → *trees*
*mountain* → *mountains*
*rock* → *rocks*
*river* → *rivers*

### Teaching Tip

Give students multiple opportunities to practice pronunciation. For example, encourage students to bring in pictures of vocabulary words from newspapers or magazines. Have students present their pictures and name the vocabulary words in them. When modeling for students, be sure to pronounce each syllable clearly and have students repeat.

### Related Vocabulary

*branch, leaf, nature*

## Practice 1 2

- 1 Say *Look.* Point to your eyes and then point to pp. 26–27, making sure all students still have their books open to those pages. Say *Listen.* Point to your ears and play **TR: A27**. Point to the appropriate object in the picture when you hear each word. Then say *Now listen and say.* Play **TR: A27** again. After students hear each word pause the audio. Have students repeat the word. Listen to make sure students are pronouncing each word correctly.

- 2 Point to your ears and then make a pointing gesture to the picture on pp. 26–27 as you say *Listen and point.* Play **TR: A28** and model listening and pointing. Point to your ears as you listen to the track, and then point to the correct picture as you say *Listen and point.* Play **TR: A28** again and have students point to the words and repeat after the audio. ✓ Say the words slowly and observe students as they point to the pictures. If students have difficulty pointing to the right picture, use Picture Cards 35–44 to review each vocabulary word one at a time.

- Form pairs of students. Have them ask each other questions about the pictures on pp. 26–27. Model with a student. Point to a tree. Say *Is it a tree?* (Yes, it is. It's a tree.)

## Wrap Up

- Put students in small groups. Pass out Picture Cards 35–44. Give each group at least one card. Then have each group show its picture card and say the vocabulary word. When all groups finish, call out a vocabulary word. Have the group with that card stand up, show the card, and say the word.

- Say *Now let's play a game. Take out paper and a pencil.* Model the game. Say *I'm going to say a word. You write it and draw a picture.* Say *Tree.* Model writing the word *tree* and drawing a simple tree. Play the game with *bird, mountain, butterfly, rock, river, ocean, sun,* and *grass.*

- Use Picture Cards 1–8 and 35–44. One by one, hold up pairs of related colors and images, such as *red* and *butterfly.* Have students connect the words. (a red butterfly)

## Recap

- Put Picture Cards 35–44 in a pile and give them to one student. Say *Pick a card. Show it. Say the word. Then ask the class to repeat.* Model by having the student show a card, say the word, and have the class repeat the word. Have the student go through the full routine with the next card, and then pass the cards to the next student. Continue until all target words have been used.

## Apply 3

- 3 Form pairs of students. Point to the model dialogue on the bottom of p. 27. Point to the animals in order and say *Freddy the frog asks. Polly the parrot answers.* Point to your ears and say *Listen.* Play **TR: A29**. Then model the dialogue with students. Say *It's yellow. What is it?* Have the class answer *It's a bird.* Then say *Now ask me. Say what Freddy says.* and have the class say *It's yellow. What is it?* Answer *It's a bird.* Then have partners take turns asking and answering with other words on pp. 26–27.

## Extend

- Review classroom objects with students as you practice the vocabulary for this unit. Hand each student a note card with one of these phrases written on it: *yellow book, white paper, red crayon, green pen, blue pencil, black table, yellow bird, green grass, blue river, black rock, blue sky, yellow sun.*
- Point to one side of the classroom and say *Read your card. Is it in the classroom? Line up here.* Point to the other side of the classroom and say *Is it in nature? Line up here.* Have students go to the correct side of the room. Have students hold up their cards. Check that students are on the correct side of the classroom. Then have students hold up their cards again and read them one at a time.
- Point to six classroom areas for each of these colors: black, white, red, blue, green, yellow. As you call out each color, have students line up in the spot that names the color of the objects on their cards. Have them read their cards again.

## Wrap Up

- Have students draw pictures of the vocabulary words. Call out one vocabulary word. For example, say *a bird.* Give students time to draw a bird and hold up and name their pictures. Repeat with the remaining words in the unit.

## Be the Expert

### Teaching Tip

**Classroom Management** Use activities that involve movement to engage students, but plan carefully. Mark out spaces in the classroom for these activities, making the boundaries very clear before you begin. If the movement is supposed to be silent, give a "silent signal" by placing your finger to your lips before you begin and during the activity as needed.

### Formative Assessment

Can students

- identify and name objects in nature?
  Hold up Picture Cards 35–44 and have students name the object on each one.
- identify and name colors in nature?
  Write and say *sky, bird, ocean, tree, river, grass, sun* and have students use colors to describe them.

**Review** For additional practice, direct students to Activity Worksheet 2.1.

## Song

**Vocabulary in the song**

**Vocabulary 1** *a bird, the sky, the sun, the ocean, a tree, a mountain, a rock*

**Vocabulary 2** *the moon*

**Grammar in the song**

**Grammar 1** use *to be* to talk about the present

**Grammar 2** ask questions with *where*

**Academic Language** *hold up*

**Resources** Workbook p. 18; Audio CD TR: A30; Video: Sc. 9—Song; Classroom Presentation Tool: Song; Teacher's Resource CD-ROM: Graphic Organizer (Word web); Picture Cards 35–44

**Materials** large signs or poster boards labeled with the words *sky, ocean,* and *mountains*

4 **Listen.** Read and sing. TR: A30

# Nature

*Where are the birds?*
*They're in the sky.*

*Where are the sun and the moon?*
*They're in the sky.*

*The sky is part of our world.*

*Where are the fish?*
*They're in the ocean.*

*Where are the waves?*
*They're in the ocean.*

*The ocean and the sky*
*are part of our world.*

*Where are the trees?*
*They're in the mountains.*

*Where are the rocks?*
*Up in the mountains.*

*The mountains and the ocean*
*and the sky, they're part of our world.*

28

## Use the Song 4

- Prepare three large posters labeled **Sky**, **Ocean**, and **Mountains**. Break the class into three groups, one for each poster. On the **Sky** poster, have students draw or paste pictures of birds, the sun, and the moon. On the **Ocean** poster, have them draw or paste pictures of waves and fish. If necessary, point to the waves on p. 26. On the **Mountains** poster, have students draw or paste pictures of mountains, rocks, and trees.
- Display the posters at the front of the class. Hold up the **Sky** poster and say *This is the sky. The sky is in our world. Birds, the sun, and the moon are in the sky. They're part of our world, too.* Repeat for the **Ocean** and **Mountains** posters.
- 4 Play **TR: A30** once as students listen to the song. When they hear *They're in the sky*, have students point to the **Sky** poster. When they hear *They're in the ocean*, have students point to the **Ocean** poster. When they hear *They're in the mountains*, have students point to the **Mountains** poster.
- Put students into three groups. Give each group one of the posters. Then have students open their books to pp. 28–29. Play **TR: A30** a second time. Have group members hold up their poster and point to the items named (the sun and the moon, trees, and rocks) as they hear each phrase.

*What colors do you see*
*in our beautiful world?*
*What colors do you see*
*in our beautiful world?*

*The colors of the rainbow,*
*the colors of the rainbow.*
*The colors of the rainbow,*
*the colors of the rainbow.*

*The rainbows and the mountains*
*and the ocean and the sky,*
*they're part of our world,*
*part of our world.*

*Our beautiful world!*

5 **Sing again.** Hold up pictures.

29

## Be the Expert

### Teaching Tip

Music and songs can dramatically change the atmosphere in a classroom, filling it with energy and enthusiasm. If students love a song, use it for more challenging activities. For example, students can write a new line or verse for the song, and create their own illustrations. Students can tap out rhythms they hear, especially in the chorus. This is a good way to call attention to syllables and intonation.

### Related Vocabulary

*fish, rainbow, waves*

## Use It Again 5

- 5 **Vocabulary 1** Hold up Picture Card 35 (a bird), show it to students, and have them say *a bird*. Hand out the Picture Cards for *a bird, a mountain, the ocean, a rock, the sky,* and *the sun.* Say *Listen. Hold up your card.* Play **TR: A30**. Have students hold up their cards when they hear the word they have. To model, hold up Picture Card 35 when you hear *birds* in the first verse.
- **Grammar 2** Play **TR: A30**. Write and read these sentences aloud: *They're in the ocean. They're part of our world.* Have students repeat the sentences. Then ask *Where are the fish?* and have students join you in a singing response. (They're in the ocean.) Ask *Where are the sun and moon?* (They're in the sky.) Then ask *Where are the rocks? Where are the trees?* (They're in the mountains.)
- **End of unit** Have students open their books to pp. 28–29 and look at the pictures. Hold up the book, point to, and say *our world, fish, the moon, a bird, the sun, colors.* Then ask students *What is in our world?* Create a word web with the phrase *our world* at the center and cluster students' ideas, which may show all the things from the song and more.

# Grammar 1

**Objectives**

Students will

- ask questions with *What is it?* and *What are they?*
- answer questions and make statements with *It's* and *They're*.

**Grammar** use *to be* to talk about the present

**Academic Language** *look, listen, circle, ask a question*

**Resources** Workbook pp. 19–20; Audio CD TR: A31–32; Video: Sc. 6—Grammar 1; Classroom Presentation Tool: Grammar 1; Teacher's Resource CD-ROM: Graphic Organizers (Three-column chart)

**GRAMMAR** TR: A31

| | |
|---|---|
| What **is** it? | It**'s** a bird. |
| What **are** they? | They**'re** birds. |

**6** **Look.** Listen and circle. TR: A32

**1**

**2**

## Warm Up

- **Recycle** Ask students questions with *is*. Point to a clock and ask *Is it a clock?* Say *Yes, it is. It's a clock.* Repeat the question, and have students repeat the answer as a group. Repeat with other objects in the classroom, such as a desk, a map, and a computer.
- Have one student hold up an object from his or her desk. Have the student ask the class *Is it (a pen)?* The class should answer *Yes, it is. It's a (pen).* Repeat the activity with other objects and students.
- **Preteach** Hold up one pencil. Ask *What is it?* Then say *It's a pencil.* Have students repeat the answer. Then hold up two pencils. Ask *What are they?* Say *They're pencils.* Have students repeat the answer. Repeat with crayons. First, hold up one crayon. Ask and say *What is it? It's a crayon.* Repeat with two crayons. Ask and say *What are they? They're crayons.*

31

## Be the Expert

### Our World in Context

Trees are an important part of our world. They provide habitats for many animals. They take in carbon dioxide and make oxygen. They also hold down the soil, which helps protect water supplies and prevent floods. In addition, trees are the source of building materials, foods (including fruits, nuts, oils, and spices), medicines, and other products. Even when trees die they are useful. Trees break down and are recycled into nutrients that many living things need to survive.

### Grammar in Depth

Contractions are very common in spoken English. Students will also encounter them in stories, as they are used in dialogue to make characters sound natural and believable. Explain to students that contractions are shortened forms of words. The contractions used on p. 30 are

*It is* = *It's*

*They are* = *They're*

When a contraction is formed, the meaning is not changed. These terms can be used interchangeably.

## Present

- Draw students' attention to the yellow grammar box at the top of p. 30. Play **TR: A31** and have students read along with the questions and answers. Point to the picture of one bird on p. 30. Cover the other two birds up. Say *One bird. It's a bird.* Point to the picture of the two birds on p. 30. Say *Two birds. They're birds.*
- **Give examples** Draw one chair on the board. Say *It's a chair.* Draw two chairs. Say *They're chairs.* Draw three chairs. Say *They're chairs.*
- Write the following on the board:

  It's a chair.

  They're chairs.

- Point to the picture of two chairs. Ask *What are they?* (They're chairs.) As students answer, point to the second sentence on the board. Repeat with other pictures. Remind students to use *They're* to talk about more than one thing. Carry two pencils as you walk around the room. Ask *What are they?* (They're pencils.) If students have difficulty choosing between *It's* and *They're*, ask *How many?*

## Practice 6

- Direct students' attention back to the yellow grammar box on p. 30. Say the questions and have students say the answers. Then have half of the class ask the questions and the other half say the answers aloud.

- 6 Explain Activity 6. Point to your ear and say *Listen.* Point to the pictures on pp. 30–31, then point to your eye and say *Look at the pictures.* Pretend to circle one of the pictures and say *Circle.*

- Point to item 1 and say *Listen.* Pause and say *Number 1.* Say *You're going to hear a question and answer. Then you're going to circle what you hear.* Play **TR: A32** and pause after item 1. Say *What is it? It's a bird.* Help students complete the first item. *It's a bird. It's one bird. Circle one bird.* Play the rest of **TR: A32**. Have students complete the other items as they listen.

## Wrap Up

Make a chart like the following on the board:

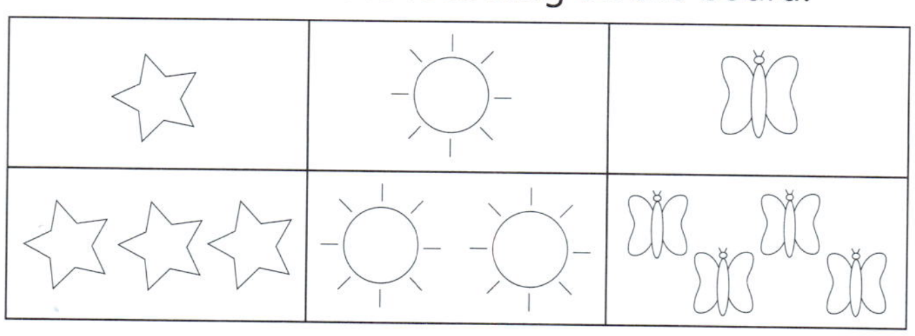

- Point to the box with two suns and ask *What are they?* Have students write a sentence that tells about the picture. (They're suns.) Continue the activity by pointing to other boxes and asking *What is it?* or *What are they?*

## Recap

- Remind students that they can use either *It is* or *It's* to talk about one thing, and either *They are* or *They're* to talk about two or more things. Draw two squares on the board. Then draw one star. Point to the squares and ask *What are they?* (They're squares.) Point to the star and ask *What is it?* (It's a star.)

## Apply

- Have students draw vocabulary words from pp. 26–27. Say *Draw one or draw two.* Give students time to draw their pictures.

- Put students in pairs. Say *Show your pictures. Your partner asks a question. Say the answer.* Model with a student. Have the student hold up his drawing. Ask *What is it?* or *What are they?* Have students use *It's* ________ or *They're* ________ to respond.

- Give students time to ask and answer questions about their pictures. Then have students repeat their dialogues for the class.

## Extend

- Have students look at pp. 30–31. Say *Let's say the colors.* Point to the picture of the first bird. Ask *What color is it?* (blue) *Blue. It's a blue bird. What is it?* (It's a blue bird.) Point to the picture of the two birds. Ask *What color are they?* (blue) *They're blue birds. What are they?* (They're blue birds.) Continue with the pictures of the green trees and orange butterflies.

## Wrap Up

- Say *I ask a question. You say the answer.* Point to an object in the classroom. Ask a student *What is it?* After the student answers, point to two objects and ask another student *What are they?* Continue asking until all students have an opportunity to answer. If students have trouble answering, write the sentence frames *It's* ________. and *They're* ________. on the board.

## Be the Expert

### Teaching Tip

**Leveling** When doing oral group work, keep individual students' abilities in mind, and try to call on students at their respective comfort levels. For example, some students may not be ready to use *They're*, which can be difficult to pronounce. A choral response, when a whole class speaks aloud together, can give students a chance to practice within the safety of a group. Alternatively, students may demonstrate understanding by drawing or writing.

### Formative Assessment

Can students

- ask questions with *What is it?* and *What are they?*

  Draw a tree. Say *Ask a question about the tree.* Draw two trees. Say *Ask a question about the trees.*

- answer questions and make statements with *It's* and *They're*?

  Point to the tree. Ask *What is it?* Point to the trees. Ask *What are they?*

# Vocabulary 2

**Objective**

Students will

- identify and name objects in nature.

**Vocabulary** *a star, a flower, a cloud, a bush, the moon*

**Academic Language** *listen, point, say*

**Resources** Workbook p. 21; Audio CD TR: A33–34; Video: Sc. 4—Vocabulary 2; Classroom Presentation Tool: Vocabulary 2; Teacher's Resource CD-ROM: Graphic Organizers (Two-column chart), Activity Worksheet 2.2; Picture Cards 35–49

**Materials** ten note cards

**7 Listen and say.** TR: A33

the moon

**8 Work with a partner.** Point and say.

**9 Work with a partner.** Guess and stick. TR: A34

1 2 3 4 5



## Warm Up

- **Recycle** Show students Picture Card 41 (a rock). Ask *Is it a bird?* (no) If necessary, model the answer *No, it isn't.* Ask *Is it a rock?* (yes)
- Play a guessing game. Show students Picture Cards 35–39 and give them time to look at them. Then turn the cards over. Choose one card, but don't let students see it. Say *Now you ask.* Write *Is it __________?* on the board. Have students ask *Is it (a butterfly)?* Answer by saying *Yes, it is* or *No, it's not*. After they guess the card, have students pick another one. Have the class ask that student questions to guess the card. Repeat the activity with several students.

## Present

- **Activate prior knowledge** On the board, draw a line for the horizon and then draw two trees and some grass. Write *the sky* above the horizon line. Ask *What's in the sky?* (birds, butterflies, the sun) Say *Yes, (birds) are in the sky.* Draw a bird in the sky and write *a bird* under it. Say *The sun is in the sky, too!* Draw the sun and write *the sun* under it.
- Say *Let's learn the names of more things in the sky.* Show Picture Card 46 and say *a cloud*. Have students say *a cloud.* Then draw a cloud in the sky and write *a cloud* under it. Repeat with Picture Card 49 (a star) and Picture Card 48 (the moon).
- Say *The sky is part of nature. Let's learn two more things in nature.* Show Picture Card 47 and say *a flower*. Repeat with Picture Card 45 (a bush), drawing pictures where they belong on the board.

- Have students open their books to p. 32. Point to each of the new vocabulary words one by one. Say each word twice, and then have students say the words. If students have difficulty, model correct pronunciation. ✓ Hold up Picture Cards 45–49 one at a time. Ask students to identify the vocabulary words.

## Practice 7 8

- 7 Say *Now listen and say.* Play **TR: A33**. Join with students in responding to the audio as a class. Then read the words aloud and have students listen and repeat them.

- Have students look at the photos on p. 32. Point to each picture as you talk about it, and have students repeat each sentence. Say A star. *A star is in the sky.* A cloud. *A cloud is in the sky.* The moon. *The moon is in the sky.* A flower. *The flower is red.* A bush. *A bush is green.*

- 8 Display Picture Cards 45–49. Put students in pairs. Say *Now you point and say.* Have one partner use the photos on p. 32. Have the other partner use the Picture Cards.

## Apply 9

- 9 Say *Look at the Unit 2 stickers on page 178.* Point to each sticker and ask *What is it?*

- Have students look at Activity 9 on p. 32. Play **TR: A34**. Then model the dialogue with a student. Put students in pairs and have partners practice the dialogue.

- Model finding a sticker in the back of the book. Do not show it to the class. Have the class ask questions to guess what it is. Model a question *Is it a cloud?* Answer by saying *Yes, it is* or *No, it isn't*. After students have correctly guessed, model sticking the sticker.

## Extend

- Make a two-column chart on the board with the headings **Sky** and **Water**. Next to it write *moon, river, sun, star,* and *ocean.* Point to *moon*. Say *This is the moon. Is the moon in the sky?* (yes) *Yes, the moon is in the sky.* Have students repeat the sentence. Write *moon* in the first column. Repeat with the other words.

## Wrap Up

- Say *I'm going to say a word. Then you're going to draw it, like this.* Say *bird* and then draw a bird on the board. Say *Now it's your turn. When I say a word, you draw.* Say *star*. Repeat with *cloud, flower,* and *bush*.

## Be the Expert

### Our World in Context

Flowers come in an almost endless variety of colors, shapes, and sizes. Flowers aren't just part of nature. They're also a way for us to express ourselves. The meanings behind different types of flowers can change around the world, but many cultures use them to show feelings. Flowers can express "happy birthday," "get well," "I love you," and even "I'm sorry for you."

### Sounds of English

**Comparing sounds: /n/ and /m/**

The sounds /n/ (su<u>n</u>) and /m/ (<u>m</u>ap) are very common in English. You pronounce them through your nose. The main difference is that you pronounce /m/ with your mouth closed, and /n/ with your mouth open and the tip of your tongue touching the top of your mouth.

Use Minimal Pair Card 47. (<u>m</u>ap, <u>n</u>ap). Have the students hold a hand in front of their noses to feel the air coming out.

Example words: ocea<u>n</u>; co<u>m</u>puter; <u>m</u>ountai<u>n</u>, <u>m</u>oo<u>n</u>, <u>n</u>u<u>m</u>ber

### Formative Assessment

Can students

- identify and name objects in nature?

  One by one, hold up Picture Cards 45–49 and ask *What is it?*

**Review** For additional practice, direct students to Activity Worksheet 2.2.

## Grammar 2

**Objectives**

Students will

- ask and answer questions with *where*.
- use *on* and *in*.

**Grammar** ask questions with *where*

**Academic Language** *answer, ask, look, partner*

**Resources** Workbook p. 22; Audio CD TR: A35–36; Video: Sc. 7—Grammar 2; Classroom Presentation Tool: Grammar 2, Teacher's Resource CD-ROM: Graphic Organizers (Word web, Three-column chart), Activity Worksheet 2.3; Picture Cards 35–49

**GRAMMAR** TR: A35

| | |
|---|---|
| **Where** is the butterfly? | It's **on** the flower. |
| **Where** are the clouds? | They're **in** the sky. |

**10** **Play with a partner.** Ask and answer. TR: A36

**11** **Look at the pictures.** Write.

1. How many birds? ______________
2. What color are the flowers? ______________
3. Where are the stars? ______________



## Warm Up

- **Preteach** Write the vocabulary words from this unit on the board. Pass out Picture Cards 35–49 to pairs of students. Then ask where each picture card is. For example, ask *Where is the bird?* Have the pair with the bird hold it up and name it. Continue until you have located all the cards.
- **Build background** Draw a word web on the board with a question mark in the center circle. Draw three outer circles. In one outer circle, write and say What. Point to the frog on p. 33. Say *What color is the frog?* (green) In another outer circle, write and say How many. Point to the stars. Ask *How many stars?* (four) In the third outer circle, write and say Where. Point to the clouds. Ask *Where are the clouds?* Say *They're in the sky.* Have students repeat.

## Present

- Write the following on the board:

| | |
|---|---|
| Where is the frog? | It's on the rock. |
| Where are the frogs? | They're on the rock. |

- Draw a frog on a rock. Ask *Where is the frog?* Say *It's on the rock.* Have half of the class ask the question and the other half answer.
- Draw another frog on the rock. Ask *Where are the frogs?* Say *They're on the rock.* Have half of the class ask the question and the other half answer.
- Draw a picture of a butterfly on a flower. Direct students' attention to the yellow grammar box at the top of p. 33. Play **TR: A35**. As students listen, point to the butterfly on the flower. For the second sentence, point to the clouds on p. 33.

## Practice 10

- Read each question in the grammar box on p. 33 aloud, and have students read the answer. Then switch roles.
- Say *Listen.* Play **TR: A36.** Read the model dialogue aloud with a student. Put students in pairs and have them practice asking and answering the question.
- Write the following phrases on the board. Read each aloud, and have students repeat after you:

| | | |
|---|---|---|
| on the flower | in the sky | in the bush |
| on the rock | in the river | in the tree |
| on the grass | | |

- Point to the picture of the frogs in the river. Ask *Where are the frogs?* Say *They're in the river.* Have students repeat.
- 10 Say *Now it's your turn. You ask and answer.* Point to one student. Say *You ask.* Point to that student's partner. Say *You answer. Take turns.* ✓ Walk around the room to check students' dialogues. If students have difficulty choosing between *on* or *in*, direct them to the phrases on the board.

## Apply 11

- 11 Hold up your book and point to item 1. Read the question aloud and point to the picture of three birds. Count *1, 2, 3. Three birds.* Say *Write three.* Write *three* on the board. Have partners complete the activity. When they finish, have students read their questions and answers aloud.

## Extend

- Write the following on the board:

| | |
|---|---|
| Where is the pen? | It's on the desk. |
| Where are the pens? | They're on the desk. |

- Place a pen on a desk. Ask *Where is the pen?* Say *It's on the desk.* Put another pen on the desk. Ask *Where are the pens?* Say *They're on the desk.*
- Place students in groups. Have them take turns putting objects on their desks and asking and answering questions about them.

## Wrap Up

- Say and write the following sentence frames. Complete the frames as a class, accepting multiple answers wherever possible: *Where is the moon? It's* ________. *Where is the frog? It's* ________. ________ *is the flower?* ________ *is the bird?*

## Be the Expert

### Grammar in Depth

The prepositions *on* and *in* have many uses in English. They can indicate position: *The book is on the desk. The cake is in the oven.* They can also be used in expressions about time: *He came on Monday. She was born in 1988.*

### Formative Assessment

Can students

- ask and answer questions with *where?*

  Hold up picture cards showing things in the sky. Ask *Where is it?* or *Where are they?*
- use *on* and *in?*

  Draw two frogs on grass on the board. Ask *Where are they?*

**Review** For additional practice, direct students to Activity Worksheet 2.3.

## Reading

**Objective**

Students will

- use words and pictures to understand rainbows.

**Reading Strategy** Use Visuals to Support Comprehension

**Academic Language** *circle, color*

**Content Vocabulary** *indigo, rain, rainbow, violet*

**Resources** Workbook pp. 24–25; Audio CD TR: A37–38; Classroom Presentation Tool: Reading; Picture Cards 1–8, 38, 41, 43, 45

**Materials** big photo or picture of a rainbow (*optional*); long strips of paper; tape; sheets of colored paper in the colors of a rainbow

**12 Listen and read.** TR: A37

# Rainbows

The sun is in the sky. Rain is in the sky. Look! A rainbow! A rainbow is red, orange, yellow, green, blue, indigo, and violet.

**13 Listen and read.** Circle *yes* or *no*. TR: A38

1. For a rainbow, the sun is in the sky. yes no
2. Ten colors are in the rainbow. yes no

34

## Warm Up

- **Build background** Show a photo of a rainbow, or draw a rainbow on the board. Say *Look. It's a rainbow!* Point to the red in the rainbow. Ask *What color is it?* (red) Write *red* on the board. Repeat for orange, yellow, green, and blue. Point to the indigo in the rainbow. Say *This color is indigo.* Have students repeat the word and write it on the board. Ask *What color looks like indigo?* (blue) Say *Blue looks like indigo.* Point to the violet in the rainbow. Say *This color is violet.* Have students repeat, and write *violet* on the board. Ask *What color looks like violet?* (purple) Say *Yes, purple looks like violet.*
- Point outside. Say *We see rainbows outside. Rainbows are in nature.*

## Present 12 13

- Direct students to p. 34. Point to and read the title aloud. Have students repeat after you. Point to the photo of the rainbow on p. 34. Ask *What is it?* (a rainbow)
- 12 **Read together** Play **TR: A37** and have students listen. Play **TR: A37** again and have students read along. Pause the audio after *A rainbow!* On the board, write *rain* + *sun* = __________. Say *Rain and sun make a rainbow.* Write *rainbow* on the line. Ask *What do rain and sun make?* (a rainbow)
- Point to the rainbow at the bottom of p. 35. Say *Listen for words that name colors. Point to the colors.* Play **TR: A37** and model pointing to the colors. Then play the audio again and have students point to the colors as they hear them.

**14** **Color the rainbow.**

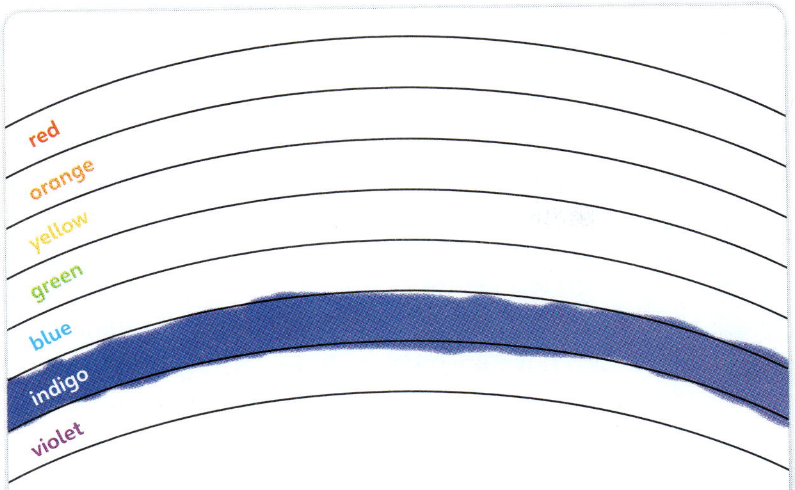


**15** **Look.** Circle things in the sky. Say.

35

## Be the Expert

### About the Photo

The photo on p. 34 shows a prism bending white light. White light is made up of many colors. When the prism bends the light, the different colors can be seen. Similarly, when light from the sun hits raindrops, the light bends, and a rainbow forms.

### Our World in Context

Sunlight is made of all the colors people can see. When rays of sun light hit drops of rain, the light slows down and bends in different directions. This divides the light into different colors. Every rainbow has colors in the same order: red at the top and violet at the bottom. Full rainbows are in the shape of a circle, but people usually only see an arc—or "bow"—because land blocks their view of the circle. People in airplanes can sometimes see the whole circle.

### Related Vocabulary

*light, nature, outside, prism*

- **13** Read the directions aloud. Say *Show me how to make a circle.* Have students draw circles in the air. Act out drawing a circle for students if necessary. Point to Activity 13. Read item 1 aloud, and then have students read it with you. Ask *What makes a rainbow?* (sun and rain) Ask *Is the sun in the sky when you see a rainbow?* (yes) Say *Circle the correct answer.*

- Have students complete item 2 on their own. Lead the class in counting the colors in the rainbow by reading aloud and counting the color words in the text on p. 34. Ask *How many colors are there in the rainbow?* (seven) Read item 2 aloud. Ask *Are there ten colors in the rainbow? Think about it. Then circle the correct answer.* ✓ Walk around the room and ask *How many colors are in the rainbow?*

- **Expand** Have students draw pictures of a rainbow. Encourage students to add as many things to their pictures as they can label.

- Remind students that they need to include two things (sun and rain) to make a rainbow. Have students share their drawings with a partner and explain what they show.

## Practice 14

- Have students open their books to p. 35. Hold up your book and point to the words in Activity 14. Say *The words name the colors of the rainbow. Let's read them together.* Read the words aloud with students.

- Point to each word again, and then have students read them aloud on their own. Say *red.* Hold up a blue crayon and ask *Is this red?* (no) Hold up a red crayon and ask *Is this red?* (yes) Repeat with the other colors of the rainbow.

- 14 Say *Let's color a rainbow.* Hold up a red crayon. Point to *red* in the picture and act out coloring the red row.

- Have students select red, orange, yellow, green, blue, and violet (or purple) crayons. Have students finish coloring the rainbow.

- **Expand** After students finish coloring their rainbows, help them learn the order of the colors. Write the numbers 1–7 on the board in a list. Point to red in the rainbow. Write *red* next to the 1 on the board. Say *Red is one. What color is two?* Affirm the correct answer *Yes, orange is two.* Write *orange* next to 2. Continue with the remaining colors. Then have students close their books. Draw a red half-circle on a paper for students to see. Ask *What color is next?* (orange) Continue until all colors are in the correct order.

## Wrap Up

- Draw pictures of a star, raindrops, a tree, and the sun. Ask *What two things make a rainbow?* (sun, rain) Have students come to the board and circle the correct pictures.

- Put students in small groups. Give each group seven long strips of paper. Have group members color each strip a different color of the rainbow. Then have each group tape the strips on a sheet of paper in the correct order of a rainbow. Have groups come to the board to show their rainbows and name the colors.

## Recap

- Draw a rainbow on the board. Say *It's a ________.* And have students finish the sentence for you. Say *For a rainbow, you need ________.* Have students complete the sentence for you. Ask *How many colors are in the rainbow?* (seven) *Who can name the colors?* (red, orange, yellow, green, blue, indigo, violet)

## Apply 15

- Point toward the sky. Say *It's blue. The sun is in it. What is it?* (It's the sky.) Say *Many things are in the sky.* Ask *What's in the sky?* (the sun, the moon, stars, clouds, birds, rainbows)

- 15 Have students open their books to p. 35. Read the directions aloud. Have students draw a circle in the air. Then hold up your book and point to the tree. Ask *What is this?* (a tree) *Is a tree in the sky?* (no) Say *No, a tree isn't in the sky. I don't circle the tree.* Then point to the stars. Ask *What are they?* (stars) *Are stars in the sky?* (yes) Say *Yes, stars are in the sky. I circle the stars.* Have students repeat the sentence. Have them circle the stars and then complete the rest of the activity independently. ✓ Walk around the room and remind students to say a sentence for each picture they circle.

## Extend

- Give out pieces of colored paper for each of the colors of a rainbow. Each student gets one piece of colored paper. Ask each student *What's your color?* Have them say the colors aloud.
- Then have students stand and move to a part of the room with enough room for them to make a rainbow. Point to specific areas and say *Red here. Orange here.* and so on. When students are all in order, have the color groups say the colors of the rainbow in the correct order. Say *You make a beautiful rainbow!*

## Wrap Up

- Display Picture Cards 1–8 on the board one at a time. Ask *Is this a color in the rainbow?*
- On the board, write *Rain and _________ make a rainbow.* Then show Picture Cards 38, 41, 43, and 45 one at a time. Ask *Does this make a rainbow?* Students should choose the sun on Picture Card 43. Write *the sun* to complete the sentence on the board.

## Be the Expert

### Reading Strategy

**Use Visuals to Support Comprehension** Visual supports can help students understand texts that give information. For example, the picture of the prism on p. 34 can help students understand how a rainbow is formed. You can explain that light from the sun is like the light in the picture. The prism is like a raindrop. When light from the sun hits raindrops, a rainbow forms.

You may also want to point to the photo of the rainbow on pp. 34–35 and explain to students that the photo at the bottom of the page shows a real rainbow. In this photo, you can see rainclouds and the light in the clouds.

### Teaching Tip

**Fluency** Provide multiple opportunities for students to practice reading aloud. Pair a more fluent reader with a less fluent one. Without describing differences between them, have fluent readers read the text aloud first. Then have less fluent readers read the same text aloud. Encourage partners to help each other read difficult words. Repeat the reading until both students feel comfortable reading the text on their own.

### Formative Assessment

Can students

- use words and pictures to understand rainbows?

  Ask *Where is a rainbow? What colors are in a rainbow? To make a rainbow, what is in the sky?*

## Writing

**Writing** Draw and write about colors.

**Objectives**

Students will

- view a writing model.
- write short sentences with *is* and *are*.
- talk about their pictures.

**Academic Language** *color, group, write*

**Resources** Workbook p. 26; Classroom Presentation Tool: Writing

The bush is green.
The flowers are red, yellow, and blue.
The birds are red and black.

**16 Color and write.**

1. The tree is ____________.
2. The ____________ is ____________.
3. The flowers are ____________.
4. The ____________ are ____________.

**17 Work in a group.** Talk about your picture.

36

### Formative Assessment

Can students

- write short sentences with *is* and *are*?
  Ask students questions such as *What color is the tree? What color are the flowers?*
- talk about their pictures?
  Have students say two sentences about their pictures.

## Present

- **Recycle** Hold up several pencils. Ask *What are they?* Say *They're pencils.* Have students repeat. Then hold up individual crayons and, for each, ask *What color is it?* Say *It's (yellow).* Have students repeat for each.
- **Spiral** Pair students. Have partners choose one crayon and two pencils. Point to a crayon. Ask *What is it? What color is it?* Help the student respond, if necessary. Point to the two pencils. Ask *What are they?* (They're pencils.)

## Write 16

- Have students open their books to p. 36. Point to the sentences and pictures at the top of the page. Say *These words tell about the pictures.*
- Say *Now let's read.* Read the first sentence as you point to the bush. Have students repeat and point to the bush in their books. Continue with the other two sentences.
- 16 Read the directions aloud. Point to *color* and say *Color the picture.* Point to *write*, read it aloud, and point to the four sentences students will complete. Say *Then write about your picture.*
- Model coloring the tree green. Read item 1 aloud. Say *The tree is ____________. What color is the tree?* (green) Say *The tree is green.* Write *green* to complete item 1. Have students complete the activity. ✔ Observe students as they complete item 2. Ask *How many birds are in the picture?* (one) On the board, write *The bird (is/are)* and have students choose the correct verb.

NATIONAL GEOGRAPHIC

# Our World

## Enjoy nature.

**18** **Look and read.**

Stop and look.
Enjoy.

Wadi Bani Khalid, Oman

**19** **Read and copy.**

I look at the trees and flowers. I enjoy nature.

___________________________________________

37

## Value

**Value** Enjoy nature.

**Objectives**

Students will

- read about enjoying nature.
- read and copy two sentences.

**Academic Language** *copy, look*

**Resources** Values Poster

## Be the Expert

### About the Photo

The photo shows a *wadi*, which is a shallow depression in a desert region. Water collects in these depressions, often forming temporary streams or pools that create a kind of oasis. The Arabic term *wadi* refers to a streambed, a temporary stream or river, or other temporary or seasonal water in southwestern Asia and northern Africa.

## Share 17

- **17** Form small groups. Have students use the sentences they wrote in Activity 16 to describe their pictures. Walk around the room, providing sentence frames such as: *The butterflies are* _________. *The flowers are* _________.
- For more fluent speakers, provide sentence frames such as *The flowers in my picture are* _________ and *The bird on the tree is* _________. Have students say the complete sentences.

## Value 18 19

- Have students look at the photo on p. 37. Point to the water and rocks and say *The water and the rocks are in nature.*
- Draw a happy face on the board. Point to the happy face and say *happy.* Point to the man in the photo and say *The man is happy in nature. He enjoys nature.* Write *enjoy* under the happy face. Then point to and read the sentence *Enjoy nature*. Explain that *enjoy nature* means to like things outside, such as mountains, flowers, rivers, and trees. Ask *Do you enjoy nature?*
- **18** Read the directions and the caption aloud. Read the caption again, slowly acting out each command: *Stop* (stop forward movement) *and look* (point to your eyes). *Enjoy* (point to your smile). Have students repeat the gestures as you read the text again.
- **19** Read the directions aloud. Model copying by writing the exact words on p. 37. Say them as you write them. Tell students to copy and read the sentences aloud.

# Project

**Objectives**

Students will

- think about and draw things in nature.
- make a mural about nature.
- complete the Unit 2 Quiz.

**Academic Language** *cut, draw, glue, make*

**Content Vocabulary** *mural*

**Resources** Assessment: Unit 2 Quiz; Picture Cards 35–49; Teacher's Resource CD-ROM: Activity Worksheet 2.4

**Materials** scissors; glue; poster board or construction paper

## 20 Make a mural about nature.

1 Cut out the pictures on page 161.

2 Draw more pictures.

3 Glue things from nature.

4 Write your name.



## Prepare

- Review the unit's vocabulary words by holding up Picture Cards 35–49 and asking *What is it?* or *What are they?* When students answer, repeat the answer as a complete sentence *Yes, it's (the sun).*
- Have students open their books to pp. 38–39. Point to the mural on p. 39. Write *mural* on the board. Say *a mural* and have students repeat. Say *A mural is a big picture. This mural is about nature. We're going to make a mural today!*
- Write the following on the board. Read it aloud, and then have students read it with you.

| |
|---|
| 1. Cut. |
| 2. Draw. |
| 3. Glue. |
| 4. Write your name. |

- Hold up the cutouts on p. 161 and model cutting them out with scissors. Then model drawing more pictures, gluing things on the paper, and writing your name. Then guide students to read the steps on p. 38 with you.
- Help students locate the nature cutouts on p. 161. Have students name each thing from nature.
- Put students in small groups and give each group a poster board to make the mural.
- Say *Make a mural about nature.* Walk among students to give help as needed.

## Share

- Have students look at the girl on p. 39. Read together what she is saying. Explain *You can talk about your mural too.* Model sharing a mural. Borrow one from a student. Hold it up so everyone can see it. Say *This mural shows nature.* Model language for sharing details. For example: *This is the sun. The sun is in the sky.*
- Have students come forward one by one to share their murals, or group four murals together as shown in the picture on p. 39 and have the group come forward. Each person should speak about his or her own mural by telling what it is about and naming things it shows.
- **Modify** To simplify the project, bring in photos and pictures from magazines instead of having students draw their own pictures. Have students work in groups to make one mural.

## Be the Expert

### Teaching Tip

Remember that some students who are not verbally fluent may be better able to express themselves through different means, such as art or movement. Give those students a chance to show their abilities. For example, if a student prefers not to speak, let him model a step in a process or share a drawing without speaking.

### Project Rubric

- ✓ Did students cut the pictures along the lines?
- ✓ Did students glue each cutout to the mural?
- ✓ Did students write their names?

### Now I Can

Ask questions such as the following:

- *What are some things in nature?*
- *What color is it?*
- *Where is it?*
- *Where are they?*

**Review** For additional practice, direct students to Activity Worksheet 2.4.

### Unit Assessment

Give the Unit 2 Quiz. Hand out the quiz and go over the instructions with students. The quiz should take 15–20 minutes.

## Video

**Vocabulary 1a** *a bird, a rock, a tree, grass, a river*

**Vocabulary 1b** *the sky, a mountain, the ocean, the sun, the moon*

**Vocabulary 2** *a flower, a bush, a butterfly, a cloud, a star*

**Grammar 1** use *to be* to talk about the present

**Grammar 2** ask questions with *where*

**Song** *Nature*

**Viewing** objects and colors in nature

**Story Time** *Where Are the Animals?*

**Resources** Student Book, pp. 24–33; Teacher's Resource CD-ROM: Graphic Organizers (Two-column chart)

## Before You Watch

- Play Scene I: Introduction. Say *This video is about nature. What do you see in nature? What animals do you see? What colors do you see?*

## While You Watch

- As students watch the video, have them listen for target words about nature.

- Provide a checklist. Write *flower, bird, rock, tree,* and *grass* in a list. Have students make a mark next to each vocabulary word when they hear it in the video.

## After You Watch

- Put students in pairs. Have pairs share their checklists and tell the words they heard. If students missed a word, play the video with the sound off.

- Replay the video with the sound off and have students use their lists to tell about what is happening in the video.

## Zoom In

### Vocabulary

- Have students raise their hands when they know a vocabulary word before Anna or Freddy says it. You can pause when students raise their hands and ask *What's the word?* Have students say the word.

### Grammar

- Form pairs of students. Pause the video at appropriate points to have pairs ask and answer these questions: *Where is the butterfly?* (on a flower) *Where is the bird?* (on the grass) *Where is the tree?* (on the mountain) *Where is the cloud?* (in the sky)

### Song

- Play Scene 9: twice. During the second viewing, have students clap each time Anna says a word that names something in nature. Pause to say *Yes, that's in nature.*

### Viewing

- Replay the segment with monarch butterflies. Ask *Where are the butterflies?* (in the sky, on the trees, on the flowers)

### Story Time

- Play Scene II: Story Time. Have half of the class read the questions. Have the other half of the class read the first sentence and all the answers.

- After a second viewing of *Where Are the Animals?*, help students make a two-column chart that shows the questions and the answers.

| Questions | Answers |
|---|---|
| Where are the birds? | in the tree<br>in the sky |
| | |

## *Where Are the Animals?*

Where is the frog? Is it on a leaf? A flower? Come explore a mountain and its many animals.

# Before You Read

- **Activate Prior Knowledge** Show the cover of the reader. Point to the title and say *The name of the book is* Where Are the Animals? Say *A bird is an animal. A frog is an animal. What other animals do you know?*

- **Predict** Ask students to guess where the animals in the book are. Encourage and accept answers such as *in nature*, *in the sky*, *on trees*, *in mountains*, *on the grass*, and so on.

- **Introduce the Strategy** Say *When you read, picture the story in your mind. Use the words to draw a picture. This helps you understand the words.* On the board, write *A blue bird is in a green tree*. Say *Draw a picture of the sentence.* Give students a few minutes to draw their picture. Say *I ask a question. Use the words and your picture to answer.* Ask *What color is the bird?* (blue) Point to the words *blue bird* in the text. Say *The words and the picture tell you the color of the bird.* Repeat with the question *Where is the bird?*

- **Preteach** Draw a leaf on the board. Say *Leaf. The leaf is green.* Draw a tree next to it. Say *The leaf is on the tree.*

# While You Read

- Read the book aloud to students. Stop every few pages to ask questions such as the following:

  p. 4: Say *Close your eyes.* Ask *Where are the birds?*
  p. 8: Ask *Where is the butterfly?* Say *Describe the butterfly.*
  p. 11: Ask *Where are the animals?* Have students say where the frogs, birds, and butterflies are. Have them use words that describe colors, numbers, and places.

# After You Read

- Form pairs. Have partners take turns asking and answering the questions on pp. 3, 5, 7, and 9.

## Unit 2 Reader

**Text Type** informational text

**Reading Strategy** Visualize

**Vocabulary** *a bird, a tree, a flower, a frog, a butterfly, a mountain*

**Grammar** use *to be* to talk about the present; ask questions with *where*

**Reading Strategy** Visualize

**Resources** Video: Sc. 11—Story Time; Classroom Presentation Tool: Story Time

## Be the Expert

### Reading Strategy

**Visualize** Encourage students to make pictures in their heads as they read or listen to a reading. Suggest they close their eyes and think about what they have read or heard. Encourage them to draw what they "see" in their minds. Visualizing helps clarify information and engage students with the content. When students make pictures in their minds, they feel connected to the text.

### Text Background

The book is set in a tropical rain forest. Animals pictured include the red-eyed tree frog and scarlet macaws. The *heliconia* on page 6 is a flower that is related to bananas.

# Audio Script

## Student Book

**TR: A27** **1** **Listen and say.**

the sky, the ocean, a bird, the sun, grass, a rock, a tree, a mountain, a butterfly, a river

**TR: A28** **2** **Listen. Point and say.**

a mountain, a butterfly, the sky, a bird, grass, the ocean, a rock, a tree, a river, the sun

**TR: A29** **3** **Work with a partner. Point. Ask and answer.**

Example
It's yellow. What is it?
It's a bird.

**TR: A30** **4** **Listen. Read and sing.**

Note: Lyrics for the song *Nature* are on pp. 76–77.

**TR: A31** **Grammar**

Note: Grammar 1 is on p. 78.

**TR: A32** **6** **Look. Listen and circle.**

1. What is it?
   It's a bird.
2. What are they?
   They are mountains.
3. What are they?
   They are trees.
4. What is it?
   It's a rock.
5. What is it?
   It's a butterfly.

**TR: A33** **7** **Listen and say.**

a star, a flower, a cloud, a bush, the moon

**TR: A34** **9** **Work with a partner. Guess and stick.**

Example
Is it a bush?
No, it isn't.
Is it a butterfly?
Yes, it is.

**TR: A35** **Grammar**

Note: Grammar 2 is on p. 84.

**TR: A36** **10** **Play with a partner. Ask and answer.**

Example
Where are the clouds?
They're in the sky.

**TR: A37** **12** **Listen and read.**

Note: Reading *Rainbows* is on p. 86.

**TR: A38** **13** **Listen and read. Circle *yes* or *no*.**

The sun is in the sky. Rain is in the sky. Look!
A rainbow!
A rainbow is red, orange, yellow, green, blue, indigo, and violet.

1. For a rainbow, the sun is in the sky.
2. Ten colors are in the rainbow.

## Workbook

**TR: 17** **1** **Listen. Look and match. Write the number.**

a river, grass, the sun, a bird, a mountain, the sky, the ocean, a tree, a rock, a butterfly

**TR: 18** **3** **Listen to the song. Circle.**

Note: Lyrics for the song *Nature* are on pp. 76–77.

**TR: 19** **4** **Listen. Write.**

The rainbows and the mountains and the ocean and the sky

They are part of our world, part of our world. Our beautiful world!

**TR: 20** **8** **Listen and look. Write.**

1. What are they?
   They're rocks.
2. What is it?
   It's a river.
3. What are they?
   They're mountains.

**TR: 21** **15** **Listen and read.**

Note: Reading *The Northern Lights* is on p. 308.

**TR: 22** **22** **Listen and circle. Color.**

1. What is it?
   It's grass.
2. What is it?
   It's a river.
3. What is it?
   It's the sun.
4. What is it?
   It's the ocean.
5. What are they?
   They're flowers.
6. What are they?
   They're stars.

# Answer Key

## Student Book

### Unit Opener SB p. 24

bug

**6** SB pp. 30–31

1. a bird, 2. mountains, 3. trees, 4. a rock, 5. a butterfly

**11** SB p. 33

1. four 2. They're red. 3. in the sky

**13** SB p. 34

1. yes, 2. no

**15** SB p. 35

stars, moon, rainbow

## Workbook

Go to pp. 306–309 for the Workbook Answer Key for this unit.

# In This Unit

**Theme** This unit is about the people in our families.

**Content Objectives**

Students will

- name family members.
- describe family members.

**Language Objectives**

Students will

- name family members.
- talk about family members.
- use numbers.

**Vocabulary**

**Vocabulary 1** *baby, brother, father, grandfather, grandmother, mother, my family, parents, a photo, sister*

**Vocabulary 2** *big, old, short, small, tall, young*

**Grammar**

**Grammar 1** use simple present of *to have* (first and second person singular)

**Grammar 2** ask questions with *who*

**Pacing Guides** LIU3

**Writing** Write about your family.

**Value** Love your family.

**Project** Make a family photo poster.

## Unit Opener

**Objectives**

Students will

- look at a photo for information.
- count people in a photo.

**Resources** Video: Sc. 1—Introduction; Classroom Presentation Tool: Unit Opener; Teacher's Resource CD-ROM: Home-School Connection Letter; Unit Opener Poster; World Map Poster

## Introduction

- **Activate prior knowledge** Review the Unit 0 number words on p. 6 *(one, two, three, four, five, six, seven, eight,* and *nine)*. Draw one stick figure on the board. Hold up one finger and say *one*. Point to the picture and say *one* until students repeat. Then draw another stick figure. Hold up two fingers and say *two*. Have students repeat. Continue until there are nine stick figures on the board. Count each figure as you point to it.
- Circle and count three of the stick figures on the board. Have students count with you. Then ask *How many?* (three) Circle four stick figures and ask *How many?* (four)
- **Build background** Have students open their books to p. 40. Point to the photo and ask *What do you see?* (people, rocks, trees) Point to the objects and say *This is a (tree).*
- Point to all three people and say *This is a family.* Point to yourself and say *I have a family. There are (four) people in my family.*

Circle and count the correct number of figures on the board. Indicate everyone in the room and say *We all have families.*

- Ask *What do you do with your family? Do you play outside? Do you go to the (ocean)?* Say *Show me what you do with your family.* Call on students to act out activities.
- Discuss the photo by asking questions such as the following:
  *How many people are in this family?* (three)
  *Do you see trees?* (yes)
  *What color are the trees?* (green)
- Point to the activity on p. 40. Read the sentence aloud with each answer option. Have students say *yes* or *no* for each.
- Read the correct answer aloud. Have students repeat after you.

## Be the Expert

### About the Photo

This photo was taken at Bryce Canyon National Park in Utah in the United States. This park has colorful rock formations known as *hoodoos*, which are shown in the background of the photo. Hoodoos are created by snow slowly carving away rock over millions of years. Today, more than one million people visit Bryce Canyon National Park each year. Hikers walk along trails and admire the colorful rocks.

### Teaching Tip

When possible, use examples from students' lives. Incorporate familiar people, places, and things they already know about. This personalizaton helps students remember what they are learning. For example, you can ask questions like *Do you walk with your family? How many people are in your family?*

# Vocabulary 1

**Objective**

Students will

- identify and use words for family members.

**Vocabulary** *my family, brother, parents, father, mother, grandmother, grandfather, sister, baby, a photo*

**Content Vocabulary** *me, pretend*

**Resources** Workbook pp. 28–29; Audio CD TR: A39–41; Video: Sc. 2—Vocabulary 1a; Video: Sc. 3—Vocabulary 1b; Classroom Presentation Tool: Vocabulary 1; Picture Cards 11, 12, 14, 52–61; Sound Card 15; Teacher's Resource CD-ROM: Activity Worksheet 3.1

**Materials** note cards

1 **Listen and say.** TR: A39

2 **Listen.** Point and say. TR: A40

## Warm Up

- **Activate prior knowledge** Review the Unit 0 words *listen, point,* and *say.* Hold up Picture Card 12 and say *Point.* Say *Show me how you point.* Point to the classroom clock and say *Point to the clock.* Then say *Now point to the board.*
- Hold up Picture Card 14 and say *Say.* Hold your hand to your mouth and say *I say my name. My name is (Mr. Ramos).* Hold up Picture Card 11 and say *Listen. Show me how to listen.* Put your hand to your ear as though you're listening to something. Keep your hand on your ear and have students repeat the action.
- Say *Listen. I'll say a word. You point.* Say *boy.* Model by pointing to a boy in the class. Say *girl.* Have students point to a girl. Say *Teacher.* Have the class point to you.

## 3 Work with a partner.

Point and ask about the family.
Pretend and answer. TR: A41

# Present

- Hold up the book, showing the photo of a family on pp. 42–43. Point to the picture and say *This is a family. Point to the people in the family.*
- Point to the picture again and ask *How many people are in the family?* (eight people) Point to each person in the photo and read the caption. Then point to each person again, read the caption, and have students repeat after you.
- Hold up Picture Cards 52–61 one at a time and have students say the target word. Then place Picture Cards 53 and 61 next to each other. Ask *Who is the brother? Point to the brother.* Students should point to Picture Card 53. Ask *Who is the sister? Point to the sister.* Students should point to Picture Card 61. Repeat with other pairs of picture cards.
- Ask students about their own families. Ask *How many brothers are in your family? How many sisters are in your family? How many babies are in your family?* Call on different students to answer.

## Be the Expert

### Vocabulary Strategy

**Compound Words** One kind of compound word is a noun that's made up of two words written together as one word. In this lesson, for example, point out the compound words *grandfather* and *grandmother.* You can show students how to separate each into two words to show which words are joined together: *grand + mother* and *grand + father.* Help students identify the smaller words within compound words as they learn them.

### Teaching Tip

If students are having difficulty with pronunciation, work with the whole group to sound out each target word. Speak slowly, saying each syllable clearly. Then have students repeat after you. Repeat each word several times, increasing speed until you are saying the words naturally. Start or end each class by practicing several words this way, and continue until students are comfortable with pronunciation.

## Practice 1 2

- 1 Hold up the book, showing the picture on pp. 42–43. Say *Listen.* Play **TR: A39**. Point to the person or object in the picture when you hear each word. Then say *Now listen and say.* Play **TR: A39** again. After students hear each word, have them repeat it. Listen to make sure students are pronouncing each word correctly. If needed, repeat the activity and help students pronounce the words correctly.

- 2 Help students follow the order of the words on **TR: A40** by pointing to the first three people named. Then have them point to the rest of the words on their own and say each word. Say *Listen, point, and say.* Play **TR: A40**. ✓ Walk around the room saying words to individual students. Have them say the words and point to them in the book. If students have difficulty, review the corresponding Picture Cards.

- Call on different students to stand up and say a word on pp. 42–43. Have the class point to the word in their books and hold up the page. Then have the class repeat the word together. Model by saying sister. Students should point to the photo of the sister and then hold their books up. Say sister and guide the class to say the word with you.

## Wrap Up

- Write the following words in two columns on the board:

| | |
|---|---|
| brother | mother |
| father | grandfather |
| sister | grandmother |
| baby | parents |

- Give each student four note cards. Pair students. Point to the first column of words. Point to one student in a pair and say *Draw a picture of each word.* Then point to the second student in the pair. Point to the second column of words. Say *Draw a picture for each word.* Say *Write the word on the back of the card.*

- Write *grandfather* on a note card. Say *My word is grandfather. I write grandfather on the back of the card. Now I draw a picture of a grandfather.* Draw a picture on the other side of the card and hold it up. Give students enough time to make their cards. One student in each pair should hold up a picture. His partner then guesses the word. Have students take turns until they have guessed all words.

## Recap

- Hold up Picture Cards 52–61 one at a time, asking students to call out the names of the family members and objects they see.

## Apply 3

- 3 Point to the model dialogue on p. 43. Play **TR: A41**. Then read the question and answer aloud and have a few students model the dialogue with you. First, ask the question and have students give the answer. Then have students ask you the question.

- Explain that *Who's* is the same as *Who is*. Write *Who's* on the board with the words *Who is* underneath. Say *Who's this? Who is this?* Have students repeat each question. Point to the baby on p. 43 and ask *Who is this?* Then ask *Who's this?* (a baby)

- Place students in pairs. Have them ask and answer questions about the vocabulary words, using the dialogue on p. 43 as a model.

## Extend

- Write the following on the board:

| | |
|---|---|
| Is it a ______? | Yes, it is. |
| | No, it isn't. |

- Hold Picture Card 53 (brother), but don't let students see which card it is. Model how to ask questions to guess the card. Ask *Is it a mother?* Model the dialogue. Say *No, it isn't. Is it a sister? No, it isn't.* Then have students ask you questions. Say *Now you ask.* Call on students to ask questions. Have them continue asking about each vocabulary word until they guess the answer.
- Put students in small groups. Give one student in each group one of the Picture Cards 52–61. Make sure the rest of the group does not see the card. Have group members ask questions until they guess correctly. Make sure students are asking and answering in complete sentences, using the patterns above.
- Collect the cards and distribute a different card to a different group member. Repeat the activity until all students have had an opportunity to hold a card and answer questions.

## Wrap Up

- Say *I'm going to draw a picture. You write the word.* Model the activity with *grandmother*. On the board, draw an older woman with glasses. Ask *Who's this?* Write and say *Grandmother. Now you answer.* Draw a picture of a baby. Ask *Who's this?* Students should write *baby* in their notebooks. Walk around the room as students write the answer. Continue drawing target words until you review all of the words.

## Be the Expert

### Teaching Tip

**Grouping** When you put students in groups, make sure each group includes a combination of students with varying language levels. One way to do this is to color-code students by language level. For example, give green cards to more advanced language learners, yellow cards to on-level learners, and blue cards to beginning students. Then you can group students by saying *Work in groups of three colors: green, yellow, and blue.* This way, students assume their groupings are simply color-based.

### Sounds of English

**Single Sounds: /ð/** The pronunciation of the /ð/ sound (mo<u>th</u>er) can be confused with the pronunciation of /d/ (<u>d</u>og), and /θ/ (tee<u>th</u>). To pronounce the /ð/ sound, have students put the tip of the tongue behind the upper teeth and push air through the gap between the teeth and the tongue. Students' vocal cords will vibrate as they pronounce the /ð/ sound.

Use Sound Card 15 (fea<u>th</u>er). Pronounce the /ð/ sound for several seconds and then say *feather*. Then say the example words.

Example words: <u>th</u>e, mo<u>th</u>er, fa<u>th</u>er, bro<u>th</u>er

### Formative Assessment

Can students

- identify and use words for family members?

  Have students open their books to pp. 42–43. Point to the people in the photo and ask *Who's this?*

**Review** For additional practice, direct students to Activity Worksheet 3.1.

## Song

**Vocabulary in the song**

**Vocabulary 1** *my family, brother, sister, baby*

**Vocabulary 2** *big, short, tall, small*

**Grammar in the song**

**Grammar 1** use simple present of *to have* (first and second person singular)

**Resources** Workbook p. 30; Audio CD TR: A42; Video: Sc. 9—Song; Classroom Presentation Tool: Song; Picture Cards 62–67

4 **Listen.** Read and sing. TR: A42

# Big or Small?

*Do you have a big family?*
*Do you have a big family?*
*Do you have a big family?*
*Yes, my family is big!*

*Do you have a little brother?*
*Do you have a little sister?*
*Do you have a little baby*
*in your family?*

*I don't have a little brother,*
*little sister, baby brother.*
*My brother is big!*

*Some are short, and some are tall.*
*I have a big family, and I love them all!*

*How many people are in your family?*
*How many people are in your family?*
*How many people are in your family?*
*Two, three, four, five or more?*

*There are two boys in my family.*
*There are two girls in my family.*

44

## Use the Song 4

- **Act it out** Draw seven stick figures on the board. Then draw three stick figures. Say *We talked about families.* Point to the first group of figures. Say *Some families are big.* Point to the second group of figures. Say *Some families are small.*
- Have students open their books and look at pp. 44–45. Ask *Is this a big family or a small family?* (big) Ask *How many people are in this family?* (six) *Who are they?* (mother, father, parents, sisters, baby)
- 4 Play **TR: A42** once, with books closed, so students can listen. Then have students open their books to pp. 44–45. Play the song a second time. Have students point to the brother, sister, and baby as they hear each one named in the song.
- Play **TR: A42**. Have students raise their hands if the answer to a question in the song is *yes* for them. Model by reading aloud the first line. Say *Do you have a big family?* Then raise your hand. Explain *I raise my hand if I have a big family.*

*There are six people in my family.*
*And I love them all!*

*Some are short, and some are tall.*
*I have a big family, and I love them all!*

*My family is big.*
*Your family is small.*

*I love the people in my family!*
*Yes, I love them all.*
*I love them all!*
*I love them all!*

5 **Sing again.** Hold up pictures.

45

## Be the Expert

### Teaching Tip

Students usually enjoy music and songs, but it can be challenging for them to hear a song just once or twice and be expected to sing along. You can break songs down into manageable chunks so students have time to get used to the rhythm of the music and the pronunciation of the words.

## Use it Again 5

- Sing or play this line from the song: *Do you have a little brother?* Have students sing the next line: *Do you have a little sister?* Then sing the following line together: *Do you have a little baby in your family?*
- Switch roles. Have students sing the first line. Sing the next line yourself, and then have everyone sing the last line together.
- Sing the first line, but pause for *brother*. Say *Do you have a little _______?* Have students sing the missing word. Repeat for *sister* and *baby* in the next two lines.
- **Vocabulary 2** Put students in six groups. Hand out Picture Cards 62–67, one to each group. Say each word and have group members hold up their card when you say the word. Then point to something big in the classroom and say *This is big.* Point to something small and say *This is small.* Provide examples for the other words.
- 5 Say *Listen to the song and sing. Listen for the word on your card. When you hear your word, stand up and show your card.* Play **TR: A42**. Have students stand and hold up their cards when they hear their word in the song. Then have groups switch cards, and play the song again.
- **Value** Have students open their books to p. 53. Play **TR: A42**. Pause after the line *I have a big family, and I love them all.* Ask *What do you do with your family?*

## Grammar 1

**Objectives**

Students will

- ask questions with *do you have.*
- answer questions with *have* and *don't have.*

**Grammar** use simple present of *to have* (first and second person singular)

**Resources** Workbook pp. 31–32; Audio CD TR: A43–44; Video: Sc. 6—Grammar 1; Classroom Presentation Tool: Grammar 1

**Materials** paper bag; three note cards

**GRAMMAR** TR: A43

| | |
|---|---|
| How many brothers **do** you **have?** | I **have** two brothers. |
| How many sisters **do** you **have?** | I **don't have** any sisters. |

**6** **Look and listen.** Draw a line. TR: A44

46

## Warm Up

- Place a book, a pencil, and two or three crayons where students can see them. Pick up the book and say *I have a book.* Pick up two crayons and say *I have two crayons.*
- On the board, write *I have* _________. Read the sentence frame aloud. Hold up one object at a time as you say the completed sentence. Have students repeat. If possible, have students hold up their own crayons and books. Repeat, and have students complete the sentence frame when you hold up an object.
- Pick up the book and the pencil. Say *I have a book and a pencil.* As you say *have* nod your head *yes.* Put down the pencil. Say *I have a book. I don't have a pencil.* As you say *have* nod your head *yes.* As you say *don't have* shake your head *no.* Put down the book. Say *I don't have a book.* Pick up a crayon and the pencil. Say *I have a crayon and a pencil.* Put down the crayon. Say *I have a pencil. I don't have a crayon.* Put down the pencil. Say *I don't have a pencil.*
- On the board, write *I don't have* _________. Read the frame aloud. Hold up each object and then put it down as you say the completed sentence. Have students repeat.

## Be the Expert

### Our World in Context

Members of a family often live together and share a house or an apartment. In many countries, it's common for parents and children to live together. In some places, other relatives, such as grandparents, live together with children and their parents. When grandparents, parents, children, and/or other relatives all live together in the same house, this is called an *extended family*.

### Grammar in Depth

The helping verb *do* is often used with *How, When, Where,* and *What* questions. For most questions, the main verb in the question is restated in the answer.

*How many brothers do you* ***have****?*
*I* ***have*** *one.*
*When do you* ***see*** *your grandparents?*
*I* ***see*** *them on Sundays.*
*Where do your grandparents* ***live****?*
*They* ***live*** *in my town.*

*What* questions with *do* ask about actions. The main verb isn't repeated in the answer.

*What does your family* ***do*** *on Saturdays?*
*My family* ***goes*** *to the park.*

# Present

- Have students open their books to p. 46. Direct students' attention to the yellow grammar box. Play **TR: A43**. Read the questions and answers aloud and have students repeat after you. Then read the questions aloud and have students read the answers. Finally, reverse roles so students ask you the questions.
- Write the following on the board:

| How many brothers do you have? | | |
|---|---|---|
| I have one brother. | I have two brothers. | I don't have any brothers. |

- Read aloud the question and sentences on the board and have students repeat them. Then ask *How many brothers do you have?* Point to the first response on the board and have a student read it aloud. Ask the question again and point to the second response. Ask the question a third time and point to the third response. Have students read each sentence aloud. Repeat with *sisters*.
- Put students in three groups. Give each group a note card with the number *0*, *1*, or *2* on it.
- Ask one group *How many sisters do you have?* Students should answer according to the number on their card. (1: I have one sister; 2: I have two sisters; 0: I don't have any sisters).

## Practice 6

- Place students in pairs and have them take turns reading the questions and answers in the grammar box on p. 46. Say *Listen to more questions and answers.* Explain that students will draw lines from the pictures of boys and girls to their answers.
- Practice with students by drawing a picture of a child (or a smiley face) on the board. Below the picture, draw two "boy" stick figures and one "girl" stick figure. Point to the picture of the child and say *This is Amina. Amina has two brothers.* Model drawing a line from the child to the two boy stick figures. Point to each stick figure and say *This is a brother. This is also a brother.*
- 6 Play **TR: A44**. Help students complete item 1. Then have students complete the activity on their own. ✓ Walk around the room and give new examples, such as *Salam has one brother and one sister. Point to the picture.* The student should point to the image of one boy and one girl. If students have difficulty, point to each image and say an accurate sentence, such as *I have two brothers.*

## Wrap Up

- Have students play a role-playing game. Have each student pretend he or she is one of the children pictured on pp. 46–47. Ask the student playing the role of Tariq *How many sisters do you have?* (I have one sister.) Then ask *How many brothers do you have?* (I don't have any brothers.) Ask the student playing the role of Ryan *How many brothers do you have?* (I have one brother.) and *How many sisters do you have?* (I don't have any sisters.) Continue in this way until all students have had a chance to answer.

## Recap

- Remind students that they can use *have, do not have,* or *don't have* to ask and answer questions. Have students role play again. This time, have them ask two questions of each student. For example, have a student ask the student playing Dao *How many brothers do you have?* (I don't have any brothers.) *How many sisters do you have?* (I have two sisters.)

## Apply

- Give students the opportunity to practice using *have* and *don't have* in sentences. Model examples such as *I have a dog. I don't have a cat.* Then walk around the room and ask students questions such as *How many cats do you have? How many dogs do you have? How many birds do you have? How many butterflies do you have?*

## Extend

- Draw and label a square, a triangle, a rectangle, a star, and a circle on the board. Then draw a collection of ten shapes made up of the ones on the board.
- Say *Draw ten shapes like the shapes on the board. You can draw as many of each shape as you want. Keep it a secret. Don't show anyone your shapes.* After students finish drawing, put them in pairs. Have students take turns asking and answering questions about their pictures. On the board, provide sentence frames such as *How many* ________ *do you have in your picture?* and *I have* ________.

## Wrap Up

- Have students write sentences using *have* and *don't have* to describe their families. Then have pairs of students exchange their sentences and read them aloud.

## Be the Expert

### Teaching Tip

Students can become discouraged if you correct them directly or say their names when you correct a mistake. To avoid this, talk about mistakes and corrections in a general way. For example, you can say *I heard "I don't have no brothers." We should say "I don't have any brothers."* Then have the entire class repeat the correct sentence.

### Formative Assessment

Can students

- ask questions with *do you have?*

  Have students ask you about the people in your family.
- answer questions with *have* and *don't have?*

  Ask students a variety of questions, including ones for which they will answer in the negative. For example, *How many big brothers do you have? How many little sisters do you have?*

# Vocabulary 2

**Objective**

Students will

- use words that describe people and objects.

**Vocabulary** *young, old, tall, short, small, big*

**Resources** Workbook p. 33; Audio CD TR: A45–46; Video: Sc. 4—Vocabulary 2; Classroom Presentation Tool: Vocabulary 2; Picture Cards 52–61; World Map Poster; Teacher's Resource CD-ROM: Activity Worksheet 3.2

**Materials** note cards

**7 Listen and say.** TR: A45

**8 Work with a partner.** Point and say.

**9 Work with a partner.** Listen. Say and stick. TR: A46

1 2 3 4 5

48

## Warm Up

- **Recycle** Use Picture Cards 52–61 to review family words. Then put Picture Cards 53, 55, 56, and 61 face down in a pile. Write *0*, *1*, and *2* on note cards and place them face down in a second pile. Have students pick a card from each pile and make a sentence. For example, *I don't have any brothers* for *0* and *brother*.

## Present

- Say *Now we're going to learn new words to talk about families.* Open the book to p. 48 and point to the first photo of the girl. Say *This is a girl. She's young. The girl is young.* Have students repeat both sentences. Point to her grandfather in the same photo and say *This is her grandfather. He's old. The grandfather is old.* Have students repeat.
- Show Picture Cards 52 and 56. Point to the baby and ask *Is she old?* (no) *Is she young?* (yes) Say *Yes, the baby is young.* Point to the grandmother and ask *Is she young?* (no) *Is she old?* (yes) Say *Yes, the grandmother is old.*
- Point to the photo of the two boys. Point to the tall boy and say *The boy is tall.* Have students repeat. Point to the short boy and say *The boy is short.* Have students repeat. Then point to the tall boy and ask *Is he short?* (no) *Is he tall?* (yes) Point to the short boy and ask *Is he tall?* (no) *Is he short?* (yes)
- Point to the photo of the small family. Say *This is a family. The family is small.* Then point to the photo of the big family. Say *The family is big.*

## Practice 7 8

- 7 Say *Listen and say.* Play **TR: A45**. Have students listen to the sentences and repeat them. Then play **TR: A45** again and have students point to the correct photos as they repeat the sentences.

- 8 Put students in pairs. One student points to a word, and the other student says the word. Model this activity with a student. Point to one of the pictures until the student says the word. Make sure students take turns pointing and saying the words.

## Apply 9

- 9 Place students in pairs. Hold up the book and point to Activity 9 on p. 48. Play **TR: A46**. Model the dialogue with a student.

- Say *Look at the Unit 3 stickers in the back of your book.* Pair students. One partner describes the picture, and the other partner responds. (Yes, she's old.) Then students place the sticker.

## Extend

- Write the following on the board:

| | | |
|---|---|---|
| big/small | young/old | tall/short |

- Hold up an eraser. Point to *big/small* and say *Pick one of the words. Use the word to write a sentence about the eraser.* (The eraser is small.)

- Show Picture Card 52 (baby). Point to *young/old* and say *Pick one. Write a sentence about the baby.* (The baby is young.)

- Draw a giraffe. Point to *tall/short* and say *Pick one. Write a sentence about the animal.* (The animal is tall.)

## Wrap Up

- Read aloud each pair of sentences below. Give students a few minutes to draw pictures for each pair. Read the sentences aloud and have students hold up the correct pictures. Have students repeat the sentences.
  1. *The sister is tall. The brother is short.*
  2. *The baby is young. The grandmother is old.*
  3. *The flower is small. The mountain is big.*

## Be the Expert

### Vocabulary Strategy

**Antonyms** Some of the vocabulary words introduced in this lesson are antonyms, or words that have opposite meanings. For example, *hot* and *cold* are opposites. In this lesson, antonym pairs include *young/old, tall/short*, and *small/big*. Teach antonym pairs together whenever possible, and be sure that students can match each word to its opposite.

### Formative Assessment

Can students

- use words that describe people and objects?

  Hold up a photo of a person or object, such as a ball, an older man, or a cow. Ask *What is it? Is it big? Is it tall? Is (he) young?*

**Review** For additional practice, direct students to Activity Worksheet 3.2.

# Grammar 2

**Objectives**

Students will

- ask questions with *who*.
- identify and describe family members.

**Grammar** ask questions with *who*

**Resources** Workbook p. 34; Audio CD TR: A47–48; Video: Sc. 7—Grammar 2; Classroom Presentation Tool: Grammar 2; Picture Cards 52–61; Teacher's Resource CD-ROM: Activity Worksheet 3.3

**GRAMMAR** TR: A47

| | |
|---|---|
| **Who**'s she? | She's my sister. She's nine. |
| **Who**'s he? | He's my grandpa. He's old! |

**10** **Play a game.** Cut out the pictures on page 163. Glue. Listen and play. TR: A48

**11** **Look at the pictures.** Write *yes* or *no*.

1. Is the grandpa old? ________________
2. Is the mother tall? ________________
3. Is the brother young? ________________

49

## Warm Up

- **Recycle** Write the words *young, old, small, big, tall,* and *short* on the board, and have students read them aloud. Hold up Picture Card 61 (sister). Model using the card to say *She's my sister. She's young. She's short.* Then have several students come to the board and pick one card from Picture Cards 52–61. Say *Tell about the person.* Point to the words on the board. Say *Use these words.*

## Present

- Have students open their books to p. 49. Direct students' attention to the yellow grammar box and play **TR: A47**. Have students listen to the recording once, and then play it again. As they listen, pause the recording as needed to give students time to repeat each question and answer.
- Write the following on the board:

| | |
|---|---|
| Who's she? | She's my ________. |
| Who's he? | He's my ________. |

- Draw a simple picture of three people on the board. Point to one picture and say *Who's he? He's my brother. He's young.* Have students practice asking you questions with *who* about the other pictures. Include a short description of each person in your answers.
- Have each student draw a picture of one family member. ✓ Call on students to hold up their pictures. Ask *Who's she?* or *Who's he?* If students have trouble, help them begin the sentence with *She's* or *He's*.

## Practice 10

- Direct students to the game board on p. 49. Point to the picture of the boy and ask *Who's he?* If necessary, model the answer by saying *He's a boy.*
- Read the directions aloud. Help students find the pictures on the top of p. 163. Give students a few minutes to cut out the pictures.
- Draw the game on the board. Number the empty boxes 1 through 8 randomly, starting with the first box in the first row. Have students use numbers 1–8 to fill all of the boxes on their game boards. Remind students to put the numbers in any order.
- 10 Play **TR: A48**. Have students listen to the recording once. Then play it again. Pause after the first description (*She's my sister. She's ten.*) and model choosing the correct picture and placing it on number 1 on the board you've drawn. Then continue the recording. Pause as needed to give students time to pick the correct picture and glue it to their boards. When students have completed their boards, have them take turns pointing to the pictures and describing the people. (She's the mother. She's short.)

## Apply 11

- 11 Write *yes* and *no* on the board. Then read the directions for Activity 11 aloud. Say *Read the questions. Look at each picture again. Write* yes *or* no. Complete item 1 with students. Read the question aloud. Ask *Who's the grandpa?* Have students point to the grandfather in Activity 10. Explain *Some people call a grandfather a grandpa.* Ask *Is the grandpa old?* (yes) Say *Yes, the grandpa is old. Write* yes *for number one.*
- Have students complete the activity. When they finish, have students read the questions and their answers aloud.

## Extend

- Have students draw pictures of their families. Then put students in pairs. Have them ask *Who's she?* and *Who's he?* about each person in their partner's picture. Encourage students to give as many details as they can about each person, using the vocabulary they've learned in this unit. Model an example, such as *She's my mother. She's old. She's tall.*

## Wrap Up

- Have a student come to the board. Give the student Picture Card 53 (brother). Ask *Who's he? Tell about him.* (He's my brother. He's short.) Model an answer for students, if needed. Continue the activity with Picture Cards 53–57 and 61 until all students have a turn.

## Be the Expert

### Grammar in Depth

The phrase *who is* can be shortened to the contraction *who's*. The contraction *who's* is different in meaning from the word *whose*, which signals ownership. *Who's* can be used at the beginning of a question to ask about the identity of a person. *Whose* can be used at the beginning of a question to ask about possession.

### Formative Assessment

Can students

- ask questions with *who?*
  Show Picture Cards 53–57 and 61 one at a time. Have students ask you a question about the cards. *(Who's she? Who's he?)*
- identify and describe family members?
  Have students look at the photo on pp. 42–43 or the illustration on pp. 44–45. Point to the family members and ask *Who's he/she? Tell about him/her.*

**Review** For additional practice, direct students to Activity Worksheet 3.3.

## Reading

**Objectives**

Students will

- compare and describe families.
- tell about their families.

**Reading Strategy** Make Connections to Personal Experience

**Academic Vocabulary** *connect*

**Content Vocabulary** *family tree, Mexico, Turkey*

**Resources** Workbook pp. 36–37; Audio CD TR: A49–50; Teacher's Resource CD-ROM: Graphic Organizers (Three-column chart); World Map Poster

**12** **Listen and read.** TR: A49

# Families Are Different

This family from Turkey is small. There are parents and a boy.

This family from Mexico is big. There is a grandfather, a grandmother, a father, and a mother. There are four brothers and one sister.

## Warm Up

- **Build background** Point to the world map. Say *This is a world map.* Locate your country on the map and point to it. Say *This is (country).* Point to it again and have students repeat after you.
- Locate Mexico on the map. Trace a path from your country to Mexico. Then point to Mexico on the map and say *This is Mexico.* Have students repeat. Point to the photo of the big family on p. 50. Say *This family is from Mexico.* Point to Mexico on the map again.
- Locate Turkey on the map. Trace a path from your country to Turkey. Then point to Turkey on the map and say *This is Turkey.* Have students repeat. Point to the photo of the small family on p. 50. Say *This family is from Turkey.* Point to Turkey on the map again.
- Ask *Where is your family from?* Call on students to say their hometown or home country. If possible, show on the map any countries other than the one you're in.

## Present 12 13

- Direct students to p. 50. Point to and read the title aloud. Have students repeat after you. Give students a moment to look at the photos. Point to the small photo and ask *Is this a big family?* (no) Point to the large photo and ask *Is this a big family?* (yes)

**13** **Listen and read.** Draw a line. TR: A50

1. The family from Mexico — has three people.
2. The family from Turkey — has nine people.

**14** **Look at this family tree.** Write.

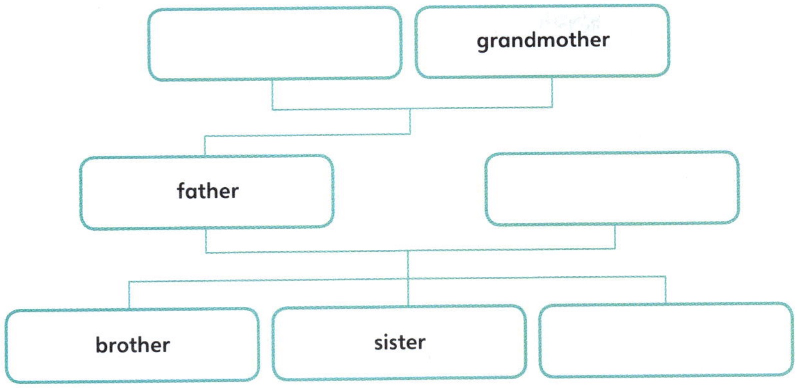


**15** **Work with a partner.** Ask and answer. Write.

| | You | Your Partner |
|---|---|---|
| Name | | |
| Family Size | | |
| Brothers | | |
| Sisters | | |

51

## Be the Expert

### Our World in Context

Mexico connects North America and Central America. It shares a border with four states of the United States, incuding California and Texas, and it borders the countries of Guatemala and Belize to the south. Turkey is located on two different continents, Europe and Asia, and is traditionally viewed as being at the crossroads between Europe and Asia.

### Teaching Tip

You can use Picture Walls to help connect students' personal experiences to the unit. For example, students can bring in pictures of their families and post them on the Picture Wall. Then you can expand activities by having students use the pictures on the Picture Wall. Place Picture Walls where students can easily see and refer to them.

- **12** **Read together** Play **TR: A49** once and have students listen as they read along with the text.
- Play **TR: A49** a second time. Pause after each paragraph to check for comprehension. ✓ Ask questions such as the following:

  **Paragraph 1:** *Is the family big or small?* (small)
  **Paragraph 2:** *How many brothers does the family have?* (four)
- Read the selection aloud and have students repeat each sentence after you. Have students point to the correct photo for each sentence.
- Point to the small photo. Say *This family is from Turkey. How many people are in the family? Let's count.* Point to the first person and then hold up one finger and say *one*. Have students repeat after you as you count. When you've finished counting, say *There are three people in this family. It's a small family.* Repeat the activity with the other photo.
- **13** Read the directions aloud. Explain to students that they will draw a line to connect words on the left with words on the right to make sentences. Play **TR: A50** and have students look at the phrases as they listen. Play **TR: A50** again and have students complete the activity. Have students read the complete sentences aloud as they point to the appropriate family on p. 50.

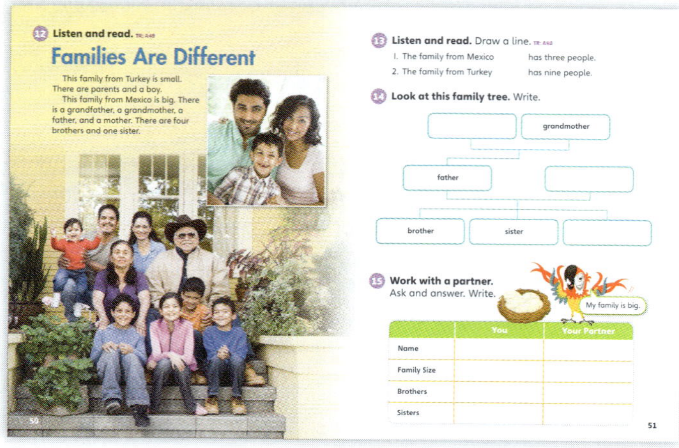


## Practice 14

- **Graphic literacy** Have students open their books to p. 51. Point to the family tree. Say *This is a family tree. A family tree shows people in a family.* Point to the top row. *Older people are on top.* Point to the bottom row. *Young people are on the bottom.*
- Read the first entry on the family tree. (grandmother) Have students repeat after you. Say *The grandmother is older. She goes on top.* Trace your finger along the connecting lines. Point to *father* on the tree and say *father*. Then place your finger back on *grandmother* and say *The grandmother is the father's mother* as you trace your finger along the connecting lines.
- Repeat with *father*, *brother*, and *sister*.
- 14 Read the directions aloud. Explain to students that they're going to complete the family tree with the names of family members. Walk through the first one with students. Say *Who else in a family is old like the grandmother?* (grandfather) Say *Yes, the grandfather is old.* Write *grandfather* in the box next to *grandmother*. Then trace your finger down the connecting lines and say *The grandfather is the father's father.* Ask *Who goes with the father? They go here.* Trace you finger to the box next to *father*.
- Have students complete the activity in small groups. Walk around the room and check students' work as they complete the activity. ✓ As you walk around the room, stop and point to a word in the family tree. Ask questions such as *Who's this? Is he old or young? Who is (his) (father)?*

## Wrap Up

- Have students write one sentence about the family from Mexico and one sentence about the family from Turkey. Ask *Is your family like the one in Turkey? Is your family like the one in Mexico? Why?* Call on different students to answer aloud.

## Recap

- Say *We read about two families. One family is big. One family is small.* Ask *Where is the big family from?* (Mexico) *Where is the small family from?* (Turkey)
- Say *I'm going to talk about each family. You say the family from Mexico or the family from Turkey.* Model by saying an example aloud, such as *The family is big.* Then say *the family from Mexico*. Continue with these sentences: *There's one boy in the family.* (the family from Turkey) *There's a grandfather in the family.* (the family from Mexico) *There's one sister in the family.* (the family from Mexico) *The family is small.* (the family from Turkey)

## Apply 15

- Hold up three crayons and two pencils. Ask *How many crayons?* (three) *How many pencils?* (two) Hold up both hands and have two students hold up their hands. Ask *How many hands?* (six)
- 15 Have students open their books to p. 51. Point to Activity 15 and read the directions aloud. Point to the column under **You** and say *Write your answers here.* Point to *Name* and then to the empty box next to it. Say *Write your name.* Point to *Family Size* and then to the empty box next to it. Ask *How many people are in your family? Write the number.* Repeat with the rows for brothers and sisters. Give students a few minutes to write their answers.
- Write the following on the board:

> What's your name?
> How many people are in your family?
> How many brothers do you have?
> How many sisters do you have?

- Pair students and say *Ask about your partner's family.* Point to the column under **Your Partner**. Say *Write your partner's answers here.*
- Have students use the questions on the board to ask their partners about their families. Then have students share what they learned about their partners' families. Prompt with questions such as *How many people are in your partner's family? How many brothers? How many sisters?*
- **Expand** Say *Use your chart to write about your family. Is it big? Is it small? How many brothers do you have?* Model by writing on the board: *My family is big. I have three brothers.*

## Extend

- Have students choose an animal and create a family tree for that animal. Refer students to the family tree on p. 51. Say *Remember, a family tree shows who is in a family.* Point to the lines that connect *grandmother* and *grandfather* to *father*. Say *These lines show that this grandmother and grandfather are the father's parents.* Repeat with the lines connecting the mother and father to the three children.
- Say *Let's make animal family trees! What's your favorite animal? Give the animal a name. Who's in its family?* Have students copy the first two rows of the family tree from p. 51. Have them write the names for grandparents and parents inside the boxes. Then have students draw one box for the animal they named and boxes for its brothers and sisters. Say *Give your animal lots of brothers and sisters... or just one or two. Draw the animal family.*
- Have students share their family trees with the class.

## Wrap Up

- Draw a three-column chart like the one below.

| | Family from Turkey | Family from Mexico |
|---|---|---|
| Family Size | | |
| Brothers | | |
| Sisters | | |

- Model how to use the chart to summarize the reading on p. 50. Use the chart to ask questions about the two families. Complete the chart with students' answers and information from the reading.

## Be the Expert

### Reading Strategy

**Make Connections to Personal Experience** Connecting what they learn to their own lives can help students understand new material. For example, when reading about other families, students can tell about their own families. When information does not directly relate to students' lives, they can make connections by giving opinions or talking about what they already know about a subject.

### Related Vocabulary

*aunt, cousin, uncle*

### Formative Assessment

Can students

- compare and describe families?

  Ask questions such as *What is the family from Mexico like? What is the family from Turkey like? Are they big or small? How many (brothers) does the family from Mexico have? How is your family like the one from (Mexico)?*
- tell about their families?

  Ask students questions such as *Who's in your family? Is your family big?*

# Writing

**Writing** Draw and write about your family.

**Objectives**

Students will

- view a writing model.
- draw and write about their families.

**Resources** Workbook p. 38; Classroom Presentation Tool: Writing

I'm Adrian. I have a big family. In this photo, you see my grandfather, my grandmother, my parents, and my other grandmother. I have one sister and one brother. In this photo, I am the baby!

**16** **Draw and write.**

I'm ______________. I have a ______________.

In this picture, you see my ______________.

I have ______________.

**17** **Work in a group.** Talk about your picture.

52

## Formative Assessment

Can students

- draw and write about their families?

  Have students display their drawings and read their sentences aloud.

## Present

- Write the following on the board:

  I'm __________. I have a __________.

- Read the sentence frames aloud. Then walk around the room. Say *Hello. I'm (Mr. Ramos). What's your name?* Say *I have a (small) family. Is your family big or small?* Encourage students to respond in complete sentences.
- Say *Today, we're going to draw and write about our families.*
- Have students look at the model and photo on p. 52. Point to the photo and say *This is one boy's family.* Ask *Does he have a big or small family?* (big). Read the model paragraph aloud. Read it aloud again and have students repeat each sentence after you. Ask *How many sisters does Adrian have?* (one)

## Write 16

- **16** Have students open their books to p. 52. Point to the blank space in Activity 16. Say *Draw a picture of your family.*
- Point to the sentence starters. Say *Look at your picture. Write about your family.* Read each sentence starter aloud. Connect them to matching sentences in the writing model.
- Remind students to spell out numbers in every sentence.

NATIONAL GEOGRAPHIC

# Our World

## Love your family.

18 **Look and read.**

Work and play together.

19 **Read and copy.**

I work and play with my family.

53

## Value

**Value** Love your family.

**Objectives**

Students will

- read about family-related values and activities.
- read and copy a full sentence.

**Academic Language** *copy*

**Resources** Values Poster

## Be the Expert

### Teaching Tip

Echo reading helps students develop oral reading skills and provides practice with stress, rhythm, and intonation. Before students read, model correct pronunciation and rhythm and have them repeat after you. If students are having trouble with pronunciation, stress, rhythm, or intonation, focus on modeling the skills until students can do them properly. Repeat the process until students seem ready to read independently.

## Share 17

- 17 Have students look at Activity 17 on p. 52. Ask a student to read the directions aloud.
- Put students in small groups. Have students use the sentences they wrote in Activity 16 to talk about their pictures. Encourage group members to ask questions. If students need additional support, model asking and answering questions with them.

## Value 18 19

- Point to the photo on p. 53. Say *This is a family.* Point to the boy. Say *He is a boy.* Point to the parents. Ask *Who are they?* (parents) Point to the father. Ask *Who is he?* (father) Repeat for mother. Ask *How many people are in this family? Is it a big family or a small family?* (three, small) *Who are the people in the family?* (the boy, the mother, and the father)
- 18 Have a student read the text under the photo of the boy. Ask *What are two things you can do with your family?* (work and play)
- 19 Say *Now let's read and copy.* Have students read the sentence silently and copy it. Remind them to use a capital letter at the beginning of the sentence and place a period at the end.

# Project

**Objectives**
Students will
- name family members.
- talk about family members.
- make a family photo poster.
- complete the Unit 3 Quiz

**Content Vocabulary** *frame, members*

**Resources** Assessment: Unit 3 Quiz; Picture Cards 52–67; Teacher's Resource CD-ROM: Activity Worksheet 3.4

**Materials** family photos (*optional*); colored paper; scissors; glue

**20 Make a family photo poster.**

Cut out the frame on page 163. Draw more frames.

Choose photos.

Glue photos and frames.

Write.



## Prepare

- Use Picture Cards 52–61 to review the family member vocabulary words students learned in this unit. Hold up the cards of family members one by one, each time asking *Who's this?*
- Have students review the vocabulary words that describe family members. Then show Picture Cards 62–67 one at a time for students to discuss.
- Have students open their books to p. 55. Point to the family photo poster the boy is holding in the photo. Say *This is a family photo poster. We're going to make family photo posters, too. This is how we're going to make them.*
- Write the following steps on the board:

  1. Cut.
  2. Choose.
  3. Glue.
  4. Write.

- Discuss the first step. Say *Cut out a frame for each photo. The frame is the outside part of the picture.* Model the shape of a frame with your hands. Direct students to the frame on p. 163 and have them cut it out. Say *This is a frame.*
- Say *We need more frames.* Model choosing and making frames from the colored paper. Say *I want to make my poster colorful. I'm going to choose frames in different colors.*

## Be the Expert

### Project Rubric

✓ Did students cut out frames for each photo?

✓ Did students write sentences about their families?

✓ Did students use unit vocabulary to talk about their family photo posters?

- Have students choose the photos they will use. If students are unable to bring in family photos, give them time to draw pictures of people in their family they would like to include on the poster.
- Say *Glue your pictures to the frames.* Show students how to glue a photo in the middle of the frame. Then say *Now write a sentence about your family. Who is in the picture?* Move around the room, making sure students understand what to do. Offer help when needed.

## Share

- Model sharing a poster. Stand in front of the class, holding up the family poster you made. Say *This is a poster of my family.* Read the sentence you wrote about your family.
- Have students come to the front of the class to share their posters. Have them describe their posters. Then have them tell who each person in the photo is. Encourage students to use words that describe. If there is time, have other students ask questions about the photo posters.

### Now I Can

Ask questions such as the following:

- *Who's in your family?*
- *Is your father tall or short? Is your grandmother young or old?*
- *How many sisters are in your family?*

**Review** For additional practice, direct students to Activity Worksheet 3.4.

### Unit Assessment

Give the Unit 3 Quiz. Hand out the quiz and go over the instructions with students. The quiz should take 15–20 minutes.

# Video

**Vocabulary 1a** *a photo, a family, brother, sister, a baby*

**Vocabulary 1b** *mother, father, parents, grandfather, grandmother*

**Vocabulary 2** *tall, short, big, small, old, young*

**Grammar 1** use simple present of *to have* (first and second person singular)

**Grammar 2** ask questions with *who*

**Song** *Big or Small?*

**Viewing** families and family members

**Story Time** *We All Pull*

**Resources** Student Book pp. 40–49

## Before You Watch

- Play Scene 1: Introduction. Pause when Anna and Freddy are introduced. Point to Anna and ask *Who's she?* (She's Anna.) Point to Freddy and ask *Who's he?* (He's Freddy.)
- Finish playing Scene 1. Then say *This video is about families.* Ask *How many people are in your family? How many brothers do you have? How many sisters do you have?*

## While You Watch

- As students watch the video, have them look and listen for words that name or describe family members.
- Say *Listen to the words Anna and Freddy say. Then you say them.* Pause the video at each image and have students repeat the target word.

## After You Watch

- Write a vocabulary item on the board. Have students draw and share pictures that show the word.

## Zoom In

### Vocabulary

- Pause the video after frames that show a family member. Repeat the term with students. Then ask *Who's (he)?* Use students' responses to make a complete sentence such as *He's the (brother).* Have students repeat the sentence.

### Grammar

- Play Scene 7: Grammar 2 and pause after Freddy asks *Who's he?* Have students try to answer the question. Then play the video again, stopping after Freddy asks a question about the next image. Continue with the remaining questions Freddy and Anna ask.

### Song

- Play Scene 9: Song. Then play *Big or Small* again. Have half the class sing the questions that start with *How many*, and the other half sing the questions that start with *Do*.

### Viewing

- Play Scene 10: Viewing. Pause the video to ask questions about the animal babies. For example, ask *What color is the baby? How many babies do you see? Is this baby tall or short?*

### Story Time

- View Scene 11: Story Time once with students.
- View *We All Pull* again. Pause and ask questions to check students' comprehension. For example, ask *Who's the first person to pull?* (grandfather) Point to the grandmother and ask *Is she tall or short?* (tall) Point to a character in the video and ask *Who's she?*

## *We All Pull*

A family wants the giant turnip in their garden. They work together to pull it out of the ground. They pull and pull and pull. Will the turnip ever come out?

## Before You Read

- **Activate prior knowledge** Review Picture Cards 52–61 with students. Hold up one Picture Card at a time and have students name the target word on it.
- Hold up the Reader. Point to the title and say *The name of the book is* We All Pull. *This story is about a family doing something together.* Have students identify the family members in the picture on the cover. (brother, grandfather, grandmother, father, mother, sister)
- **Introduce the strategy** Say *We do things in order.* Model coloring a picture. Hold up a piece of paper. Say *First, I get out paper.* Draw a small picture on the paper and say *Next, I draw a picture.* Color the picture and say *Then I color the picture.*
- Say *A story tells what happens in order. First, we read about the first thing that happens. Then we read about the second thing that happens. The story is over when we read about the last thing that happens.*

## While You Read

- On the board, write the numbers 1–6 in a list. Next to number 1, write *Grandfather pulls*. Say *This is the first thing that happens. Let's listen to the story to see what happens next.*
- Read the book aloud. Stop after every few pages and ask questions to help students think about what they already know. Help them use this information to figure out each answer.

  p. 4: *Who is the second person who pulls?* (the grandmother)
  p. 5: *Who pulls next? What word describes him?* (the father; strong)
  p. 6: *Who pulls after the father? What words tell about her?* (the mother; big)
  p. 7: *Who's this? What does she do?* (the sister; She pulls.)

## After You Read

- Point to the numbered list on the board. Point to number 1 and say *The grandfather pulls first.* Ask *Who pulls next?* (grandmother) Next to number 2, write *grandmother*. Point to the remaining numbers and have students identify the remaining characters in the order in which they pulled.

## Unit 3 Reader

**Text Type** folktale

**Vocabulary** *big, grandfather, grandmother, tall, father, mother, sister, small, young, family*

**Grammar** use simple present of *to have* (first and second person singular)

**Reading Strategy** Identify Sequence of Events

**Resources** Video: Sc. 11—Story Time; Classroom Presentation Tool: Story Time; Teacher's Resource CD-ROM: Graphic Organizers (Two-column chart); Picture Cards 52–61

## Be the Expert

### Reading Strategy

**Identify Sequence of Events**

Identifying the sequence of events helps students be active readers. Help students identify the sequence of events while reading *We All Pull*. Stop reading every few pages and ask questions about the sequence of events in the story. Use words such as *first, next, last, before,* and *after* in your questions.

### Text Background

*We All Pull* is based on a Russian folktale about a farmer's huge turnip, and how it's pulled from the ground. Many versions of this story have been told and published. In some versions, it takes the farmer's entire family and help from his farm animals to finally pull the turnip from the ground.

## Student Book

### TR: A39 1 Listen and say.

my family — It's a photo of my family.
brother — He's my brother.
parents — They're my parents.
father — He's my father.
mother — She's my mother.
grandmother — She's my grandmother.
grandfather — He's my grandfather.
sister — She's my sister.
baby — She's a baby.
a photo — It's a photo.

### TR: A40 2 Listen. Point and say.

my family, brother, parents, father, mother, grandmother, grandfather, sister, baby, a photo

### TR: A41 3 Work with a partner. Point and ask about the family. Pretend and answer.

Who's this? The sister.

### TR: A42 4 Listen. Read and sing.

Note: Lyrics for the song *Big or Small?* are on pp. 104–105.

### TR: A43 Grammar

Note: Grammar 1 is on p. 106.

### TR: A44 6 Look and listen. Draw a line.

1. Mark, how many brothers do you have?
   I have one brother.
2. Carmen, how many brothers do you have?
   I have two brothers.
3. Tariq, how many sisters do you have?
   I have one sister.
4. Clare, how many sisters do you have?
   I have one sister. I have one brother, too.
5. Julia, how many brothers and sisters do you have?
   I have a brother and a sister.
6. Dao, how many sisters do you have?
   I have two sisters.
7. Ryan, how many brothers do you have?
   I have one brother.
8. Aisha, how many sisters do you have?
   I have one sister.

### TR: A45 7 Listen and say.

young — The girl is young.
old — The grandfather is old.
tall — The boy is tall.
short — The boy is short.
small — The family is small.
big — The family is big.

### TR: A46 9 Work with a partner. Listen. Say and stick.

1. The grandfather is old. Yes, he's old. My turn.

### TR: A47 Grammar

Note: Grammar 2 is on p. 112.

### TR: A48 10 Play a game. Cut out the pictures on page 163. Glue. Listen and play.

1. Who's she? She's my sister. She's ten.
2. Who's she? She's my grandma. She's old.
3. Who's he? He's my little brother. He's three.
4. What's this? It's a photo of my parents.
5. Who's he? He's my father. He's tall.
6. Who's she? She's my mother. She's short.
7. Who's he? He's my grandpa. He's old.
8. What's this? It's a photo of my family.

### TR: A49 12 Listen and read.

Note: Reading *Families Are Different* is on p. 114.

### TR: A50 13 Listen and read. Draw a line.

This family from Turkey is small. There are parents and a boy. This family from Mexico is big. There is a grandfather, a grandmother, a father, and a mother. There are four brothers and one sister.

1. The family from Mexico has nine people.
2. The family from Turkey has three people.

## Workbook

### TR: 23 1 Listen. Look and match. Write the number.

family, brother, baby, father, grandmother, mother, parents, sister, a photo, grandfather

**TR: 24** **3** **Listen to the song. Check.**

Note: Lyrics for the song *Big or Small?* are on pp. 104–105.

**TR: 25** **4** **Listen. Write.**

Some are short, and some are tall.
I have a big family, and I love them all!

**TR: 26** **5** **Listen. Circle.**

1. Do you have any sisters?
   Yes, I do.
   How many sisters do you have?
   I have two sisters.
2. How many brothers do you have?
   I don't have any brothers.
3. How many sisters do you have?
   One. I have a baby sister.
4. Do you have a big sister?
   I don't have a big sister.

**TR: 27** **6** **Look and listen. Write.**

Hi, I'm Lisa. I have a big family. I have a big brother. I have a little brother. I have a big sister. And I have a baby sister, too!

**TR: 28** **11** **Listen. Write the number.**

1. Who's she? She's my sister.
2. Who's he? He's my father.
3. Who's she? She's my grandmother.
4. Who's she? She's my mother, with my baby brother.
5. Who's he? He's my grandfather.
6. Who's he? He's my brother.

**TR: 29** **13** **Listen. Draw a line.**

This is me. This is my grandfather.
This is my mother. This is my father.
We are a small family.

**TR: 30** **15** **Listen and read.**

Note: Reading *Families Around the World* is on p. 311.

**TR: 31** **21** **Listen and circle.**

1. She's my sister.
2. He's my grandfather.
3. She's my mother.
4. She's young.
5. It's small.
6. It's short.

## Answer Key

# Student Book

**Unit Opener** SB p. 40

three

**6** SB pp. 46–47

Mark: one brother
Carmen: two brothers
Tariq: one sister
Clare: one sister and one brother
Julia: one brother and one sister
Dao: two sisters
Ryan: one brother
Aisha: one sister

**11** SB p. 49

1. yes, 2. no, 3. yes

**13** SB p. 51

1. The family from Mexico has nine people.
2. The family from Turkey has three people.

**14** SB p. 51

grandfather, mother, sister / brother

# Workbook

Go to pp. 309–312 for the Workbook Answer Key for this unit.

## Review: Units 1-3

**Vocabulary** U1–U3

**Grammar** U1–U3

**Content Vocabulary** *heads, tails*

**Resources** Workbook pp. 40–41

**Materials** coins, playing pieces (such as buttons, tokens, or other small, flat objects)

- **Play the game** Explain that students will play a game. Have them open their books to pp. 56–57. Give students time to look at the images on the two pages. Then point to the picture of the crayon. Ask *What is it?* (It's a crayon.) *What color is it?* (It's orange.) Point to the flowers. Ask *What are they?* (They're flowers.) *How many flowers?* (Two.)
- Have students find the pictures of the coin on p. 56. Read the caption aloud. Then hold up a coin for students to see. Point to the "heads" side and say *This is heads.* Point to the "tails" side and say *This is tails.* Walk around and show the coin to students. Have several students try tossing it and saying *heads* or *tails.*
- Direct students' attention to the word *Start* on p. 56. Demonstrate how to put a playing piece over the word to begin the game. Then toss the coin in the air. If it lands on "heads," demonstrate moving the playing piece forward one space in the game. If it lands on "tails," demonstrate moving forward two spaces.
- Model playing the game. Point to a student and say *Play with me, please.* Toss the coin and move the playing piece (one space). Ask *What is it?* Prompt the student to respond. (It's a crayon.) Model taking turns. Flip the coin. Have your partner move the same playing piece forward (two spaces.) Prompt the student to ask you the question *What is it?* Say *(It's a tree.)*

## Be the Expert

### Teaching Tip

When students answer questions out loud, have them repeat the question before they answer. When students work in pairs, have them do the same thing. Repeating a question before answering it will help students identify any errors in the question. Additionally, it will serve as a check that students are listening to one another and answering appropriately.

- Have students read the model dialogue on p. 57. Then say *Now it's your turn. Play! Take turns. When it's your turn, move one or two spaces. Then ask a question.* Have students play the game in pairs. Give a coin and a playing piece to each pair. Remind them to ask and answer questions.
- Monitor students as they play the game. Accept responses such as the following: *A crayon. An orange crayon. It's an orange crayon. Birds. Three birds. The birds are in the sky.* Make sure students understand that they keep moving along the game route until they reach the word *Finish*.
- **Sentence frames** If students need help thinking of questions and answers, write examples on the board:

| | |
|---|---|
| What is it? | Yes, it is. |
| What color is it? | What are they? |
| How many? | They're ______. |
| Is it a ______? | Who's she? |
| It's ______. | Who's he? |
| No, it isn't. | |

- **Modify** To modify the game, have pairs work in unison to complete each step in the game at the same time. Provide instructions such as *Player One, toss the coin!* and *Player One, ask about the photo. Player Two, answer.*

# In This Unit

**Theme** This unit is about homes.

**Content Objectives**

Students will

- describe houses.
- identify furniture and rooms in houses.

**Language Objectives**

Students will

- name rooms in a house.
- name furniture.
- talk about actions they do at home.

**Vocabulary**

**Vocabulary 1** *a bathroom, a bed, a bedroom, a dining room, a kitchen, a lamp, a living room, a mirror, a sofa, a TV*

**Vocabulary 2** *cleaning, cooking, eating, sleeping, taking a bath, watching TV*

**Grammar**

**Grammar 1** ask and answer questions with *Is there?* and *There is*

**Grammar 2** use verbs with the *-ing* ending (present progressive)

**Pacing Guides** LIU4

**Writing** Write about your bedroom.

**Value** Be neat.

**Project** Make a plan of rooms in a house.

## Unit Opener

**Objectives**

Students will

- identify objects in a photo.
- complete a description of a house.

**Resources** Video: Sc. 1—Introduction; Classroom Presentation Tool: Unit Opener; Teacher's Resource CD-ROM: Home-School Connection Letter; Picture Cards 1–9; Unit Opener Poster

**Materials** photo of a house

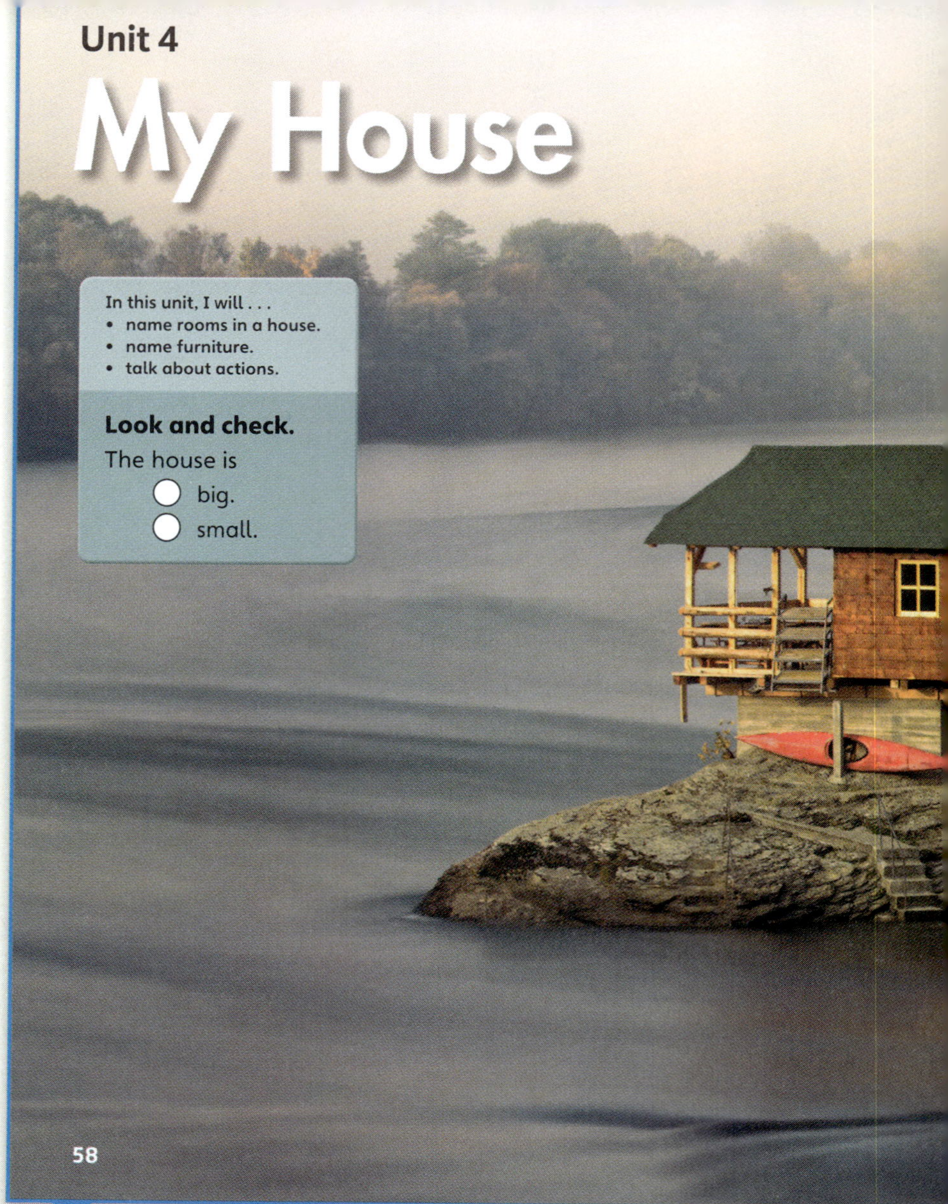


## Introduce

- **Recycle** Review colors and shapes: *black, blue, green, orange, purple, red, white, yellow, circle, rectangle, square, star, triangle.* Hold up Picture Card 1. Say *red*. Repeat with Picture Cards 2–8. Then hold up Picture Card 9 and ask *What shapes are these?* (square, triangle, circle, rectangle, star)
- Point to objects around the classroom and ask *What is the shape? What is the color?*
- Say *The name of this unit is "My House."* Ask *Are we in a house?* (no) *No, we are in school.* Then hold up a photo of a house and ask *Is this a house?* (yes) *Yes, this is a house.*
- Say *Open your books to page 58. This house is in a river.* Point to the red kayak under the house and say *People use this to go places.* Then ask questions to encourage discussion of the photo, for example:

  *What do you see in the photo?* (a house, trees, a rock, a river)
  *Where is the house?* (on a rock, in a river)

Drina River, Serbia

*What shape is the house?* (a rectangle)
*Is the house big or small?* (small)

- Guide students through the activity on p. 58. Read *The house is* and each option aloud. Have students repeat after you. Have students say *yes* or *no* after each option. Have students read the correct completed sentence aloud.
- Write the following on the board:

> The house is ________.
> It's on a ________.

- Read the first sentence frame aloud and model completing it. For example, write and say *The house is small.* Have students use the frames to tell about the house in the photo.
- Then ask students to tell you the colors of their houses. Call on each student and ask *What color is your house?* Ask a few students to describe the shapes of their houses.

## Be the Expert

### About the Photo

The house in the photo is on the Drina River in Serbia, a Balkan country in southeastern Europe. Forty-five years ago, a group of young people who regularly swam in the river thought of building the house after resting on the rock during their swims. One of the swimmers later built the small one-room house. Today the house is a popular attraction in the area.

### Teaching Tip

**Classroom Management** When you ask a question, have each student write an answer before having any student speak an answer aloud. This gives all students time to think of an answer and the language to express it. In addition, even if you have only one student answer aloud, every student has an opportunity to form an answer and participate.

### Related Vocabulary

*kayak, waves, window*

# Vocabulary 1

**Objectives**

Students will

- name rooms in a house.
- name objects in a house.

**Vocabulary** *a living room, a lamp, a dining room, a bedroom, a TV, a kitchen, a sofa, a bathroom, a mirror, a bed*

**Academic Language** *point*

**Resources** Workbook pp. 42–43; Audio CD TR: A51–53; Video: Sc. 2—Vocabulary 1a; Sc. 3—Vocabulary 1b; Classroom Presentation Tool: Vocabulary 1; Teacher's Resource CD-ROM: Graphic Organizers (Three-column chart), Activity Worksheet 4.1; Picture Cards 52–58, 68–77; Sound Card 31

**Materials** drawing paper (*optional*); note card with *Place* and *Thing* written on opposite sides

1 **Listen and say.** TR: A51

2 **Listen.** Point and say. TR: A52

60

## Warm Up

- **Recycle** Hold up Picture Card 58. Say *This is a family.* Hold up Picture Card 52 and ask *Who's this?* (a baby) Continue with Picture Cards 53–57. Repeat words as necessary.
- **Activate prior knowledge** Say *Some families live in a house. What things are in a house?* Model an example, such as *books*. Write students' responses on the board and add to the list if needed. (*clock, crayons, computer, paper, pens, pencils, table, chairs, desk*)
- **Set the stage** Say *In my house, there's a black table. There are four black chairs. There are many books in my house. There's a computer.* As you say each sentence, draw a picture of it on the board.

3 **Point.** Ask and answer. TR: A53

## Present

- Hold up Picture Cards 68–77 one at a time. Say each word. Hold up the cards again, this time having students say the words with you.
- Have students open their books to pp. 60–61. Say *There are different places in a house. They're called rooms.* Point to each room in the picture, and have students say the name of the room with you.
- Say *Rooms have things in them.* Point to the bedroom. Say *This bedroom has a bed.* Point to the bed and say *bed.* Point to the lamp in the living room and say *The living room has a lamp.* Point to the TV and say *There's a TV in the living room.* Point to the sofa and say *There's a sofa in the living room, too.* Draw students' attention to the bathroom, point to the mirror, and say *The bathroom has a mirror.* Pretend to look in a mirror, fix your hair, and say *I'm ready!*
- Say *Now I'm going to name a room. Find the room in the picture.* Say *kitchen* and have students point to the correct room on the page. Continue with the remaining rooms.

## Be the Expert

### Vocabulary Strategy

**Classifying and Categorizing**

Students can categorize words to help them recall vocabulary terms. Students can use two- or three-column charts to sort words according to categories such as **Things, Place,** and **Actions.** Extend beyond this unit's vocabulary lessons by reviewing terms students learned in earlier units, pointing to objects and locations in the classroom and gesturing to show actions. Write things, places, and actions in the proper columns on the chart.

### Teaching Tip

Pause after you ask questions in class and before you call on someone. Tell students you want to give them time to think of an answer. To give students even more time to prepare, write several questions on the board before you ask them for answers.

### Related Vocabulary

*floor, plants*

## Practice 1 2

- 1 Hold up pp. 60–61. Say *Listen.* Play **TR: A51**. As you hear each word and sentence, point to the room or object in the picture. Then say *Now you say the words.* Play **TR: A51** again. Pause after each word and sentence and have students point to the word and repeat it. Listen to make sure students pronounce each word correctly. As necessary, repeat words until students pronounce them correctly.

- 2 Say *Open your books to pages 60 and 61. Listen. When you hear a word, point to it in the picture. Then say the word.* Play **TR: A52**. Have students point to each word and say it aloud. ✓ Ask *Where's the dining room?* Have students point. Repeat with other rooms and objects.

## Wrap Up

- Hand out drawing paper to each student. Say *Draw a room. Draw things inside the room.* After students have drawn their rooms, say *What room is it? Write the word on the back of your paper.* Then put students in small groups. Have students show their pictures. The group should guess which room is shown. Ask students to present their pictures and tell about them. On the board, provide sentence frames such as *This is a (living room). It has a (sofa). This is a (kitchen.) It has (a table) and (chairs).*

## Recap

- Hold up Picture Cards 68–77 one at a time. For each card, ask *What is it?* Then ask *Is it a place? Is it a thing?* Have the class answer together.

## Apply 3

- Point to the elephant on p. 61 and say *Eddie the elephant asks a question.* Play the first voice of **TR: A53** only. ("What is it?") Point to the parrot and say *Polly the parrot answers.* Play the second voice on **TR: A53**. ("It's a mirror.") Then play the rest of the model dialogue.

- Say *Now we're going to ask and answer.* Play **TR: A53** again. Pause after each sentence and have students repeat it.

- 3 Point out the model dialogue. Say *Let's read what Eddie the elephant and Polly the parrot say.* Read the parts of the dialogue and have students repeat. Say *Now I'll point and ask a question. Then you answer.* Hold up your book and point to the lamp. Ask *What is it?* Call on a student to answer. Then ask another student *Where is it?* Say *Now it's your turn to ask and answer.*

- Place students in groups of three or four. Have them take turns pointing to parts of the picture on pp. 60–61 and asking and answering questions. Write the following sentences on the board for reference:

> What is it? It's a ________.
>
> Where is it? In the ________.

## Extend

- Assign each student a room from pp. 60-61. Draw and hand out a three-column chart with the headings **Room**, **What's in it?**, and **Big or small?** Point to the first column and say *Write the name of the room here.* Point to the second column and say *Write what's in it here.* Write examples of things on the board. Ask *What's in a kitchen?* Model the answer aloud: *tables, chairs*. Then point to the last column and ask *Is the room big or small?* Say *Write the answer here.*

| Room | What's in it? | Big or small? |
|---|---|---|
| | | |
| | | |

- As students work, write the following on the board: *The __________ has __________. It's __________.* When students are done with their charts, say *Make sentences. Copy the words on the board. Then finish the sentences. Use your charts to help you.*

## Wrap Up

- Have students form a circle. Hold up a note card with *Place* written on one side and *Thing* written on the other side. Say *I'm going to show a card. If you see* Place, *name a room in a house. If you see* Thing, *name something in a house.* Hold up the card and have students respond. Then hand the card to a student. Say *Now it's your turn. Hold up the card for the class.* Have students pass the card around the circle so each student has a chance to hold it up and elicit a response from the class.

## Be the Expert

### Teaching Tip

**Classroom Management** Have students practice taking turns. Give one student a small object, such as a pencil or a note card. Have the student say her name and then pass the object to the next student. Have the second student say his name. Continue until every student has held the object and said his name. Whenever students need to take turns on an activity, repeat this as practice, or remind them to pass an object back and forth to show whose turn it is.

### Sounds of English

**Single Sounds: /uː/**

The sound /uː/ (bl<u>ue</u>) can be difficult for beginning students. To demonstrate /uː/, round your lips like you are blowing. Show that, unlike the sound /ɒ/ (cl<u>o</u>ck), you say the sound with your mouth barely open.

Use Sound Card 31 (m<u>oo</u>n) to help students pronounce the long form of /uː/. Then have students say *boot*. Point out that the /uː/ sound in *boot* is not as long as the /uː/ in *moon*.

Example words: bl<u>ue</u>, r<u>oo</u>m, comp<u>u</u>ter, classr<u>oo</u>m

### Formative Assessment

Can students

- name rooms in a house?

  Hold up one of Picture Cards 68–72 and ask *What is this?* Have students name the room. Repeat with other cards.

- name objects in a house?

  Hold up one of Picture Cards 73–77 and ask *What is this?* Have students name the object. Repeat with other cards.

**Review** For additional practice, direct students to Activity Worksheet 4.1.

# Song

**Vocabulary in the song**

**Vocabulary 1** *bedroom, bed, kitchen*

**Vocabulary 2** *sleeping, eating*

**Grammar in the song**

**Grammar 1** ask and answer questions with *Is there?* and *there is*

**Content Vocabulary** *apartment, spoon, backyard, ball*

**Resources** Workbook p. 44; Audio CD TR: A54; Video: Sc. 9—Song; Classroom Presentation Tool: Song; Picture Cards 69, 70, 72

4 **Listen.** Read and sing. TR: A54

# My Home

*Where do you live?*
*I live in an apartment.*
*Where do you live?*
*I live in a house.*

*Where do you sleep?*
*I sleep in the bedroom.*
*Is there a bed?*
*Yes, there is.*

*At home, my home,*
*at home, where I live.*

*Where do you eat?*
*I eat in the kitchen.*
*Is there a spoon?*
*Yes, there is.*

62

## Use the Song 4

- **Set the stage** Say *I live in a small house. It's my home. I eat in the kitchen. I read in the living room. I sit on the sofa. I have a small TV. I have a blue bedroom. I have a small bed.*
- Hold up your book and have students look at pp. 62–63. Point to the house and ask *What is it?* (a house) *What color is it?* (yellow and blue) Ask *Who lives in the house?* (the girl)
- 4 Say *Listen.* Play **TR: A54**. Then say *Open your books to page 62. Listen and read.* Play **TR: A54** again. Encourage students to point to the words as they listen to the song. Pause after each verse to make sure no one falls behind. Say *Now read and sing.* Play **TR: A54** again. Have students read the words and sing along. It may require several attempts for the whole class to sing together successfully.
- Divide the class into two groups. Tell one group *You sing the questions.* Tell the other group *You sing the answers.* Play **TR: A54** again. Have each group sing its part. Students should be silent for the chorus.

## Use It Again 5

- 5 **Vocabulary 1** Put students in two groups. Have one group draw a bedroom and the other group draw a kitchen. Both groups should label their pictures. Say *Listen for your word. When you hear it, stand up and show your picture!*

## Be the Expert

### Teaching Tip

A song's tune and repetition can help students remember vocabulary and grammar. Having students add to the song can help them gain confidence with new grammar and vocabulary. If possible, print out or make copies of the song with a new verse partially completed. Have students complete the verse and then sing the revised song.

### Related Vocabulary

*bike, sidewalk, wall*

Play **TR: A54** and have students stand for *bedroom* and *kitchen*.

- Put students in pairs and have them use the target words to write a new verse for the song. Write the following example on the board to guide students. Tell students to change the underlined words.

  *Where do you <u>sit?</u>*
  *I <u>sit</u> in the <u>living room.</u>*
  *Is there a <u>sofa?</u>*
  *Yes, there is.*

- Have each pair sing their new verse.
- **Vocabulary 2** Say *Listen.* Play **TR: A54**. Pause after the second verse and ask *What room is for sleeping?* (bedroom) Resume **TR: A54** and pause after the fourth verse. Ask *What room is for eating?* (kitchen) Finish playing the song.
- **Grammar I** Play **TR: A54**. Pause after the second verse and ask *Is there a bedroom?* (Yes, there is.) *Is there a bed?* (Yes, there is.) Ask similar questions after the fourth and fifth verses. Then finish playing the song. Hold up pp. 62–63. Ask *Is there a girl?* (Yes, there is.) *Is there a tree?* (Yes, there is.)
- Write *baby, butterfly, mountain,* and *sun* on the board. Place students in pairs. Point to the words on the board and say *Take turns. Ask questions with* Is there. *Look at the picture on pages 62 and 63. Answer with* Yes, there is *or* No, there isn't. Visit students as they ask and answer questions, helping them as needed.

# Grammar 1

**Objectives**

Students will

- ask questions with *Is there?*
- answer questions with *there is* and *there isn't.*

**Grammar** ask and answer questions with *Is there?* and *there is*

**Academic Language** *check*

**Resources** Workbook pp. 45–46; Audio CD TR: A55–56; Video: Sc. 6—Grammar I; Classroom Presentation Tool: Grammar I

**Materials** drawing paper; 10 note cards, each with one unit vocabulary term

**GRAMMAR** TR: A55

| | |
|---|---|
| **Is there** a table in the kitchen? | Yes, **there is.** |
| **Is there** a sofa in the kitchen? | No, **there isn't.** |

6 **Look.** Listen and check. ✔ TR: A56

1. ◯ yes ◯ no
2. ◯ yes ◯ no
3. ◯ yes ◯ no
4. ◯ yes ◯ no
5. ◯ yes ◯ no
6. ◯ yes ◯ no

64

## Warm Up

- **Activate prior knowledge** Write *Places* and *Things* next to each other on the board. Say *Places in a house are called rooms. What rooms are in a house?* Call on several students to answer, and write their answers under *Places*. Ask *What things are in a house?* Call on several students, and write their answers under *Things*.
- Point to each word under *Things*. Ask a question about each one, such as *Where is the (mirror) in a house?* (bedroom, bathroom) *What shape is it?* (rectangle, circle, square) Use students' answers in a complete sentence. Have students repeat the sentence after you.

## Present

- Have students open their books to p. 64. Say *Look at the yellow grammar box.* Read the questions and answers aloud and have students repeat. Then read the questions aloud and have students say the answers.
- Play **TR: A55**. Pause after each sentence and have students repeat it.
- Write the following on the board:

> Is there ___________?
>
> Is there ___________ in the ___________?
>
> Yes, there is. No, there isn't.

65

## Be the Expert

### Grammar in Depth

The word *there* has several meanings in English. For example, it can be used to tell about location: *The book is there. Please stand over there.* In the song for this unit, *there* is used with a form of the verb *to be* to tell *(There is)* or ask *(Is there?)* about a situation.

Note that the English words *there, they're,* and *their* sound the same but have different spellings and meanings. *They're* is a contraction of *They* and *are*: *They're birds. Their* shows possession by more than one person, animal, or thing: *The students are here. Their bus is outside.*

### Teaching Tip

Ask students to give you examples of when they might hear English spoken outside of class. TV, movies, and music are all possible answers. Some students may have friends or family members who speak some English. Begin class by having students report new English words and phrases they hear or see outside of school.

- Point to p. 65 and ask *Is there a living room?* Model the answer *Yes, there is.* Point to the living room at the lower right on p. 65. Then point to the second sentence frame on the board and ask *Is there a sofa in the living room?* Point to the sofa and then to the first answer on the board and say *Yes, there is.* Have students repeat.
- Point to the second sentence frame again and ask *Is there a bed in the living room?* Point to the second answer on the board and say *No, there isn't.* Have students repeat.
- Say *Now I ask and you answer.* Point to the picture of the living room and ask *Is there a sofa in the living room?* (Yes, there is.) Then ask *Is there a bed in the living room?* (No, there isn't.)
- Say *Look around the classroom.* Ask *Is there a board in the classroom?* (Yes, there is.) *Is there a mountain in the classroom?* (No, there isn't.)

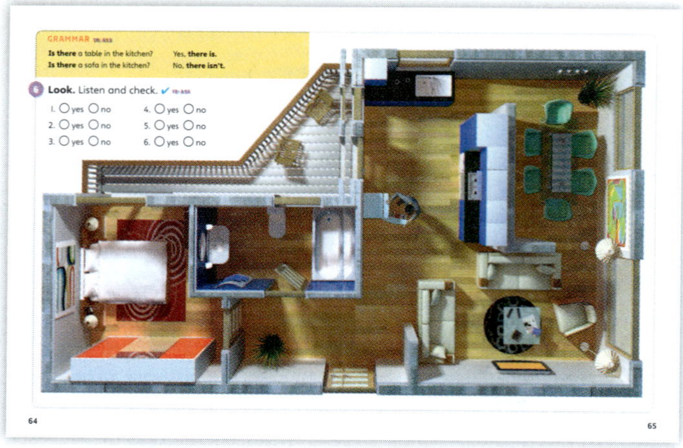


## Practice 6

- 6 Say *Look at the picture on pages 64 and 65. Listen and look. Check* yes *or* no. Play **TR: A56**. Pause after the question for item 1 and say *Look at the living room. Is there a sofa in the living room?* Give students time to think about the answer. Resume **TR: A56**. Pause after the answer for item 1 and say *Yes, there is. Check* yes *in the circle next to number 1.* Make sure students check the correct circle.

- Say *Listen again.* Continue playing **TR: A56**, pausing after each question to let students answer and then pausing again after each answer so students can verify their answers. ✓ Point to the bedroom on p. 64. Ask *Is there a TV in the bedroom?* If students have difficulty, review the picture with students.

## Wrap Up

- Write *Yes, there is* and *No, there isn't* on the board. Say *I ask a question. You answer.* Ask questions about objects that are and aren't in the classroom, such as *Is there a clock in the classroom? Is there a pencil in the classroom? Is there a sofa in the classroom? Is there a river in the classroom?* Have students answer and point to any objects that are in the classroom.

- Put students in pairs and have them ask and answer questions about items in the classroom. Have students share their dialogues with the class.

## Recap

- Ask *Is there a book in the classroom?* Point to a book and say *Yes, there is.* Say *Open your books to page 64. Look at the picture. Ask questions with Is there.* Model asking *Is there a bedroom in the house?* (Yes, there is.) Have several students ask questions to the class. The class should answer with *Yes, there is* or *No, there isn't.*

## Apply

- Place students in pairs and make sure each student has paper and a pen or pencil. Say *Tell about your house. What rooms are in your house? What things are in the rooms? Write words.* Give students enough time to make a list of words about their houses.

- Say *Now take turns. Ask questions about places and things in a house. Answer questions. Use your words.* Model the activity. Ask *Is there a table in the dining room?* Model the answer. *Yes, there is.*

- As partners talk, walk around the room and ask students about rooms in their houses, such as *Is there a mirror in the bedroom? Is there a table in the bathroom?* Try to elicit both *yes* and *no* answers from students.

## Extend

- Give drawing paper and crayons to students. Say *Draw one room in a house. Draw three things in the room. Color the picture.*
- Place students in pairs. Tell students to turn their pictures over so the other student cannot see it.
- Say *Guess the three things your partner drew. Ask questions with Is there. Your partner answers "Yes, there is," or "No, there isn't." Draw the things the room has. Take turns.* Model the activity. Ask a student *Is there a table?* If there is, draw a table on the board. Ask *Is there a bed?* If there is, draw it on the board. If there's not, don't draw it. When students finish, have them compare their pictures. Give groups a minute to talk about their drawings.

## Wrap Up

- Set out a pile of note cards with the words *a kitchen, a dining room, a bathroom, a bedroom,* and *a living room.* Then set out a second pile of note cards with the words *a mirror, a bed, a TV, a lamp,* and *a sofa.*
- Have students take turns choosing one card from each pile and making a question with the words on the cards. Hold up two cards and say *I have (bathroom) and (bed). I ask "Is there a (bed) in the (bathroom)?" Look at the picture to answer.* Point to the picture on pp. 64–65 and say *No, there isn't.*
- Have each student choose two cards, ask a question, and then return the cards to the piles. While students study the picture and decide on an answer, mix up the cards so the next student will get a new combination. Continue until all students have an opportunity to participate.

## Be the Expert

### Teaching Tip

When possible, have students collect visuals that show new vocabulary. By drawing or cutting out pictures, all students become more actively involved in learning—and kinesthetic learners are accommodated. If you have students use this option more than once, ask them to keep a "vocabulary portfolio" of their drawings or cutouts.

### Formative Assessment

Can students

- ask questions with *Is there?*

  Put students in pairs and have them ask questions with *Is there* about the picture on pp. 60–61. Then have pairs share one of their questions with the class.

- answer questions with *there is* and *there isn't.*

  Ask questions about the classroom, such as *Is there a table in the classroom?* and *Is there a mirror in the classroom?* Have students answer with *Yes, there is* and *No, there isn't.*

# Vocabulary 2

**Objective**

Students will

- use words for actions.

**Vocabulary** *sleeping, cleaning, cooking, taking a bath, eating, watching TV*

**Resources** Workbook p. 47; Audio CD TR: A57–58; Video: Sc. 4—Vocabulary 2; Classroom Presentation Tool: Vocabulary 2; Picture Cards 29, 68–83; Teacher's Resource CD-ROM: Activity Worksheet 4.2

**7 Listen and say.** TR: A57

sleeping

cleaning

cooking

taking a bath

eating

watching TV

**8 Work with a partner.** Point and say.

**9 Work with a partner.** Listen. Say and stick. TR: A58

1 2 3 4 5



## Warm Up

- **Recycle** Use Picture Cards 29 and 68–77 to review words for rooms and objects in a house. Hold up Picture Card 29. Ask *What is it?* (a table) Hold up Picture Card 72 (a kitchen), point to the table, and ask *Where is the table?* Then ask questions with *Is there*. For example, ask *Is there a sofa in the kitchen?* (No, there isn't.) *Is there a table in the kitchen?* (Yes, there is.)

## Present

- Hold up Picture Card 81. Say *sleeping*. Act out *sleeping*. For example, put your hands together against your face. Have students say the word after you and repeat the action. Hold up Picture Card 79 and say *cooking*. Act out cooking something in a pot. Have students say the word and repeat the action. Repeat with Picture Cards 80 and 82–83. Act out each action word as you say it. Have students act out along with you.
- Open the book to p. 66 and point to the first photo. Say *She's in the bedroom. What is she doing?* Model the answer. *She's sleeping.* Have students repeat. Then point to the next photo and say *They're in the kitchen. What are they doing?* (They're cleaning.) Continue pointing to each photo, asking questions about the photos and having students answer using the target words.

## Practice 7 8

- Say *Listen.* Play **TR: A57**.
- 7 Say *Now listen and say.* Play item 1 only from **TR: A57**. Say *Sleeping. She's sleeping.* Have students listen to the audio and repeat. Continue with the words and sentences for all six photos.

- 8 Put students in pairs. Have students point to one of the photos in Activity 7, say the word, and use it in a sentence. Model this activity with a student. Ask a student to point to one of the photos. If the student points to the second picture, for example, say *Cleaning. They're cleaning.* Make sure students take turns pointing, saying the word, and using it in a sentence. ✓ Point to the photo for *sleeping*. Ask *Is she eating?* (No, she's sleeping.)

## Apply 9

- 9 Point to Activity 9 on p. 66. Read the directions aloud. Play **TR: A58**. Model the dialogue with a student. Then have partners practice reading the dialogue together.
- Say *Look at the Unit 4 stickers in the back of your book.* Point to the stickers one at a time and ask *What is he doing? What is she doing?* Make sure students can identify each sticker.
- Have partners continue the activity, taking turns choosing a sticker and saying the word in a complete sentence. Walk around the room as students place their stickers, offering help as needed.

## Extend

- Write *sleeping* and *bedroom* on the board. Point to each word and have students say it aloud. Then write *She's sleeping in the bedroom*. Have students repeat the sentence. Write *watching TV*. On the board, write *He's ________ in the living room*. Have students think about an activity that takes place in the living room. (watching TV) Say and write *He's watching TV in the living room.* Have students repeat the sentence.
- On the board, write the following:

He's cooking in ________.

She's watching TV in ________.

He's taking a bath in ________.

She's eating in ________.

- Read the sentence frames aloud and have students complete each sentence accurately.

## Wrap Up

- Ask *What do people do in houses?* Act out the actions for *sleeping, cleaning, cooking, taking a bath, eating*, and *watching TV*. Prompt students to name each action.
- Put Picture Cards 78–83 face down on a desk. Pair students. Have a pair of students come to front of the classroom and act out one of the target words. The class guesses. Have students take turns until all pairs have had an opportunity to participate.

## Be the Expert

### Vocabulary Strategy

**Base Words and the Suffix *-ing***

You can add the suffix *-ing* to a verb to show that the action is happening now. For example, *I am cooking*. The suffix *-ing* can also be added to a verb to turn it into a gerund. Gerunds function as nouns. For example, *I like cooking*.

### Related Vocabulary

*broom*

### Formative Assessment

Can students

- use words for actions?

Show students Picture Cards 78–83. Ask *What's she doing?* or *What's he doing?*

**Review** For additional practice, direct students to Activity Worksheet 4.2.

## Grammar 2

**Objective**

Students will

- use verbs that end in *–ing*.

**Grammar** use verbs with the *–ing* ending (present progressive)

**Academic Language** *point*

**Resources** Workbook p. 48; Audio CD TR: A59–60 ; Video: Sc. 7—Grammar 2; Classroom Presentation Tool: Grammar 2; Picture Cards 53–57, 61, 68, 70–72, 74, 78–83; Teacher's Resource CD-ROM: Activity Worksheet 4.3

**GRAMMAR** TR: A59

| | |
|---|---|
| Where's your mother? | She's in the kitchen. She**'s cooking.** |
| Where's your brother? | He's in the living room. He**'s watching TV.** |

**10** **Play a game.**
Point. Ask and answer. TR: A60

**11** **Look at the pictures.** Write.

1. How many frogs are there? ____________________
2. What color is the sofa? ____________________
3. Where is the TV? ____________________

67

## Warm Up

- **Activate prior knowledge** Write the numbers 1–10 on the board. Then draw a circle, a triangle, and a square. Have students stand up. Say *I'll ask questions about numbers and shapes. I call your name. You come here and point to the number or shape.* Make sure students understand the activity. Ask *Where is number seven? Come and point.* Call a student by name and have her come to the board. Say *Thank you! You may sit down.* Continue with other numbers and shapes until all students are sitting down.

## Present

- Have students open their books to p. 67 and find the grammar box. Point to the first question and read it aloud. Then point to the first part of the answer and say *Read it with me: She's in the kitchen.* Ask *What's she doing?* Say *She's cooking. Read the next question and answer with me.*
- Say *Listen.* Play **TR: A59**. Have students listen to the audio once. Then say *Now you say the sentences* and play the track again. Pause after each sentence and have students repeat it. Pay attention to students' pronunciation.
- Write the following on the board:

| |
|---|
| She is → She's |
| He is → He's |
| Where's ______? ______ in the classroom. |

- Point to *She is* and *She's*. Say *She is a girl. She is means the same thing as She's.* Point to *He is* and *He's*. Say *He is a boy. He is means the same thing as He's.*

- Point to the sentence frames and model asking and answering several questions, such as *Where's the teacher? She's in the classroom. She's talking. Where's (Ahmad)? He's in the classroom. He's sitting down.*

## Practice 10

- 10 Have students open their books to p. 67 and find Activity 10. Say *Let's play a game.* Point to the mascots and say *Polly the parrot and Mia the monkey are asking and answering questions. Let's listen.* Play **TR: A60**. Have students point to the first picture of the frog. Ask *Where's the frog?* (He's in the dining room. He's eating.) Play **TR: A60** again.
- Place students in pairs. Say *Now it's your turn. Point and ask "Where's the frog?"* Point to the second picture in the row. Say *You point and ask. Your partner answers. Take turns.*
- Have partners take turns pointing to the pictures and asking *Where's the frog?* Walk around the room to make sure partners are taking turns. If necessary, explain that they do not have to go through the pictures in order. They should ask about all of the pictures. ✓ Point to pictures at random and ask *Where's the frog?*

## Apply 11

- 11 Read the directions aloud. Make sure students understand they are looking at the pictures from Activity 10. Read item 1 aloud. Say *Let's count frogs.* Point to each frog and count aloud. Say *There are eight frogs.* Write the number 8 on the board. Say *Write eight on the line.* Students might also point out that there are nine frogs if the one on TV is counted.
- Have students complete the activity. When they finish, check their answers as a group. Ask *What color is the sofa?* (orange) *Where is the TV?* (in the living room)

## Extend

- Put students in pairs. Have pairs draw a house with people in a kitchen, dining room, living room, and at least one bedroom. Say *Write sentences. Say what the people are doing.* Model. Show Picture Card 68 (a bathroom) and say *She's cleaning the bathroom. She's taking a bath.* Give students enough time to complete the activity. Then have students share their pictures and sentences with the class.

## Wrap Up

- Place Picture Cards 53–57 and 61 face down in a pile on a desk. Place Picture Cards 68, 70–72, and 74 in another pile face down. Have two students come to the front of the class. One student takes a card from the first pile and asks *Where is the (brother)? What's he doing?* The second student picks a card from the the second pile and answers *He's in the (kitchen). He's eating.* Continue with several pairs of students.

## Be the Expert

### Grammar in Depth

Use the present progressive to tell about an action that is happening right now. The action may or may not continue for a time. Words and phrases such as *right now, now, this minute, this instant,* and *presently* indicate that the present tense is being used: *She's running right now.*

### Teaching Tip

**Grouping** To help students remember to take turns asking and answering questions in pairs or small groups, have a supply of note cards with large question marks written on them. Give one card to each pair or group. Explain that the student asking the question should hold the card, and then give it to another student, who will ask the next question. Monitor pairs or groups during the activity to make sure the card moves from student to student.

### Formative Assessment

Can students

- use verbs that end in *–ing?*

  Point to one of the pictures in Activity 10 and ask *Where's the frog?* Prompt students to also tell what the frog is doing.

**Review** For additional practice, direct students to Activity Worksheet 4.3.

## Reading

**Objectives**

Students will

- compare and contrast houses.
- talk about different types of houses.

**Reading Strategy** Making Connections to Personal Experience

**Content Vocabulary** *different, houseboat, inside, outside*

**Resources** Workbook pp. 50–51; Audio CD TR: A61–62; Classroom Presentation Tool: Reading

**12 Listen and read.** TR: A61

# Houses Are Different

Most houses have kitchens, living rooms, and bedrooms inside, but the outside of houses can be very different.

Is there a house here?

a houseboat

Kerala, India

**13 Listen and read.** Look. Circle. TR: A62

1. Some houses are on the water. yes no
2. Most houses have kitchens. yes no

68

## Warm Up

- **Build background** On the board, draw a square house with a door and two windows. Ask *What is it?* (a house) Draw a rectangular building with lots of windows. Say *This is a house, too.* Have each student draw a picture of a house. Encourage them to be creative. Give them enough time to finish their drawings.
- Place students in pairs. Say *Tell about the house in your picture. What color is it? What shape is it? What rooms are there?* Give pairs time to describe their drawings to each other. Then collect the drawings from students and post them on the board. Sweep your hand over the pictures and say *Houses are different. Let's learn about houses.*

## Present 12 13

- Have students open their books to p. 68. Point to and read the title aloud. Say *Read it with me: Houses Are Different.* Point to the photo of the car house. Read the caption aloud. Ask *What is it?* (a car, a house) Say *It's a house! It's different.* Then point to the photo of the houseboat and say *This is a houseboat. It's a house on a river! It's different, too.* Point to the collection of drawings on the board and say *These houses are different.*

**14** **Look at the shapes.** Draw a line.

1. circle
2. rectangle
3. square
4. triangle

**15** **Look at the houses.** What shape are they? Draw a line.

1. circle    2. rectangle    3. square    4. triangle

**16** **What shape is your house?** Circle.

circle    rectangle    square    triangle

69

## Be the Expert

### About the Photos

This photo shows a houseboat in Kerala, India. Kerala is a state in the southwest of India on the Malabar Coast. The region has 44 rivers, in addition to countless canals, lakes, and lagoons. In the past, people used houseboats to move goods such as rice. Today, houseboats—like the one in the photo, which is called a *kettuvallam*—often carry tourists. The number of houseboats has grown so much that river crowding has become an environmental concern.

The inset photo is of the Auto Residence, or "crazy car house," near Salzburg, Austria. It was designed by architect Markus Voglreiter. He spent about 750,000 euros to change a 1970s-style house into an energy-efficient "eco house" in the shape of a Volkswagen Beetle.

- **12** **Read together** Say *Listen.* Play **TR: A61**. Say *Now you read.* Play **TR: A61** again. Pause after each sentence and have students repeat it aloud. Pause after *inside* to check for comprehension. Ask *What rooms do most houses have?* (kitchens, living rooms, bedrooms). Ask *Are they inside or outside of the house?* (inside). At the end of the audio, ask *Are the outsides of houses different?* (yes)
- Have pairs of students read the paragraph aloud to each other. Offer help with pronunciation as needed.
- Point to the photo of the houseboat. Say *Point to the outside of the house.* Ask *Where is the inside?* Have students point.
- **13** Read the directions aloud. Draw a circle on the board. Say *Draw a circle around the answer.* Play **TR: A62** and have students read along in their books. Pause the audio after the word *different*.
- Write *water* on the board. Say *A river has water.* Point to the water in the photo. Resume **TR: A62** with number 1. Pause after *water*. Have students circle their answers. Play number 2. Have students circle their answers.

12 **Listen and read.** TR: A61

Houses Are Different

Most houses have kitchens, living rooms, and bedrooms inside, but the outside of houses can be very different.

Is there a house here?

a houseboat

Kerala, India

13 **Listen and read.** Look. Circle. TR: A62

1. Some houses are on the water. yes no
2. Most houses have kitchens. yes no

68

14 **Look at the shapes.** Draw a line.

1. circle
2. rectangle
3. square
4. triangle

15 **Look at the houses.** What shape are they? Draw a line.

1. circle 2. rectangle 3. square 4. triangle

16 **What shape is your house?** Circle.

circle rectangle square triangle

69

## Practice 14 15

- Write and draw the following on the board:

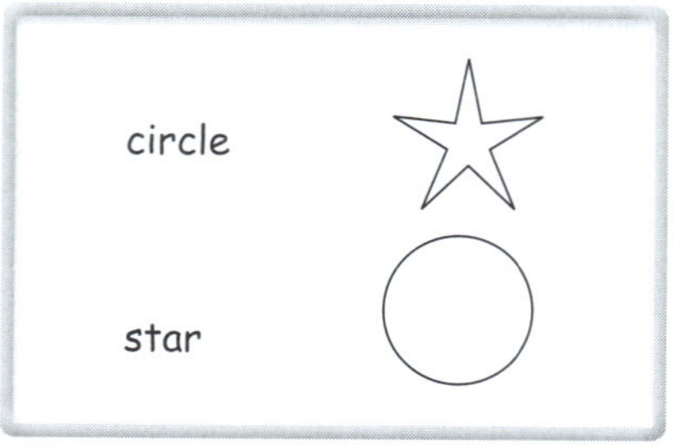


- Point to *circle* and read it aloud. Say *Circle.* Point to each shape and ask *Is this a circle?* Give students time to think and answer. Draw a line to connect *circle* with the circle shape. Say *I draw a line.* Repeat for *star,* but have a student draw the connecting line.
- 14 Have students open their books to p. 69. Read the directions aloud. Say *Now it's your turn. Look at the shapes. Draw a line from the word to the shape.* Give students time to complete the activity.
- 15 Point to the photos in Activity 15 and read the directions aloud. Say *Let's do one together.* Point to item 1 and read it aloud: *Circle. I know what a circle is.* Point to the circle photo in Activity 14. Say *One house is a circle. The directions say to draw a line. Draw a line from the word to the house that looks like a circle.* Model drawing the connecting line. Say *Now you do the rest.* Have students complete the activity. ✓ Walk around the room and say the name of shapes aloud. Have students point to the correct photo.

## Wrap Up

- On the board, draw two houses that are different shapes, such as a square and a triangle. Put a window or a door in each to show that they are houses. Have students name each shape. Then ask *Are the houses different? How are they different?*

## Recap

- Say *Houses can be different. Some houses are different on the outside. Some houses are different on the inside.* Ask *What rooms are in a house?* (kitchen, living room, bedroom) *What are some shapes of houses?* (circle, rectangle, square, triangle)

## Apply 16

- 16 Draw a circle, rectangle, square, and triangle on the board. Point to each shape and ask *What is it?* After students name them, label the shapes. Ask *What shape is your house?* Point to the circle and ask *Is your house a circle? Raise your hand.* Continue for the other shapes.
- Direct students' attention to Activity 16. Read the directions aloud. Ask *What shape is your house? Circle the shape.*

## Extend

- Take a class survey about students' houses. Draw the following chart on the board:

| Shape | | Color | |
|---|---|---|---|
| triangle | | red | |
| square | | white | |
| rectangle | | yellow | |
| circle | | brown | |

- Point to *red* and say *Show me something that's red.* Have students point. Repeat for *white* and *yellow*. Say *Brown is another color.* Point to things in the room that are brown. Repeat the word *brown* each time. Say *Some houses are brown.*

- Point to the first column under Shape. Read each option and ask *Is your house a (triangle)? Raise your hand.* Ask *How many have triangle houses?* Count how many students raise their hands for each option. Write numbers in the second column. Repeat for *Color.* If students' houses are a different color, ask *What color is your house?* Add rows to the chart for other colors as needed.

## Wrap Up

- On the board, write *It's* ________. Call on a student and ask *What color is your house?* (It's red.) Ask another student the same question. Ask the class *Are the houses different colors?* (yes/no) Repeat with more pairs of students. If time allows, repeat the activity with shapes.

## Be the Expert

### Reading Strategy

**Making Connections to Personal Experience** Making connections to personal experience helps students become engaged with a text and remember it. Students can connect to a text by asking questions such as *What does this remind me of in my own life? Do I know something about this topic?*

### Related Vocabulary

*boat, car*

### Formative Assessment

Can students

- compare and contrast houses?

  Point to the photos on p. 69. Ask *How are the houses the same? How are they different?*

- talk about different types of houses?

  Point to the photos on p. 68. Ask students to tell you about the houses.

## Writing

**Writing** Write about your bedroom.

**Objectives**

Students will

- use a writing model.
- draw and write about their bedrooms.

**Content Vocabulary** *rug*

**Resources** Workbook p. 52; Classroom Presentation Tool: Writing

**Materials** markers

### Formative Assessment

Can students

- draw and write about their bedrooms?

  Have students show their pictures and read two sentences from their paragraphs aloud.

I'm Teddy. This is my bedroom. My bed is blue. I have a red rug under my bed. There is a lamp on a small table.

**17** **Draw and write.**

I'm ______________. This is ______________.

My ______________ is ______________.

I have ______________.

There is ______________.

**18** **Work in a group.** Talk about your picture.

70

## Present

- Say *Today you'll draw and write about a room. What rooms are in your house?* (bedroom, bathroom, living room) *Do you have a bedroom? What color is it?*
- On the board, write *My house has* ______. and have students write one sentence about their houses. Then play an accordion game. Say *My house has a yellow bedroom.* Ask the first student in the first row to stand up and say his or her sentence. Then the next student takes a turn. Continue until all students have read their sentences.

## Write 17

- Have students open their books to p. 70. Read the paragraph aloud. Read it again, having students repeat each sentence after you. Then call on individual students to read each sentence.
- **17** Read the directions aloud. Say *Draw a picture of your bedroom. What color is it? What's in it?* When students finish their drawings, say *Now write about your bedroom.* Model by drawing a picture of a bedroom. Color the walls yellow and write *This is my bedroom* on the board. Ask *What color is it?* (yellow) Point to the second sentence and say *My bedroom is yellow.*
- Read each of the other sentence frames, helping students complete their sentences. Remind students to check their spelling.

NATIONAL GEOGRAPHIC

# Our World

## Be neat.

**19** **Look and read.**

**20** **Read and copy.**

I am neat. I clean my room.

______________________________

______________________________



## Value

**Value** Be neat.

**Objectives**

Students will

- read about home-related values and activities.
- read and copy two sentences.

**Academic Language** *copy*

**Resources** Values Poster

## Be the Expert

### Teaching Tip

Teach students to be respectful of other cultures. Help them avoid using negative words to describe houses or things and ideas from other cultures that may be unfamiliar to them. Teach and encourage students to use words such as *different* and *interesting*.

## Share 18

- **18** Have students look at Activity 18. Read the directions aloud.
- Divide the class into small groups. Have students talk about their drawings and read their sentences aloud. Encourage other group members to ask questions. Say *Tell about your picture. Read your sentences. Do your sentences tell about your picture?* Encourage others in the group to ask questions. If students need additional support to ask or answer questions, model asking and answering questions with students.

## Value 19 20

- Point to the photo on p. 71. Say *This is a bedroom.* Point to the bed. Ask *What is this?* Have students point to and name other things they recognize in the photo.
- Read the value sentence on p. 71 aloud: *Be neat.* Explain the meaning of the word *neat.* (to keep things where they belong) Move around your desk putting things away, straightening up. Say *I'm neat. My room is clean. My desk is clean. Are you neat? Raise your hand if you're neat.*
- **19** Direct students' attention to the activity. Read the directions aloud. Read it again as students repeat after you. Then read the two sentences below and have students repeat after you. Have students read them again on their own. Ask *Do you clean your room? Raise your hand.*
- **20** Read the directions for Activity 20 aloud. Have students read the sentences silently and then copy them. Remind students to copy the words exactly.

## Project

**Objectives**

Students will

- think about and draw rooms in a house.
- create a plan of rooms in a house.
- complete the Unit 4 Quiz.

**Academic Language** *organize*

**Content Vocabulary** *furniture*

**Resources** Assessment: Unit 4 Quiz; Picture Cards 68–77; Teacher's Resource CD-ROM: Activity Worksheet 4.4

**Materials** scissors; glue; drawing paper; crayons; poster board

**21 Make a plan of rooms in a house.**

1 Cut out the pictures on page 165. Draw more pictures.

2 Organize the pictures.

3 Glue the pictures.

4 Write your name.

72

## Prepare

- Review the vocabulary words students learned for rooms and household objects in this unit. Hold up Picture Cards 68–77, one by one, giving students a chance to call out the name of each room or object. As you show each card, ask *What is it?*
- Have students open their books to pp. 72–73. Point to the plan of the house on p. 73. Say *This is a plan of rooms in a house. It shows different rooms. Let's make a plan of rooms in a house.*
- Distribute poster board. Model drawing horizontal and vertical lines to show the different rooms in a house. Have students draw lines for the rooms in their house.
- Read the instructions on p. 72 aloud. Then say *Turn to page 165.* Help students find the correct pictures on p. 165. Hold up a pair of scissors. Say *Cut out the pictures.* Distribute drawing paper and crayons to students. Ask *Do the rooms need more furniture? Let's draw it.*
- Help students organize their pictures. Ask *What rooms and furniture go together? Is there a sofa in the bathroom?*
- Say *Now let's glue the pictures. Do they look like rooms in a house?* Have students glue their pictures onto the poster board. Remind students to write their names on their plans.

## Be the Expert

### Project Rubric

✓ Did students cut out pictures?
✓ Did students organize pictures?
✓ Did students glue pictures?

## Share

- Model sharing a poster. Stand in front of the class, holding up a plan similar to the one shown on p. 73. Say *This is a plan of rooms in a house. There are four rooms. This is the bedroom. There's a sofa in the living room. There's a refrigerator in the kitchen.*
- Have students come to the front of the class to share their plans. Have them describe the rooms, the furniture, and other objects in the rooms. To help students get started, ask *How many rooms are there? Is there a living room?*
- **Modify** If less time is available, put students into groups of four. Have each person in the group create one room. Then have students combine their rooms to form a plan of four rooms. Each student in the group can describe one room in the house.

### Now I Can

Ask questions such as the following:

- *What room do we eat in?*
- *What is there in a living room?*
- *What do you do in a kitchen?*

**Review** For additional practice, direct students to Activity Worksheet 4.4.

### Unit Assessment

Give the Unit 4 Quiz. Hand out the quiz and go over the instructions with students. The quiz should take 15–20 minutes.

## Video

**Vocabulary 1a** *a bed, a lamp, a mirror, a sofa, a TV*

**Vocabulary 1b** *a kitchen, a bathroom, a living room, a dining room, a bedroom*

**Vocabulary 2** *cooking, eating, watching TV, sleeping*

**Grammar 1** ask and answer questions with *Is there?* and *there is*

**Grammar 2** use verbs with the *–ing* ending (present progressive)

**Song** *My Home*

**Viewing** rooms and furniture in homes

**Story Time** *The Three Bears*

**Resources** Student Book, pp. 58–67

## Before You Watch

- Play Scene 1: Introduction. Say *This video is about rooms in a house. It's also about what's in the rooms.*

## While You Watch

- As students watch the video, have them look and listen for rooms in a house. Say *Look and listen for rooms in a house. Can you name one?* (a living room) Ask students to listen for objects in the rooms. Say *What's in a living room?* (a sofa)

- Pause the video as necessary to allow students time to say the words. Have them use the images to give short explanations for each word or use the words in complete sentences.

## After You Watch

- Play parts of the video with the sound off. Have students explain what's happening on screen. Then have students roleplay Anna's and Freddy's parts, using the target words.

## Zoom In

### Vocabulary

- Pause the video before Freddy names a room, an object, or an action. Ask students to name the target word. Then start the video again and have students check their answers.

### Grammar 1

- Play Scene 6: Grammar 1 without pausing. Then play it again, and pause after each question Anna asks. Have students answer with a complete sentence. Continue with the remaining questions.

### Song

- View Scene 9: Song once with the audio off. Have students read the lyrics together. Play *My Home* again, this time with the audio. Have students listen as they read.

### Viewing

- Play a few seconds of Scene 10: Viewing without the audio. Have students tell what they think the segment is about. Ask *What do you see?*

### Story Time

- View Scene 11: Story Time with students.

- View *The Three Bears* again. Play all the way through without pausing. After students have viewed *The Three Bears* twice, play it again, pausing the video at each new scene. Ask questions about the room and objects in the room.

## *The Three Bears*

Three bears leave their house and go for a walk. What happens when a little girl comes into their house and discovers their food, their chairs, and their cozy beds?

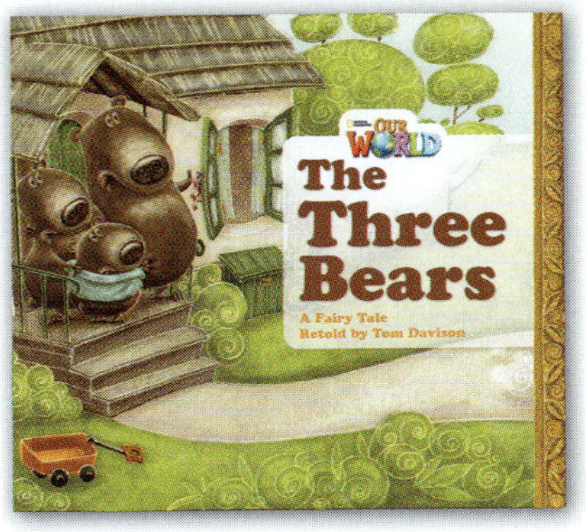


## Before You Read

- **Activate prior knowledge** Hold up the Reader and point to the title. Say *The name of the book is* The Three Bears. *It's about a girl who walks into a house. The house is the three bears' house!*
- **Introduce the strategy** Say *Sometimes a story doesn't tell why something happens. We have to figure it out. First, we read what happens. Next, we think about what we know. Then we put it together. We understand why it happens.*
- Model using the strategy to make an inference. Point to p. 2 of the Reader and read the sentence aloud. Point to the picture and ask *Who's looking in the window?* (a little girl) *Why is she looking in the window?* **Think Aloud** Read the sentence aloud again and say *The story doesn't tell. I have to figure it out. The story tells that the bears are leaving. I know that people look in windows to see what's inside. I think the girl wants to go inside the house. I read to find out!*

## While You Read

- Read the book aloud to students. Stop every few pages and ask questions to help students think about what they already know. Help them use this information to figure out each answer.

  p. 4: *What is Goldilocks doing?* (eating) *Where does Goldilocks eat Baby Bear's food?* (in the kitchen)
  p. 6: *What is Goldilocks doing now?* (sleeping)
  p. 9: *Where does Baby Bear find Goldilocks?* (in his bed)

- As you read, stop and ask questions to help students make inferences about the story. For example, ask *Why is Goldilocks eating Baby Bear's food? Why is she in bed?*

## After You Read

- Show students clues on pp. 4–6 that help them make inferences. Ask questions about each page. Have students answer in complete sentences. For example, point to the chair on p. 5 and then point to Goldilocks. Say *Is Goldilocks too big for the chair? Yes, she is. She's breaking the chair because she's too big for Baby Bear's chair.*

## Unit 4 Reader

**Text Type** fairy tale

**Reading Strategy** Make Inferences

**Vocabulary** *kitchen, eating, living room, bedroom, sleeping, bed*

**Grammar** use verbs with the *–ing* ending (present progressive)

**Resources** Classroom Presentation Tool: Story Time; Video: Sc. 11—Story Time

## Be the Expert

### Reading Strategy

**Make Inferences** Readers often have to make inferences, or guesses, about a character and his or her actions. The reader has to "read between the lines." A writer doesn't always say why something happens or why a character acts a certain way, but through pictures or other words, the reader makes an inference. Help students make inferences about characters by reminding them to ask questions such as *Why is he doing that? Why is he saying that?*

### Text Background

*The Three Bears* is a fairy tale first written by British author Robert Southey in the late 19th century. Fairy tales are a type of folktale that often contain magical beings, including talking animals. The oldest fairy tales were originally spoken aloud. Fairy tales often show how to deal with problems in life.

## Student Book

**TR: A51 1 Listen and say.**

| | |
|---|---|
| a kitchen | It's a kitchen. |
| a dining room | It's a dining room. |
| a bathroom | It's a bathroom. |
| a mirror | It's a mirror. |
| a bedroom | It's a bedroom. |
| a bed | It's a bed. |
| a living room | It's a living room. |
| a TV | It's a TV. |
| a sofa | It's a sofa. |
| a lamp | It's a lamp. |

**TR: A52 2 Listen. Point and say.**

living room, lamp, dining room, bedroom, TV, kitchen, sofa, bathroom, mirror, bed

**TR: A53 3 Point. Ask and answer.**

Example
What is it?
It's a mirror.
Where is it?
In the bathroom.

**TR: A54 4 Listen. Read and sing.**

Note: Lyrics for the song *My Home* are on pp. 134–135.

**TR: A55 Grammar**

Note: Grammar 1 is on p. 136.

**TR: A56 6 Look. Listen and check.**

1. Is there a sofa in the living room?
   Yes, there is.
2. Is there a bed in the living room?
   No, there isn't.
3. Is there a table in the dining room?
   Yes, there is.
4. Is there a lamp in the bedroom?
   Yes, there is.
5. Is there a chair in the kitchen?
   No, there isn't.
6. Is there a TV in the bathroom?
   No, there isn't.

**TR: A57 7 Listen and say.**

| | |
|---|---|
| sleeping | She's sleeping. |
| cleaning | She's cleaning. |
| cooking | He's cooking. |
| taking a bath | He's taking a bath. |
| eating | She's eating. |
| watching TV | He's watching TV. |

**TR: A58 9 Work with a partner. Listen. Say and stick.**

Example
1. He's cooking.
   Ok. My turn. 2.

**TR: A59 Grammar**

Note: Grammar 2 is on p. 142.

**TR: A60 10 Play a game. Point. Ask and answer.**

Example
Where's the frog?
He's in the dining room. He's eating.

**TR: A61 12 Listen and read.**

Note: Reading *Houses Are Different* is on p. 144.

**TR: A62 13 Listen and read. Look. Circle.**

Most houses have kitchens, living rooms, and bedrooms inside, but the outside of houses can be very different.

1. Some houses are on the water.
2. Most houses have kitchens.

## Workbook

**TR: 34 3 Listen to the song. Circle.**

Note: Lyrics for the song *My Home* are on pp. 134–135.

**TR: 35 5 Listen. Circle.**

1. Is there a table in the kitchen?
   Yes, there is.
2. Is there a TV in the bathroom?
   No, there isn't.

3. Is there a sofa in the bedroom?
No, there isn't.
4. Is there a mirror in the bedroom?
Yes, there is.
5. Is there a sofa in the bathroom?
No, there isn't.
6. Is there a bed in the bedroom?
Yes, there is.
7. Is there a table in the bathroom?
No, there isn't.
8. Is there a mirror in the kitchen?
No, there isn't.

**TR: 36** (6) **Look and listen. Write.**

1. Is there a TV in the living room?
Yes, there is.
2. Is there a bed in the kitchen?
No, there isn't.
3. Is there a lamp in the bathroom?
No, there isn't.
4. Is there a lamp in the living room?
Yes, there is.

**TR: 37** (11) **Listen. Circle.**

1. Where's your mother?
She's in the kitchen. She's cleaning.
2. Where's your brother?
He's in the bedroom. He's sleeping.
3. Where's your sister?
She's in the living room. She's watching TV.
4. Where's your grandfather?
He's in the dining room. He's eating.

**TR: 38** (15) **Listen and read.**

Note: Reading *A House in the Trees* is on p. 315.

# Answer Key

## Student Book

### Unit Opener SB p. 58

small

(6) SB pp. 64–65

1. yes, 2. no, 3. yes, 4. yes, 5. no, 6. no

(11) SB p. 67

1. eight, 2. orange/pink, 3. in the living room

(13) SB p. 68

1. yes, 2. yes

(14) SB p. 69

1. line to orange circle
2. line to blue rectangle
3. line to green square
4. line to red triangle

(15) SB p. 69

1. line from circle to fourth house
2. line from rectangle to first house
3. line from square to third house
4. line from triangle to second house

## Workbook

Go to pp. 313–316 for the Workbook Answer Key for this unit.

# In This Unit

**Theme** This unit is about clothes and colors.

**Content Objective**

Students will

- identify and discuss clothing.

**Language Objectives**

Students will

- name clothes.
- name colors.
- say what people are wearing.

**Vocabulary**

**Vocabulary 1** *a dress, gloves, a hat, a jacket, pants, a shirt, shoes, a skirt, socks, a T-shirt*

**Vocabulary 2** *brown, a closet, pink, purple, a shelf*

**Grammar**

**Grammar 1** use *I/he/she* + verb + *ing* to ask and answer questions

**Grammar 2** ask and answer questions with *that* and *those*

**Pacing Guides** LIU5

**Writing** Write sentences about clothes.

**Value** Take care of your clothes.

**Project** Dress a stick puppet.

## Unit Opener

**Objectives**

Students will

- look at a photo for information.
- complete a sentence.

**Resources** Video: Sc. 1—Introduction; Classroom Presentation Tool: Unit Opener; Teacher's Resource CD-ROM: Home-School Connection Letter; Graphic Organizers (Word web); Unit Opener Poster; World Map

## Introduce

- **Recycle** Say *Let's talk about colors.* Write the word *colors* on the board. Read it aloud. Circle the word and then draw a word web around it. Point to or hold up classroom objects of different colors. Ask about each item *What color is it?* Inside each outer circle, write a color that students say. Continue until the word web has 6–8 outer circles.

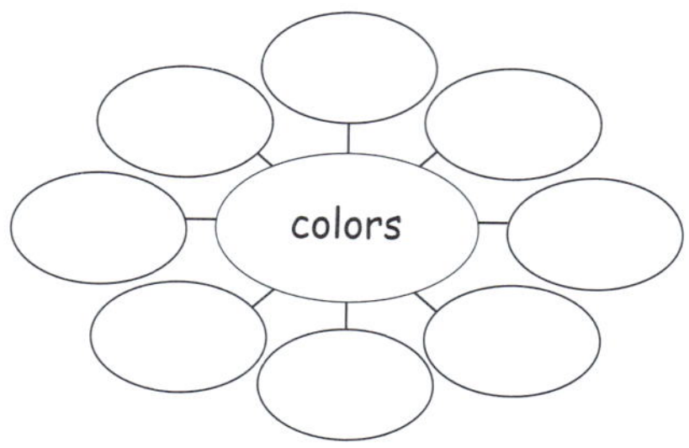


- **Set the stage** Have three students stand with you. Point to your clothes and to their clothes. Say *These are clothes. Clothes are things we wear.* Have the students go back to their seats. Ask the

class *What are your clothes?* Touch your shirt and pants or skirt. Indicate for students to do the same. Say *Clothes are cool!*

- Direct students' attention to the photo on pp. 74–75. Ask questions to guide discussion of the photo:

  *What do you see?* (a girl)
  *How many?* (one)
  Point to the girl's shirt. Ask *What color is it?* (blue)

- Say *This girl is from Guatemala. Guatemala is a country in Central America. Look at the colors in the photo.* Point to the girl's shirt and ask *What other colors do you see?* (black, pink, green, purple, red, white)

- Guide students through the activity on p. 74. Say *I see a lot of one color in this photo.* Ask *What color is it?* (blue) Read the sentence stem aloud. Say *Her clothes are ________.* Use a hand signal to get the class to call out the answer. (blue) Say *That's right. Her clothes are blue.*

## Be the Expert

### About the Photo

Guatemala produces beautiful fabrics made of cotton and wool. Different villages have their own unique patterns and colors. People can tell where a cloth is made by its colors and patterns, which include shapes, stripes, flowers, and animals.

Today, many weavers in Guatemala use the same type of backstrap looms that their Maya ancestors used over a thousand years ago. Many people still dye cloth the traditional way, with natural materials such as plants, tree bark, and minerals.

### Teaching Tip

**Classroom Management** Signals and gestures are a good way to reinforce or demonstrate what students need to do. Use gestures to support statements such as *Let's listen* or *Let's say it together*. The same movement should be repeated each time for a word or phrase.

As students become familiar with classroom routines, add gestures and expanded language. For example, point when you say *Now it's your turn*.

### Related Vocabulary

*cloth, shapes*

# Vocabulary 1

**Objectives**

Students will

- name clothes.
- say what people are wearing.

**Vocabulary** *a hat, gloves, a skirt, a jacket, a dress, pants, a shirt, a T-shirt, socks, shoes*

**Content Vocabulary** *wearing*

**Academic Language** *listen, point, say*

**Resources** Workbook pp. 54–55; Audio CD TR: B2–4; Video: Sc. 2—Vocabulary Ia; Video: Sc. 3—Vocabulary Ib; Classroom Presentation Tool: Vocabulary I; Picture Cards 68, 70–72, 74, 84–93; Sound Cards 25, 29; Teacher's Resource CD-ROM: Activity Worksheet 5.I

**Materials** examples of clothing in different sizes: infant, child, and adult (*optional*)

1 **Listen and say.** TR: B2

2 **Listen.** Point and say. TR: B3

## Warm Up

- Mix Picture Cards 68, 70–72, and 74 with Picture Cards 84–93. Select cards at random and have students tell you what each card shows. Repeat several times.
- Call on students to help you sort the pictures into two groups. Ask *Which cards show rooms in a house? Put them here.* Then ask *Which cards show clothes? Put them there.* Point to the first set of cards and ask *What are they?* (rooms in a house) Point to the second set of cards and ask *What are they?* (clothes)

## Present

- **Set the stage** Point to the clothes you're wearing. Say *These are clothes. I wear clothes. You wear clothes. We all wear clothes. We're all wearing clothes.* Then point to each item of your clothing. Act out putting on different types of clothing. Name each item as you put it on. For example, say *my shirt* or *my shoes*.

## Be the Expert

### Vocabulary Strategy

**Using a Dictionary** When students look up words in a dictionary, they need to look at more than just the first letter of a word. Introduce this skill with words that begin with different letters. Have students put words such as *dress*, *jacket*, and *shirt* in alphabetical order. Then give them three words that start with the same letter, such as *shirt*, *socks*, and *skirt*. Tell them that to find these words in a dictionary, they need to look at the second letter of each word. Have them underline the second letter in each *(h, o, k)*. Students need to organize the words in ABC order according to these letters.

### Teaching Tip

It can be helpful to draw from students' experiences when presenting new vocabulary. However, some students may be self-conscious about discussing personal issues, including clothing. When you ask students to share personal information, consider their comfort levels and cultural attitudes. Ask only those students who offer to participate. Use pictures from the Student Book and other classroom books, posters, and materials to support students.

Then point to each item of your clothing. Say *I'm wearing (a blue shirt, black pants, black shoes).* Say *I like my clothes!*

- Have students open their books to pp. 76–77. Point to each photo as you say the target word. For each word, point out whether you or a student is wearing that article of clothing. Point to the photo again and repeat the word.
- **Contextualize** Say *We all wear clothes! Let's talk about our clothes.* On the board, draw a chart with six to eight columns. Write different clothing words across the top. List students' names in the first column. Ask *Who's wearing a (T-shirt)? Raise your hand.* Have students point to their T-shirts. Put a check mark by the students' names. Say *(Amanda and Tranh) are wearing T-shirts* and have the class repeat.

| | T-shirt | pants | socks | shirt | shoes | skirt |
|---|---|---|---|---|---|---|
| Mei | | | | ✓ | ✓ | ✓ |
| Amanda | ✓ | ✓ | ✓ | | ✓ | |
| Tranh | ✓ | ✓ | ✓ | | ✓ | |

## Practice 1 2

- 1 Say *Now listen and say.* Play **TR: B2**. Ask students to repeat the words. Help them pronounce the words correctly.
- 2 Have students open their books to pp. 76–77. Say *Listen.* Play **TR: B2** again. Point to the appropriate picture when you hear each item of clothing. Say *Now listen. Then point and say.* Play **TR: B3**. Help students follow the order of the words by pointing to the first three items named. ✓ Walk around the room, saying words to individual students. Have them point to the clothes in the book.
- Walk around the room, pointing to the photos on pp. 76–77. As you randomly point to the photos, have students name the clothes. If students have difficulty, replay **TR: B2**.

## Wrap Up

- Place students in groups of three. Say *I have clothes. Let's talk.* Give a few pieces of clothing to each group or hand out Picture Cards 84–93. Stand with two students. Hold up a T-shirt (Picture Card 93). Ask one student *What is it?* (a T-shirt) Ask the other student *What color is it?* (red) Have groups repeat the activity. One student holds up an item of clothing, and the next student says what it is. The third student then names the color. Have students take turns.

## Recap

- Say *Let's use the words we learned*. Hold up Picture Cards 84–93 one at a time. For each card, ask *What is it?* or *What are they?* Then show the cards again and say *Tell me more.* For example, say *It's a hat. Is it big? Is it red?*

## Apply 3

- 3 Have students look at the model dialogue on p. 77. Point to the monkey mascot and say *Look at Mia the monkey. She points to her shoes and asks* What are they? Then point to the elephant and say *Look at Eddie the elephant. He says* They're shoes. You're wearing shoes. Say *Listen.* Play **TR: B4**.
- Say *Look at me.* Point to something you're wearing and ask *What is it?* or *What are they?* Then change position as if you were someone else. Answer in a higher, lower, or different voice and say *It's (a shirt). You're wearing (a shirt).* Then model the dialogue with a student.
- Pair students. Say *Now you try it!* Have each pair act out the dialogue with different articles of clothing. Students should take turns asking and answering questions.

## Extend

- Say *Let's talk about our clothes.* Form small groups of three or four students. Have each group sit in a circle and tell what someone in the group is wearing. Model some examples. Say *Ivan is wearing a yellow shirt. He's wearing blue pants and black shoes.* Write the words *yellow, black,* and *blue* on the board. Read them aloud with students. Have students use colors to describe their classmates' clothing.

## Wrap Up

- Have students stand in a circle. Point to a student and ask the student next to him *What is (Ivan) wearing?* The student should answer in a complete sentence. Model by saying *Yes, (Ivan) is wearing (a red shirt).* The student answering then asks the next student *What am I wearing?* Continue around the circle until all students have had a turn asking and answering.

## Be the Expert

### About the Photo

The photo of the two women on p. 76 was taken in Guilin, a city in southern China. The two women are wearing traditional clothing of the Miao people. Handcrafted materials and brightly colored clothing are important aspects of Miao history and culture. The hills behind the women are terraced rice paddies in the countryside outside the city of Guilin. The terraces were made by hand, and they make the hillsides look like giant staircases.

### Sounds of English

**Comparing Sounds: /ɪ/ and /æ/**

The /ɪ/ sound (pi̲cture) and the /æ/ sound (ha̲t) can be difficult to distinguish because they are both pronounced with the tongue at the front of the mouth.

To make the /ɪ/ sound, lower your jaw slightly. The sides of your tongue should touch your teeth. To make the /æ/ sound, lower your jaw even farther and place the tip of your tongue behind your lower teeth.

Use Sound Cards 25 (i̲nsect) and 29 (a̲pple).

Example words: bi̲g, pi̲cture, ki̲tchen; pa̲nts, bla̲ck, a̲lphabet

### Formative Assessment

Can students

- name clothes?

  Show Picture Cards of clothes and ask *What is it?* or *What are they?*

- say what people are wearing?

  Point to a student in the classroom and ask *What is she wearing?*

**Review** For additional practice, direct students to Activity Worksheet 5.1.

## Song

**Vocabulary in the song**

**Vocabulary 1** *shoes, pants, shirt, skirt, hat*

**Vocabulary 2** *brown, purple, pink*

**Grammar in the song**

**Grammar 1** use *I/he/she* + verb + *ing* to ask and answer questions

**Resources** Workbook p. 56; Audio CD TR: B5; Video: Sc. 9—Song; Classroom Presentation Tool: Song; Picture Cards 84–87

4 **Listen.** Read and sing. TR: B5

# My Clothes

*What are you wearing?*
*What are you wearing?*
*I'm wearing my brown shoes,*
*and I really like them.*

*What are you wearing?*
*What are you wearing?*
*I'm wearing my purple pants,*
*and I really like them.*

***I like my shoes!***
***I like my pants!***
***I like my shirt!***
***I like my skirt!***

78

## Use the Song 4 5

- **Predict** Have students open their books to pp. 78–79. Say *It's time for a song. Look at the words and pictures in your book.* After 30 seconds, have students close their books. Say *I think this song is about clothes. What do you think the song is about?* Prompt students to describe the clothes they saw and the words they recognized.
- Say *I think this song is about colors, too.* Repeat the process, asking students to talk about the pictures and words in their books.
- 4 Say *Open your books again. Now listen and read.* Play **TR: B5**. Play the song again and have students sing.
- 5 Place students in four groups, and assign each group one of the following: *shoes, pants, shirt,* and *skirt.* Have students draw and label the item. Encourage students to use the correct colors for each of the clothing items in their pictures. Play **TR: B5** again. Pause after each verse. Have students stand up and show their pictures when they hear their clothing item in the song.

*What are you wearing?*
*What are you wearing?*
*I'm wearing my orange shirt,*
*and I really like it.*

*What are you wearing?*
*What are you wearing?*
*I'm wearing my pink skirt,*
*and I really like it.*

**CHORUS**

*Oh, you look nice.*
*Thank you.*
*Nice hat.*
*Nice shoes.*
*Nice shirt.*

**5 Sing again.**
Hold up pictures.

79

## Be the Expert

### Teaching Tip

**Grouping** To help maintain order in the classroom during group activities, give group members a minute or two at the beginning of each activity to organize and review any materials they receive. Give them the same amount of time at the end of the activity to put materials away or return them to you.

### Related Vocabulary

*hanger*

## Use It Again

- **Vocabulary 1** Put students in four groups. Give each group one of Picture Cards 84–87. Write the following sentence frame on the board:

  I'm wearing my ________.

- Say *My word is* T-shirt. *I sing* I'm wearing my T-shirt, and I really like it! Play the first verse of the song. Pause after the questions. Have groups take turns singing the complete sentence, one group at a time.
- **Grammar 2** Put students in pairs. Have each partner point to an item of clothing the other is wearing and ask *What's that?* Prompt partners to answer *That's my (blue shirt).* Then have them do the same with *What are those?* (Those are my shoes.) Play the first verse of the song. Have one student sing or chant the last two lines but use words for what he is wearing. Have the other student sing or chant the chorus. Then have partners switch and repeat the activity.
- **Vocabulary 2** Point to the picture on pp. 78–79. Ask questions such as *What's purple? What's brown? What color is the girl's skirt?* Then play and sing the song, but pause when you hear *brown*, *purple*, and *pink*. Have students sing the vocabulary words that follow.

# Grammar 1

**Objective**

Students will

- ask and answer questions about what people are wearing.

**Grammar** use *I/he/she* + verb + *ing* to ask and answer questions

**Academic Language** *answer, ask, color, draw, partner*

**Resources** Workbook pp. 57–58, Audio CD TR: B6–8; Video: Sc. 6—Grammar I; Classroom Presentation Tool: Grammar I; Teacher's Resource CD-ROM: Graphic Organizers (Word web)

**Materials** magazine or printed-out photos of people of different ages wearing various clothes; 40–50 note cards

**GRAMMAR** TR: B6

What **are** you **wearing?**

**I'm wearing** a red dress.
My sister**'s wearing** a green dress.

**6** **Listen and find.** Color. TR: B7

80

## Warm Up

- **Recycle** Hold up a Student Book and show the family portrait on p. 50 (Unit 3). Say *Let's play a game. I tell you about someone, and you tell me who it is. Ready?* Say *Look at the photo. She's wearing a purple shirt. Who is it?* (the grandmother) *He's wearing blue pants, a blue shirt, and brown shoes. Who is it?* (the brother) *He's wearing blue pants, a brown hat, and a jacket. Who is it?* (the grandfather)
- Give students printed-out photos or magazine photos of people of different ages wearing various clothes. Then put students in pairs. Have them take turns showing their pictures, giving clues about the clothes people are wearing, and challenging their partners to a game of Guess Who? Model with a picture, saying sentences such as *She's wearing socks and a purple shirt. Who is it?* Have a student point to the correct person on the page.

**7** **Draw and color.** What are you wearing? Talk. TR: B8

81

## Be the Expert

### Our World in Context

Some people wear special clothes called *uniforms*. These clothes show that the people wearing them are part of a group. They may be players on a sports team, students at a school, or workers at a factory. Public workers, such as police officers and firefighters, wear uniforms. Their uniforms make it easy for people to know who they are. Workers who have dangerous jobs wear uniforms that protect them.

### Grammar in Depth

The present progressive tense describes an action that is happening now, or at the moment. The action happens while the person writes or speaks: *He's wearing pants (now). You're wearing shoes (now).* The present progressive may also be used to tell about future actions: *He's wearing a hat to the party (next week).* The simple present, on the other hand, is for general facts: *The hat is red.* (It's always red, now and at other times.) The simple present is also used to tell how often something happens: *I wear a hat every day.*

## Present

- Draw students' attention to the yellow grammar box at the top of p. 80. Play **TR: B6** and have students follow along in their books.
- Write the following on the board:

| |
|---|
| I am wearing shoes. = I'm wearing shoes. |
| He is wearing shoes. = He's wearing shoes. |
| She is wearing shoes. = She's wearing shoes. |

- Read each sentence aloud, pointing to yourself for *I*, to a male student for *he*, and to a female student for *she*. Have students repeat after you. Point to each pair of sentences and explain that both sentences have the same meaning.
- Point to the word *sister's* on p. 80.
  **Think Aloud** *The word* sister's *reminds me of other words I know, like* he's *and* she's. *I can say* She's wearing a hat *or* She is wearing a hat. She is *and* she's *mean the same thing. I think* my sister's *means the same thing as* my sister is.
- Ask a student *What are you wearing?* Have the student use the sentences on the board to help her respond. Then ask another student *What is he/she wearing?* Continue until all students have had an opportunity to answer a question.

## Practice 6

- 6 Point to the four black-and-white drawings on p. 80. Say *These pictures do not have colors. I wonder what the people are wearing. Let's listen and find out.*

- Hold up your book and point to the first drawing. Say *Look at page 80. The two girls are sisters. What are they wearing?* Say *Listen. Then color.* Play the first item of **TR: B7**. Say *Now it's time to color. One girl is wearing a blue dress and blue socks. Color her dress and socks blue. Her sister is wearing a green dress and green socks. Color the dress and socks green.*

- Play item 2 of **TR: B7**. Have students repeat the colors of the clothes aloud. Then have them color the clothes. ✓ Point to the girl and ask *What's she wearing?* (a yellow T-shirt and a black skirt) Repeat with the lady in the drawing.

- Remind students to listen carefully. For the next two pictures, they will color three things. Play item 3 of **TR: B7**. Ask *Who's wearing blue pants?* (the boy)

- Play item 4 of **TR: B7** and say *Listen. What color is the boy's shirt?* (blue) *What color is Grandma's dress?* (green and white) Have students color their pictures.

## Wrap Up

- Put students in groups of four or five. Prepare eleven note cards for each group with the following words or phrases: *The dad; is wearing; are wearing; I'm; My grandfather; My sister's; wearing; gloves; You; The brothers;* and *pants.*

| | | |
|---|---|---|
| My sister's | wearing | pants. |
| I'm | wearing | gloves. |
| The brothers | are wearing | gloves. |

- Have students make as many sentences as they can with the word cards. Have them write each sentence on a piece of paper. Then have one person from each group take turns reading the sentences aloud and writing them on the board.

## Recap

- Draw stick figures of a mom, a dad, a boy, and a girl on the board. Leave room to add clothes to each. Point and say *This is a mom, a dad, a brother, and a sister.* Draw pants and a shirt on the stick figure of the father. Say *The dad is wearing pants and a shirt.* Point to the other family members one at a time and ask *What's (she) wearing?* As students offer ideas, say and draw them. Ask *What are they wearing?* Keep the pictures on the board.

## Apply 7

- 7 Form pairs of students. Have everyone look at the top of p. 81. Say *Now you talk, draw, and color. Let's listen first.* Play **TR: B8**. Point to the mascots at the bottom of the page. Model the dialogue with a student.

- Say *Ask your partner* What are you wearing? *Your partner answers, and then asks you the same question. Take turns talking. Then draw a picture of yourself, and color your clothes.*

- **Expand** Collect students' drawings. Hold up a drawing and ask *What's he wearing?* Call on different students to answer. Then ask *Who is it?* See if students can guess. Repeat with more drawings.

## Extend

- Tell students to imagine that a family (a grandmother, father, and sister) is visiting the classroom. Ask *What are they wearing?* Make word webs for three different family members: **grandmother**, **father**, and **sister**. Attach sample answers to each web. (shirt, pants, gloves, and hat) Put students in three groups and tell them to complete the webs.
- Have group members tell what their word webs show. Help students frame their replies as *The (grandmother's) wearing* ________. On the board, write a list of words students can use to describe the clothing: *big, small, old, white, red, blue, brown.* Remind students that these words come before the clothes words. Students may use sentences such as *The grandmother's wearing a big hat.*

## Wrap Up

- Write and say the following sentence frames. Have students work in pairs to complete them.

| |
|---|
| I' ________ a ________ dress. |
| He' ________ a ________ jacket. |
| She' ________ shoes and ________ socks. |
| My grandmother' ________ ________ gloves. |

- When students are finished, have them come to the board to write their answers. Then read the completed sentences together as a class.

## Be the Expert

### Teaching Tip

Provide immediate positive feedback to students. Say *Yes! Very good!* or *Excellent job!* when a student follows directions, answers a question correctly, or helps a classmate. It's also important to provide positive feedback and support to students who answer incorrectly. Say *Good try! You said (blue) very well, but (this dress is red).* Then direct the student to the part of the book that provides help or reteach the missed concept.

Positive feedback encourages students to practice their new skills and builds trust between students and teachers.

### Formative Assessment

Can students

- ask and answer questions about what people are wearing?

  Ask *What are you wearing?* and *What is he/she wearing?* and have students answer in complete sentences.

# Vocabulary 2

**Objectives**

Students will

- name colors.
- identify clothes.

**Vocabulary** *pink, purple, brown, a shelf, a closet*

**Academic Language** *circle, partner, point, turn*

**Resources** Workbook p. 59; Audio CD TR: B9–11; Video: Sc. 4—Vocabulary 2; Classroom Presentation Tool: Vocabulary 2; Teacher's Resource CD-ROM: Graphic Organizers (Two-column chart), Activity Worksheet 5.2; Picture Cards 1–8, 84–93

**Materials** items of clothing (*optional*)

**8 Listen and say.** TR: B9

**9 Work with a partner.** Point and say.

**10 Listen and read.** Circle. TR: B10

1. Is there a black hat? yes no
2. Is there a purple hat? yes no

**11 Work with a partner.** Listen. Say and stick. TR: B11

1 2 3 4 5

82

## Warm Up

- **Spiral** Say *Open your books to page 35. Do you remember the rainbow? Let's say the colors.* Point to each band in the rainbow and have students say the color. Change the order and repeat several times. Then say *I point to a color, and then to a student.* Point to (green), and then point to a student wearing a (green shirt). Say *If I point to green, you say* I have a green shirt.
- Next, put Picture Cards 1–8 and 84–93 in two separate piles. Have a student come to the front of the class and pick one card from each pile. Have him use the cards to form a sentence, for example, *She has blue pants.*

## Present 8

- **Set the stage** Act out neatly folding clothes (real or imaginary) and putting them in a closet. *I put clothes in the closet.* Open the closet door and say *There's a shelf in the closet. I put clothes on the shelf.* Run a hand along an imaginary shelf or, if your classroom has a shelf, use it.
- 8 Say *Open your books to page 82. Listen and say.* Play **TR: B9**. Point to each item as it's mentioned and pause after you hear *One hat is brown.* Point to each color word again and say *Pink. One hat is ________.* Have the class provide a choral response. Repeat with the purple and brown hats.
- Point to the closet and say *Let's look in the closet. Listen and say.* Play the rest of **TR: B9**. Say each sentence aloud and have students repeat after you.

## Practice 9 10

- 9 Form pairs of students and say *Now you point and say.* Model with a student. Point to an object in the picture, and have the student say the word. Prompt the student to point to a different object and have you name the word.

- 10 Say *Now you listen, read, and circle.* Say *Let's do the first one together.* Play the first item on **TR: B10**. Model *Is there a black hat? I look at the picture. There's no black hat. I circle no.* Play the second item on **TR: B10** and have students do it on their own. ✓ Students may arrive at the correct answer by chance. If they circled *yes*, ask them to point to the purple hat to confirm their comprehension.

## Apply 11

- 11 Form pairs. Say *Let's do a sticker activity.* Have a student help you model the dialogue. Ask *Where's the green hat?* Have the student find the correct sticker, answer the question, and put the sticker on number 1. Switch roles and have the student ask you where something is. Play **TR: B11** and have pairs follow along. Then have them place the rest of the stickers on their own.

- **Expand** When students have finished the sticker activity, have them write a complete sentence about one of the stickers they used.

## Extend

- Ask students to think about the ways you keep your classroom clean and neat. Work together to brainstorm a list of things you put away in the closet or on a shelf. Write students' suggestions on the board.

- Have students point out objects around the room that are pink, purple, or brown. Ask them whether the objects should be put away in the closet or on the shelf.

## Wrap Up

- Make a two-column chart on the board. Write the headings **Colors** and **Not colors** at the top of each column. Write the following words on the board, next to the chart: *brown, closet, pink, purple, shelf.* Have students copy the chart and write the words in the correct columns. Then review the chart as a class.

| Colors | Not colors |
|---|---|
| brown | closet |
| pink | shelf |
| purple | |

## Be the Expert

### Teaching Tip

If students have difficulty repeating sentences, break the sentences up into chunks and have students repeat each word or phrase. For example: *There's/a shelf/in the closet. There are/ shoes/in the closet.* After practicing a few times, ask students to put the chunks together and say the whole sentence.

### Formative Assessment

Can students

- name colors?

  Point to items in the classroom that are pink, brown, or purple. Have students say the colors of the items.

- identify clothes?

  Point to shoes, a shirt, a dress, or a jacket that you or a student is wearing. Have students complete this sentence: *She/He is wearing* ________.

**Review** For additional practice, direct students to Activity Worksheet 5.2.

# Grammar 2

**Objectives**

Students will

- ask questions with *that* and *those*.
- answer questions with *that is* and *those are*.

**Grammar** ask and answer questions with *that* and *those*

**Academic Language** *draw lines, match, play a game*

**Resources** Workbook p. 60; Audio CD TR: B12–13; Video: Sc. 7—Grammar 2; Classroom Presentation Tool: Grammar 2; Teacher's Resource CD-ROM: Activity Worksheet 5.3

**Materials** items of clothing that include things in pairs; large bag or box with lid; paper bags

**GRAMMAR** TR: B12

| | |
|---|---|
| What**'s that?** | **That's** my orange T-shirt. |
| What **are those?** | **Those are** my purple shoes. |

**12** **Play a game.** Ask and answer. Draw lines. TR: B13

**13** **Look at the pictures.** Write.

1. What color are the gloves? ____________________
2. What color is the hat? ____________________
3. Is there a jacket? ____________________

83

## Warm Up

- **Spiral** Play a "What is it?" game. Put different items of clothing in a big bag or large box. Have a student reach in and select an item to show the class. Ask *What is it?* Say *Yes, it's a (T-shirt). It's a (white T-shirt).*
- Have pairs of students take turns picking an item from the bag or box and then asking and answering questions about it. If a student can't identify an item, say *No, it isn't a (blue shirt). It's a (blue skirt).*

## Present

- Draw a hat on the board. To the right of the hat, draw three shirts. Stand at a distance and point to the hat. Say *That's a hat.* Then point to the group of shirts and say *Those are shirts.* Lead students in chorally identifying the drawings as you point to them. Explain *We use the words that and those to tell about things that are not close to us.* Point to a desk at a slight distance from you. Say *That's a desk.* Point to several desks at the same distance. Say *Those are desks.*
- Write the number 1 above the hat, and the number 3 above the shirts. Explain *We use the word that to tell about one thing.* (Hold up one finger.) *That hat. We use those to tell about two or more things.* (Hold up three fingers.) *Those shirts.* Have students repeat the phrases with you.
- Direct students' attention to the yellow grammar box at the top of p. 83. Read each question and answer aloud. Have students listen carefully as you play **TR: B12** twice. Call on students to read the questions and answers aloud.

## Practice 12

- Form pairs. Say *It's time to play a game.* Direct students' attention to the model dialogue on p. 83. Draw a pair of socks on the board. Move toward the middle or back of the room and read the question as though you were Mia the monkey pointing to the socks in the distance. Ask *What are those?* Then act out the Eddie the elephant's voice and answer *Those are socks.*

- Say *Let's listen.* Play **TR: B13**. Say *You say it now.* ✔ Point to pictures of clothing and ask *What's that?* or *What are those?* Students' answers should begin with *That's* or *Those.*

- 12 Hold up your book and say *Work with a partner. You point to a picture and ask* What's that? *or* What are those? *Your partner answers. Draw a line from the clothes* (indicate the bottom row of pictures) *to the colors* (indicate the top row of pictures) *that match.*

- Point to the socks and say *Those are socks. Those socks are red and white.* Draw a line connecting the socks to the red and white swirl. Say *Now it's your turn. Ask and answer. Then draw lines to match.*

## Apply 13

- 13 Read the directions for Activity 13 aloud. Then point to item 1 and ask *What color are the gloves?* Model answering. Hold up your book and point to the picture of the blue gloves. Say *The gloves are blue.*

- Have students complete the activity on their own. When they have finished, ask them to read the questions and their answers aloud.

## Extend

- Put students in pairs. Have students point to different objects in the classroom and ask *What's that? or What are those?* Model by pointing to the clock and asking *What's that?* Have partners point and ask each other three questions. Then call on different students to point to a classroom object and ask the class a question.

## Wrap Up

- Give a small paper bag to each student. Have students choose one object to put inside the bag. Then put students in pairs. Say *Ask your partner* What's that? *Your partner answers* That's my *(red pen).* Model with a student. Then give students a minute to choose an object.

- After students finish the activity, have pairs ask each other questions using *What are those?* Model by pointing to the paper bags of one pair and asking *What are those?*

## Be the Expert

### Grammar in Depth

The words *that* and *those* are pronouns when they take the place of nouns. Instead of saying *The hat and the jacket are mine*, you can say *Those are mine. That* and *those* can also be used as adjectives to tell about a particular person or thing: *That girl is smart* and *Those shoes are big.*

Whether *that* and *those* are used as pronouns or adjectives, they communicate relative distance from the speaker. *This* and *these* (introduced in Unit 6) refer to something closer to the speaker. *That* and *those* usually refer to things that are farther away.

### Formative Assessment

Can students

- ask questions with *that* and *those*?
  Point to a single object and prompt students to ask questions about its color with *that*. Point to multiple objects and have students ask questions with *those*.
- answer questions with *that is* and *those are*?
  Point to a single object and ask *What's that?* Have students answer in complete sentences. Repeat with multiple objects and ask *What are those?*

**Review** For additional practice, direct students to Activity Worksheet 5.3.

## Reading

**Objectives**

Students will

- use photos and maps to compare and contrast.
- talk about clothes worn by people all over the world.

**Reading Strategy** Compare and Contrast

**Academic Language** *check, draw a line*

**Content Vocabulary** *costume*

**Resources** Workbook pp. 62–63; Audio CD TR: B14–16; Classroom Presentation Tool: Reading; Teacher's Resource CD-ROM: Graphic Organizers (Venn diagram); Picture Cards 84–97

**Materials** a rolled piece of paper or a paper towel roll to be used as a "spyglass" (*optional*); crayons or colored markers; note cards; a soft (cloth or foam) ball

**14** **Listen and read.** TR: B14

# Clothes Are Fun!

People all over the world wear special clothes on special days. Sometimes they are clothes from the past.

**15** **Listen and read.** Look. Circle *yes* or *no*. TR: B15

1. The children from Turkey are wearing shoes. yes no
2. The girls from Korea are wearing dresses. yes no



## Warm Up

- **Activate prior knowledge** Form groups of four. Give each group one or two cards from Picture Cards 84–97. Say *Talk about the clothes. What is it? What color is it? Write sentences.* Give students five minutes to discuss and write about their cards. Then have groups present their cards and read aloud their sentences to the class.

## Present 14 15

- **Graphic literacy** Have students open their books to pp. 84–85. Read the title aloud to students. Then point out the photos and the map. Say *I see four photos and a map of the world.* Say *The words by the photos are labels.* Read the photo labels on pp. 84–85 aloud: *Korea, Turkey, Peru, Spain.* Say *The labels name countries.* Guide students to match the four labels to the words on the map. Read each country name again as you point to the corresponding photo. Say *The map shows where the people in the photos are from.* Have students read the labels with you as they point.

- **14** **Read together** Say *Now let's listen.* Play **TR: B14** and have students read along. Play the track a second time, pausing at the end of each sentence.

**16** **Look at Activity 14.** Check ✔ the costume colors.

| | from **Turkey** | from **Peru** | from **Korea** | | from **Turkey** | from **Peru** | from **Korea** |
|---|---|---|---|---|---|---|---|
| black | | | | pink | | | |
| blue | | | | purple | | | |
| brown | | | | red | | | |
| green | | | | yellow | | | |
| orange | | | | white | | | |

**17** **Look.** Draw a line.

1. hat
2. jacket
3. pants
4. shirt
5. dress

**18** **Work with a partner.** What are you wearing today? Ask and answer. **TR: B16**

85

## Be the Expert

### About the Photo

The large photo on p. 84 shows two South Korean girls at a railway station in Seoul, wearing traditional clothes. The family is traveling for the three-day *Chuseok*, or Harvest Moon festival. The photo at the top right shows children in traditional dress, marching in a parade in Ankara, Turkey. The girls from Peru are wearing many layers of warm clothes because the temperature in the Andes, where they live, does not reach beyond 21° Celsius (70° Fahrenheit) for much of the year. The photo on p. 85 shows the Jerez Horse Fair in Andalusia, Spain.

### Related Vocabulary

*horse, train*

- After the first sentence, ask *Who is this about?* (people all over the world) Stretch out your hands to emphasize the idea of "all over the world." *What do people all over the world do?* (wear special clothes on special days) Ask *What's an example of a special day?* (a birthday) After the second sentence, say *We read about writing in the past. Now we're reading about clothes from the past.*

- **15** Point to the directions and read them aloud. Say *Listen first.* Point to the first item. Play **TR: B15**, and pause after item 1.

- Say *It says,* The children from Turkey are wearing shoes. *Let's look for the photo that says* Turkey. Point to the photo and label. Say *Here it is. The children are wearing white shoes.* Read item 1 again and say *I circle yes.* Model circling.

- Have students complete item 2 on their own. ✔ Ask *Are the girls from Korea wearing dresses?* (yes) *Are they wearing shoes?* (yes)

## Practice 16 17

- **16** Read the direction line aloud. Say *We have to look at the photos in Activity 14.* Point to the chart and have students read the colors. Say *Costumes are the clothes people are wearing in the photos.* Point to the column for Turkey. Say *Let's start here. It says* from Turkey. *Now let's find the photo that says* Turkey. Point to the photo on p. 84. Ask *Are there black clothes? No, there are no black clothes.* Continue with the other colors, until you can answer *yes.* (pink) Say *Are there pink clothes? Yes, there are pink clothes. I put a check there.*

- Form pairs and have partners complete the chart. ✓ Observe students as they read across and down the chart. If students need additional support, model reading across a row and down a column. Review the completed chart as a class.

- **17** Point to Activity 17. Say *Now we're going to draw lines* (pick up a pencil and act out drawing a straight line) *from the words to the photo. Let's do the first one together.* Say *One. hat.* Ask *Is there a hat?* Say *Point to the hat.* Point to the hat and then say *I draw a line from the word* hat *to the hat in the photo*. Model drawing the first line. Have students do the other items on their own. Then review the items as a class.

## Wrap Up

- Have students look at the photos on p. 84. Ask *Who's wearing a dress? Point. Tell what she's wearing.* Then have students look at the photo on p. 85. Ask *Who's wearing a dress? Point. Tell what she's wearing.* Point to the dresses. Ask *What colors are the same?* Guide students by saying *I see* pink *here. I see* pink *here, too.* Have students list colors that are the same. Then have students list colors that are different.

## ▸ Recap

- Say *Let's play "I See."* Use a piece of paper or a paper towel roll to make a spyglass. Look through it at articles of clothing in the classroom, such as shirts, shoes, dresses, and pants. Say *I see a red shirt.* Ask *What other clothes are red in the classroom?* Ask *What clothes are blue in the classroom?* Point and say *Those clothes are red. Those clothes are blue. They're different colors.*

## Apply 18

- **18** Point to the frog and elephant at the bottom of p. 85. Say *Listen and follow along in your book.* Play **TR: B16**.

- Form pairs. Say *Now you ask and answer. Take turns.*

- **Expand** Have pairs make a Venn diagram to compare their clothes. Explain the three sections of the diagram: Student 1, both students, Student 2. For the overlapping section, they can list any clothing or color they are both wearing. When students are done, ask them to do a show-and-tell of their work with another pair.

## Extend

- Put students in groups of four or five. Give colored markers or crayons to students and have them draw some special clothes. Say *Use many colors! Make the clothes beautiful!* When students are finished, have group members ask and answer questions about the clothes: *What is it? It's (a skirt). What color is it? It is (blue and yellow).*

- Then ask *Who drew a (skirt)? Show me.* Have students hold up their pictures. Ask *Who drew (pants)? Show me.* Say *Skirts and pants are different clothes.* Have students repeat. Point to the (skirts) and ask *What color are they?* Repeat for the pants. Ask *What is the same? What is different?* Repeat for other items of clothing.

## Wrap Up

- Have students stand in a circle. Ask *Are you wearing (a white T-shirt)?* Toss a soft ball to a student wearing (a white T-shirt). Have the student answer *Yes, I'm wearing (a white T-shirt).* Have that student ask a similar question and toss the ball to another student. (Are you wearing a blue shirt?) Continue until all students have had a turn.

## Be the Expert

### Reading Strategy

**Compare and Contrast** Many students identify information more easily when it's sorted for them visually. A Venn diagram is an ideal tool to help students organize information in order to compare and contrast. Write similarities, or details shared by both items, in the overlapping area in the middle of a Venn diagram. Differences, or details specific to each item, belong on either side of the diagram.

### Teaching Tip

Help students use visuals such as photos, charts, and graphs to understand text. Direct students' attention to the headings, labels, and captions that accompany their reading selections. For a chart, have them use their fingers to follow a horizontal row and a vertical column to the place where they meet. Then ask a simple question students can answer with the information they find in that cell.

### Formative Assessment

Can students

- use photos and maps to compare and contrast?

  Have students look at the photos and map on p. 84. Have them point to each photo and the matching country on the map. Ask *What color shoes are the girls from Korea wearing? What color shoes are the children from Turkey wearing?*

- talk about clothes worn by people all over the world?

  Point to one of the photos on p. 84 and ask *Where are they? What's she wearing? What are they wearing?*

## Writing

**Writing** Write sentences about clothes.

**Objectives**

Students will

- view a writing model.
- write about clothes.

**Academic Language** *group*

**Resources** Workbook p. 64; Classroom Presentation Tool: Writing

**Materials** crayons, colored pencils, or colored markers

### Formative Assessment

Can students

- write about clothes?

Have students write a sentence about an item of clothing and its color.

The girl is wearing a red shirt and a black and red skirt. The boy is wearing a white shirt, a blue jacket, and brown pants.

**19** **Color and write.**

The girl is wearing ________________.

The boy is wearing ________________.

**20** **Work in a group.** Talk about your picture.



## Present

- Write the following on the board.

| Who | + | is wearing | + | what. |
|---|---|---|---|---|

- Say *Let's write sentences that tell who is wearing what.* Expand the idea with an organizer, such as the one below. Have students help you brainstorm names and items of clothing. Add other possible subjects, such as *The boy* and *The girl*. Then form pairs and have students use the following chart to say and write as many sentences as they can:

| Who | | What |
|---|---|---|
| Amit | is wearing | a hat. |
| The boy | | shoes. |
| Rachel | | gloves. |

## Write 19

- Have students open their books to p. 86. Point to the pictures at the top of the page. Ask *What do you see?* (a girl, a boy) Ask *What is the girl wearing?* (a red shirt, a black and red skirt, black shoes) Ask *What is the boy wearing?* (a white shirt, a blue jacket, brown pants, a red hat, black shoes)
- Say *Now let's read the sentences.* Read the first sentence. Then have students read it with you. Continue with the other sentence. Ask *Do the sentences tell what the pictures show?* (yes)
- **19** Read the directions aloud. Then read the two sentence stems. Say *Color the picture of the girl and boy. Then write sentences that tell what they're wearing.* Make sure students understand that the first sentence is about the girl (on the right).

NATIONAL GEOGRAPHIC

# Our World

## Take care of your clothes.

**21** **Look and read.**

Put away your clean clothes.

Mandawa, India

**22** **Read and copy.**

I take care of my clothes.

______________________________________

______________________________________

87

## Value

**Value** Take care of your clothes.

**Objectives**

Students will

- read about clothes-related values and activities.
- read and copy a full sentence.

**Resources** Values Poster

## Be the Expert

### Teaching Tip

When students talk about classmates, encourage them to point and also use the classmate's name. If students are unsure of a classmate's name, remind them of the language to use to ask. Have them say a sentence about the classmate using his or her name. Then have them repeat the sentence using *he* or *she*. This will help reinforce basic conversational skills as well as give students additional practice using pronouns.

## Share 20

- **20** Form small groups. Have students use their sentences to tell the group about their pictures.
- **Modify** If you have time, or if students are eager for a challenge, have group members ask and answer questions about their pictures. Model pointing to an item of clothing in a drawing, and ask *What's that?* or *What are those?* Explain that the writer should answer.

## Value 21 22

- **21** Write *put away clothes* on the board. Pretend to fold up the item of clothing and place it on a shelf or other neat surface of your classroom. As you do so, say *I take care of my clothes. I put away my clothes.* Say *Now let's look and read.* Point to *Put away your clean clothes* on p. 87. Read it aloud. Then have students read it aloud with you.
- **22** Write *Take care of your clothes* on the board. Act out washing, ironing, folding, and putting away clothes. As you do so, say *I take care of my clothes. I keep my clothes clean and neat. I put them away. I fold my clothes and put them on a shelf. I put clothes in my closet.* Read the directions for Activity 22 aloud. Say *Copy.* Model copying by writing the exact words on p. 87. Say them as you write them. Tell students to copy, and remind them to use a capital letter for the word *I*. When students finish, have them read their writing aloud.

# Project

**Objectives**

Students will

- think and write about clothes.
- create a stick puppet.
- complete the Unit 5 Quiz.

**Academic Language** *cut out, choose, glue*

**Resources** Assessment: Unit 5 Quiz; Picture Cards 84–96; Teacher's Resource CD-ROM: Activity Worksheet 5.4

**Materials** scissors, glue, craft sticks

**23 Dress a stick puppet.**

1 Cut out the pictures on page 167.

2 Choose a head.

3 Glue the clothes.

4 Glue the puppet to the stick.

88

## Prepare

- Review the new clothing and color words by holding up each Unit 5 Picture Card and asking *What is it?* or *What are they?* After students name each item or color, use the word in a complete sentence, such as *Yes, that's a skirt* or *Yes, those are brown pants.*

- Have students open their books to pp. 88–89. Hold up the book and point to the stick puppet the boy on p. 89 is holding. Say *The boy has a stick puppet. He says* He is wearing a blue T-shirt. Point to the pants and shoes and ask *What else is the puppet wearing?* (black pants, white shoes) *You can make a stick puppet, too. Let's find out how to make one.*

- Work along with students, making your own stick puppet and modeling as you go. Begin by having students look at picture 1 on p. 88. Ask *What do we do first?* (cut out pictures) *Let's turn to page 167 and cut out all the pictures. Remember to cut along the lines.* Read step 2 and model choosing a head. Read step 3 and model choosing clothes. Hold up the clothes and say *Put the glue on the side that does not show. It goes on this side.* Flip the picture over and demonstrate gluing clothes to the body. When students finish, say *It's time to glue the puppet to the stick.* Model the final step.

## Share

- Ask a student to come to the front of the room with his or her puppet. Role-play the character of your puppet. Ask the student's puppet *What are you wearing?* or *What are those?* or *What is that?* Prompt the student to speak as though he is the puppet. (*I'm wearing a pink hat* or *Those are black pants.*) Direct the student to ask you questions, and answer them.
- Form pairs. Have each student role play his or her puppet. Walk around the room to make sure students are taking turns asking and answering questions about clothes and colors. Then have pairs come forward to share their dialogues.

## Be the Expert

### Our World in Context

People have been making and using puppets and puppet-like figures since at least the 5th century BCE. The earliest puppets were probably shadow puppets that came to life on a wall with sunlight or firelight. Puppets were very popular during the Middle Ages in Europe, when people used *marionettes*, or string puppets, to tell stories. Students can see examples of this type of puppet in the pictures on pp. 96–97.

### Project Rubric

✓ Did students cut the pictures along the lines?

✓ Did students glue the head and clothes in the correct positions?

✓ Did students talk about their puppets through questions and answers?

### Now I Can

Ask questions such as the following:

- Hold up Picture Cards of clothes and ask *What's that* or *What are those?*
- Hold up Picture Cards of clothes and ask *What color is it? What colors are they?*
- Point to a stick puppet and ask *What is it wearing?*

**Review** For additional practice, direct students to Activity Worksheet 5.4.

### Unit Assessment

Give the Unit 5 Quiz. Hand out the quiz and go over the instructions with students. The quiz should take 15–20 minutes.

## Video

**Vocabulary 1a** *a jacket, pants, a skirt, a shirt, socks*
**Vocabulary 1b** *a dress, shoes, a T-shirt, a hat, gloves*
**Vocabulary 2** *pink, purple, brown, a closet, a shelf*
**Grammar 1** use *I/he/she* + verb + *ing* to ask and answer questions
**Grammar 2** ask and answer questions with *that* and *those*
**Song** *My Clothes*
**Viewing** clothes and colors
**Story Time** *The King's New Clothes*
**Resources** Student Book, pp. 74–83; Teacher's Resource CD-ROM: Graphic Organizers (Two-column chart, Word web); Picture Cards 2, 7, 94, 96

## Before You Watch

- Play the Introduction. When Anna speaks, ask *Who's that?* (Anna) *What is Anna wearing?* (a hat and gloves)

## While You Watch

- Draw a two-column chart on the board with the headings **Clothes** and **Colors.** As students watch the video, have them list words that name clothes and words that name colors. Model by writing *jacket* under **Clothes** and *brown* under **Colors.**
- Pause the video as necessary to allow students to record the words.

## After You Watch

- Put students in pairs and have them compare their charts.
- Ask students to share what they learned by playing the roles of Anna and Freddy. The student playing Anna says the sentence stems *Those are* __________ and *That is* __________. The student playing Freddy completes the sentences. Then the students switch roles.

## Zoom In

### Vocabulary

- Play Scenes 2–4. Stop the video from time to time to have students say the vocabulary words before Freddy does, or to name things before Anna does.

### Grammar

- Play Scene 7. Pause occasionally to identify clothing items with *that* or *those*. Say *One jacket. Do you say that jacket or those jacket?* (*that jacket*)

### Song

- Play Scene 9 to review vocabulary. Give groups Picture Cards for *purple*, *orange*, *brown*, and *pink*. Have students hold up the appropriate card when they hear a color in the song. For more practice, divide the class in half, and have one half sing questions and the other half sing answers.

### Viewing

- Replay the scene, pausing during the segment of children playing in the snow. Lead students to draw conclusions about where people live from the clothes they wear. Make statements, such as *The sun is shining. This is a warm place.*
- Work with students to create two word webs with the names of clothes. In the center of the first web, draw the sun. In the center of the second web, draw a snowflake or snowman.

### Story Time

- At the end of *The King's New Clothes*, point to the girl in the blue dress and ask *What does she tell the king?* Explain that folktales often teach a lesson about the right way to act. Ask *What does the story teach us?* (Tell the truth.)

## *The King's New Clothes*

A tailor makes "magic" clothes for a king. But no one can see these "magic" clothes! Will the tailor trick the silly king?

## Before You Read

- **Build background** Hold up the cover of the book and say *The title of the story is "The King's New Clothes."* Turn to p. 2 and point to the king. Explain *This is the king. He is wearing a crown.* Point to the crown and pantomime placing a crown on your head.
- **Introduce the strategy** Have students open their readers to p. 2. Call on a student to read what the king says. Ask *What does the king love?* (clothes) Point to the clothes in the picture and ask *What are those?* (Those are clothes.) Have students follow along as you read the dialogue on p. 3. Say *I wonder if the king is really smart. Does he know* (point to your head) *lots of things? Let's read to find out.*

## While You Read

- Read the book aloud. Stop every few pages to sum up the story and ask questions that require students to draw conclusions.
    - p. 5: Ask *What's the king wearing?* (a white T-shirt) Point to the picture of the jacket above the king's head on p. 4. Ask *What does the king think he's wearing?* (a magic jacket) *What do some people say?* (That jacket is beautiful.) *Is that true?* (no)
    - p. 7: Ask *Is the king wearing a new hat?* (no) Point to the boy speaking on p. 7 and ask *What does the boy say?* (That hat is beautiful.) *Look at his eye. He is winking* (wink at students) *at the other people. That's a clue. Does the boy see a hat?* (no)
    - p. 7: Point to the girl and ask *What does the girl say?* (What hat?) *Why is she laughing?* Act out laughing. (The king is not wearing a hat.)

## After You Read

- Form groups of four. Have each group count off. Say *Student 1, you are the king.* Say *Student 2, you are the girl.* Say *Students 3 and 4, you are the other people in the story.* Have each group role-play one of these scenes.

## Unit 5 Reader

**Text Type** folktale

**Vocabulary** *a jacket, a hat, shoes, socks, a T-shirt*

**Grammar** use *I/he/she* + verb + *ing* to ask and answer questions; ask and answer questions with *that* and *those*

**Reading Strategy** Draw Conclusions

**Resources** Video: Sc. 11—Story Time; Classroom Presentation Tool: Story Time

## Be the Expert

### Text Background

Versions of this folktale, about an emperor who is tricked by his tailor into believing that his clothes are beautiful and magical, have been told in many countries for many years. The version here is adapted from the story made famous by Danish author Hans Christian Andersen. His story has been translated into more than 100 languages and is loved throughout the world.

### Reading Strategy

**Draw Conclusions** Good readers combine what they know with words and pictures to figure out things the text doesn't directly state. Help students apply the strategy by presenting it like a math problem, such as $A + B = ?$. Write details for A and B. The question mark (?) represents the conclusion. Encourage students to "add up" the details to draw a conclusion.

## Student Book

**TR: B2** (1) **Listen and say.**

| | |
|---|---|
| a hat | She's wearing a hat. |
| gloves | She's wearing gloves. |
| a skirt | She's wearing a skirt. |
| a jacket | He's wearing a jacket. |
| a dress | She's wearing a dress. |
| a T-shirt | He's wearing a T-shirt. |
| pants | He's wearing pants. |
| socks | She's wearing socks. |
| a shirt | He's wearing a shirt. |
| shoes | He's wearing shoes. |

**TR: B3** (2) **Listen. Point and say.**

a skirt, pants, a hat, shoes, gloves, socks, a shirt, a jacket, a dress, a T-shirt

**TR: B4** (3) **Point. Ask and answer.**

What are they?
They're shoes. You're wearing shoes.

**TR: B5** (4) **Listen. Read and sing.**

Note: Lyrics for the song *My Clothes* are on pp. 162–163.

**TR: B6 Grammar**

Note: Grammar 1 is on p. 164.

**TR: B7** (6) **Listen and find. Color.**

1. What are you wearing?
   I'm wearing a blue dress and blue socks.
   My sister's wearing a green dress and green socks.
2. What are you wearing?
   I'm wearing a yellow T-shirt and a black skirt.
   My mom's wearing an orange shirt and white pants.
3. What are you wearing?
   I'm wearing a red T-shirt, blue jeans, and red shoes.
   My dad is wearing a jacket, a blue shirt, and pants.
4. What are you wearing?
   I'm wearing a black jacket, a blue shirt, and black pants. My grandma's wearing a green hat, a green and white dress, and green shoes.

**TR: B8** (7) **Draw and color. What are you wearing? Talk.**

What are you wearing?
I'm wearing a blue T-shirt.

**TR: B9** (8) **Listen and say.**

| | |
|---|---|
| pink | One hat is pink. |
| purple | One hat is purple. |
| brown | One hat is brown. |
| a shelf | There's a shelf in the closet. |
| a closet | There are shoes in the closet. |

**TR: B10** (10) **Listen and read. Circle.**

1. Is there a black hat?
2. Is there a purple hat?

**TR: B11** (11) **Work with a partner. Listen. Say and stick.**

Where's the green hat? It's on the shelf. My turn.

**TR: B12 Grammar**

Note: Grammar 2 is on p. 170.

**TR: B13** (12) **Play a game. Ask and answer. Draw lines.**

What are those? Those are socks.

**TR: B14** (14) **Listen and read.**

Note: Reading *Clothes Are Fun!* is on p. 172.

**TR: B15** (15) **Listen and read. Look. Circle yes or no.**

People all over the world wear special clothes on special days. Sometimes they are clothes from the past.
1. The children from Turkey are wearing shoes.
2. The girls from Korea are wearing dresses.

**TR: B16** (18) **Work with a partner. What are you wearing today? Ask and answer.**

What are you wearing?
I'm wearing a white shirt, blue pants, and black shoes.

## Workbook

**TR: 39** (3) **Listen to the song. Write. Read. Draw lines to match. Color.**

Note: Lyrics for the song *My Clothes* are on pp. 162–163.

**TR: 40** **5** **Listen. Write.**

1. What are you wearing? I'm wearing a skirt.
2. What are you wearing? I'm wearing a jacket.
3. What are you wearing? I'm wearing a T-shirt.
4. What is your brother wearing?
   My brother's wearing pants.

**TR: 41** **6** **Listen. Look at the chart. Read. Check.**

What's your mother wearing?
My mother's wearing a white shirt and a red skirt.
She's wearing black shoes.
What's your father wearing?
My father's wearing a blue shirt and black pants.
He's wearing black socks and black shoes.

**TR: 42** **10** **Listen. Look at the picture. Color.**

1. Color the shelf brown.
2. Color the hat purple.
3. Color the skirt pink.
4. Color the shoes brown.
5. Color the gloves purple.

**TR: 43** **12** **Listen. Write the number.**

1. What's that? That's my dress.
2. What are those? Those are my socks.
3. What are those? Those are my gloves.
4. What's that? That's my jacket.
5. What's that? That's my shirt.
6. What are those? Those are my shoes.

**TR: 44** **15** **Listen and draw a line.**

1. What are those? Those are socks.
2. What's that? That's a skirt.
3. What are you wearing? I'm wearing pants.
4. What are those? Those are gloves.
5. What are you wearing?I'm wearing a dress.

**TR: 45** **16** **Listen and read.**

Note: Reading *Clothes for Work* is on p. 318.

## Answer Key

## Student Book

### Unit Opener SB p. 74

blue

**6** SB p. 80

first line: 1st figure, blue dress and blue socks; 2nd figure, green dress and green socks, 3rd figure, yellow shirt and black skirt; 4th figure, orange shirt and white pants

second line: 1st figure, red shirt, blue jeans, and red shoes; 2nd figure, jacket, blue shirt, and pants; 3rd figure, black jacket, blue shirt, and black pants; 4th figure, green hat, a green and white dress, and green shoes

**10** SB p. 82

1. no, 2. yes

**13** SB p. 83

1. The gloves are blue.
2. It's pink
3. No, there isn't.

**15** SB p. 84

1. yes, 2. yes

**16** SB p. 85

Answers may vary. Suggested answers.

Turkey: pink, purple, red, white
Peru: black, blue, green, orange, pink, purple, red, yellow, white
Korea: blue, green, orange, pink, red, yellow

**17** SB p. 85

1. line to boy's hat
2. line to boy's jacket
3. line to boy's pants
4. line to boy's shirt
5. line to girl's dress

## Workbook

Go to pp. 316–319 for the Workbook Answer Key for this unit.

## In This Unit

**Theme** This unit is about toys and the things we have and want.

**Content Objective**

Students will

- identify and describe toys, possessions, and wants.

**Language Objectives**

Students will

- name and describe toys.
- talk about wants.
- talk about possession.

**Vocabulary**

**Vocabulary 1** *a ball, a bike, a car, a drum, a game, a kite, a puppet, a top, a train, a truck*

**Vocabulary 2** *a board game, a doll, a puzzle, a robot, a teddy bear*

**Grammar**

**Grammar 1** use simple present of *want* (first, second, and third person singular)

**Grammar 2** ask and answer questions with *this* and *these*

**Pacing Guides** LIU6

**Writing** Write about a favorite toy.

**Value** Share your toys.

**Project** Make a cup-and-ball toy.

## Unit Opener

**Objectives**

Students will

- analyze a photo.
- name the colors of toys.

**Resources** Video: Sc. 1—Introduction; Classroom Presentation Tool: Unit Opener; Teacher's Resource CD-ROM: Home-School Connection Letter; Unit Opener Poster

**Materials** two toys, such as an action figure and a toy car

Unit 6

# My Toys

In this unit, I will . . .

- name and describe toys.
- talk about wants.
- talk about possession.

**Look and circle.**

The toys are

| | |
|---|---|
| blue | green |
| red | yellow |
| black | pink |

90

## Introduce

- **Set the stage** Hold up a toy action figure and say *This is a toy.* Move the toy so that it walks, stands, and lies on its side. Ask *What can it do?* Say *It can walk. It can stand up.* Hold up a toy car and say *It's a toy car.* Move the car as you make sound effects: *beep, beep, vroom, vroom!* Ask students to name the colors of the toys. Hold up a toy. Ask *What color is it?*

- Ask *Do you play with toys?* Raise your hand and say *Raise your hand if you play with toys.* Say *We play with toys!* Write the following sentence frames on the board, and have students use them to tell about playing with toys.

  I play with ________.
  We play with ________.

- **Recycle** Say *Open your book to pages 90 and 91. Count the toys.* Say *Three toys.* Have students count to three aloud. Point

Santa Fe, New Mexico

91

## Be the Expert

### About the Photo

The photo was taken in Santa Fe in the state of New Mexico, in the United States. Sante Fe, founded in 1610, is one of the oldest cities in the United States. After New Mexico became part of the United States in 1848, Santa Fe became the capital of the Territory of New Mexico in 1853. When New Mexico became a state in 1912, Santa Fe became the capital of the state.

### Our World in Context

Children all over the world play with toys. In the past, many toys were made from wood, cloth, and other natural materials. Today, many toys are made from plastic instead. Children often use toys to copy what their mothers, fathers, and other adults do. They play house with dolls. They "go to work" and drive in toy cars.

### Related Vocabulary

*camera, cowboy, cowgirl, movie*

to the blue toy on p. 91 and ask *What color is this toy?* (blue) Encourage discussion of the photo with these questions:

*How many toys?* (three)
*What color are the toys?* (yellow, blue, red)
*What else do you see? What color is it?* (blue sky, white clouds, blue mountain, brown rock, green trees)

- Direct students' attention to the activity on p. 90. Read the sentence stem aloud. Ask *What color are the toys?* After students have named the colors, say *Circle the colors.* Review the answers as a class.

- **Contextualize** Have students work with partners to brainstorm ideas for their own "toy story." Tell them to each choose one toy. Say *Tell your partner about your toy. What can it do? What color is it?* After students take turns describing their toys, have them work together to draw a scene from their stories. Call on students to share their work.

# Vocabulary 1

**Objectives**
Students will
- name toys.
- identify different toys.

**Vocabulary** *a top, a puppet, a bike, a truck, a car, a kite, a ball, a drum, a game, a train*

**Academic Language** *answer, ask, partner*

**Resources** Workbook pp. 66–67; Audio CD TR: B17–19; Video: Sc. 2—Vocabulary 1a; Sc. 3—Vocabulary 1b; Classroom Presentation Tool: Vocabulary 1; Picture Cards 98–107; Sound Card 36; Teacher's Resource CD-ROM: Activity Worksheet 6.1

**Materials** examples of the toys shown on pp. 92–93 (*optional*)

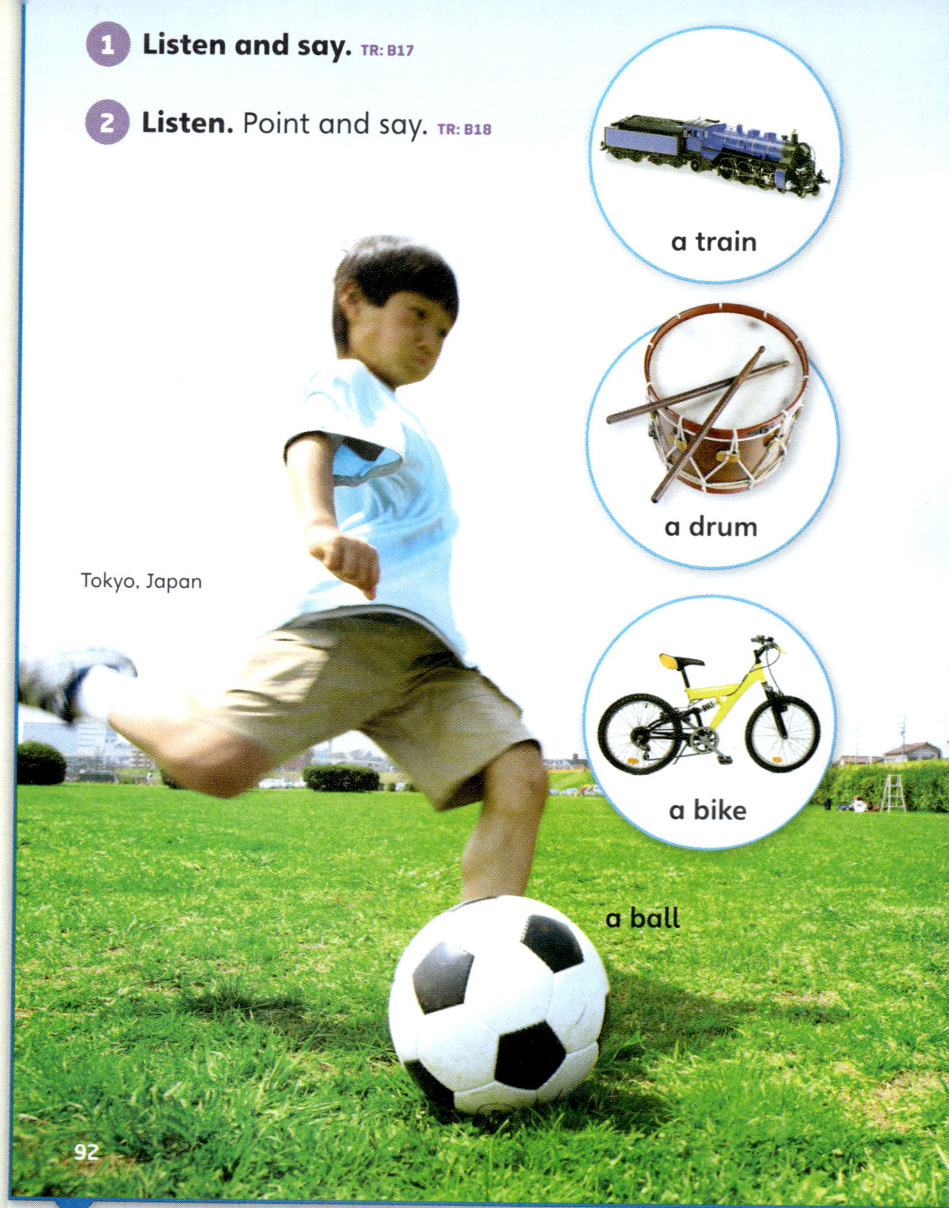


## Warm Up

- **Preteach** Post Picture Cards 98–107 around the room. Point to the cards and say *These are toys.* Then have students take out paper and crayons. Say *Pick a toy. Draw a picture of it.*
- When students are finished, have them hold up and share their pictures with the class. Ask a student *Is it a (train)?* as you point to a picture of a train. Students may answer *yes* or *no*. Continue until all students have had a chance to share their pictures.

## Present

- Have students open their books to pp. 92–93. Point to the photo of the train, say *a train,* and then say *The train is purple.* Pretend to move a toy train and make a train sound: *choo-choo!*

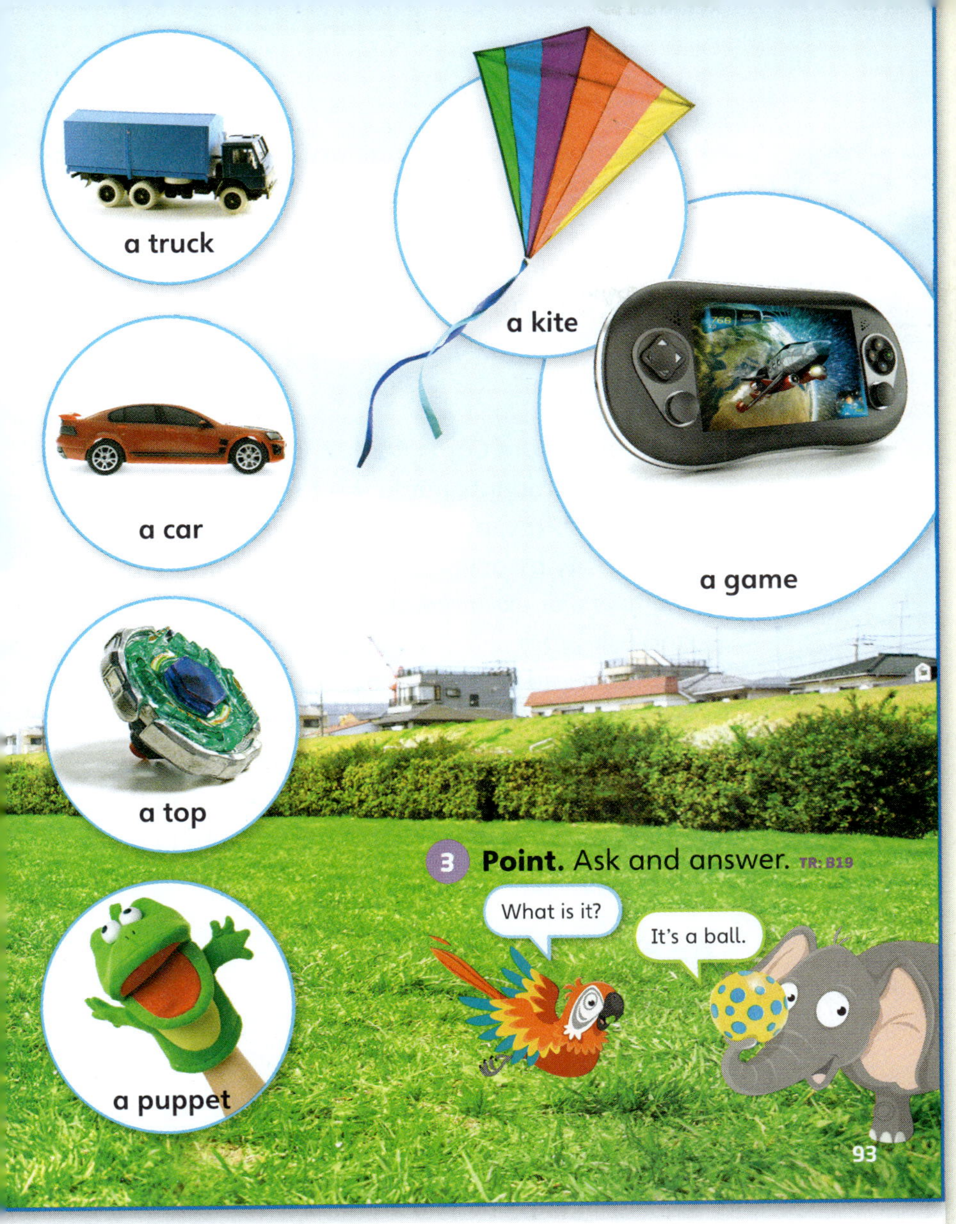


- Point to the photo of the drum, say the word aloud, and say *It's a drum!* Pretend to hit a drum and make sounds like a drum: *boom, bam, bam!*

- Point to each remaining word, say it aloud, and then say sentences such as the following: *I see a bike!* Pretend to ride a bike around the room. *It's a ball.* Pretend to kick a ball. *This is a big truck.* Pretend to drive a truck and make a loud truck horn noise. *It's a car. The car is red.* Pretend to drive a sports car and make typical car and tire noises. *I see a top.* Pretend to spin a top. *A puppet!* Pretend to have a puppet on your hand and change your voice as you say *Hello, class!* Say *A kite! The kite is in the sky.* Pretend you are flying a kite. *A game. Games are fun.* Pretend to play a handheld video game.

## Be the Expert

### Our World in Context

The boy in the photo is in Tokyo, Japan. He's kicking a soccer ball. Soccer, also known as football, is the most popular team sport in the world, with more than 1.3 billion fans. Soccer-like games date back thousands of years to Ancient Greece and China.

Because the game has simple rules and equipment, soccer can be played almost anywhere. All that is needed is a ball and an open space.

In many places around the world, children make handmade soccer balls. They shape a ball out of plastic bags and wrap it with rope, yarn, or twine made from tree bark.

### Teaching Tip

Help students learn and remember new words by showing them examples of real objects. When possible, give students a chance to hold, touch, and move the objects. For example, when teaching the word *kite*, it's good to show a picture of a kite, and even better if students hold or fly an actual kite.

Students have different learning styles, so seeing, holding, touching, and moving an object appeals to a wide range of learning styles and strengthens the learning experience.

## Practice 1 2

- 1 Say *It's time to listen and say. Say everything you hear: a train. I have a train.* Motion for students to say the words and sentence with you as you repeat them. Ask *Are you ready?* Play **TR: B17**. As students repeat each word and sentence, make sure they pronounce the words correctly.

- 2 Say *Now it's time to listen, point, and say.* Say *Listen. I say a bike. I point to a bike.* Point to the photo of a bike and say *a bike* again. Ask *Are you ready?* Play **TR: B18**. ✓ Point to a photo on pp. 92–93, and ask *What is it?* If students have difficulty, provide support by saying the name and asking them to repeat it.

- Put students in pairs and have them open their books to pp. 92–93. Have one student hold up a Picture Card from 98–107. Have the other student find the matching picture in the book and say the words. Model by showing Picture Card 107 (a truck). Hold up your book and point to the photo of the truck on p. 93. Say *A truck. Here is a truck.* Have students take turns holding up picture cards and finding and saying the vocabulary words in the book.

## Wrap Up

- Review the lesson's vocabulary with the pictures on pp. 92–93. Say *I'm a toy. I start with the letter p. What am I?* (a puppet) Repeat with the letters *k* (a kite), *c* (a car), *d* (a drum), *g* (a game), *b* (a ball, a bike), and *t* (a truck, a top, a train).

## Recap

- Hold up Picture Cards 98–107, one at a time, and have students name the toys. After students name each toy, put students in two groups. Begin the activity by acting out an action for one of the toys. For example, act out playing a drum and ask *What is it?* Have students respond *It's a drum.* Hold up the correct card. Have the class continue the activity. Students in one group should act out actions for the toys, and students in the other group ask *What is it?* Students doing the acting respond *It's a* ________ , and hold up the correct card.

## Apply 3

- 3 Point to the bottom of p. 93. Say *There's Polly the Parrot! And there's Eddie the Elephant. What are Polly and Eddie saying? Let's listen.* Play **TR: B19**. Have students follow along in their books as you read the question and answer aloud. Hold up your book as you point to the ball. Ask a student *What is it?* Prompt the student to answer *It's a ball.*

- Have students form pairs. Say *Point to a photo and ask "What is it?" Your partner tells you what it is. Take turns.* ✓ Walk around the room, making sure that partners are taking turns and correctly naming the different photos.

- **Expand** Say *Let's put some words in ABC order!* On the board, write the following vocabulary words:

| | | |
|---|---|---|
| train | kite | puppet |
| drum | car | |
| bike | game | |

- Point to *bike*. Ask *What is it?* (bike) *What's the first letter?* (b) Motion to all of the words and ask *Does any word begin with a?* (no) Say *Bike is the first word.* Erase *bike* and start a new list of words, beginning with *b: bike*. Say *What comes next? Does a word begin with c?* (yes) *What is it?* (car) Write *c: car* in the list under b: *bike*. Continue in this manner until you have alphabetized all of the words. Say *Now the words are in ABC order!*

## Extend

- Display Picture Cards 98–107. Work with students to sort the cards into groups. For example, ask *What toys have blue?* (truck, kite, game, top) *Let's put them together.* Hold up the four cards and say *The toys have blue.* Lead students in sorting the images on the cards in other ways, such as by size.
- After students have sorted the toys different ways, have them sort the toys by popularity. See if students can rank the toys from most favorite to least favorite. Then ask *What toy do you like most? Why?* Help students answer, if necessary.

## Wrap Up

- Say *Let's play a game. I say a word. You draw it.* Model with the word *train*. Say *train*. Draw a picture of a train. Then hold it up. Say *Now you draw.* Say each target word for students to draw.
- Once students have completed their drawings, have them share them with the class. Ask each student to stand, show his or her drawing, and say *It's a* ________.

## Be the Expert

### Sounds of English

**Single Sounds: /ʌ/** The sound /ʌ/ (s<u>u</u>n) is a relaxed vowel sound. Your tongue should be relaxed but pressing down slightly in the back of your mouth. Your jaw will drop slightly, and your lips shouldn't be rounded.

Use Sound Card 36 (<u>u</u>mbrella) to help students hear and produce the sound.

Example words: tr<u>u</u>ck, dr<u>u</u>m, p<u>u</u>zzle, p<u>u</u>ppet, grandm<u>o</u>ther

### Teaching Tip

Use gestures and movements to reinforce the meaning of academic language such as *listen*, *point*, and *say*. Following these directions should become effortless for students in order for them to focus on learning new words, grammar skills, and concepts in class.

### Related Vocabulary

*soccer*

### Formative Assessment

Can students

- name toys?

  Have students name the toys on pp. 92–93.
- identify different toys?

  Hold up or display Picture Cards for three different toys. Ask *What picture shows the (car)? What picture shows the (game)? What picture shows the (drum)?* Have students select the correct pictures.

**Review** For additional practice, direct students to Activity Worksheet 6.1.

## Song

**Vocabulary in the song**

**Vocabulary 1** *a drum, a bike, a kite, a ball, a train*

**Vocabulary 2** *a doll*

**Grammar in the song**

**Grammar 1** use simple present of *want* (first, second, and third person singular)

**Resources** Workbook p. 68; Audio CD TR: B20; Video: Sc. 9—Song; Classroom Presentation Tool: Song; Picture Cards 98–99, 101, 103, 106, 109

**Materials** a box; toys such as a toy car, a toy train, and a puppet; note cards

4 **Listen.** Read and sing. TR: B20

# Let's Play!

*Do you want to play?*
*Do you want to play with me?*
*Do you want to play?*
*Do you want to play with me?*
*Do you want to play?*
*Do you want to play with me?*
*Yes, I do! Yes, I do!*

*Do you want to bang on a drum?*
*No, I don't.*
*Do you want to ride a bike?*
*No, I don't.*
*Do you want to fly a kite?*
*Yes, I do.*
*I want to fly my kite with you!*

94

## Use the Song 4

- **Build background** Place toys in a box, and put the box on a shelf in your classroom. Point to the shelf and the wall. Say *There's a shelf on the wall.* Point to the box. Say *There's a box on the shelf.* Take down the box and take out the toys. Say *There are toys in the box.*

- Put the toys back in the box and place the box of toys on the shelf. Say the following lines of the song as you act out with movements: *There is a shelf on the wall* (point to and touch the shelf), *a box on the shelf* (touch the box), and *toys in the box* (point inside the box). Then say *Now let's do it together.*

- 4 **Act it out** Form six groups. Assign each group a toy and an action: banging on a drum, riding a bike, flying a kite, dressing a doll, kicking a ball, and playing with trains. Play **TR: B20** and cue each group to perform its action as they sing along. Cue the entire class to perform the "box on the shelf" part of the song.

- Play **TR: B20** a second time. Give each group one of the Picture Cards 98–99, 101, 103, 106, and 109. Have students hold up the appropriate card when they hear the toy's name.

*There is a shelf on the wall,*
*a box on the shelf,*
*toys in the box.*
*Toys for girls and boys!*

*Do you want to dress my doll?*
*No, I don't.*
*Do you want to kick a ball?*
*No, I don't.*
*Do you want to play with trains?*
*Yes, I do.*
*I want to play with you!*
*Choo choo choo!*

**CHORUS**

*Let's play!*

5 **Sing again.** Hold up pictures.

95

## Be the Expert

### Our World in Context

This song uses the onomatopoetic words *choo, choo, choo* to convey the sound a train whistle makes. An onomatopoetic word is an imitation of the sound something makes. Because onomatopoetic words make use of the sounds of a given language, they differ from language to language, some a great deal, some only slightly.

For example, an English-speaking person would describe the sound a cat makes as "meow." A Spanish-speaking person would describe it as "miau." And a Chinese-speaking person would say "miāo." Regardless of the exact words, understanding the meaning would probably be apparent, which is what makes onomatopoetic words so helpful.

### Teaching Tip

To help students become familiar with the concept of varying musical beats, play a variety of songs, each with a different beat. For each song you play, mark the beat by clapping, tapping your feet, or tapping your fingers on your desk. Then play each song again, asking students to mark the beat any way they prefer: clapping, tapping their feet, or tapping their fingers on their desks.

## Use It Again 5

- 5 **Vocabulary 1** Prepare a set of note cards numbered 1–5. Write the following on the board: *1. a drum; 2. a bike; 3. a kite; 4. a ball; 5. a train.* Give each student a note card. Have students write their words on one side of the card and draw pictures on the other side. Then play **TR: B20**. Have students sing along. Have them stand and show their pictures when they hear their words. Have them say their words when they hear them sung.
- **Vocabulary 2** Write the following on the board:

| | | |
|---|---|---|
| Do you want to ________ | ? | No, I don't. |
| Do you want to ________ | ? | No, I don't. |
| Do you want to ________ | ? | Yes, I do. |

- Put students in pairs. Have pairs use the target words to complete the new verse. Then have pairs take turns singing their completed verse.
- **Grammar 1** Use the song to practice questions and answers. Sing *Do you want to bang on a drum?* Have students sing *No, I don't.* Continue singing questions and answers from the song. Have half of the class sing a question and the other half sing the answer.

# Grammar 1

**Objective**
Students will
- make sentences with *want* and *wants*.

**Grammar** use simple present of *want* (first, second, and third person singular)

**Academic Language** *find, guess, number, sentence*

**Resources** Workbook pp. 69–70, Audio CD TR: B21–24; Video: Sc. 6—Grammar 1; Classroom Presentation Tool: Grammar 1; Teacher's Resource CD-ROM: Graphic Organizers (Tree); Picture Cards 98–107

**Materials** note cards

**GRAMMAR** TR: B21

| | |
|---|---|
| **Do** you **want** a kite? | No, I **don't.** |
| **Do** you **want** a puppet? | Yes, I **do.** |

**6** **Listen and find.** Draw a line. TR: B22

96

## Warm Up

- **Recycle** Say *I have; you have; she has.* Start a chant. Clap, snap, or tap as you say each pronoun. Have students join in. Make hand motions to show *I, you,* and *she.* Start the chant off slowly, and pick up the pace as students join in. Then hold up Picture Cards 99, 102, and 104 for *a bike, a game,* and *a puppet.* Help students expand the chant. Say *I have (a bike), you have (a bike), she has (a bike).* Repeat for *a game* and *a puppet.*

- **Spiral** Start a new chant. Say *I want, you want, he wants.* Clap, snap, or tap as you say each pronoun. Hold up the Picture Cards and have students extend the chant with you *I want (a game), you want (a game), she wants (a game),* and so on.

## Present

- Have students open their books to p. 96. Draw students' attention to the yellow grammar box at the top of the page. Read the first question aloud. Have students repeat the phrase in two chunks: *Do you want ... a kite?* Read the answer aloud and then have students repeat.

- Ask students to follow along in their books as you play **TR: B21**. Students can take turns reading the two questions and answers in the grammar box. Say *Now you say a different answer. Tell me that you want a kite. Tell me that you don't want a puppet.* Ask several students the two questions. Listen for the correct use of *do* and *don't.*

**GRAMMAR** TR: B23

| | |
|---|---|
| **Does** she **want** a ball? | Yes, she **does.** |
| **Does** he **want** a ball? | No, he **doesn't.** He **wants** a truck. |

**7 Listen and circle.** TR: B24

1. Yes, he does. He wants a train.

   No, he doesn't. He wants a drum.

2. Yes, she does. She wants a puppet.

   No, she doesn't. She wants a car.

3. Yes, he does. He wants a game.

   No, he doesn't. He wants a kite.

4. Yes, she does. She wants a top.

   No, she doesn't. She wants a ball.

97

## Be the Expert

### Our World in Context

One of the oldest toys in the world is the puppet. Before people could write, puppets were used to educate and entertain. Puppets are still popular. Common types are hand puppets, like Freddy the frog in the videos, and rod puppets.

Hand puppets fit over a puppeteer's hand. The puppeteer uses his fingers to move the puppet's heads and arms. Rod puppets are more realistic than hand puppets because the puppeteer can manipulate the puppet's entire body. Thin rods are connected to the puppet's arms and legs, and one thick rod runs through the body and head. The puppeteer uses the rods to move the body in a realistic manner.

### Grammar in Depth

A helping verb, also called an auxiliary verb, is used with a main verb. The helping verb has no meaning on its own. The common helping verb *do* (*does*) is used to ask questions (*Do you want a puppet? Does he want a ball?*) and to stand for the main verb in some constructions. (*No, he doesn't. Yes, she does.*) It is also used to show emphasis (*I do want you to pass the test.*) and to make negative statements. (*I don't like that.*)

- **Explain** Use Tree diagrams to show two answers to the same question.

  Do you want a puppet?

  Yes, I do. | No, I don't.

  Does he want a bike?

  Yes, he does. | No, he doesn't.

- Model saying the completed questions and answers aloud. Then have students take turns asking and answering the questions.

- Put students in three groups. Tell the first group *You ask the question.* Point to the *Yes* sentence, and tell the second group *You answer with Yes.* Point to the *No* sentence, and tell the third group *You answer with No.* Switch until all groups have read each frame once.

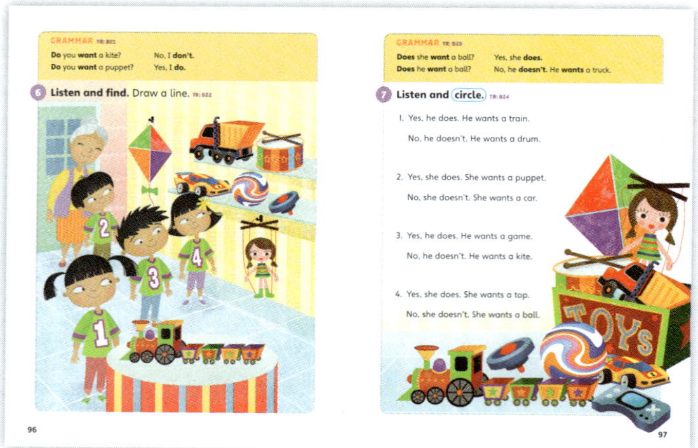


## Practice 6 7

- 6 Read the directions for Activity 6 aloud. Say *Listen to the boys and girls. Let's start with girl number 1. Let's find her in the book.* Play only the first conversation on **TR: B22**.
- Model completing the first item. Ask *Does girl number 1 want a kite?* (No, she doesn't.) *Does she want a top?* (Yes, she does.) Model drawing a line from girl number 1 to the toy top. Say *She wants a top. I draw a line from the girl to the top.*
- Before students complete the remaining items, review the names of the toys in the picture. Point out the marionette under the shelves and explain *This is a puppet.* Say *Now listen and draw a line.* Play **TR: B22** again. ✓ Check to make sure students are drawing lines from the correct child to the toy he or she wants.
- Draw students' attention to the yellow grammar box at the top of p. 97. Read the questions and answers aloud, or play **TR: B23**. Say *We're talking about* he *and* she, *so we say* does *and* doesn't. *Say these words with me:* She does, he does. She doesn't, He doesn't.
- 7 Hold up a book and point to Activity 7. Read the directions aloud. Say *Now listen and circle.* Draw a circle on the board or in the air as you say *circle*.
- Say *Listen. What does the boy want? Circle the answer.* Play only the first conversation on **TR: B24**. Repeat the narrator's question *Does he want a train?* (No, he doesn't.) Ask *What does Mark want?* (He wants a drum.) Say *Look at the answers. Read the sentences.* Ask *Does Mark want a train? No, he doesn't. He wants a drum.* Say *That's the right answer. Let's circle it.*
- Form pairs. Play the rest of **TR: B24**. Have students work together to listen, read, and circle. To support listening comprehension, show a Picture Card each time a toy is mentioned in the dialogue. Then show the card again when the narrator asks the question.

## Wrap Up

- Say *I want a ball. I don't want a train.* Ask *Do I want a train?* Motion for students to answer chorally. (No, you don't.) Repeat with *He wants a puppet. He doesn't want a truck. Does he want a puppet?* (Yes, he does.) *She doesn't want a kite. She wants a top. Does she want a kite?* (No, she doesn't.) *What does she want?* (She wants a top.)

## Recap

- Draw an imaginary line through the middle of the room, dividing the class into two groups. Tell students on one side that they are the *Yes* group. Students on the other side are the *No* group. Ask *Do you want a (truck)?* and point to someone in the *No* group (No, I don't. No, she doesn't.), someone in the *Yes* group (Yes, I do. Yes, he does.), or yourself (Yes, you do. No, you don't.).

## Apply

- Have students role play shopping at a toy store. One student plays the role of the salesperson and asks *Do you want a ________?* The customer answers *Yes, I want a ________* or *No, I don't. I want a ________.* Have students take turns. The salesperson should ask about the customer and the customer's child (to practice using sentences with *he* and *she*).

## Extend

Use a chart to conduct a class survey. Ask students these questions: *Do you want a ball? Do you want a bike? Do you want a truck?* If the student says *yes*, then record a check mark in the chart.

| | ball | bike | truck |
|---|---|---|---|
| Lily | ✓ | | |
| Ben | | ✓ | ✓ |
| Karin | | | ✓ |

- After you survey the class, call on students to sum up the information in the chart. Help them understand that if there is no check mark, the student doesn't want the toy. Ask them to say and write sentences that tell who wants and doesn't want a toy.

## Wrap Up

- Form groups. Give each group eight note cards with the following word or words on them: *do, you, does, he, I, want, wants, a drum*

- Have students use the cards to form as many questions and answers as they can. Groups should write each sentence they form. Point out that they don't have to use each card in every sentence. Model by forming and writing the sentence *I want a drum.*

## Be the Expert

### Our World in Context

The puppet shown in the pictures on pp. 96–97 is a marionette, also called a string puppet. This type of puppet is manipulated from above by strings attached to a control. A simple marionette has strings attached to each leg, each hand, each shoulder, each ear, and the base of the spine. Some marionettes have many strings—the more strings there are, the more sensitive the movement.

### Teaching Tip

Encourage students to use English outside the classroom. For example, encourage them to use *Do you want* ________ and *Yes, I do / No, I don't* when they're with family and friends. Take time during class to have students tell how they used English outside the classroom.

### Formative Assessment

Can students

- make sentences with *want* and *wants*?

  Say *I want a train. She doesn't want a ball.* Ask *Do I want a train? Does she want a ball?* Have students answer *yes* and *no*. Prompt them to use complete sentences.

# Vocabulary 2

**Objectives**

Students will

- name toys.
- identify different toys.

**Vocabulary** *a robot, a teddy bear, a board game, a puzzle, a doll*

**Academic Language** *stick, sticker*

**Resources** Workbook p. 71; Audio CD TR: B25–27; Video: Sc. 4—Vocabulary 2; Classroom Presentation Tool: Vocabulary 2; Teacher's Resource CD-ROM: Graphic Organizers (Word web), Activity Worksheet 6.2; Picture Cards 108–112

**Materials** toys such as a doll, puzzle, board game, and teddy bear (*optional*)

**8 Listen and say.** TR: B25

a robot

a teddy bear

a puzzle

a board game

a doll

**9 Work with a partner.** Point and say.

**10 Listen and read.** Circle *yes* or *no*. TR: B26

1. Does he want a robot? yes no
2. Does he want a puzzle? yes no

**11 Work with a partner.** Listen. Say and stick. TR: B27

1 2 3 4 5



## Warm Up

- **Activate prior knowledge** On the board write *table, shirt, kite*. Read the words aloud with students. Say *You know a lot of words about toys. One of these things is a toy. What is it?* (kite) Model answering with a complete sentence *A kite is a toy.* Repeat with new sets of words, such as *sky/cat/puppet* and *ball/desk/cloud*.

- Expand the list to four words and include two toys. For example, write *T-shirt, bike, sofa*, and *drum*. Say *Now there are four words. Two are toys. What are they?*

## Present

- In a robot voice, say *My name is ZR5. I have many friends. I have many toys. They're in the classroom now. Would you like to meet them?* One by one, introduce students to ZR5's "friends." Hold up a doll, or point to the photo of the doll on p. 98, and say, in a robot voice, *This is my friend. She's a doll.* Hold up a teddy bear and say *This is my friend, too. He's a teddy bear.* Say *I play board games with my friends. I make puzzles with my friends.* Encourage students to play the role of the robot and introduce classmates to its friends and toys.

- Hold up Picture Cards 108–112 one at a time, say the word, and have students repeat. Then shuffle the cards, show them one at a time, and have students say the target word.

## Practice 8 9 10

- 8 Have students open their books to p. 98. Say *Listen and say.* Play **TR: B25**. ✓ Point to a photo and ask *What is it?* If students have difficulty, replay **TR: B25**.
- 9 Pair students. Read the directions and model the activity with a student. Point to a photo and have the student say the word. Then have the student point and you say the word.
- 10 Say *Now listen to two people talking. Then answer questions.* Do item 1 with the class. Play item 1 on **TR: B26**.
- Say *Number 1 says* Does he want a robot? Yes or no? *I circle* no. *Now you do number 2.* Play only item 2 on **TR: B26**.

## Apply 11

- 11 Put students in pairs and play **TR: B27**. Have partners practice the dialogue.
- Say *Let's do a sticker activity.* Help students find the stickers in the back of their books. Model the sticker activity with a student. Peel off the doll sticker, point to the first box, and say *Number 1. I have a doll.* Place the doll sticker in the box. Have the student peel off a sticker, point to the second box, and use the following sentence and sentence frame: *I don't. I have a ________. Number 2.* Have students work to complete the activity by placing the stickers in their books.

## Extend

- Write the following on the board (without the answers).

1. Sit to play. Play with friends. Try to win. (board game)
2. Put me together. I am a picture. (puzzle)
3. I'm brown. I sit on a bed. I sleep. (teddy bear)
4. I'm a girl. I sit. I stand. (doll)
5. I'm many colors. I sit. I stand. I make noises. (robot)

- Put students in pairs. Say *Let's play a game. Read the sentences. Then write the name of the toy.* Review answers as a class.

## Wrap Up

- Give each student a word web graphic organizer and draw one on the board. In the center circle write *Toys.*
- Have students name the toys from the lesson, as you write each one in an outer circle. Have students copy onto their webs. To start, show a Picture Card and ask *What is it?* Have students use the following sentence frame to respond: *It's a ________.*

## Be the Expert

### Vocabulary Strategy

**Compound Words** In English, words are combined in a variety of ways. There are three forms of compound words: the closed form, in which the words are joined together (*notebook, softball*); the hyphenated form (*eight-year-old*); and the open form (*teddy bear, board game*).

Forming plurals and possessives of compound words can be tricky with open-form compound words. The *s* in the plural form is added at the end of the second word in a compound word. So, *teddy bear* becomes *teddy bears* and *board game* becomes *board games.*

### Teaching Tip

**Classroom Management** Help students become good, active listeners by having them use complete sentences when they respond to a question. Instead of replying *Yes* or *No*, encourage them to repeat the question in their answer.

Practice question-and-answer exchanges with students until they become familiar with the routine. For example, when you or another student asks *Do you want a ________?*, have the student respond *Yes, I want a ________* or *No, I don't want a ________.* By restating the question in the answer, you will know that the student has heard the question correctly and is actively listening.

### Formative Assessment

Can students

- name toys?

  Point to the teddy bear, doll, puzzle, board game, and robot on p. 98. Have students name each toy.
- identify different toys?

  Say *teddy bear, doll, puzzle, board game,* and *robot.* Have students point to the correct photo on p. 98.

**Review** For additional practice, direct students to Activity Worksheet 6.2.

## Grammar 2

**Objective**

Students will

- ask questions with *this* and *these*.

**Grammar** ask and answer questions with *this* and *these*

**Academic Language** *check, cut out, partner*

**Resources** Workbook p. 72; Audio CD TR: B28–30; Video: Sc. 7—Grammar 2; Classroom Presentation Tool: Grammar 2; Teacher's Resource CD-ROM: Activity Worksheet 6.3

**Materials** two cut-outs each of a teddy bear, doll, truck, puzzle, robot, and top for each pair of students (*optional*)

**GRAMMAR** TR: B28

| | |
|---|---|
| **Is this** your teddy bear? | No, **it** isn't. It's Sonia's teddy bear. |
| **Are these** your puppets? | No, **they** aren't. They're Mark's puppets. |

**12** **Look.** Listen and read. Check ✔ *yes* or *no*. TR: B29

| | yes | no |
|---|---|---|
| 1. Is this Anna's puzzle? | ○ | ○ |
| 2. Are these Ken's robots? | ○ | ○ |

**13** **Play a game.** Cut out the cards on page 169. Ask and answer. Play with a partner. TR: B30

99

## Warm Up

- **Recycle** Point to an object far from you, such as a clock. Ask *What's that?* Prompt students to answer *That's a (clock).* Then point to multiple objects far from you, such as books. *What are those?* (Those are books.)
- Say *We use* that *to ask about one thing that's far away. We use* those *to ask about two or more things that are far away.*

## Present

- Have students open their books to p. 99. Read aloud the grammar box.
- Point to the boy with the bear and say *He has a teddy bear.* Play **TR: B28**. Pause after the first exchange and have students repeat. Say *He uses the word* this *because the teddy bear is close to him and the girl.* Play the rest of **TR: B28**.
- Then write the following on the board.

| | | |
|---|---|---|
| Is this your doll? | No, it isn't. | Yes, it is. |
| Are these your dolls? | No, they aren't. | Yes, they are. |

- Read the first row of sentences aloud. Point to *this* and say *Use* this *to ask about one thing.* Pick up a student's book and ask *Is this your book?* Point to *Yes, it is* on the board and have the student read it aloud. Ask a different student *Is this your book?* Point to *No, it isn't,* and have the student read it aloud. Then say *No, it isn't. It's (Li's) book.*
- Read the second row of sentences aloud. Say *Use the word* these *to ask about more than one thing.* Pick up a student's pencils and ask *Are these your*

*pencils?* Have the student use the sentences on the board to answer. ✔ Have students ask you questions about items on your desk using *Is this* or *Are these*.

## Practice 12

- 12 Say *It's time to listen and read.* Point to Activity 12. Read the directions aloud. Say *We're going to check yes or no.* Make a check mark in the air or write one on the board as you say *check*.
- Play the first item on **TR: B29**. Model completing the item. Say *I read question one. It says* Is this Anna's puzzle? *I check* no. *You do the next one.* Play the next item on the track. Ask *Did you hear the words* this robot *or* these robots? (these robots) Ask *Did Ken answer* yes *or* no? (yes) Review answers as a class.

## Apply 13

- 13 Form pairs. Direct students' attention to Activity 13 on p. 99. Say *Let's play a game.* Play **TR: B30**. Explain *One person asks a question about a toy. The other person answers.* Help students find the cards on p. 169 and cut them out. Have students put the cards with toys in one pile and the cards with children in a second pile.
- Model playing the game. Pick a card from the first pile. Ask *Is this your (puzzle)?* Pick a card from the second pile. Say *No, it's not. It's (Tina's) puzzle.* Then put students in pairs and have them play the game.

## Extend

- Pair students and give each pair two cut-outs each of a teddy bear, doll, truck, puzzle, robot, and top. Place all twelve cards face down on one student's desk, four across in three rows. Mix the cards up for each pair. Don't let students see which cards are placed where.
- Start the matching game by modeling how to play. Turn over a card in one row, and then turn over a card in another row. If they match, take the cards and say *These are (toys).* If they don't match, turn the cards back over, say *No match*, and let a student take a turn. Continue until all cards have been turned over and matched. The player with the most cards wins.

## Wrap Up

- Hold up different classroom objects, such as a pen, crayons, and a book, one at a time. Have students ask questions using *Is this* or *Are these*. Model *Is this your pencil? No, it isn't. It's (May's) pencil.*

## Be the Expert

### Grammar in Depth

*This* and its plural form, *these*, are often used as demonstrative pronouns to indicate a person or thing that is near, or has just been pointed out: *This is my doll. These are my dolls.* When used to refer to a person or thing that is nearer in place than another person or thing, *this* (*these*) is often used with *that* (*those*): *This is my doll. That's Tina's doll. These are my dolls. Those are Tina's dolls.*

When *this* and *these* modify nouns, they function as adjectives. Note the difference in the following sentences. In the first set of sentences, *this* and *these* are pronouns; in the second set of sentences, they are adjectives:

*This is my truck.*
*These are my trucks.*

*This truck is mine.*
*These trucks are mine.*

### Formative Assessment

Can students

- ask questions with *this* and *these?*

  Hand students a classroom object, such as a pencil. Have students ask you *Is this your (pencil)?* Repeat, using more than one of an item, such as crayons. Have students ask you *Are these your (crayons)?*

**Review** For additional practice, direct students to Activity Worksheet 6.3.

## Reading

**Objectives**

Students will
- analyze photos for information.
- read a story.
- talk about teddy bears.

**Reading Strategy** Visualize

**Content Vocabulary** *heart, museum*

**Resources** Workbook pp. 74–75; Audio CD TR: B31–33; Classroom Presentation Tool: Reading; Teacher's Resource CD-ROM: Graphic Organizers (Two-column chart); Picture Card 112; World Map Poster

**Materials** drawing paper; photos of famous museums; a board game, puzzle, doll, and robot (*optional*)

14 **Listen and read.** TR: B31

# We ❤ Teddy Bears

People around the world love teddy bears. Children play with them and sleep with them. There are even teddy bear museums! This popular museum is in Korea. It has big bears and small bears, girl bears and boy bears. There are teddy bears for everyone!

100

## Warm Up

- **Activate prior knowledge** Display a teddy bear or Picture Card 112 and ask *What is this?* (a teddy bear) Say *Yes. This is a teddy bear.* Say *Do you like teddy bears?*
- **Build background** Write and say museum and have students repeat after you. Say *A museum is a special place we can go. We can see many different things in a museum.* Show photos of famous and different museums around the world, and have students talk about the photos. Locate the Korean peninsula on a world map and say *Today we'll read about a teddy bear museum. It's in South Korea. Some of the teddy bears in the museum are big. Some are small.*

## Present 14 15

- Have students open their books to p. 100. Point to the title of the passage. Say *Look at the blue words. What is this story about?* (teddy bears)
- Point to the heart. Say *This is a heart.* Point to your heart, then point again to the heart in the title. Say *It means love. The title of this story is We Love Teddy Bears. Do you love teddy bears? What do you love?* Allow a few students to answer. As students answer, write sentences such as the following on the board. Have students take turns reading the sentences aloud.

(Maria) ❤ (butterflies).

**15** **Listen and read.** Circle *yes* or *no*. **TR: B32**

1. There are teddy bear museums. yes no
2. This museum is in China. yes no
3. It has big bears and small bears. yes no

**16** **Look and write.**

1. How many teddy bears are small? _____
2. How many are big? _____
3. How many colors are the bears? _____
4. How many have shirts? _____

**17** **Work with a partner.** What are your favorite toys? Ask and answer. **TR: B33**

101

## Be the Expert

### About the Photo

The Teddy Bear Tower Museum is located in a tower, high above Seoul in South Korea (the Republic of Korea). The museum uses teddy bears in exhibits about the city's past, present, and future. This photo shows an exhibit in the museum. The teddy bears are wearing traditional Korean dress, paying respect to the country's past.

### Teaching Tip

**Fluency** Reading with expression, or feeling, develops students' reading fluency and comprehension. Model reading a passage, such as *We Love Teddy Bears*, with expression. Then have pairs of students take turns reading the passage to each other. Encourage them to read as though they were speaking. As examples, point out the two sentences with exclamation points. Explain that these marks tell readers to read the sentences with excitement and surprise.

### Related Vocabulary

*place, soft, visit*

- **14** **Read together** Say *Let's listen.* Play **TR: B31** once and have students listen. Play it again and have students read along. Pause to check their understanding. Ask questions such as the following:

  **Sentence 1:** *Who loves teddy bears?* (people around the world)

  **Sentence 2:** *What do children do with teddy bears?* (play with them, sleep with them)

  **Sentence 4:** *Where is the teddy bear museum?* (Korea)

- **15** Say *Now let's listen and read.* Play the first item on **TR: B32.** **Think Aloud** Say *Number 1 says* There are teddy bear museums. *I look back at the story. I look quickly for the word* museums. *I see it! Sentence 3 says* There are even teddy bear museums. *Number 1 is right. I circle* yes. Model circling the correct answer.

- Play the rest of **TR: B32** and have students complete items 2 and 3 on their own. ✓ Ask *Where is the museum?* (Korea) Say *Point to the sentence that tells where the museum is.*

## Practice 16

- 16 Direct students' attention to Activity 16 and say *Look at item 1.* Then read it aloud. Point to the photo on p. 101. Say *Point to a big bear. Now point to a small bear. How many small bears do you see? Count them. Write the number on the line.* Have students use the photo to complete items 2–4. ✓ Ask *What color are the teddy bears?* (brown, white)

## Wrap Up

- Give students two sheets of drawing paper. Ask them to draw something else they might see at the Teddy Bear Museum on one sheet and the words they would use to tell about it on the other. Once students have completed their drawings and written their words, have them describe their drawings to the class using the words they wrote.

## Recap

- Say *I learn new things when I read. After I read, I can go back and quickly look for information on the page.* Have students look at p. 100 and scan the text for one thing they learned about the museum.

## Apply 17

- 17 Have students open their books to p. 101. Point to Activity 17 and read the directions aloud. Say *Listen.* Play **TR: B33**. Practice the dialogue with a student. Model expanding the answer into a complete sentence: *My favorite toys are my teddy bear and my drum.*

- Form pairs. Say *Ask and answer. Take turns.* Walk around the room, making sure students are correctly naming toys and using the plural form *are*.

- **Expand** Write the following target vocabulary words on the board:

| | | |
|---|---|---|
| a teddy bear | a puzzle | a kite |
| a board game | a doll | a game |
| a robot | a truck | a top |
| a car | a train | a puppet |
| a ball | a bike | a drum |

- Say *Pick a favorite toy from the unit. Draw a picture of it. Write the name of the toy.* Give students enough time to draw their pictures. Then put students in small groups. Have them exchange drawings within their groups. One student in the group begins the activity by looking at the drawing she has and asking another student a question, using the following sentence frame: *Is this your (truck)?* The other student responds *Yes, it's my (truck)* or *No it isn't. It's (Maria's) (truck).*

## Extend

- Work with students to create a class toy museum. Set aside a place for the museum, such as a shelf, the top of a bookcase, or a table. Display examples of toys or have students draw pictures of toys, such as a teddy bear, robot, board game, puzzle, and doll. Form small groups and have students make museum labels for each item. Labels should include the toy's name and information about the toy, such as *His name is Teddy. He's a brown bear. He's wearing a blue hat and white T-shirt.*

## Wrap Up

- Ask students to name their favorite toys. Draw a two-column chart on the board to make a tally, such as the one shown below.

| | |
|---|---|
| ball | // |
| bike | ~~////~~ /// |
| car | ~~////~~ // |
| kite | / |
| puppet | / |
| train | ~~////~~ ~~////~~ |
| | |

- Point to the tally marks for *kite*. Count the marks aloud. Ask *How many?* (one) Repeat for other toys, counting the number of tally marks, or votes. Make sure you count the marks for the toys that received the most votes. Say *(Train) and (bike) are the favorites.* If students disagree about favorite toys, say *(Two) students like (a ball). (Seven) students like (a car). It's OK to like different things!*

## Be the Expert

### Reading Strategy

**Visualize** When students learn to read, they often begin with picture books, many of which have bright colors and vivid scenes. These images help young readers visualize the accompanying text and learn new words and syntax. Images also help students understand the story better, since they can picture what is happening.

Good readers continue to visualize, making use of vivid words that create the pictures in their minds. As you read the selection, ask students which words help them picture what the teddy bears look like. (big, small, girl, boy)

### Related Vocabulary

*information*

### Formative Assessment

Can students

- analyze photos for information?

  Have students point to and describe details in the photo on p. 100.
- read a story?

  Point to a sentence in the passage, and have students read the sentence aloud.
- talk about teddy bears?

  Have students describe the different teddy bears they see on pp. 100–101.

# Writing

**Writing** Write about a favorite toy.

**Objectives**

Students will

- view a writing model.
- draw and write about a favorite toy.
- use a period at the end of a sentence.

**Resources** Workbook p. 76; Classroom Presentation Tool: Writing

### Formative Assessment

Can students

- draw and write about a favorite toy?
  Use the following prompts to have students draw and write about a favorite toy: *What's your favorite toy? What color is it? Where do you play with it?*
- use a period at the end of a sentence?
  On the board, write *My favorite toy is a puzzle* and leave out the period. Have students tell you where to place the period.

My favorite toy is my doll.
Her name is Kate. She is small.
She is wearing a pink dress.
I play with her in my bedroom.
She sleeps with me in my bed.

**18** **Draw and write about your favorite toy.**

My favorite toy is ______________________

______________________

______________________

**19** **Work in a group.** Talk about your picture.

102

## Present

- **Brainstorm** Help students list words for toys until you have most or all of the vocabulary words on the board. Go through the list and ask *Is this your favorite toy?* If no one raises a hand, cross the toy off the list. Make sure each student identifies a favorite toy.
- Say *Let's read what someone wrote about her favorite toy.* Have students open their books to p. 102. Point to the writing model. Read each sentence aloud, modeling correct pronunciation and intonation.
- Read the passage again. Pause after each sentence to emphasize key details.
- Have students choral read with you. Then ask *What does she tell about?* (her favorite toy, what it looks like, where she plays with it, what it does)

## Write 18

- **18** Read the directions aloud. Point to the blank space and say *Draw your favorite toy here.* Point to the lines below and say *Write about your favorite toy here. Tell about your toy.* Point to the writing model and say *Read this again for ideas.*
- If necessary, ask questions to help guide students' descriptions, such as *What is its name? Is it big or small? What color is it? Where do you play with it?* Remind students to write a period at the end of sentences that tell about their toy.

NATIONAL GEOGRAPHIC

# Our World

## Share your toys.

**20 Look and read.**

Share your toys with your friends.

**21 Read and copy.**

I share my toys with my friends.

______________________________

______________________________

103

## Value

**Value** Share your toys.

**Objectives**

Students will

- read about sharing.
- read and copy a full sentence.

**Academic Language** *copy*

**Content Vocabulary** *share*

**Resources** Values Poster

## Be the Expert

### Teaching Tip

As students copy sentences, reinforce the left-to-right concept of print. Point to each word as they work, moving a finger from left to right. Alternatively, write the sentence on the board. Run your finger from left to right as students copy the sentence, or read it aloud.

## Share 19

- 19 Form small groups. Have students take turns reading their writing, showing their drawings to their group, and responding to others. Before students begin sharing, review different ways of responding to a classmate's writing. Write the following phrases on the board: *You said* ________. *I think* ________. *I like* ________. Model and say *You said your favorite toy is a robot. I think robots are fun. I like robots.*

## Value 20 21

- 20 Have students open their books to p. 103. Say *Do you like toys? Do you like to play with toys? Do you like to play with friends?* Encourage students to answer the questions aloud. Say *Let's look and read. I'll read first and then you read with me.* Read the text in white type: *Share your toys with your friends.*
- On the board, write *I don't share my toys.* Draw a sad face next to it, and read the sentence aloud in a sad voice. Act out bringing a toy close to your body in a selfish way. Say *I don't share my toys.*
- Then write *I share my toys.* Draw a happy face next to it. Read the sentence aloud in a happy voice, and act out handing a toy to a student. Say *I share my toys.*
- 21 Say *Now it's time to read and copy.* Point to Activity 21. Read the sentence aloud, and have students read it chorally. Then say *Now write the sentence.* If students need help, have them check the sentence in the book and count the words. Have them count the words in their writing.

## Project

**Objectives**

Students will

- think and write about toys.
- make a cup-and-ball toy.
- complete the Unit 6 Quiz.

**Content Vocabulary** *cup, hole, pull, string, tie, tape*

**Resources** Assessment: Unit 6 Quiz; Picture Cards 98–112; Teacher's Resource CD-ROM: Activity Worksheet 6.4

**Materials** a cup; string about 30 centimeters (10 inches) long; buttons; small ball for each student; tape; pencils with sharp points; markers or crayons

**22 Make a cup-and-ball toy.**

1 Decorate your cup. Write your name.

2 Make a hole in the bottom of the cup.

3 Pull string through the hole. Tie and tape the string.

4 Fix the string to a small ball. Play!

104

## Prepare

- Hold up Picture Cards 98–112 one by one to review the unit vocabulary. Then fan out the cards and say *These are all toys. Today we're going to make a toy.*
- Hold up each item as you say its name. Say *We'll use a cup, a piece of string, a button, tape, and a ball to make our toys. We will use (markers/crayons), too.*
- Distribute materials and have students do the first step with you. Say *Write your name on your cup.* Model. Say *Decorate your cup.* Model drawing squiggles, circles, designs, or pictures on your cup. Say *I decorate my cup.* Point to the picture on p. 105 and say *She decorated her cup. There are so many colors!*
- Say *Now use your pencils to make a hole in the bottom of your cup.* Model making the hole with a sharp pencil point.
- Say *Now put down your cups. Watch me.* Pick up the button and string, saying *button, string*. Show students how to thread the button and knot the string. Then model pulling the string through the cup until the button blocks the hole. Say *Now it's your turn. Tie the string. Pull the string through the hole.*
- Next, model tying the string around the ball, and then taping it to the ball. Say *Now I tie and tape the string to the ball.* Have students complete the step. Say *Now it's your turn. Tie and tape the string to the ball.*

**Now I can . . .**

- ○ name and describe toys.
- ○ talk about wants.
- ○ talk about possession.

105

## Be the Expert

### Teaching Tip

Acting out words is a fun way to have students remember target vocabulary. The associations that students make when they are acting or guessing often create lasting impressions. For example, a student can act out his or her favorite toy for the class: he can act out the sounds it makes, how it moves, how it feels, and what he does with it.

### Project Rubric

- ✓ Did students write their names on and decorate their cups?
- ✓ Did students poke a hole in the bottom of the cup?
- ✓ Did students pull string through the hole and tape it?
- ✓ Did students fix the string to a ball?

- Walk around the classroom as students work, and offer help as needed. When students have finished, point to a completed toy and ask *What is it?* (a cup-and-ball toy)

## Share

- Model sharing your toy by saying *This is a cup-and-ball toy,* and showing how you can use it to get the ball in the cup. Then ask the class to join you in getting the ball in the cup at the same time. Call out *1, 2, 3, Go!* and encourage everyone to flip the ball into the cup at the same moment. Then have pairs or small groups share in the same way.
- **Modify** Consider punching holes in the cups before students begin. You might also consider doing this step, or others, for students whose eye-hand coordination is less developed.

### Now I Can

Ask questions such as the following:

- *What is your favorite toy? What does it look like?*
- *Do you want a drum?*
- *Is this your teddy bear?*

**Review** For additional practice, direct students to Activity Worksheet 6.4.

### Unit Assessment

Give the Unit 6 Quiz. Hand out the quiz and go over the instructions with students. The quiz should take 15–20 minutes.

# Video

**Vocabulary 1a** *a ball, a car, a game, a truck, a top*

**Vocabulary 1b** *a drum, a puppet, a train, a bike, a kite*

**Vocabulary 2** *a board game, a puzzle, a doll, a teddy bear, a robot*

**Grammar 1** use simple present of *want* (first, second, and third person singular)

**Grammar 2** ask and answer questions with *this* and *these*

**Song** *Let's Play!*

**Viewing** playing with toys

**Story Time** *The Toys*

**Resources** Student Book pp. 90–99; Teacher's Resource CD-ROM: Graphic Organizers (Word web)

## Before You Watch

- Play Scene 1: Introduction. Say *This is a video about toys. Let's say all the words we know about toys.* Write all suggestions from students on the board.

## While You Watch

- Hand out blank word webs and have students write *Toys* in the center circle. As they watch the video, have them use the web to write the names of toys they hear or see.
- Pause the video as necessary to allow students to fill in their webs.

## After You Watch

- Form pairs. Have partners read their webs to each other and check for any missing words. Then play parts of the video again with the sound off. Have students use their webs to tell what is happening in the video.

## Zoom In

### Vocabulary

- Pause after each word in Scenes 2–4. Have students say the target word for each image and use the word in a sentence.

### Grammar

- While viewing Scene 7: Grammar 2, pause at various frames and ask *Is this a (ball)? Are these (robots)?* Have students respond with *No, it isn't. It's a* ________. or *No, they aren't. They're* ________.

### Song

- Use Scene 9 to review words that name toys and the phrases *Do you want* and *Yes, I do.* Have students form groups. Assign a verse to each group. Play *Let's Play!* again. Have each group sing its assigned verse.

### Viewing

- Play the video without audio and freeze on several frames. Ask *What toys are children playing with?* Have students describe what else is happening in the video. (two girls are on bikes, boys are playing drums)

### Story Time

- View Scene 11. Pause the video and ask sequence questions such as *What happens first?* (The girl comes home.) Pause again and ask *Who helps Doll put away the toys?* (Puppet) Ask *Where is Doll at the end?* (sleeping on the floor)
- On a second viewing, emphasize visual details in *The Toys*. Pause after the first frame and ask *Where is the girl?* Students can point to the picture of the girl's legs in the window. Focus on details by pausing after the third frame. Ask *How are Puppet and Doll alike?* (They both act like people. They stand up. They point. They tell toys where to go.) After the last frame, call attention to one more detail by asking *What's Puppet doing?* (He's on the shelf saying "shhh!")

# Unit 6 Reader

**Text Type** fantasy

**Reading Strategy** Summarize

**Vocabulary** *a car, a robot, a teddy bear, a ball, a puppet, a doll*

**Grammar** use simple present of *want* (first, second, and third person singular); ask and answer questions with *this* and *these*

**Academic Language** *main idea, summarize*

**Resources** Picture Cards 98–112; Classroom Presentation Tool: Story Time; Video: Sc. 11—Story Time; Teacher's Resource CD-ROM: Graphic Organizers (Two-column chart)

## *The Toys*

When a little girl leaves her room, what happens to her toys? Does her puppet stay on the shelf? Does her doll sit quietly on her bed? Or does something more interesting happen?

## Before You Read

- **Build background** Say *What is a fantasy? It's a story that isn't true. Some fantasies even have toys that talk!*
- **Introduce the strategy** Say *This story is about a doll. There are other toys, too. The story tells about where the other toys go.* Say *We're going to read the story. Then we're going to say what happened in the story.*
- **Predict** Say *A girl leaves her house. Her toys stay home. They do something amazing! What do you think they do?* Prompt as needed, asking *Do the toys stay on the shelf? Do they go to the closet? Do they play?* Record some predictions. Then ask *What do you think happens when the girl comes home?* Record more predictions. Then say *Let's read to find out.*

## While You Read

- Read the book aloud to students. Stop every few pages to ask questions that require students to summarize.
  - pp. 2–3: *Why do the toys say "Oh no?"* (They're out in the room, and the girl is home.)
  - pp. 4–7: *What do the toys do?* (They hide.)
  - pp. 10–11: *What does the girl see?* (a clean room)

## After You Read

- Draw a two-column chart with the headings **Toy** and **Where the Toy Goes.** Have students list each toy in the first column (car, robots, teddy bear, and so on) and list where the toys go in the second column (under the table, in the boxes, onto the dresser, and so on).
- Have students sum up the story. Ask *What does Doll do in this story?* (Doll cleans up the room. Doll makes the room neat. Doll puts away the toys.)

## Be the Expert

### Reading Strategy

**Summarize** Summarizing means retelling the most important parts of a story. Summarizing helps students understand and remember what they read. To summarize fiction, have students tell what happens at the beginning, middle, and end of a story. Students should use their own words to retell the story.

### Text Background

Fantasies are stories that are distinguished by personified (or "talking") toys, animals, or objects. Many fantasies have perfectly realistic settings, although fantastic things happen in them. Although themes, points of view, and styles can all vary in fantasies, these stories often have a humorous tone or include humorous events.

## Student Book

**TR: B17** **1** **Listen and say.**

| | |
|---|---|
| a train | I have a train. |
| a drum | I have a drum. |
| a bike | I have a bike. |
| a ball | I have a ball. |
| a truck | I have a truck. |
| a car | I have a car. |
| a top | I have a top. |
| a puppet | I have a puppet. |
| a kite | I have a kite. |
| a game | I have a game. |

**TR: B18** **2** **Listen. Point and say.**

a top, a puppet, a bike, a truck, a car, a kite, a ball, a drum, a game, a train

**TR: B19** **3** **Point. Ask and answer.**

What is it? It's a ball.

**TR: B20** **4** **Listen. Read and sing.**

Note: Lyrics for the song *Let's Play!* are on pp. 190–191.

**TR: B21** **Grammar**

Note: Grammar 1, 1st chart, is on p. 192.

**TR: B22** **6** **Listen and find. Draw a line.**

1. Do you want a kite?
   No, I don't.
   Do you want a top?
   Yes, I do.
2. Do you want a car?
   No, I don't.
   Do you want a truck?
   Yes, I do.
3. Do you want a drum?
   No, I don't.
   Do you want a puppet?
   Yes, I do.
4. Do you want a train?
   No, I don't.
   Do you want a ball?
   Yes, I do.
   Thank you, Grandma!

**TR: B23** **Grammar**

Note: Grammar 1, 2nd chart, is on p. 193.

**TR: B24** **7** **Listen and circle.**

1. Look, Mark, a train!
   No thanks. I want a drum.
   Does he want a train?
2. Look, Mary. This puppet is cute.
   Yes it is. I want the puppet!
   Does she want a puppet?
3. Look at this kite, Ken.
   A kite? No, I want a game.
   Does he want a game?
4. Look, Sonia. A top.
   No, I don't want a top. I want a ball.
   Does she want a top?

**TR: B25** **8** **Listen and say.**

| | |
|---|---|
| a robot | I have a robot. |
| a teddy bear | I have a teddy bear. |
| a board game | I have a board game. |
| a puzzle | I have a puzzle. |
| a doll | I have a doll. |

**TR: B26** **10** **Look. Listen and read. Circle *yes* or *no*.**

1. Do you want a robot? No, I have a robot.
2. Do you want a puzzle? Yes, I do. Thanks!

**TR: B27** **11** **Work with a partner. Listen. Say and stick.**

Number one. I have a board game.
I don't. I have a robot. two.

**TR: B28** **Grammar**

Note: Grammar 2 is on p. 198.

**TR: B29** **12** **Look. Listen and read. Check yes or no.**

1. Anna, is this your puzzle? No, it isn't. It's Lucy's puzzle.
2. Ken, are these your robots? Yes, they are. They're my robots.

**TR: B30** **13** **Play a game. Cut out the cards on page 169. Ask and answer. Play with a partner.**

Are these your tops?
No, they aren't. They're Tina's tops.

**TR: B31** **14** **Listen and read.**

Note: Reading *We Love Teddy Bears!* is on p. 200.

**TR: B32** **15** **Listen and read. Look. Circle yes or no.**

People around the world love teddy bears. Children play with them and sleep with them. There are even teddy bear museums! This popular museum is in Korea. It has big bears and small bears, girl bears and boy bears. There are teddy bears for everyone!

1. There are teddy bear museums.
2. This museum is in China.
3. It has big bears and small bears.

**TR: B33** **17** **Work with a partner. What are your favorite toys? Ask and answer.**

What are your favorite toys?
My teddy bear and my drum.

## Workbook

**TR: 46** (3) **Listen to the song. Check.**

Note: Lyrics for the song *Let's Play!* are on pp. 190–191.

**TR: 47** (4) **Listen. Write.**

1. Do you want to bang on a drum? No, I don't.
2. Do you want to ride a bike? No, I don't.
3. Do you want to fly a kite? Yes, I do.
   I want to fly my kite with you!
4. Do you want to dress my doll? No, I don't.
5. Do you want to kick a ball? No, I don't.
6. Do you want to play with trains? Yes, I do.
   I want to play with you! Choo choo choo!

**TR: 48** (5) **Listen and read. Circle.**

1. Do you want a truck? No, I don't.
2. Do you want a game? No, I don't.
3. Does she want a puppet? Yes, she does.
4. Does he want a kite? No, he doesn't.
5. Do you want a train? Yes, I do.
6. Does she want a ball? No, she doesn't.

**TR: 49** (6) **Listen and read. Draw a line.**

1. Do you want a car? Yes, I do. I want a car.
2. Does she want a drum? Yes, she does. She wants a drum.
3. Does he want a ball? No, he doesn't. He wants a kite.
4. Do you want a train? No, I don't. I want a bike.

**TR: 50** (7) **Listen. Write.**

1. Do you want a ball? No, I don't.
2. Does she want a truck? No, she doesn't.
3. Does she want a train? Yes, she does.
4. Do you want a bike? Yes, I do.

**TR: 51** (12) **Listen and write.**

1. Is this your robot? Yes, it is.
2. Are these your teddy bears? No, they aren't.
3. Are these your puzzles? No, they aren't.
4. Is this your board game? No, it isn't.
5. Are these your robots? Yes, they are.
6. Is this Mia's puppet? No, it isn't.
7. Is this Anya's drum? Yes, it is.
8. Are these Ivan's puzzles? Yes, they are.

**TR: 52** (15) **Listen and read.**

Note: Reading *We Love Kites* is on p. 321.

**TR: 53** (21) **Listen and circle.**

1. Does he want a top? Yes, he does.
2. Does she want a drum? No, she doesn't.
3. Is this your robot? No, it isn't.
4. Are these your cars? No, they aren't. They're Mateo's cars.
5. Do you want a puppet? No, I don't. I want a car.
6. Do you want a truck? Yes, I do.

# Answer Key

## Student Book

**Unit Opener** SB p. 90

blue, red, yellow

(6) SB p. 96

line from child 1 to top, line from child 2 to truck
line from child 3 to puppet, line from child 4 to ball

(7) SB p. 97

1. No, he doesn't. He wants a drum.
2. Yes, she does. She wants a puppet.
3. Yes, he does. He wants a game.
4. No, she doesn't. She wants a ball.

(10) SB p. 98

1. no, 2. yes

(12) SB p. 99

1. no, 2. yes

(15) SB p. 101

1. yes, 2. no, 3. yes

## Workbook

Go to pp. 319–322 for the Workbook Answer Key for this unit.

**Vocabulary** U4–U6

**Grammar** U4–U6

**Content Vocabulary** *heads, tails*

**Resources** Workbook pp. 78–79

**Materials** coins, playing pieces (buttons, tokens, or other small, flat objects)

- **Play the game** Say *Let's play a game!* Have students open their books to pp. 106–107. Point to the photos. Say *Look at all the photos.* Give students a few moments to look at the pages. Ask *Is there a lamp?* (Yes, there is.) Ask *Where's the lamp?* Say *Point to it.* Have students point to the photo of the lamp on p. 107. Then ask *Is there a train?* (No, there isn't.)
- Hold up the Student Book so the class can see it. Point to the photo of the hat on p. 107. Ask *What's that?* (That's a pink hat.) Then point to the photo of the boy wearing a blue shirt on p. 106. Ask *What is he wearing?* (He's wearing a blue shirt.)
- Show students a coin. Point to the "heads" side and say *This is heads.* Show the coin to students. Point to the "tails" side and say *This is tails.*
- Model playing the game. Choose a student to play with you. Put a playing piece on *Start* and toss the coin. Say *This is tails. I move two spaces.* Move two spaces and count aloud. Point to the photo on the space. Say *I ask my partner a question about the picture.* Say *I ask "What is he wearing?" My partner answers.* (He's wearing a jacket.)
- Model taking turns. Have the student playing with you toss the coin. Say *That's (heads). Move (one space).* Prompt the student to ask *What's that?* Say *(That's a doll.)*
- Point to the model dialogue at the bottom of p. 107. Have students read it aloud together. Then pair students. Hand out a coin and a playing piece to each pair. Say *Now you play the game! Look. Ask questions and answer. Take turns.* Allow time for pairs to play the game.

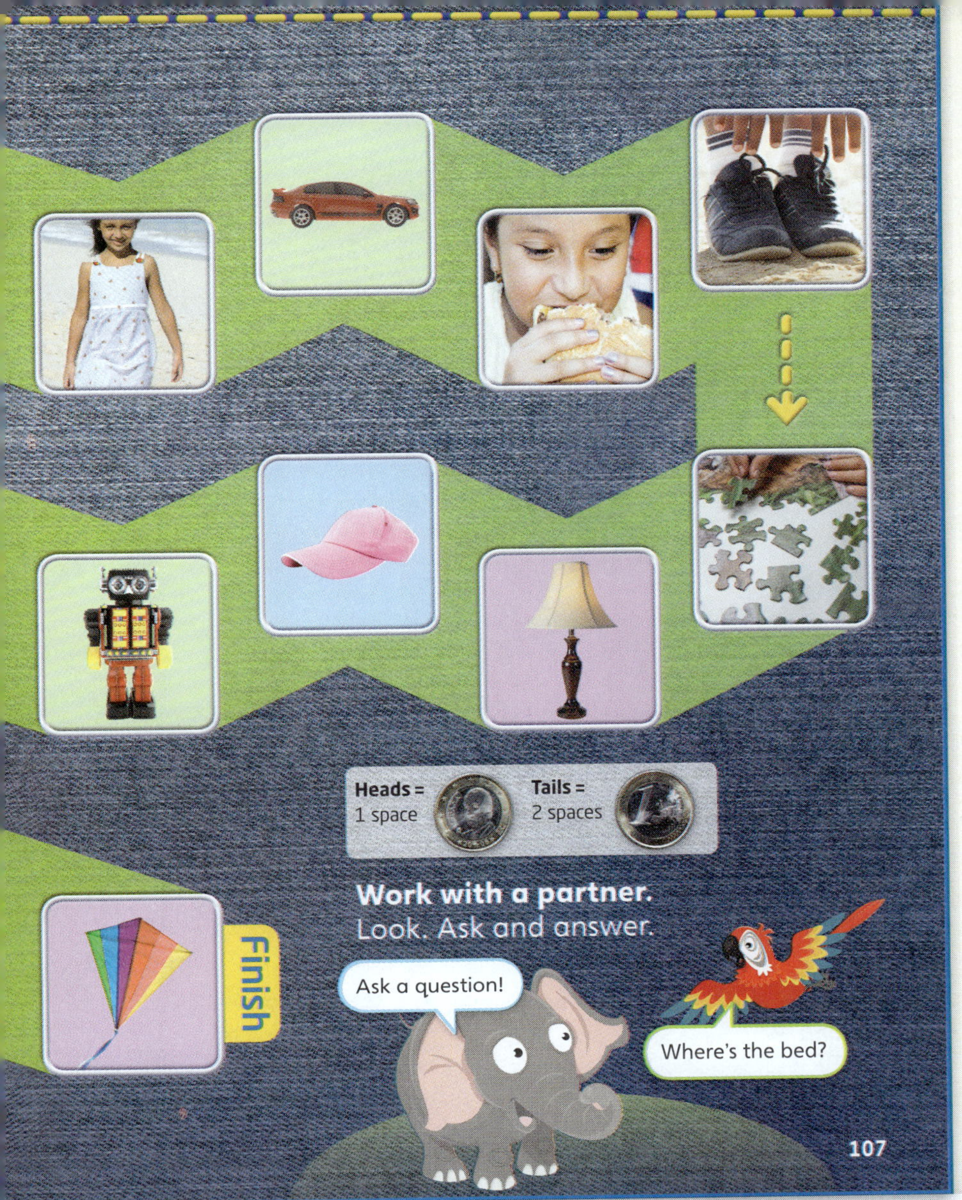


## Be the Expert

### Teaching Tip

All students, including students learning English, benefit from regular encouragement during class. As students work in groups, walk around the room and visit each pair or group. Observe students as they perform activities and compliment them on any responses that are especially strong. Students who are confident and motivated are likely to try harder and better remember what they learn.

- **Sentence frames** If students need help thinking of questions and answers, write examples on the board:

| | |
|---|---|
| Is there a ______? | What are those? |
| Yes, there is. | Those are ______. |
| No, there isn't. | Do you want ______? |
| What is she wearing? | Yes, I do. |
| She's wearing ______. | No, I don't. |
| What's that? | Is this ______? |
| That's a ______. | Are these ______? |

- **Modify** If less class time is available, put students into small groups instead of pairs. For the coin toss, have heads count for two spaces and tails count for three spaces.
- Have students who need more support ask and answer *Yes/No* questions, such as *Is there a bed in the bedroom? Is that a (car)? Are those (socks)?*

# In This Unit

**Theme** This unit is about parts of the body and physical activities.

**Content Objectives**

Students will

- identify and describe parts of the body.
- identify physical activities.

**Language Objectives**

Students will

- name parts of the body.
- talk about parts of the body.
- talk about actions.

**Vocabulary**

**Vocabulary 1** *an arm, an ear, an eye, feet, a foot, hair, a hand, a head, a leg, a mouth, a neck, a nose*

**Vocabulary 2** *jump, long hair, run, strong arms, walk*

**Grammar**

**Grammar 1** use singular possessive adjectives (*my, your, his, her*)

**Grammar 2** use *can* to talk about ability

**Pacing Guides** LIU7

**Writing** Write about a costume.

**Value** Be clean.

**Project** Make a robot.

## Unit Opener

**Objectives**

Students will

- look at a photo for information.
- complete a sentence.

**Resources** Video: Sc. 1—Introduction; Classroom Presentation Tool: Unit Opener; Teacher's Resource CD-ROM: Home-School Connection Letter; Unit Opener Poster; World Map Poster

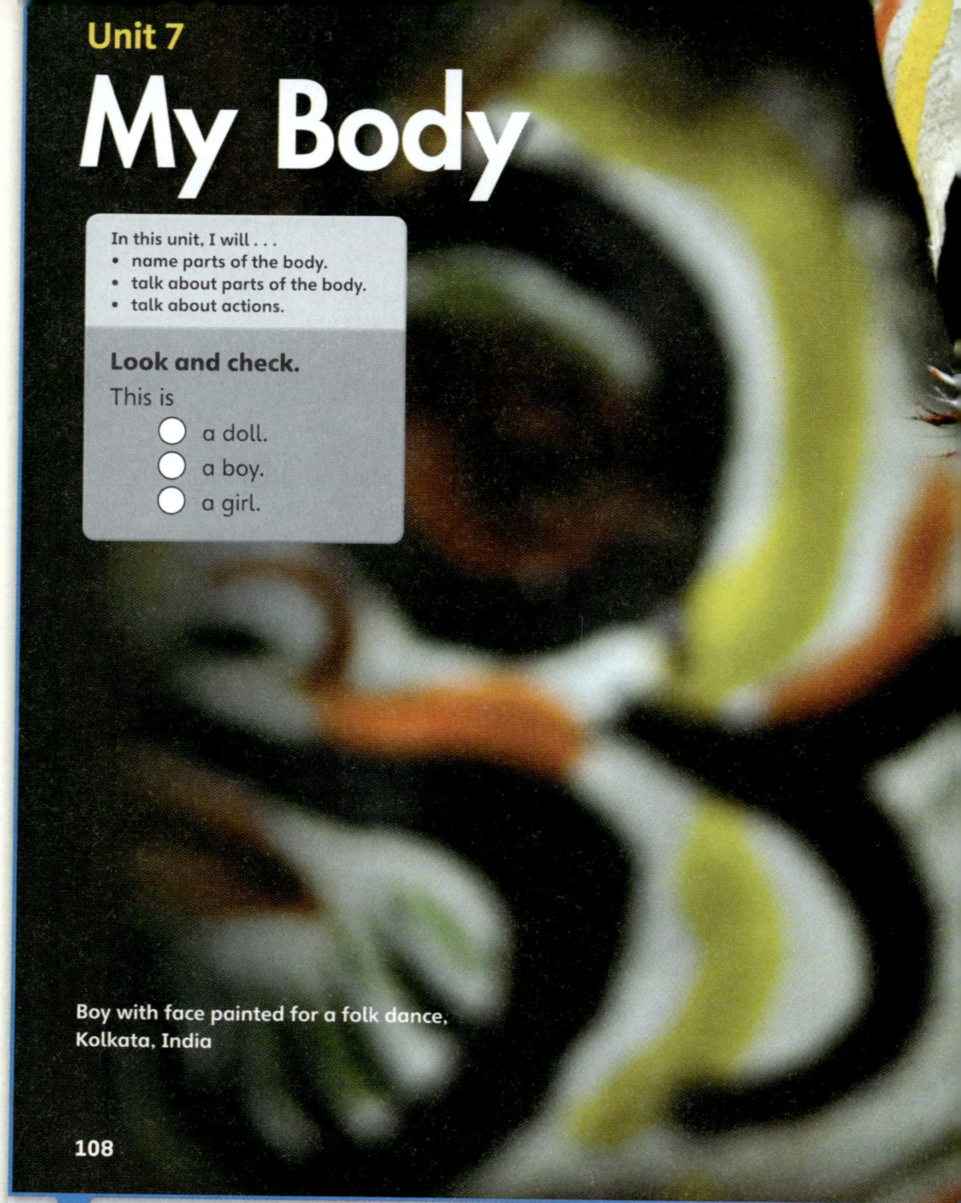

Unit 7

# My Body

In this unit, I will . . .

- name parts of the body.
- talk about parts of the body.
- talk about actions.

**Look and check.**

This is

- ◯ a doll.
- ◯ a boy.
- ◯ a girl.

Boy with face painted for a folk dance, Kolkata, India

108

## Introduce

- Have students open their books to pp. 108–109 and look at the photo. Ask questions such as the following:

  *What do you see?* (colors, shapes, a boy/a person)
  *What colors do you see?* (red, orange, white, yellow, black)
  *What shapes do you see?* (circles, lines)

- **Set the stage** Use your finger to trace the area around both your eyes. Ask *What color is here on the boy?* (red, white) Point to your nose and ask *What colors are here?* (red, white) Trace the area above your upper lip and ask *What color is here?* (black) Point to your chin and ask *What color is here?* (black) Point to your mouth and ask *What color is here?* (red, black) As you trace or point to each feature on your own face, have students copy your movements.

## Be the Expert

### About the Photo

This photo shows a boy in Kolkata, India. The boy's face is painted for a folk dance. Face and body painting are ancient arts found across cultures. Depending on the culture, face and body paint can represent a special rite, a ceremony, or belonging to a social group.

Some people also do it for fun. In many parts of the world, face painting is still very popular in circuses, at parties and fairs, and at sports events.

### Our World in Context

Kolkata, one of India's largest cities, has a diverse population made up of many cultures. For arts, it may be the most important of all of India's cities. It is a center of classical music and dance, Bengali drama, and many folk-dancing traditions.

- Guide students through the activity on p. 108. Read aloud the sentence stem and each answer choice one at a time. For each choice, ask students to raise their hands if they think the answer is true. Then confirm the correct answer.
- **Explain** Read the caption on p. 108 aloud and point to India on the World Map Poster. Explain *This boy lives in India. He's wearing paint for a special dance. Do you go to dances or do other special things? Do you see people wearing paint? What other things do you see?* Discuss students' answers.
- Gesture to your body, pointing from your head to your feet. Say *This is my body. In this unit, we're going to learn words for parts of the body.*

## Vocabulary 1

**Objective**

Students will

- name parts of the body.

**Vocabulary** *feet, hair, an eye, a leg, an arm, a mouth, a hand, a foot, a head, a nose, an ear, a neck*

**Content Vocabulary** *left, right*

**Resources** Workbook pp. 80–81; Audio CD TR: B34–36; Video: Sc. 2—Vocabulary 1a; Sc. 3—Vocabulary 1b; Classroom Presentation Tool: Vocabulary 1; Teacher's Resource CD-ROM: Graphic Organizers (Two-column chart, Word web), Activity Worksheet 7.1; Picture Cards 85–86, 88, 90, 92, 113–124; Sound Card 9

**Materials** picture books; children's dictionary (*optional*)

1 **Listen and say.** TR: B34

2 **Listen.** Point and say. TR: B35

110

## Warm Up

- **Preteach** Clap as you chant *We clap with our hands!* Have students repeat several times. Then hold up your right hand and say *This is my hand.*

- On the board, draw a large outline of a hand. Write *hand* in the middle. Say *We do many things with hands.* Form groups of four. Ask students to brainstorm things people do with their hands, such as clap, write, and color. Have students come to the board and add words to the hand outline. As students add words, ask them to complete the sentence frame *We* ________ *with hands.*

## Present

- Say *Open your books to pages 110 and 111.* Point to the boy's hand on the ground. Say *Look at his hand! He's using his hand to hold his body up!* When you say *body*, outline the boy's entire body. Show the pictures on pp. 110–111 and say *These pictures show*

*parts of the body.* Point to the boy's head. Say *a head.* Then point to your own head. Say *This is my head. Now point to your head.* Repeat with each body part shown on p. 110.

- Point to the circled picture on p. 111. Say *This picture shows parts of the face.* Point to and say each word in the circled picture as you point to the same part of your face. Say *This is my nose. Now point to your nose.* Repeat with each word shown in the circled picture on p. 111.
- Point to the picture of the jumping boy on p. 111. Say *Look! He has brown hair.* Point to your hair. Say *I have (brown) hair. Point to your hair. What color is it?* Say *His hand is at the end of his arm.* Say *arm* as you do a sweeping motion down toward your hand. Say *Point to your arm. Now point to your hand.* Say *His feet are at the ends of his legs.* Say *legs* as you do a sweeping motion down toward your feet. *Point to your legs. Now point to your feet.*

## Be the Expert

### Vocabulary Strategy

**Using a Dictionary** Learning how to use a dictionary is an important lesson for any language learner. Explain to students that words in a dictionary are listed in alphabetical, or ABC, order.

Guide words at the top left and top right corners show the first and last words on each page. Readers can find definitions for words that come between those words in alphabetical order.

Give students practice finding words in a dictionary. Open a dictionary and read the guide words at the top. Then ask students if a certain word could be found on that page.

### Related Vocabulary

*body, face*

## Practice 1 2

- 1 Have students open their books to p. 110. Say *It's time to listen and say. Look at the picture on this page.* Play **TR: B34**. Pause after the first item and have students repeat. Say *I have a right foot* and pick up and shake your right foot. Have all students repeat the sentence and pick up and shake their right feet. Repeat with *left foot*. Then continue **TR: B34** pausing after *I have a head*.

- Point to the picture of the boy jumping on p. 111. Continue **TR: B34**. Point to each body part as it's named. Pause after *I have two feet*.

- Next, point to the picture of the boy in the circle. As you play the rest of **TR: B34**, walk around the room to make sure that students are pronouncing the words correctly. Listen for *an* with *ear* and *eye*. Replay **TR: B34** and have students say each term after they hear it.

- 2 Say *Now listen. Then point and say. Point to pictures on both pages.* Put students in pairs and have them point to the correct body parts in the pictures as you play **TR: B35**. Walk around the room, offering help as needed. Regroup students as a class. Replay **TR: B35** and have students point to and say each term.

- **Explain** Hold up two fingers. Say *We have two feet.* Hold up one finger and say *We have one head.* Make a two-column chart on the board with the headings **We have 1** and **We have 2**. Model the first example in each column with *head* and *feet*. Then have students tell you how to complete the chart.
✓ Point to a word in the chart. Have a student say the word and point to the appropriate place on his or her body, or to one of the pictures in the book.

| We have 1 | We have 2 |
|---|---|
| head | feet |
| neck | arms |
| | |

- If students ask where hair should appear in this chart, explain that we have many strands of hair—so many that we can't count them. Demonstrate by pointing to your own hair or the hair of a student. Add the word to a third column, or to the side of the chart.

## Wrap Up

- Put Picture Cards 113–124 face down on a desk. Have a student come to the front of the class. Say *Let's play a game. Pick a card. Don't show it! Then point to the part on your body. Class, you guess the word.* Model with Picture Card 120 (*a head*). Then have students take turns choosing a card until all students have a turn.

## Recap

- On the board, draw a word web. Include the term **My Body** in the center circle. Draw a secondary circle and ask *What word can I write here?* Continue adding circles and words until students have said all or most of the vocabulary words.

## Apply 3

- 3 Have students open their books to p. 111. Point to the dialogue at the bottom of the page and say *Look at Mia the Monkey and Freddy the Frog! Let's listen to what they're saying.* Read the question and answer aloud, or play **TR: B36**. Hold up your hands. Ask students the question and have them answer.

- Write the following on the board:

> What are these? They're ________.
>
> What is this? It's ________.

- Model asking and answering the question about other body parts, such as your eyes and neck.
- Form pairs. Have students use the questions and sentence frames on the board to ask and answer questions. Say *Point to a part of your body and ask "What are these?" or "What is this?"* Point to the sentence frames and say *Your partner answers with "They're" or "It's."* ✓ Point to your ear and ask *What's this?* If students have difficulty, use Picture Cards 113–124 to review the target words.
- **Expand** Review the names of each clothing item as you hand out Picture Cards 85–86, 88, 90, and 92. Say *Let's play a game. I'll say and show a part of the body. You hold up the correct clothes.* Hold up Picture Cards 116 and 119–121 for *feet, hand, head,* and *leg.* As students hold up the matching card, say *Yes, we wear (gloves) on our (hands).*

## Extend

- Use the classic children's dance "The Hokey Pokey" to give students practice following directions and understanding the parts of the body. First, have students form a circle. Then show them how to tell left from right. Hold your arms straight out in front of you, with your palms facing away from you and the thumbs of each hand at right angles to the rest of your fingers. Have students copy you. Say *Look at your hands. Look for the letter L. That letter shows the left side of your body. Your right side is the other side of your body.*
- Call as you act out the lyrics *Put your left foot in. Put your left foot out. Put your left foot in. And shake it all about!* Vary the instructions to include *left arm, right foot,* and so on.

## Wrap Up

- On the board, draw an outline of a face, including eyes, nose, ears, and mouth. Form pairs. Have students copy the outline and label the face parts. Repeat with an outline of a body. Pairs can show and tell about their drawings with another pair.

## Be the Expert

### Sounds of English

**Single sounds: /h/**

The /h/ sound is uncommon in many languages, but is used in many common English words (*h*ave, *h*ow, *h*ere). Because the sound is very different from the other sounds of English, it may be difficult for your students. To pronounce /h/, place your tongue at the bottom of your mouth, with the tip behind your bottom teeth, and breathe out quickly.

Use Sound Card 9 (hippo).

Example words: hat, hair, hand, head

### Teaching Tip

There may be cultural or sensitivity issues that make students uncomfortable pointing to their bodies or other people's bodies. Carefully assess students' comfort levels before initiating an activity. Appropriate alternatives include pointing to photos or pictures in a book, including favorite picture books, with large pictures of the characters. A character's face and body parts may be used instead.

### Formative Assessment

Can students

- name parts of the body?

  Hold up Picture Cards 113–124 and have students name them. Then say the words and ask students to point to the correct picture.

**Review** For additional practice, direct students to Activity Worksheet 7.1.

## Song

**Vocabulary in the song**

**Vocabulary 1** *a leg, feet, a mouth, a hand*

**Vocabulary 2** *walk, jump*

**Grammar in the song**

**Grammar 1** use singular possessive adjectives (*my, your, his, her*)

**Grammar 2** use *can* to talk about ability

**Resources** Audio CD TR: B37; Video: Sc. 9—Song; Workbook p. 82; Classroom Presentation Tool: Song; Picture Cards 116, 119, 121, 122

**Materials** note cards

4 **Listen.** Read and sing. TR: B37

# My Body

***My body, my body!***
***It's fun to move my body!***
***My body, my body!***
***Can you dance with me?***

*Legs, legs. Move your legs.*
*Legs, legs. Move your legs.*
*Legs, legs. Move your legs.*
*Can you walk with me?*

*Feet, feet. Move your feet.*
*Feet, feet. Move your feet.*
*Feet, feet. Move your feet.*
*Can you jump with me?*

**CHORUS**

112

## Use the Song 4 5

- **Build background** Perform a few dance steps or just a simple rhythmic stepping from side to side with a light swinging arm motion. Ask *Can you dance with me?* Give the motion to rise and see if students can follow along for a few steps.
- Move your arms while you dance. Say *I move my arms. Do you?* Have students move their arms. Then move your legs while you dance. *I move my legs. Do you?* Have students move their legs. Move your feet while you dance. *I move my feet. Do you?* Have students move their feet. Then give the signal to sit down. Say *I move my body. You move your body, too. We dance.*
- 4 **Act it out** Play **TR: B37** and act out each verse, such as moving your legs and pretending to walk for the first verse. Play the song again and have students act out the song with you. Finally, play the song a third time, and have students act out the moves and sing along.
- 5 Put students in four groups and give each group one of the following Picture Cards: 116 (feet), 119 (a hand), 121 (a leg), and 122 (a mouth). Play **TR: B37** and have the group with the appropriate card hold it up when they hear the verse with their word.
- Play **TR: B37** again and have group members sing and act out their verses. The whole class should sing and act out the chorus and final verse.

*Mouth, mouth. Move your mouth.*
*Mouth, mouth. Move your mouth.*
*Mouth, mouth. Move your mouth.*
*Can you sing with me?*

*Hands, hands. Move your hands.*
*Hands, hands. Move your hands.*
*Hands, hands. Move your hands.*
*Can you clap with me?*

**CHORUS**

*My body, my body!*
*I love to move my body!*
*My body, my body!*
*Can you dance with me?*

**5** **Sing again.**
Hold up pictures.

113

## Be the Expert

### Teaching Tip

**Grouping** Some students may be able to sing or read the song after listening to it the first time. Be sure they comprehend what they are saying. If they do, you may want to pair them with students who are struggling. Students with different strengths and abilities help one another learn.

## Use It Again

- **Vocabulary 1** Play **TR: B37** and, as each body part is mentioned in the song, have students point to it on their bodies. Then point to your legs and say *I move my legs!* Ask students to do the same. Continue in the same manner, having students act out an action and complete the sentence frame. *I move my* ______ for the vocabulary words *feet*, *mouth*, and *hand*.
- **Vocabulary 2** Give each student two note cards. Have students write *walk* on one and *jump* on the other and draw a picture for each. Say *Listen to the song. When you hear one of your words, hold up your card.* Play **TR: B37**. Make sure students hold up their cards so you can see them.
- **Grammar 1** Put students in pairs. Play the song and have students point to themselves each time they hear the word *my* and point to their partners each time they hear the word *your*.
- Sing the song with students. Pause for each instance of *my* or *your*, and have students sing the word.
- **Grammar 2** Draw students' attention to the question at the end of each verse: *Can you (walk, jump, sing, clap, dance) with me?* Say *Everybody stand up.* Have students sing or say each question, performing each action as they do so.

# Grammar 1

**Objective**

Students will

- use *my, your, his,* and *her* to describe themselves and others.

**Grammar 1** use singular possessive adjectives (*my, your, his, her*)

**Resources** Workbook pp. 83–84; Audio CD TR: B38–41; Video: Sc. 6—Grammar 1; Classroom Presentation Tool: Grammar 1

**Materials** several colors of chalk or markers; drawing paper; colored pencils or crayons

**GRAMMAR** TR: B38

**My** hair is brown. **My** eyes are brown.
**Your** hair is brown. **Your** eyes are brown.

**6 Look and listen.** Write the number in the box. TR: B39

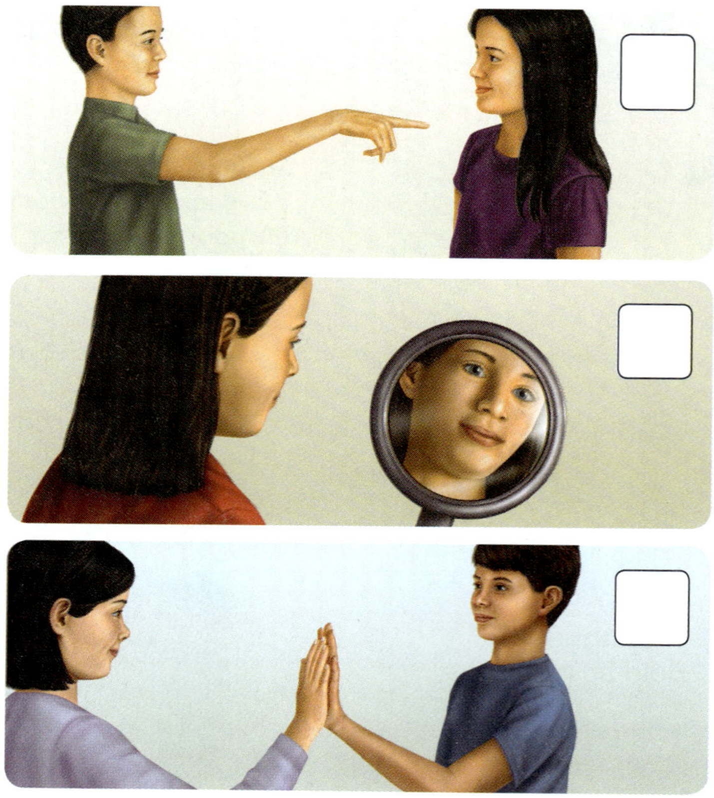

114

## Warm Up

- **Set the stage** Point to your eyes and say *I have (blue) eyes.* Ask the class *What color eyes do I have?* (blue) Point to your hair and say *I have (black) hair.* Then ask *What color hair do I have?* (black)
- Point to a female student and ask *(Miji), what color hair do you have?* Say to the student *You have (brown) hair.* Then say to the class *(Miji) has (brown) hair. She has (brown) hair.* Ask the class *What color hair does (Miji) have?* (brown) Repeat the process with a male student.
- Say *Now we're going to learn more ways to talk about how you and other people look.*

**GRAMMAR** TR: B40

**His** hair is brown. **His** eyes are brown.
**Her** hair is brown. **Her** eyes are brown.

**7** **Look and listen.** Draw a line. TR: B41

1. Her ears are small.
2. His feet are big.

115

## Be the Expert

### Our World in Context

The range of natural hair colors includes shades of blonde, red, brown, and black. Hair color is determined by the amounts of two natural pigments (colors) in the body: dark brown and reddish. The more dark brown pigment that exists, the darker a person's hair will be.

The range of natural eye colors includes blue, gray, green, hazel, and brown. The amount of natural pigments in the body determines eye color.

### Grammar in Depth

Possessive adjectives include *my, your, her, his, our, their,* and *its*. They need to be followed by a noun. For example, *My shirt is blue.* Possessive pronouns include *mine, yours, hers, his, ours,* and *theirs*. They can stand alone. For example, *The shirt is mine.*

Students may confuse the possessive adjective *its* with *it's*. The literal meaning of *its* is "belonging to it." *It's* is a contraction of the words *it is*. Remind students that when they are talking about possession, they should use *its*—not *it's*.

# Present

- Have students open their books to p. 114. Point to the yellow grammar box at the top. Read the text. Play **TR: B38** twice. During the second playing, ask students to read along.
- **Model** Point to your own hair and say *My hair is (black).* Point to a student and say *Your hair is (brown).* Point to your own eyes and say *My eyes are (blue).* Point to a student and say *Your eyes are (brown).*
- Draw the following chart on the board:

| I | you | a girl | a boy |
|---|---|---|---|
| my | your | her | his |

- **Explain** Say *When I talk about me, I use* my. *When I talk about you, I use* your. *When I talk about a girl, I use* her. *When I talk about a boy, I use* his.
- Form pairs. Have partners choose to be Student 1 or Student 2. Say *Student 1, talk to your partner. Tell about your hair. Tell about your partner's hair.* (My hair is black. Your hair is brown.) *Student 2, tell about your eyes. Think of someone else. Tell about his or her eyes.* ✓ Point to a boy's desk. Ask *Is this his desk or her desk?* Point to a girl's pencil. Ask *Is that her pencil or his pencil?*

## Practice 6 7

- 6 Have students open their books to p. 114. Read the directions aloud. Hold up your book and point to the three boxes. Play only the first item on **TR: B39**. Say *I listen to number one. I look for the picture of someone with blue eyes. Here it is.* Point to the second picture. *It's the girl with the mirror. I write number one in that box.* Write *1* in the box and show your answer to students. Say *You do the rest.* Play the other two items on **TR: B39**. When students are finished, review what each picture shows.
- Point to the yellow grammar box at the top of p. 115. Read the sentences aloud or play **TR: B40**. Say *We talk about a girl. We say* her *eyes and* her *hair.* Her *and* girl *both have the -er sound. We talk about a boy. We say* his *eyes and* his *hair.*
- 7 Say *Now look, listen, and draw a line.* Play **TR: B41**. Pause after the first item. Point to item 1 in the book and say *Her ears are small. Who is this about? Draw a line from the sentence to the picture.* Play the rest of **TR: B41** and repeat with the second item.
- Review the items by having a student read each sentence aloud and having others show where to draw the lines.

## Wrap Up

- Draw outline figures of a boy and girl on the board. Give them both hair but different size feet and hands. Use chalk or markers to draw different colored pants and shirts. Say and write the following sentence frames and have students work in pairs to complete them: *Her ______ are ______. Her ______ is ______. His ______ are ______. His ______ is ______.*
- When pairs finish, call on students to read their sentences. Write all of the possible sentences on the board. Label the girl *her* and the boy *his*. Then draw lines to connect each sentence with one of the drawings. Write labels around the pictures, such as *her shirt, her feet, his pants,* and *his hair.*

## Recap

- List these vocabulary words on the board: *arm, ear, eye, feet, foot, hair, hand, head, leg, mouth, neck, nose.* Point to the word *head*. Ask *How do we talk about a girl's head?* (her head) Then point to the word *hand*. Ask *How do we talk about a boy's hand?* (his hand) Continue alternating between a boy and a girl until you have asked about all of the vocabulary words.

## Apply

- Write *his* and *her* on the board. Hand out drawing paper and colored pencils or crayons to each student. Say *Draw a picture of a boy or a girl. Color your picture. Then write about your picture.* Model the activity. Draw a picture of a boy with black hair, brown eyes, a white shirt, and blue pants. Say *This is my brother.* Write sentences on the board, such as *His hair is black. His shirt is white.* Read the sentences aloud.
- Allow time for students to draw their pictures. Walk around the room as students work to make sure they are writing sentences that include *his* or *her*. Then call on students to present their drawings to the class and read their sentences aloud.

## Extend

- Play the Name Game. Model first with yourself, changing voices and positions as you ask the question *Is your name (Mrs. Cho)?* and answer *No, my name is (Mrs. Shah).* Go around the room asking each student a question. Vary the questions to include the names of other students, as in *Is her name (Graciela)? Is his name (James)?* Repeat the correct answer. Say, for example, *Yes, his name is (James).*
- In large classes, act out the game for students. Break students into groups and have them play the game.

## Wrap Up

- Form groups of four and have students count off. Say *Student 1, talk about yourself. Student 2, use your. Student 3, talk about a boy. Student 4, talk about a girl.* Draw a body on the board with small feet, big eyes, and a silly nose. As you point to each body part, have group members take turns identifying it using *my, your, his,* and *her.* As needed, provide these examples: *My feet are small. Your feet are small. His feet are small. Her feet are small.*

## Be the Expert

### Teaching Tip

**Grouping** When students work in groups, be sure each one plays an active role. One way to ensure this is by having groups count off and assigning each group member a specific task by number.

You might also consider assigning tasks based on students' strengths. For example, a student who is skilled at writing might be assigned the task of taking notes. A student who displays drawing skills might be given the task of creating illustrations.

When group members take an active role in the learning process, they are more likely to master important concepts and remember what they learn.

### Formative Assessment

Can students

- use *my, your, his,* and *her* to describe themselves and others?

  Ask questions such as *Are my eyes brown? Are your arms short? Is his hand big?* and *Is her hair black?* Have students answer in complete sentences.

# Vocabulary 2

**Objectives**

Students will

- use action words.
- describe parts of the body.

**Vocabulary** *long hair, strong arms, jump, run, walk*

**Content Vocabulary** *short*

**Resources** Workbook p. 85; Audio CD TR: B42–43; Video: Sc. 4—Vocabulary 2; Classroom Presentation Tool: Vocabulary 2; Teacher's Resource CD-ROM: Activity Worksheet 7.2

**8 Listen and say.** TR: B42

**9 Work with a partner.** Point and say.

**10 Work with a partner.** Say and stick. TR: B43

1 2 3 4 5

116

## Warm Up

- **Recycle** On the board, write *sit down, stand up, point,* and *clap.* Act out each term as you say it aloud. Have students repeat each action and term.
- Say *One person pretends to do something. You guess what it is. Watch me. I do this* (clap your hands). *You say "You are clapping."* Have students choose a word from the board to act out. Then say *Today, we will learn words for other ways to move.*

## Present

- **Give examples** Point to your legs and feet and say *I use my legs and feet to walk.* Walk around the front of the class. Say *You use your legs and feet to walk, too.* Say *I use my legs and feet to jump.* Jump up and down. Say *You use your legs and feet to jump, too.* Say *I use my legs and feet to run.* Run in place. Say *You use your legs and feet to run, too.*
- Draw a stick figure on the board with short legs. Say *His legs are short.* Then draw a stick figure with long legs. Say *Her legs are long.* Write *short* and *long* under the corresponding figures. Then draw two faces, one with long hair and one with short hair. Say *long* and *short* as you write them under the pictures. Ask *Is her hair short? Is his hair long?*
- Demonstrate *strong* by piling up many books. Pretend to strain as you lift the pile, or make multiple attempts at lifting, with some huffing, puffing, and wiping of your brow, before you succeed. When you lift the pile, say *I am strong! I have strong arms.* Lift one arm, bend it at the elbow, and flex your muscle. Say *This arm is strong.*

## Practice 8 9

- 8 Say *Turn to page 116. It's time to listen and say.* Play **TR: B42** and have students repeat the words. ✓ Jump in place and ask *Did I run or jump?* If students have difficulty, play **TR: B42** again.
- Point to the pictures. Encourage students to answer your questions using details in the pictures. Say *Point to the picture. Answer in a complete sentence.* Ask *Who is running?* (He is running.) *Who has long hair?* (She has long hair.) *Who is walking?* (She is walking.) *Who's jumping?* (She is jumping.) *Who has strong arms?* (He has strong arms.)
- 9 Read the directions aloud. Point to the pictures on p. 116. Explain *I point to the boy with the books. I read the words strong arms. That boy has strong arms.* Form pairs. Say *Now you point and say. Take turns.*

## Apply 10

- 10 Read the directions aloud and say *It's time for stickers.* Help students locate the stickers. Play **TR: B43**. Point to the monkey and say *It's Mia the Monkey and Eddie the Elephant!* Read the model dialogue aloud. Then say *I find the sticker of a boy with long legs. I peel off that sticker and put it on number one.*
- Form pairs. Have partners work together to complete the activity.

## Extend

- Group students. Write *run*, *walk*, and *jump* on the board. Say *Where do you run, walk, or jump? Write sentences.* Provide models on the board: *I run in the park. I walk to school. I jump in the grass.* Have groups write at least three sentences. Then have group members read their sentences aloud.

## Wrap Up

- Write *strong* and *long* on the board. Then write the following:

| | | |
|---|---|---|
| walk | jump | run |
| walks | jumps | runs |
| walking | jumping | running |

- Say *Use one word from the board in a sentence.* (He's walking.) Then say *Use two words in one sentence.* (He's walking and jumping.) *Use three words in one sentence.* (She is walking, jumping, and running.) Continue the challenge to include four and five words. Write students' sentences on the board. Read the sentences aloud and have students clap when they hear the target words.

## Be the Expert

### Our World in Context

Many animals are skilled jumpers. The common house mouse can jump more than 30 centimeters (12 inches) high. The jumping viper snake, native to Central America, is only about 0.6 meters (2 feet) long but can jump 1 meter (3 feet) to attack its prey. Australian red kangaroos can jump a length of 8 meters (25 feet).

### Formative Assessment

Can students

- use action words?

  Act out walking, running, and jumping. Ask *What am I doing?*
- describe parts of the body?

  Draw a figure with long legs and long hair. Say *Tell me about her legs. Tell me about her hair.* Act out picking up something heavy. Say *Tell me about my arms.*

**Review** For additional practice, direct students to Activity Worksheet 7.2.

# Grammar 2

**Objective**

Students will

- make sentences with *can*.

**Grammar** use *can* to talk about ability

**Resources** Workbook p. 86; Audio CD TR: B44–45; Video: Sc. 7—Grammar 2; Classroom Presentation Tool: Grammar 2; Teacher's Resource CD-ROM: Graphic Organizers (Four-column chart, Word web), Activity Worksheet 7.3

**Materials** scissors; glue

**GRAMMAR** TR: B44

I **can** walk. She **can** jump.
**Can** you run? Yes, I **can.** I have strong legs!

**11** **Play a game.** Cut out the pictures on page 171. Glue. Listen and play. TR: B45

**12** **Look at the pictures.** Write *yes* or *no*.

1. Can the boy run? ________
2. Can the baby jump? ________
3. Can the mother cook? ________



## Warm Up

- **Preteach** Walk across the room. Say *I can walk.* Jump once or twice. Say *I can jump.* Run across the room. Say *I can run. I can read, write, listen, and sing, too. I can do many things.* Ask *Can you do many things?* Model the answer *Yes, we can.* Have students join you in saying and acting out *We can jump. We can read.*

## Present

- Point out the grammar box on p. 117 and play **TR: B44**. Say *We're learning a new word today. The word is can.* Write *can* on the board.
- Make a four-column chart on the board. Brainstorm activities with students and list them on the board. (ride a bike, jump rope) Have students copy the chart and use the activities to fill in the first column. Then put students in groups of three. Have them use *can* to ask and answer questions about the activities. Have them record what they hear in their charts. Tell students to add a column to record what they can do.

| | I can | (Luis) can | (Sara) can |
|---|---|---|---|
| ride a bike | ✓ | ✓ | ✓ |
| jump rope | ✓ | | ✓ |
| cook | ✓ | ✓ | |

- Have groups take turns sharing their charts with the class.

## Practice 11

- **11** Say *Turn to page 171. Let's cut out the pictures.* As students find the pictures, walk around the room and give out scissors and glue.

- Have students turn to p. 117 and find Activity 11. Say *First, let's write numbers.* Model numbering the grid from 1 to 4 and 6 to 9. Begin at the top left, and follow along from left to right as if reading. Point out that the frog is where 5 would be.
- Say *Now listen, then glue. Let's try one together.* Play only number 1 on **TR: B45**. Model *I hear number one. I find number one.* Point to the top left square that you labeled 1. *She says "I can jump." I find the picture of a girl jumping. I glue it here.* Say *Now you do it.* Play the rest of **TR: B45**. To help them remember what they hear, suggest that students quietly repeat what the boy and girl say.
- **Expand** Point to the pictures for *jump, read,* and *draw.* Say *These pictures show what the girl can do.* On the board, make a word web with **She can** in the center. Have students use their pictures to name action words for the web. Add each action to the web and ask students to tell what the girl can do. Repeat the activity with a **He can** web and the words *run, sing,* and *write.*

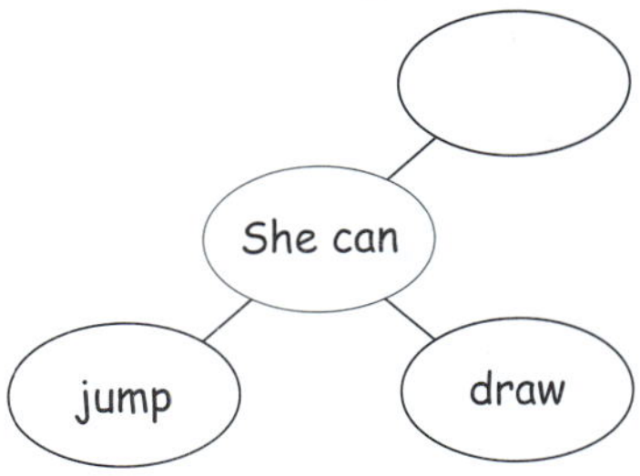


## Apply 12

- Point out Activity 12 on p. 117. Form pairs and have each pair use the pictures from Activity 11 to answer the questions. Have them write *yes* or *no.*

## Extend

- Have students look back at the picture on the top right of p. 116. Ask *What can the children do?* Say *Tell me in writing. Write three sentences. Tell what each one can do.* (She can jump rope. He can run. She can walk.)

## Wrap Up

- Form pairs. Say *What can you do? Let's show, not tell, two things you can do.* Say *Other pairs guess what you can do.* Model by acting out the action of writing. Ask *What can I do?* (You can write.) Give pairs a few minutes to decide what to act out, and then have them join other pairs to act out and identify actions using the sentence frame *You can* ________ .

## Be the Expert

### Grammar in Depth

To talk about ability in the present or future tense, use the word *can.* The word *can* is always followed by the simple form of a verb, such as *jump* (not *jumps, jumping, jumped,* or *to jump*). For example, *I can jump high.* (present) *I can help you tomorrow.* (future) To talk about ability in the past, use the word *could.* For example, *When I was a child, I could jump high.*

### Teaching Tip

Correcting students is necessary, but it's important to provide feedback in a positive way. Consider using nonverbal cues. For example, you can use gestures to indicate errors, or even make a tiny red "flag" and hold it up when students make a grammar error.

The gentlest way to correct students is to restate their response correctly and ask them to repeat it. The goal is to keep students motivated. Always acknowledge what students do well to reinforce learning and build confidence.

### Formative Assessment

Can students

- make sentences with *can?*

  Ask *Can you draw? Can he run? Can she jump?* Have students answer in complete sentences.

**Review** For additional practice, direct students to Activity Worksheet 7.3.

## Reading

**Objectives**

Students will

- describe sculptures.
- identify main idea and details.

**Reading Strategy** Identify Main Idea and Details

**Academic Language** *main idea, details*

**Content Vocabulary** *artist, balloon, dog, horse, sculptures*

**Resources** Audio CD TR: B46–47; Workbook pp. 88–89; Classroom Presentation Tool: Reading

**Materials** a figurine or object to convey the idea of sculpture; pictures of different robots

**13 Listen and read.** TR: B46

# Sculptures Are Fun

Some artists draw and paint. Some artists make sculptures. They make people and animals. Look at the man with a hat. His arms and legs are big. His horse's head is small. Look at the balloon dog. Its legs are big. Its ears are long. Artists can make many fun things!

Fernando Botero's *Man on Horse*

Jeff Koons' *Balloon Dog*

**14 Listen and read. Circle.** TR: B47

1. There are **two three** sculptures.
2. Some arms and legs are **big. old.**
3. We can see a dog with **long short** ears.



## Warm Up

- **Build background** Point to the sculptures on p. 118. Say *These photos show sculptures. Sculptures are art.* Show the sculpture or object you brought to class. Say *A sculpture is a thing. I can touch it.* Touch it. *I can walk around it. I can look all around it.* Walk around it. Write the word *sculpture* on the board and say it slowly, syllable by syllable. Say *Say it with me. Sculpture.*

## Present 13 14

- **13** Have students open their books to p. 118. Say *Let's read the title together.* Hold up your book, point to the title, and say *Sculptures Are Fun. Sculptures are art. How are they fun? Let's find out.*
- **Read together** Play **TR: B46** once and have students listen. Then play **TR: B46** a second time, telling students to read along as they listen. Pause after sentence 5. Say *Look at the man with the hat. Tell me about his arms and legs.* (They're big.) Play sentence 6 and pause. Say *Tell me about his horse's head.* (It's small.) *Let's write those words on the board.*

| man | horse |
| --- | --- |
| big arms and legs | small head |

**15** **Read and check ✔.**

| MAN | legs | arms |
| --- | --- | --- |
| big | ✔ | |
| small | | |

| DOG | legs | ears |
| --- | --- | --- |
| big | | |
| long | | |

**16** **Look.** Circle and write.

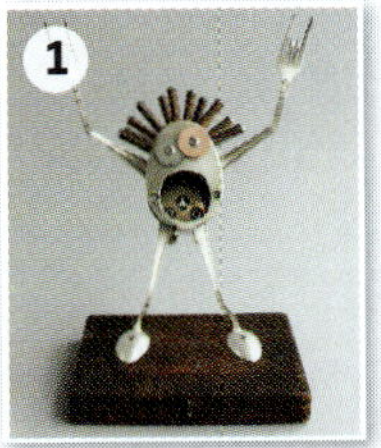

1. My robot **doesn't have** **has** hair.
   It **doesn't have** **has** 1 head.
   It **doesn't have** **has** ______ eyes.

2. My robot **doesn't have** **has** ears.
   It **doesn't have** **has** ______ big hands.
   It **doesn't have** **has** ______ short legs.

3. My robot **doesn't have** **has** ______ eyes.
   It **doesn't have** **has** ______ long arms.
   It **doesn't have** **has** ______ leg.

**17** **Work with a partner.** Choose a robot. Talk about your robots. Are your robots the same or different?

119

## Be the Expert

### About the Photo

Jeff Koons' *Balloon Dog* is not made from a balloon. Like many of his sculptures, it's made of stainless steel. Koons wants viewers to walk around the dog and see their reflections in it.

Fernando Botero's sculpture *Man on Horse* is typical of the oversized people and animals in his sculptures and paintings.

Both Botero and Koons use humor in their art, helping to make modern sculpture accessible to all.

### Teaching Tip

If students are engaged and interested by the art in these photos, take advantage of the "teachable moment." For example, you can review and recycle vocabulary (Does the dog have eyes? Does it have a neck? Does it have feet?).

Consider having interested students use clay or another suitable material to sculpt their own figures of people or animals. Hands-on activities help students make personal connections to lesson content, and enhance their learning experience.

- Continue **TR: B46**, pausing after Sentence 8. Say *Tell me about the dog's legs.* (They're big.) Play sentence 9 and pause. Say *Tell me about its ears.* (They're long.) ✔ Ask *Are the dog's legs big or small?* (They're big.) If students have difficulty answering the question, replay Sentences 7–9.

- **14** Point to Activity 14 on p. 118. Say *Now let's listen and read. Then circle the answer.* Model the activity for students by completing item 1. Play **TR: B47**, pausing after item 1. Read the sentence aloud. Say *I'll look at the pictures. Then I'll count the sculptures.* Hold up the book so students can see p. 118. Point to each sculpture and count it by saying *The dog is one. The man on the horse is two. There are two sculptures. I'll circle the word two. You circle it, too.*

- Have students complete items 2 and 3 on their own. Review the correct answers with the class.

13 **Listen and read.**

## Sculptures Are Fun

Some artists draw and paint. Some artists make sculptures. They make people and animals. Look at the man with a hat. His arms and legs are big. His horse's head is small. Look at the balloon dog. Its legs are big. Its ears are long. Artists can make many fun things!

Fernando Botero's *Man on Horse*

Jeff Koons' *Balloon Dog*

14 **Listen and read.** Circle.

1. There are **two three** sculptures.
2. Some arms and legs are **big. old.**
3. We can see a dog with **long short** ears.

118

15 **Read and check** ✓.

| MAN | legs | arms |
|---|---|---|
| big | ✓ | |
| small | | |

| DOG | legs | ears |
|---|---|---|
| big | | |
| long | | |

16 **Look.** Circle and write.

1. My robot **doesn't have has** hair.
   It **doesn't have has** 1 head.
   It **doesn't have has** ______ eyes.
2. My robot **doesn't have has** ears.
   It **doesn't have has** ______ big hands.
   It **doesn't have has** ______ short legs.
3. My robot **doesn't have has** ______ eyes.
   It **doesn't have has** ______ long arms.
   It **doesn't have has** ______ leg.

17 **Work with a partner.** Choose a robot. Talk about your robots. Are your robots the same or different?

119

## Practice 15 16

- 15 Have students open their books to p. 119 and look at Activity 15. Say *Now we'll read and check. The first one is done. Let's look at it.* Say *The green box says* Man. *Next to* Man *is the word* legs. *Look at the sculpture of the man and horse on page 118. Look at his legs. Are they big or small?* Point to the headings **big** and **small**. Say *They're big. I check that box.*

- Have students complete the box by looking at the man's arms. Then say *Now let's look at the next green box. It says* Dog. *Look at the dog's legs on page 118. Are they big or small?* Have students complete the activity on their own. When they are finished, review each answer.

- 16 Say *Now look at Activity 16. Let's look, circle, and write the answer. Look at number* one. Read the first sentence aloud with both answer choices. Say *Look at picture* one. Point to the picture and say *This robot has hair. I circle* has. Read the complete sentence aloud. Model a process for circling and writing the answers for the rest of item 1. Say *Now you try it.* Have students complete the activity on their own. When students are finished, review each answer in the same manner that you modeled.

## Wrap Up

- Put students in pairs and have them pick one of the sculptures they read about, draw it, and write two or three sentences describing it. Then have pairs share their pictures and sentences with the class.

## Recap

- Write the following on the board:

| Man | Horse | Dog |
|---|---|---|
| big arms and legs | small head | big legs and long ears |

- Have students look for more details that describe the man, horse, and dog. Say *I'm going to say some words about the man, the horse, or the dog. When you hear the words, say "man," "horse," or "dog."*

- Model the activity by saying *Big legs. Look at the board, or in your books, on page 118. Who has big legs?* (the man, the dog) *The man and dog have big legs, so you say "man" and "dog." Ready?* Have students say the words aloud.

## Apply 17

- 17 Form pairs. Hold up your book and point to the robots on p. 119. Say *Pick a robot: Robot 1, Robot 2, or Robot 3.* Say *Talk about your robot.* Say and write on the board the following questions to help students get started: *Does your robot have eyes? How many eyes does it have? Does it have hands? What color are they? Does it have hair? Does it have legs? How many legs does it have?*

- Allow time for pairs to discuss their chosen robots. Ask *Is your robot the same as or different from your partner's robot?* Have students refer to the questions on the board to help them answer.

- **Expand** Bring in pictures of different robots, with and without arms, legs, heads, and feet. Ask students to tell you if the robots have arms, legs, heads, and feet. On the board, make a list of details for these robots. Write **Robots** at the top of the list.

## Extend

- Write the following details on the board:

| | | |
|---|---|---|
| red hands | one leg | hair |
| big mouth | two eyes | a long mouth |
| two legs | two arms | long arms |

- Divide the class into three groups. Assign each group one of the robots on p. 119. Ask students to cover Activity 16 so they can't see it, choose the words on the board that describe their assigned robot, and use those words to write two or three sentences about the robot. Model sentences for students by saying *My robot has hair. It has a big mouth. It has two legs.*

## Wrap Up

- Write the following on the board:

| |
|---|
| The horse has __________. |
| The man has __________. |
| The dog has __________. |

- Ask students to read the sentence frames and complete each sentence with a phrase about the horse, the man, or the dog on p. 118.

## Be the Expert

### Reading Strategy

**Identify Main Idea and Details** The main idea is the most important point in a passage or text. The main idea is often stated in a sentence that appears at or near the beginning of the first paragraph. Sometimes the main idea appears elsewhere. The title of a passage may give clues about the main idea, as with *Sculptures Are Fun*.

Supporting details are usually found within the body of the text. Details tell more about the main idea of the passage.

### Related Vocabulary

*art, museum*

### Formative Assessment

Can students

- describe sculptures?

  Point to a sculpture on p. 118. Ask *What does it have?*

- identify main idea and details?

  Ask *What's fun about the dog sculpture?*

## Writing

**Writing** Write about a costume.

**Objectives**

Students will

- view a writing model.
- draw and write about a costume.

**Content Language** *spider, costume*

**Resources** Workbook p. 90; Classroom Presentation Tool: Writing

### Formative Assessment

Can students

- draw and write about a costume?

  Have students share their pictures and write two new sentences about them.

I'm Antoni. I have two eyes, one nose, and one mouth. I have two arms and two legs. I like spiders. My spider costume has eight eyes and eight legs. I'm a cool spider!

**18** **Draw a costume and write.**

I'm ______________________. I have ______________.

I have ______________________________________.

My ________________ costume has ________________

__________________________________________.

**19** **Work in a group.** Talk about your picture.

120

## Present

- **Contextualize** Pretend to put on a costume. Say *I put on my costume. I'm a spider! I have eight legs!* Act out putting on one leg at a time. *I put on one leg at a time!*
- Write *costume* on the board. Say it aloud with students. Say *A costume is clothes you wear. You wear the clothes to pretend to be something. You can pretend to be a robot. What other things can you pretend to be?* Say *Today, you'll draw and write about a costume. Let's read first.*
- Have students open their books to p. 120. Say *Look at the picture. What is it?* (a boy) *Yes, it's a boy. He's wearing a costume. How many legs does he have?* (eight) *That's right. Eight! He has eight legs! A spider has eight legs!* Then read the words aloud. Reread and have students read aloud with you.

## Write 18

- **18** Point to the empty box on p. 120. Say *Draw your costume here.* Give students enough time to draw.
- Write the following on the board:

| | | | |
|---|---|---|---|
| head | nose | leg | ear |
| hair | mouth | feet | neck |
| eye | arm | hand | |

- Point to the words on the board. Say *Let's read the words.* Read aloud with students. Point to the writing frames on p. 120 and say *Write about your costume here.* Point to the first sentence frame and say *Start with your name.* Point to the second sentence frame and say *Tell about the parts of your body.* Tell students to use some of the words

NATIONAL GEOGRAPHIC

# Our World

## Be clean.

**20** **Look and read.**

Wash your hands.
Wash your body.
Brush your teeth.

**21** **Read and copy.**

I wash my body. I am clean.

_______________________________________

_______________________________________

121

## Value

**Value** Be clean.

**Objectives**

Students will

- read about body-related values and activities.
- read and copy two short sentences.

**Academic Language** *copy*

**Resources** Values Poster

## Be the Expert

### Teaching Tip

**Leveling** Check in with students on a regular basis to determine their level of proficiency with each set of vocabulary words and grammar structures. Students may learn certain topics very quickly but need additional help with others. Don't assume that a student who has been successful in the past will not need intervention in the future.

### Related Vocabulary

*bracelet, faucet, water*

on the board in their sentences. Remind them to use the writing model on the top of the page as a guide for their own sentences.

## Share 19

- **19** Divide the class into four or five groups. Point to Activity 19 at the bottom of p. 120. Say *Talk about your pictures. Use your sentences.* ✓ Walk around and ask questions, prompting students to describe their pictures.

## Value 20 21

- Have students open their books to p. 121. Ask *What's in the photo?* (hands, water) Say *It's a girl. She's washing her hands with water.* Point to the title and say *Look at the title. What does it say?*
- **20** Raise your hands and say *These are my hands.* Act out washing your hands. Pretend to turn the water on and off. Say *I wash my hands.* Point to your body and say *This is my body.* Act out washing your body and say *I wash my body.* Point to your teeth and say *These are my teeth. My teeth are in my mouth.* Act out brushing your teeth. Say *I brush my teeth.* Read the sentences on p. 121. Reread them and have students join you.
- **21** Say *It's time to read and copy.* Point to Activity 21. Have students read the sentences silently and then copy them. Remind them to use a capital letter at the beginning of each sentence and a period at the end. Have students read the sentences aloud.

## Project

**Objectives**

Students will

- make a robot.
- name parts of the body.
- complete the Unit 7 Quiz.

**Resources** Assessment: Unit 7 Quiz; Picture Cards 113–124; Teacher's Resource CD-ROM: Activity Worksheet 7.4

**Materials** scissors; glue; markers or crayons; colored construction paper; heavy card stock

22 **Make a robot.** Work with a partner.

**Cut out the body.**

**Cut out a card.**

**Write the numbers.**

**Cut out or draw parts.**
**Glue them.**



## Prepare 22

- Review vocabulary by holding up Picture Cards 113–124 and asking *What's this?* or *What are these?* After students name each body part, use the word in a complete sentence, such as *Yes, my head is on my neck.*
- Say *Open your books to pages 122 and 123.* Hold up the book and point to the robot on p. 123. Say *This is a robot. Today, you will make a robot.* Ask *How many heads does the robot have?* (two) *How many eyes does it have?* (five) *How many legs and feet does it have?* (three) *What color are its arms?* (yellow)
- 22 Have students work in pairs to plan their robots. Say *Now we will make robots.*

Write the following steps on the board:

1. Cut out the body.
2. Cut out a card.
3. Write the numbers.
4. Cut out or draw parts. Glue them.

- Have students look at the first picture on p. 122. Hand out colored paper and say *Cut out your robot's body.* Model cutting out a large shape for the robot's body. Give time for groups to do the same.
- Point to the second picture. Hand out card stock to each pair and say *Cut out the same shape you cut out before.* Model cutting out the same shape (but smaller) that you cut out in step 1.
- Point to Eddie the elephant in the third picture. Say *Eddie is writing numbers.* Explain that students

**Now I can . . .**

- ○ name parts of the body.
- ○ talk about parts of the body.
- ○ talk about actions.



## Be the Expert

### Our World in Context

Robots are now a reality. One example is that scientists have invented a "robofish" named Grace. Grace has been developed to swim in the world's waterways, flapping its tail when it needs extra energy. An internal pump pushes water in and out of Grace's body, allowing the robofish to glide through water. A battery pack system helps Grace move upward and downward. Grace is designed to monitor water conditions, including temperature and levels of pollution.

### Teaching Tip

Think carefully about the mix of students you group for a project. Place students with different language abilities together. Placing a more fluent student with a student who is still struggling will help give both students a chance to learn from each other's abilities.

### Project Rubric

✓ Did students create a robot plan?

✓ Did students cut out and glue their robot parts?

✓ Did students accurately tell about their robot's body parts?

should write numbers to plan how many body parts to include. They should write four numbers between 1–6 to show how many heads, arms, and legs their robots will have. Model this step, if necessary.

- Point to the fourth picture. Say *Cut out or draw the body parts.*
- Say *Now make your robot! Glue the parts together and color.*
- **Modify** Help students be realistic. You might suggest that students make no more than four of any one body part.

## Share

- Write on the board: *Its name is* ________ *. It has* ________ *heads. It has* ________ *eyes.* Students can use these frames as they present.
- After each pair introduces its robot, have the class ask two questions about the robot. Have each partner answer one question.

### Now I Can

Ask questions such as the following:

- *What is this?* or *What are these?*
- *What color is your hair? What color are your eyes?*
- *What can you do with your feet?*

**Review** For additional practice, direct students to Activity Worksheet 7.4.

### Unit Assessment

Give the Unit 7 Quiz. Hand out the quiz and go over the instructions with the students. The quiz should take 15–20 minutes.

## Video

**Vocabulary 1a** *an arm, a hand, a leg, feet*

**Vocabulary 1b** *a head, an eye, a nose, a mouth, an ear*

**Vocabulary 2** *jump, walk, run*

**Grammar 1** use singular possessive adjectives (*my, your, his, her*)

**Grammar 2** use *can* to talk about ability

**Song** *My Body*

**Viewing** parts of the body; actions and words that describe the body

**Story Time** *My Body, Your Body*

**Resources** Student Book, pp. 108–117

## Before You Watch

- Play Scene I: Introduction. Say *This video is about the body.* Draw a teddy bear on the board and have students tell you what to add. Label the parts of its body, including its eyes, nose, mouth, ears, arms, hands, legs, and feet.

## While You Watch

- Have students look and listen for target words that name parts of the body and actions. Say *Write each word you see and hear on a sheet of paper.*

## After You Watch

- Put students in pairs and have them compare their lists. Then play "Who Heard?" Chant *Who heard (clap, clap) this word (clap, clap): Jump.* Model the answer: *I heard (clap, clap) this word (clap, clap): Jump.* Repeat the activity for each target word that students listed.

## Zoom In

### Vocabulary

- Point to each word and ask the class to say it as it appears. Pause the video as Freddy the frog practices each vocabulary word for a body part. Play the video again to hear what Freddy says.

### Grammar

- As students watch the boy and girl doing different tasks, ask relevant questions, such as *Can he walk? Can she run?* Ask as many questions as possible. Cover up the sentences on the screen, if possible.

### Song

- Use the song to review words that name parts of the body. As you play the song, have students point to each body part on themselves or in a picture. Then replay the song. Have students copy each action that Anna and Freddy perform.

### Viewing

- Stop after each animal to ask questions such as *Are its ears small?* (elephant) *Are its legs long?* (giraffe) *Is its mouth big?* (lion) *What can it do?* (kangaroo, cheetah) Have students answer in complete sentences.

### Story Time

- View Scene II: Story Time. Pause each time Anna says something about a body part, such as "My eyes are brown. Are your eyes brown, too?" Have students answer the question.

- View *My Body, Your Body* a second time, without pausing. After students have viewed the video twice, play it again and pause at still images. Ask questions such as *Are her eyes brown? Is his mouth big?*

### *My Body, Your Body*

Read as children and animals compare parts of their bodies. Are the girl's eyes like the frog's? Is the boy's mouth like the hippo's? Is the girl's hair like the llama's?

## Before You Read

- **Predict** Hold up the Reader. Say *Look at the title. Let's read it together. My Body, Your Body. What do you think this is about? Let's read to find out!*
- **Introduce the strategy** Say *We can tell how things are the same.* Point to your hair and say *I have hair.* Point to a student's hair and say *(Abdul) has hair. We both have hair.*
- Say *We can also tell how things are different. I have (brown) hair. (Abdul) has (black) hair. Our hair is different.*
- Draw a Venn diagram on the board with the labels **What the child says** and **What the animal says.** Say *Look and listen to what the children and animals say.* Point to the first circle and say *Write what the child says.* Point to the second circle and say *Write what the animal says.*

## While You Read

- Read the book aloud to students. Stop every few pages to ask questions and help students fill in the Venn diagram.

  p. 4: *What color are the girl's eyes?* (brown)
  p. 5: *What does the frog say?* (My eyes are red.)

- Add this information to the diagram. Continue with other pages in the book.

## After You Read

- Put students in pairs and have them compare their Venn diagrams and discuss any differences. Then complete the overlap part of the Venn diagram as a class. Ask *What do the children and animals both have?* Have students help you add things that are the same, such as two eyes, one head, and one body.

## Unit 7 Reader

**Text Type** nonfiction text

**Reading Strategy** Compare and Contrast

**Vocabulary** *an eye, a mouth, hair, long hair, an ear, a nose*

**Academic Language** *both, different, same*

**Grammar** use singular possessive adjectives *(my, your, his, her)*

**Resources** Classroom Presentation Tool: Story Time; Video: Sc. II—Story Time; Teacher's Resource CD-ROM: Graphic Organizers (Venn diagram)

## Be the Expert

### Reading Strategy

**Compare and Contrast** Students compare things to tell how they are alike; they contrast things to tell how they are different. Words such as *both, alike,* and *same* signal similarities. Words such as *but, however,* and *unlike* signal differences.

Help students grasp the concepts of *alike* and *different* by holding up two familiar classroom objects, such as a magazine and a book, and discussing ways they are similar and different.

### Text Background

*My Body, Your Body* is a nonfiction text. The purpose of a nonfiction text is to inform readers about a topic. Information in a nonfiction text may be organized into different sections with different headings. Nonfiction texts often include text features such as photos, drawings, tables, charts, diagrams, and other visual aids that help readers better understand the subject matter.

## Student Book

**TR: B34** (1) **Listen and say.**

| | |
|---|---|
| a foot | I have a right foot. I have a left foot. |
| a leg | I have two legs. |
| a neck | I have a neck. |
| a head | I have a head. |
| hair | I have brown hair. |
| an arm | I have two arms. |
| a hand | I have two hands. |
| feet | I have two feet. |
| an ear | I have two ears. |
| an eye | I have two eyes. |
| a nose | I have a nose. |
| a mouth | I have a mouth. |

**TR: B35** (2) **Listen. Point and say.**

Feet, hair, an eye, a leg, an arm, a mouth, a hand, a foot, a head, a nose, an ear, a neck

**TR: B36** (3) **Work with a partner. Point. Ask and answer.**

Example
What are these?
They're hands.

**TR: B37** (4) **Listen. Read and sing.**

Note: Lyrics for the song *My Body* are on pp. 220–221.

**TR: B38** **Grammar**

Note: Grammar 1, 1st chart, is on p. 222.

**TR: B39** (6) **Look and listen. Write the number in the box.**

1. My eyes are blue.
2. Your hand is big. My hand is small.
3. Your hair is black.

**TR: B40** **Grammar**

Note: Grammar 1, 2nd chart, is on p. 223.

**TR: B41** (7) **Look and listen. Draw a line.**

1. Her ears are small.
2. His feet are big.

**TR: B42** (8) **Listen and say.**

| | |
|---|---|
| long hair | That girl has long hair. |
| strong arms | That boy has strong arms. |
| jump | She is jumping rope. |
| run | He is running. |
| walk | She is walking. |

**TR: B43** (10) **Work with a partner. Say and stick.**

Example
1. His legs are long.
Yes, they're long. My turn.

**TR: B44** **Grammar**

Note: Grammar 2 is on p. 228.

**TR: B45** (11) **Play a game. Cut out the pictures on page 171. Glue. Listen and play.**

1. I can jump.
2. I can walk.
3. I can run.
4. I can cook.
5. The frog can hop.
6. I can read.
7. I can sing.
8. I can draw.
9. I can write.

**TR: B46** (13) **Listen and read.**

Note: Reading *Sculptures Are Fun* is on p. 230.

**TR: B47** (14) **Listen and read. Circle.**

Some artists draw and paint. Some artists make sculptures. They make people and animals. Look at the man with a hat. His arms and legs are big. His horse's head is small. Look at the balloon dog. Its legs are big. Its ears are long. Artists can make many fun things!

1. There are two sculptures.
2. Some arms and legs are big.
3. We can see a dog with long ears.

## Workbook

**TR: 57** (3) **Listen to the song. Use words from the box. Write.**

Note: Lyrics for the song *My Body* are on pp. 220–221.

**TR: 58** **4** **Listen and draw. Use words from the box.**

Note: Lyrics for the song *My Body* are on pp. 220–221.

**TR: 59** **5** **Listen and read. Circle.**

1. I have a small nose. My nose is small.
2. She has green eyes. Her eyes are green.
3. You have small hands. Your hands are small.
4. He has a red mouth. His mouth is red.
5. I have small hands, and you have small hands. Our hands are small.

**TR: 60** **6** **Listen and read. Circle.**

1. My baby sister has small feet. Her feet are small.
2. I have big feet. My feet are big.
3. My father is tall. His hands are big.
4. My baby sister is small. Her hands are small.
5. My nose is small. Is your nose small?

**TR: 61** **11** **Listen. Write.**

1. Can the boy jump?
   No. He can walk.
2. Can his sister jump?
   Yes, she can jump.
3. Can the mother run?
   Yes, she can run.
4. Can the baby run?
   No. He can sleep.

**TR: 62** **16** **Listen and read.**

Note: Reading *Polar Bears* is on p. 324.

# Answer Key

## Student Book

**Unit Opener** SB p. 108

a boy.

**6** SB p. 114

3, 1, 2

**7** SB p. 115

1. line to girl's ears
2. line to boy's feet

**12** SB p. 117

1. yes, 2. no, 3. yes

**14** SB p. 118

1. two, 2. big, 3. long

**15** SB p. 119

| MAN | legs | arms |
|---|---|---|
| big | ✓ | ✓ |
| small | | |

| DOG | legs | ears |
|---|---|---|
| big | ✓ | |
| long | | ✓ |

**16** SB p. 119

1. has; has, 1; has, 2
2. doesn't have; has, 2: has, 2
3. has; has, 2; has, 1

## Workbook

Go to pp. 322–325 for the Workbook Answer Key for this unit.

# In This Unit

**Theme** This unit is about food and drinks.

**Content Objectives**

Students will

- identify and name different foods and drinks.
- describe preferences.

**Language Objectives**

Students will

- name food.
- talk about likes and dislikes.
- talk about their favorite foods and drinks.

**Vocabulary**

**Vocabulary 1** *a banana, cheese pizza, a salad, an orange, an apple, rice, a sandwich, a cookie, soup, chicken, an egg, fish*

**Vocabulary 2** *tea, orange juice, water, lemonade, milk*

**Grammar**

**Grammar 1** use *like* in the simple present (first and second person singular)

**Grammar 2** use the indefinite articles *a* and *an*

**Pacing Guides** LIU8

**Writing** Write about favorite foods.

**Value** Eat good food.

**Project** Make a placemat.

## Unit Opener

**Objectives**

Students will

- identify parts of a photo.
- complete a sentence.

**Resources** Video: Sc. 1—Introduction; Classroom Presentation Tool: Unit Opener; Teacher's Resource CD-ROM: Home-School Connection Letter; Unit Opener Poster; World Map Poster; Picture Cards 129, 130, 136

**Content Vocabulary** *vegetables*

**Materials** an orange and an orange half; a glass or cup

Unit 8

# Good Food

In this unit, I will . . .

- name food.
- talk about likes and dislikes.
- talk about my favorite food.

**Look and check.**

She sells

○ flowers.

○ fruit.

○ vegetables.

Kasbah, Rabat, Morocco

124

## Introduce

- **Build background** Say *The name of this unit is "Good Food."* Hold up an orange and say *This is an orange.* As you smell it, say *Mmmm! Oranges are good food! I can eat the orange.Or I can make orange juice.* Hold an orange half over a cup and pretend to squeeze out some juice. Say *Mmmm! Orange juice.*
- Write the word *fruit* on the board. Say *An orange is a fruit.* Hold up Picture Cards 129, 130, and 136 (an apple, a banana, an orange). Say *Apples, bananas, and oranges are all fruit. Fruit is good food.* Encourage students to think about and name other fruits they know.
- **Set the stage** Say *I'm walking.* Act out walking and wiping your brow as though you're hot and tired. Say *I want a drink.* Pick up the cup and pretend to take a drink from it. Say *Mmm. Orange juice. I like orange juice.* Smile as you say *That was good!* Ask *Do you like orange juice?*

- Have students open their books to pp. 124–125 and look at the photo. Ask questions to encourage discussion of the photo.

  *What do you see?* (oranges, flowers, a table, a person)
  *What colors do you see?* (orange, white, blue, red, black, yellow, green)
  *What's in the person's hand?* (two oranges)

- Guide students through the activity on p. 124. Read the sentence stem and the three choices aloud. Make a check mark in the air and ask *What answer do we check?* Say *She sells* and point to the woman in the photo. Ask *What does she sell?* (oranges) *Are oranges flowers?* (no) *Are oranges fruit?* (yes) Read the complete sentence aloud. Then have students read it with you.

## Be the Expert

### About the Photo

The photo shows an orange juice stand in Morocco, a country in North Africa. The stand is located in the *kasbah* of Rabat, the capital city of Morocco. Kasbah is a North African term for the area of a city where a fortress once stood. A kasbah often has a market or market area. The original fortress in Rabat's Kasbah of the Oudayas was built in the 12th century.

### Our World in Context

Oranges are a type of citrus fruit. They have a tough outer rind and a juicy and sweet inner flesh. The orange is thought to be native to tropical regions of Asia. Today, oranges are grown in subtropical and tropical North America, South America, Australia, northern and eastern Mediterranean nations, and South Africa.

### Related Vocabulary

*glasses, peels*

# Vocabulary 1

**Objective**

Students will

- identify and name foods.

**Vocabulary** *a banana, cheese pizza, a salad, an orange, an apple, rice, a sandwich, a cookie, soup, chicken, an egg, fish*

**Resources** Workbook pp. 92–93; Audio CD TR: B48–50; Video: Sc. 2—Vocabulary Ia; Sc. 3—Vocabulary Ib; Classroom Presentation Tool: Vocabulary I; Teacher's Resource CD-ROM: Graphic Organizers (Venn diagram), Activity Worksheet 8.I; Picture Cards I29–I40; Sound Card I7

**Materials** cafeteria tray, napkin, fork, and spoon; two sticky notes per student; lunch bag or lunch box (*optional*)

1 **Listen and say.** TR: B48

2 **Listen.** Point and say. TR: B49

## Warm Up

- **Set the stage** Stand up and act out laying a napkin, fork, and spoon on a cafeteria tray. Act out selecting food in a cafeteria. Pick up the tray and say *Let's eat! I want good food!* Act out picking up three food items and placing them on the tray. Then sit down and act out eating each food item. Have students copy your actions. Say *Mmmm, it's good!* Have students repeat after you.
- **Activate prior knowledge** Call on students and ask them to name a food they eat. Say *Show me how you eat the food.* Students should act out eating the food. Say *Now let's learn some new words about good foods!*

## Present

- **Contextualize** Show the photos of foods on pp. 126–127. Point to one of the bananas and say *A banana. Bananas are yellow.* Ask *Who eats bananas?* Call for a show of hands. Model using students' names, for example, *(Andrés) eats bananas.*

rice

soup

an egg

a sandwich

chicken

fish

a cookie

**3 Work with a partner.**
Point. Ask and answer. TR: B50

127

- Point to the apple and say *An apple. Apples grow on trees. Who eats apples?* Continue for the remaining foods.
- Display Picture Cards 129–140 on the board. Give each student two sticky notes. Ask students to put their notes on two foods they want to eat today. Then hold up and name each card. Have students count the number of sticky notes on each card. As students count, create a chart like the one below.

| | | | |
|---|---|---|---|
| a banana | 7 | cheese pizza | 12 |
| an orange | 6 | rice | ___ |
| an apple | ___ | a cookie | ___ |
| an egg | 1 | soup | ___ |
| a sandwich | ___ | chicken | ___ |
| fish | 6 | a salad | 4 |

- Explain what the chart shows. Say *(Six) students want (fish) today. Only (one) student wants (an egg) today.* Ask other questions such as *How many students want soup today?*

## Be the Expert

### Vocabulary Strategy

**Multiple-meaning Words** Explain that many words in English have more than one meaning. Point out that students have learned two meanings for the word *orange*. One is a color. One is a fruit.

Review other words that have multiple meanings and have students share the different meanings they know: *star* (a star can be in the sky; a star can be a shape); *top* (a top can be a toy; top can mean the top of the page).

### Sounds of English

**Single Sounds: /tʃ/**
The /tʃ/ sound (watch) can be difficult for some students to pronounce. To demonstrate the /tʃ/ sound, put the tip of your tongue on the area above your upper teeth. Press your teeth together and push your lips out. Use your tongue to push out the air as you say the sound. Your vocal cords should not vibrate.

Use Sound Card 17 (chicken). Have students pronounce /t/ and /ʃ/ separately, and then bring the sounds closer together so that they are saying /tʃ/.

Example words: chair, picture, kitchen, sandwich

## Practice 1 2

- 1 Hold up and point to the banana, and say *A banana. I want a banana.* Motion for students to say it with you as you repeat. Then ask *Are you ready?* Say *It's time to listen and say.* Play **TR: B48**. Listen to students as they say the words and sentences, correcting pronunciation when necessary.

- 2 Say *Now it's time to listen, point, and say.* Before you play the next track, review the foods shown. Then play **TR: B49**. ✓ Point to the photo of rice and ask *What is this?* If students have difficulty, play **TR: B49** again and have students point to the correct picture as they listen to and then say each word.

- Have students count off by five and form groups. Say *Group one, you start. Point to a photo. Group two, you name the photo, and then you point to a new photo.* The activity continues until the fifth group points to a photo for the first group to name. If the class is small, have students count off by three instead of five.

## Wrap Up

- Mix up Picture Cards 129–140 and put them in one stack. Give the stack of cards to a student. Say *Pick up a card. Say what it is. Then we'll all repeat.* Model the activity. Have students play, naming the cards, and then mixing the stack and passing it to the next student. Continue until all students have had a turn.

## Recap

- Say *We learned about good foods.* Hold up Picture Cards 129–140 one at a time and have students name the foods. For each food, ask *Do you want ______?*

## Apply 3

- 3 Point to the model dialogue at the bottom of p. 127. Say *Look who it is! It's Mia and Polly! Let's listen to what they're saying.* Play **TR: B50**.

- Point to each mascot and ask *What is (Mia) saying?* Model the dialogue with a student. Hold up your book or Picture Card 136 and point to the orange. Ask *What is it?* (It's an orange.)

- Have students form pairs. Explain that they will practice the dialogue with all of the photos on pp. 126–127. Say *First you ask, and then your partner answers. Take turns.* ✓ Walk around the room and make sure that pairs are correctly naming all of the pictures. If not, provide context sentences such as *It's cheese pizza. Many students in our class like cheese pizza.*

## Extend

- Choose five cards from Picture Cards 129–140 and put them in a bag or box. Have students guess what they are. Prompt them to use the sentence frame *Is it ________?* When students guess a correct item, pull out the card, and ask *What is it?* After students name it again, write the word on the board. Continue until all five items have been named.

- Display the same five picture cards. Form pairs. Have pairs make a Venn diagram comparing and contrasting **Your Food** and **My Food.**

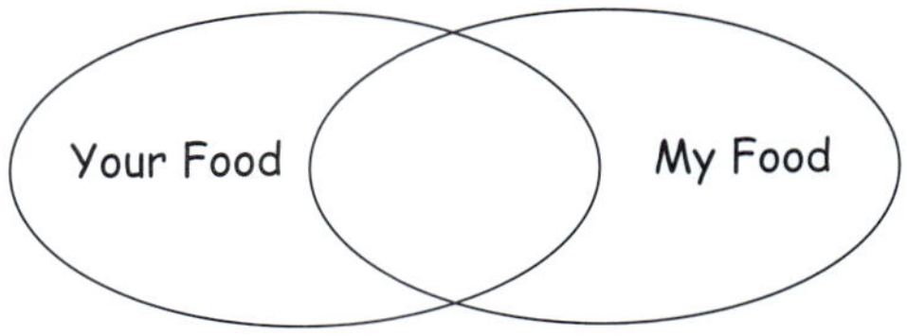


- Write the following on the board:

> You eat ________ and ________.
> I eat ________ and ________.
> You and I eat ________.

- Help students tell about their diagrams by completing sentence frames. Adjust the number of blanks based on the information in their diagrams.

## Wrap Up

- Say *Let's talk about the new foods!* Go around the room and have students stand up and name a food. Record each answer on the board until all vocabulary words are shown. Next to the list, write *Yes, I want ________.* and *No, I don't want ________.* Point to the first item on the list and ask a student *(Sung), do you want (chicken)?* Have the student use one of the sentence frames on the board to respond. Repeat for the remaining items on the list.

## Be the Expert

### Teaching Tip

Students who feel valued and supported in class are likely to take an active role in the learning process. Create a classroom atmosphere in which students do not need to be overly concerned about making mistakes. At the beginning of class, explain to students that they're learning new things and that making mistakes is a natural and expected part of learning.

Be sure to emphasize that making fun of other people's mistakes is not acceptable in your class. This type of atmosphere will encourage students to take chances and try new things. It will also support students' efforts to learn.

### Formative Assessment

Can students

- identify and name foods?

  Point to the photos of the foods on pp. 126–127 and have students name them. Hold up Picture Cards of three different foods and ask *Where is the (rice)? Where is the (soup)? Where is the (fish)?*

**Review** For additional practice, direct students to Activity Worksheet 8.1.

## Song

**Vocabulary in the song**

**Vocabulary 1** *cheese pizza, apple, cookie, banana, chicken, salad, oranges*

**Vocabulary 2** *water*

**Grammar in the song**

**Grammar 1** use *like* in the simple present (first and second person singular)

**Grammar 2** use the indefinite articles *a* and *an*

**Resources** Workbook p. 94; Audio CD TR: B51; Video: Sc. 9—Song; Classroom Presentation Tool: Song

**Materials** Picture Cards 129–130, 132–133, 136, 138

4 **Listen.** Read and sing. TR: B51

# Yes, Please!

*Pizza?*
*I like pizza!*
*Yes, I do! Yes, I do! Yes, I do!*
*I like pizza!*
*Yes, I do!*
*I like it very much!*

*Apples?*
*I like apples!*
*Yes, I do! Yes, I do! Yes, I do!*
*I like apples!*
*Yes, I do!*
*I like them very much!*

***Do you want a cookie?***
***Do you want some cheese?***
***Do you want a banana?***
***Yes, please!***

*Chicken?*
*I like chicken!*
*Yes, I do! Yes, I do! Yes, I do!*
*I like chicken!*
*Yes, I do!*
*I like it very much!*

128

## Use the Song 4

- **Predict** Say *It's time for a song! Open your books to pages 128 and 129. Look at the picture. What do you think the song is about?* Pause to allow students to answer. Say *Raise your hand if you think the song is about clothes.* Pause for a moment. Say *Raise your hand if you think it's about toys.* Pause for a moment. Say *Raise your hand if you think it's about good food.* Explain that students can look at the words and pictures to guess what the song is about.
- **Build background** Say *There are many ways to say you want to eat something. You already know some. Let's write them.* Write and say *Do you want a banana?* Ask *What's the answer*? (Yes, I do. Yes, I want a banana.) Record these answers below the question. Say *There's another answer, too: Yes, please!* Write *Yes, please!* below the other two answers. Have students say it with you. Say *Yes, Please! is the name of the song.*
- 4 Before students listen to the song, chant the words to them. Then play **TR: B51** as students read along. Replay the song and have students sing along.
- Divide the class into six groups. Assign each group one of the following foods from the song: *pizza, apples, a cookie, chicken, salad, oranges*. Then write on the board *Yes, please! I want* ________. Say *I'm going to point to you and ask a question. Use your food and the words on the board to answer.* Point to the *pizza* group and ask *Do you want pizza?* (Yes, please! I want pizza.) Repeat the process for the other five groups and words.

*Salad?*
*I like salad!*
*Yes, I do! Yes, I do! Yes, I do!*
*I like salad!*
*Yes, I do!*
*I like it very much!*

**CHORUS**

*Oranges?*
*I like oranges!*
*Yes, I do! Yes, I do! Yes, I do!*
*I like oranges!*
*Yes, I do!*
*I like them very much!*

*Water?*
*And I like water!*
*Yes, I do! Yes, I do! Yes, I do!*
*I like water!*
*Yes, I do!*
*I like it very much!*

**CHORUS**

*Yes, please!*
*Yes, PLEASE!*

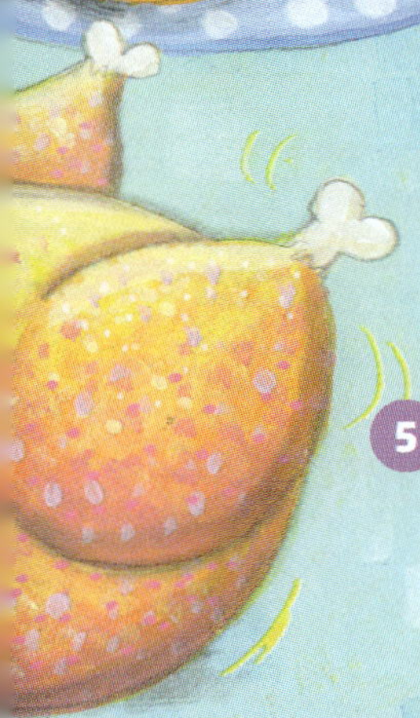

5 **Sing again.**
Hold up pictures.

129

## Be the Expert

### Teaching Tip

Provide opportunities for students to use new vocabulary in different contexts. The more they say, hear, read, and write new words, the more easily they will learn and remember them.

You can have students roleplay scenes at a restaurant or market, create illustrated menus, make an alphabet book of new foods, watch a video of a simple cooking demonstration, or take a guided tour of a local market.

### Related Vocabulary

*bowl, plate*

## Use It Again 5

- 5 **Vocabulary I** Put students into pairs. Hand each pair one of the following Picture Cards: 129 (an apple), 130 (a banana) 132 (chicken) 133 (a cookie) 136 (an orange) 138 (a salad). Have one partner name the pictured item and the other use that word in a sentence. Then play **TR: B51**.
- When students hear the word on their cards, they should hold up the card and then act out eating the pictured food. Pause the song as needed to give students time to perform the action. For more practice, have pairs exchange cards and repeat.
- **Grammar I** Play **TR: B51**. Have students raise their hands every time they hear the phrase *I like* mentioned in the song. Then write the following on the board: *Yes, I do. I like* ________. *No, I don't. I don't like* ________. Call on a particular student and ask *(Irina), do you like (salad)?* Repeat with other foods mentioned in the song. Remind students to use the words on the board to answer appropriately.

# Grammar 1

**Objective**

Students will

- ask and answer questions with *like.*

**Grammar** use *like* in the simple present (first and second person singular)

**Resources** Workbook pp. 95–96; Audio CD TR: B52–55; Video: Sc. 6—Grammar 1; Classroom Presentation Tool: Grammar 1; Picture Cards 98–112, 129–140; Teacher's Resource CD-ROM: Graphic Organizers (Tree diagram); Sound Card 17

**Materials** note cards; lunch bag or lunch box (optional)

**GRAMMAR** TR: B52

| | |
|---|---|
| **Do** you **like** apples? | No, I **don't.** I **don't like** apples. |
| **Do** you **like** bananas? | Yes, I **do.** I **like** bananas. |

6 **What do they like?** Listen and find. Circle and write. TR: B53

1. ______ 2. ______ 3. ______

130

## Warm Up

- **Recycle** Show Picture Cards 98–112 one at a time and have students name each toy. Have students write the name of their favorite toy on a piece of paper. Model writing *bike* on a piece of paper along with your name. Hold up your paper for students to see. Point to your name and say *Write your name, too.* When students have finished, collect the papers. Discuss students' favorite toys. Say *(Juan) wrote (truck). Juan wants a (truck)!* Ask *What does Juan want?* (a truck)

## Present

- Write the following on the board:

Do you want soup?
- Yes, I do. I want soup.
- No, I don't. I don't want soup.

Do you like soup?
- Yes, I do. I like soup.
- No, I don't. I don't like soup.

**GRAMMAR** TR: B54

**Do** you **like** fish? No, I **don't.** I **don't like** fish.
**Do** you **like** chicken? Yes, I **do.** I **like** chicken.

7 **What do they like?** Listen and find. Circle and write. TR: B55

1. ____________ 2. ____________ 3. ____________

131

## Be the Expert

### Our World in Context

Half of the world's population depends on rice as a staple food, including nearly all of East and Southeast Asia. In English, people say "How are you?" but some Chinese people ask "Have you had your rice today?" instead.

The rice plant is a member of the grass family. It is characterized by long, flat leaves, and can grow to a height of 1.2 meters (4 feet). Rice is grown on watery land in tropical, subtropical, and temperate climates. The earliest evidence of rice cultivation comes from China, dating to 7000–5000 BCE.

### Grammar in Depth

When asking questions with *want*, an article—such as *a*, *an*, or *the*—is used before the noun. For example: *Do you want an apple?* When asking questions with *like*, the plural form of the noun is usually used. For example: *Do you like apples?* One exception is noncount nouns, such as salad, chicken, or pizza: *Do you like pizza?*

### Teaching Tip

Think about how much time you spend talking versus how much time your students spend talking. Try to aim for having students speak 70 percent of the time.

- Read the first question and two possible answers aloud and have students repeat. Say *We answer questions with* want *using* do *and* don't.
- Say *We answer questions with* like *using* do *and* don't, *too.* Read the second question and two answer choices and have students repeat.
- Draw students' attention to the yellow grammar box at the top of p. 130. Read the questions and answers aloud, or play **TR: B52**. Point to the first answer and explain No, I don't *means the same thing as* No, I don't like apples. Repeat for the second example. Then play **TR: B52** again and have students choral read the questions with you. Play the track a third time and have students choral read the answers with you.

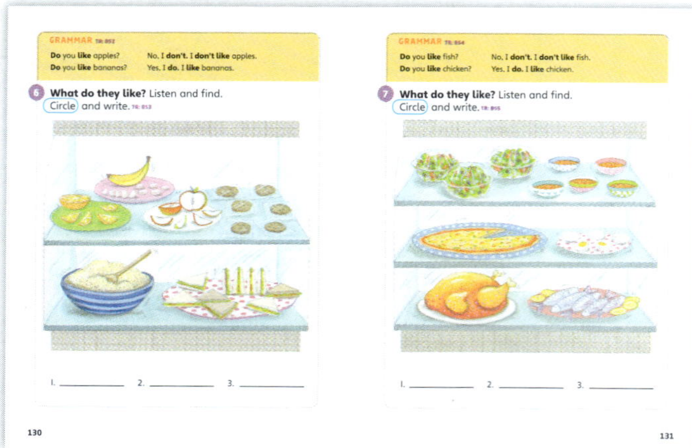


## Practice 6 7

- Point to the pictures of food on p. 130. Say *Let's name the food in this picture.* Hold up your book and point to the orange. Ask *What's this?* (an orange, orange pieces) Say *Yes, it's an orange. I like oranges.* Repeat for the other foods.
- 6 Say *Now we're going to listen to what other people like. Let's do one together.* Play number 1 of **TR: B53**. Say *This person likes oranges, so I circle the oranges. I don't circle the bananas.* Point to the bottom of the page where the numbers are and say *Then I write oranges next to number one. You write oranges there, too.*
- Form pairs. Say *Listen. Then circle. Then write.* Play number 2 of **TR: B53**. Say *What does the person like?* (cookies)
- 7 Draw students' attention to the yellow grammar box at the top of p. 131. Read the questions and answers aloud, or play **TR: B54**. Have students repeat after you. Then write the following on the board:

| I like ... | |
|---|---|
| Add *-s* or *-es* | Don't add *-s* or *-es* |
| apples, bananas, cookies, eggs, oranges, sandwiches | chicken, fish, pizza, rice, salad, soup |

- Have students read this information aloud. Help them understand that when they talk about the foods they like, they should not add *–s* or *–es* to the foods in the right column.
- Say *Now you try. Listen and find. Then circle and write.* Play **TR: B55**. Play one track at a time and ask *What does the person like?* Have students circle and write answers. If students cannot answer, play the track again. Have students point to each food as it is named to determine if the problem is vocabulary recognition or listening comprehension. If it's the former, do a Picture Card review. If it is the latter, provide practice with the dialogue and have students repeat the last thing they hear.

## Wrap Up

- Give one note card to each student. Say *Write the name of a food you like.* Model writing *fish* on your card and adding your name. Hold up the card for students to see. Say *Put your card face down on your desk. Let's play the game "Find Someone Who."* Point to your eyes as you say *Watch what I do.* Go to a student's desk. Ask *Do you like (chicken)?* Prompt the student to say *Yes, I do. I like chicken*, or *No, I don't. I don't like chicken.* If the student says *yes*, say *I guessed the food!* If the student says *no*, say *I didn't guess the food.* Have students try to guess the food on three classmates' cards. Say *Can you guess right all three times? Let's see!*

## Recap

- Hold up a real or imaginary lunch bag or box. Point to it and say *There are foods I like in here. What foods do I like?* Have students guess several foods. As they name each one, say *No, that's not in here. I don't like (oranges)* or *Yes, that's in here. I like (sandwiches).*

## Apply

- Turn Activity 7 on p. 131 into a game of What Do You Like? Form pairs. Then write the following on the board:

> Do you like ___________?
>
> No, I don't. I don't like ___________.
>
> Yes, I do. I like ___________.

- Have partners ask each other questions about the three pairs of pictured foods. Model with a student. Point to the first pair of foods and ask *Do you like salad?* After the student responds, ask *Do you like soup?* The student should use one of the sentence frames on the board to answer each question. Then have the student ask you the same questions. Then say *Now you play. Use the words on the board to help you.*

- **Expand** Have pairs choose one shelf from the picture on p. 131. Ask students to write two sentences. One sentence tells what they like. The other sentence tells what they don't like.

- **Modify** Some students may have difficulty writing sentences. If this is the case, refer them to the sentence frames on the board. Other students may be able to focus on more shelves and write additional sentences.

## Extend

- Form groups. Give each group six note cards, each with one of the words below. Have students form as many questions and answers as they can. Students should write each sentence before they rearrange the cards to form a new sentence.

| | | | |
|---|---|---|---|
| you | I | do | don't |
| like | apples | | |

## Wrap Up

- Form groups of four. Have one student in each group act out serving food to the other three students. Call three students to the front of the room and model a role play such as this: Say to one student *Hi, (Isabel)! Do you like fish?* Point to an imaginary plate of fish to be served. Isabel shakes her head *no* and says *No, I don't. I don't like fish.* She then points to an imaginary salad and says *I like salad!* Pretend to serve the food and say *Okay, Isabel, here's your salad.* Repeat with the other two students. Have group members take turns playing the roles of server and guests.

## Be the Expert

### Teaching Tip

Model using facial expressions and gestures when talking about likes and dislikes. Students who smile or nod their heads when they say *yes* and *like* convey meaning in two ways to their partners. Likewise, students who frown or shake their heads add an extra layer of meaning to a negative response or a statement of dislike.

### Formative Assessment

Can students

- ask and answer questions with *like?*

  Provide the frame *Do you like ________?* Ask questions about familiar items in your classroom. Have students use the frame to ask and answer questions.

# Vocabulary 2

**Objective**
Students will
- identify and name drinks.

**Vocabulary** *tea, orange juice, water, lemonade, milk*

**Resources** Workbook p. 97; Audio CD TR: B56–58; Video: Sc. 4—Vocabulary 2; Classroom Presentation Tool: Vocabulary 2; Teacher's Resource CD-ROM: Graphic Organizers (Two-column chart), Activity Worksheet 8.2; Picture Cards 129–145

**Materials** lunch bag or lunch box (*optional*); empty plastic cup (*optional*); empty plastic pitcher (*optional*)

**8** **Listen and say.** TR: B56

**9** **Work with a partner.** Point and say.

**10** **Listen and read.** Circle *yes* or *no.* TR: B57

1. Does she like orange juice? yes no
2. Does he like water? yes no

**11** **Work with a partner.** Say and stick. TR: B58

132

## Warm Up

- Take out a lunch bag or lunch box and place it on your desk. Put an empty plastic pitcher nearby. Act out removing food from the lunch bag and eating several bites. Then take a plastic cup out of the lunch bag. Pick up the pitcher and pour yourself an imaginary cup of something to drink. Act out taking a drink from the cup, and have students copy your actions. Say *Mmmm. I like this. It's good!* Have students repeat after you.

## Present

- **Give examples** On the board, make a word web with the word *drinks* in the center circle. Say *Today, we're going to learn words for drinks.* Hold up Picture Cards 141–145. Say each word and then add it to your word web.
- Say *Open your books to page 132. Look at these photos of drinks.* As you point to each drink, say its name aloud. Have students repeat the words aloud.
- Ask *Which drink is white?* (milk) *Which drink is brown?* (tea) *Which drink is orange?* (orange juice) Model a small cup with your hands. *Which drink is in a small cup?* (tea) Model a large glass with your hands. *Which drinks are in big glasses?* (orange juice, water, lemonade)
- Point to each drink individually and ask *Do you like (lemonade)?* Model the answer *Yes, I do. I like lemonade.*
- Say *I like milk. Let's drink milk together.* Act out taking a big gulp of milk. Signal students to do the same. Hold out your hand as though it has a glass of milk in it. Then ask *What is it?* (It's milk.) If time allows, repeat for all of the drinks.

## Practice 8 9 10

- 8 Say *Now, listen and say.* Emphasize listening by placing your hand to your ear and nodding. Play **TR: B56**. Make sure students pronounce each word and syllable correctly.
- 9 Form pairs. Say *Point to a drink. Your partner says its name. Take turns.* Again, listen for correct pronunciation, and make sure students are taking turns.
- 10 Have students continue to work with their partners. Say *Now listen. Read the sentence and circle yes or no.* Say *Let's do one together.* Play only number 1 on **TR: B57**. Model by saying *She says she doesn't like orange juice. She likes lemonade.* Hold up your book, point to item 1, and read the question aloud. Make a circle in the air as you say *I circle no. She doesn't like orange juice. What does she like?* (lemonade)
- Say *Work with your partner and do number two.* Play number 2 on **TR: B57** and have partners complete item 2 on p. 132. ✓ Ask *What picture shows water?* Have students point to the correct picture.

## Apply 11

- 11 Form pairs and say *Let's do a sticker activity.* Ask students to look at Activity 11 on p. 132. Read the model dialogue aloud or play **TR: B58**. Then have pairs practice reading the model dialogue.
- Ask *What drink do you like? Tell your partner. Then put the sticker on number 1.* Model this step for students. Say *Your partner says she likes another drink. Put that sticker on number 2. Take turns. Put five stickers in your book.*

## Extend

- Make a two-column chart on the board. Write the headings **Drinks** and **Foods.** Hold up Picture Cards 129–145 one by one, name them, and have students write each in the correct column. Review the chart as a class.

| Drinks | Foods |
|---|---|
| lemonade | an apple |
| milk | a banana |
| orange juice | cheese pizza |

## Wrap Up

- Say *Let's play the game "What Am I?" I tell you about me. You tell me what I am.* Model *I'm hot. I'm brown.* (tea) Continue with other clues such as *I'm orange. I'm cold. I'm made with oranges.* (orange juice) *I'm yellow. You drink me on hot days.* (lemonade) *I'm white. I'm cold.* (milk) *I have no color.* (water)

## Be the Expert

### Teaching Tip

At the end of class, have students write on note cards one new thing they learned or one question they still have about the lesson content. Collect these cards before students leave the classroom. Notes like these can provide valuable information about how well students comprehend key lesson concepts.

### Formative Assessment

Can students

- identify and name drinks?

  Have students point to pictures of drinks as you randomly name them. Then point to each picture and have students name it.

**Review** For additional practice, direct students to Activity Worksheet 8.2.

# Grammar 2

**Objective**

Students will

- use the words *a* and *an* correctly.

**Grammar** use the indefinite articles *a* and *an*

**Resources** Workbook p. 98; Audio CD TR: B59–60; Video: Sc. 7—Grammar 2; Classroom Presentation Tool: Grammar 2; Picture Cards 129–131, 133, 134, 136, 138, 139; Teacher's Resource CD-ROM: Activity Worksheet 8.3

**Materials** note cards; different colors of chalk or whiteboard markers

**GRAMMAR** TR: B59

**an** apple **an** egg **an** orange **a** banana **a** cookie **a** sandwich

**12** **Play a game.** Play with a partner. Find and say. Draw lines. TR: B60

**13** **Look at the pictures.** Write.

1. Is there a frog? No, there isn't a frog.
2. Is there an orange? ____________________
3. Is there a sandwich? ____________________
4. Is there an eraser? ____________________

133

## Warm Up

- Write *a* and *an* on the board. Display Picture Cards 129–131, 133, 134, 136, 138, and 139 one at a time. Read the target words aloud, emphasizing *a* or *an* and pointing to it on the board. Have students repeat.
- Give each student two note cards. Have students write *a* and *an* on separate cards. Then show the picture cards again one at a time. As students say each target word, have them hold up the correct card (*a* or *an*).

## Present

- **Give examples** Say *Today, we'll learn about the words* a *and* an. Write the following terms on the board. Use different colors for *a* and *an*.

| |
|---|
| a pizza, a sandwich, a banana |
| an apple, an orange, an egg |

- Say *Sometimes we use* a *to tell about one thing.* Point to the terms with *a* and read them aloud. Then say *Sometimes we use* an *to tell about one thing.* Read aloud the terms with *an*. Beneath these terms, write the letters *a, e, i, o,* and *u*. *We use* an *if the word begins with the letter* a, e, i, o, *or* u. Circle the initial vowels in *apple, orange,* and *egg*.
- Point to *apple* and ask *What letter does* apple *begin with?* (a) *Do we use* a *or* an? (an) Repeat for the remaining words.

- Have students open their books to p. 133. Read the grammar box aloud or play **TR: B59**. Say *Each word names one thing. An apple is one apple. A cookie is one cookie.* Play **TR: B59** again and have students repeat each term.

## Practice 12

- 12 Keep students focused on p. 133. Hold up your book and point to Polly the parrot as you read the words *Look! It's an apple* or play **TR: B60**. Point to the apple in the second row. Then ask a student to read Mia the monkey's part of the dialogue and point to the green swirl of color in the first row. Say *Let's draw a line from the green color* (move your hand in a spiral motion) *to the green apple.*

- Form pairs. Say *Work together. Say the sentences. Find the pictures. Draw lines.* Play **TR: B60** again to review the dialogue. Walk around the room to make sure pairs are drawing lines between matching pictures in each row. ✓ Point to a swirl of color and ask *What is it?*

## Apply 13

- 13 Point to Activity 13. Say *It's time to look and write. Let's do one together.* Say *Is there a frog?* Make sure students know they are looking for pictures in Activity 12. Say *I look at the pictures. I don't see a frog.* On the board, write *No, there isn't a frog.* Say *Now you try it.* When students are finished, review the answers as a class.

## Extend

- Divide the class into two large groups. Tell one group *You're the a group.* Tell the other group *You're the an group.* Draw a line down the middle of the board and label the sides **a** and **an.** Have students go on an "amazing adventure" around the classroom. They should find things they can name and count using their assigned word (*a* or *an*). As group members identify objects, have them write the words on the board with a or an. When students have finished, review the lists they created as a class.

## Wrap Up

- Say and write the following sentence frames. Have students copy them and decide whether to write *a*, *an*, or nothing in the blank: *I want* ________ *apple.* (an) *I want* ________ *banana.* (a) Review the answers and complete the sentence frames on the board.

## Be the Expert

### Grammar in Depth

The words *a* and *an* are articles. *A* and *an* are known as indefinite articles because they refer to any one of a group. The word *the* is known as a definite article because it refers to a particular noun.

*A* and *an* are only used with singular count nouns, or nouns that can be counted, such as *apple*, *orange*, and *egg*. These articles are not used with noncount nouns, or nouns that refer to groups of things, such as *rice*.

### Teaching Tip

Good pronunciation is important when introducing new vocabulary to students. With some words, however, it's not a good idea to over-enunciate or insist on a single pronunciation. One such word is *an*. That is because there are two perfectly acceptable and common ways to pronounce *an* in English.

First, *an* can be pronounced /æn/ with the short *a* sound in *man*, especially when referring to it in isolation or calling attention to it as a word. In everyday speech, especially when we are speaking or reading rapidly, *an* is usually pronounced as /ən/ with the unstressed schwa sound.

### Formative Assessment

Can students

- use the words *a* and *an* correctly?

  Say the following singular nouns and have students say them again, using *a* or *an*: *banana*, *egg*, *sandwich*.

**Review** For additional practice, direct students to Activity Worksheet 8.3.

**Objectives**

Students will

- summarize text.
- talk about food sculptures.

**Reading Strategy** Summarize

**Content Vocabulary** *vegetables, sculptures, real, examples*

**Resources** Workbook pp. 100–101; Audio CD TR: B61–63; Classroom Presentation Tool: Reading

**Materials** a simple fruit sculpture, such as an orange with pushpins for eyes and a mouth (*optional*); fruits and vegetables shown in the sculpture (*optional*); photo of sculpture created with food (*optional*)

**14 Listen and read.** TR: B61

# Fun Food

Every day, people eat food. Every day, people play. Some people play with food! They make pictures of people or animals from fruits and vegetables. Some make sculptures. Many people like to make animals. Some of these animals look real, and some animals look like they are from stories. Some food sculptures look like toys. These are all examples of fun food. Just don't eat them!

You can eat everything in this picture!

134

## Warm Up

- **Build background** Say *Today we're going to read about sculptures. A sculpture is art. It's a thing you can touch.* Say *We're going to read about sculptures made from fruits and vegetables. Who can name some fruits?* (apples, bananas, oranges) Say *Let's make a picture of a fruit sculpture. It's going to look like a person.*
- Draw an orange on the board. Say *This is the head. What can we add to the head?* (eyes, ears, mouth, arms, legs, feet) If you prepared an orange sculpture, show it. Otherwise, draw any kind of decorated orange on the board. Say *Our sculpture could look like this.* Ask *What does it have? What doesn't it have?*

## Present 14

- **Preview** Have students open their books to p. 134. Hold up your book, point to the title, and ask *Who wants to read the title?* (*Fun Food*) Say *This is about fun food. Let's look at the photo before we read.* Point to the caption and say *This sentence tells about the photo. It says* You can eat everything in this picture! *Wow, the people, the cars, and even the houses are made of food!*
- **Preteach** Point to the photo on p. 134 and say *I see some fruit. Can you find an orange? Point to it.* Point to the broccoli stalk shaped like a tree. Ask *What does this food look like?* (a tree) Say *That's right!* Then point to the red pepper and ask *What does this food look like?* (a house) Say *Yes, it looks like a house. It's a food sculpture. That's fun! Let's read about this fun food.*

**15 Listen and read.** Look. Circle *yes* or *no.* TR: B62

1. People can make sculptures with food. yes no
2. People don't make animals with food. yes no
3. Some animals look real. yes no

**16 Match.**

cookie

orange

apple

banana

**17 Look at the photo on page 134.** Write.

1. Are there any trees? ______________________
2. Are there any people? ______________________
3. Are there any houses? ______________________
4. Are there any clouds? ______________________

**18 Work with a partner.** Ask and answer.
What are your favorite foods? TR: B63

135

## Be the Expert

### Teaching Tip

The first time students read a passage, have them underline words or phrases they don't know. Afterward, discuss these words and phrases, and, as best as you can, create meaningful context for them. For example, in this passage, you may need to help students with the word *examples* by naming several fruits and saying they are all examples of fruit. Then reread the passage.

### Related Vocabulary

*boat, broccoli, cabbage, carrot, cucumber, mushroom, okra, pear, pepper, radish, squash, strawberry, watermelon, wheels*

- **14 Read together** Play **TR: B61** and have students listen. Play the track a second time and ask students to read with you, sentence by sentence. Then play the track a third time and have students read along silently. Pause at the ends of sentences to check comprehension. Ask questions such as the following:

  **Sentence 5:** *What can people make from fruits and vegetables?* (sculptures)

  **Last sentence:** *What do some sculptures look like?* (toys, animals) *Why does the writer say not to eat the fun food?* (Then you won't have the sculptures.)

- **Think Aloud** Model summarizing what you read aloud. Say *We read about fun food. People make pictures and sculptures from food. The food looks like real animals, animals from stories, and toys.*

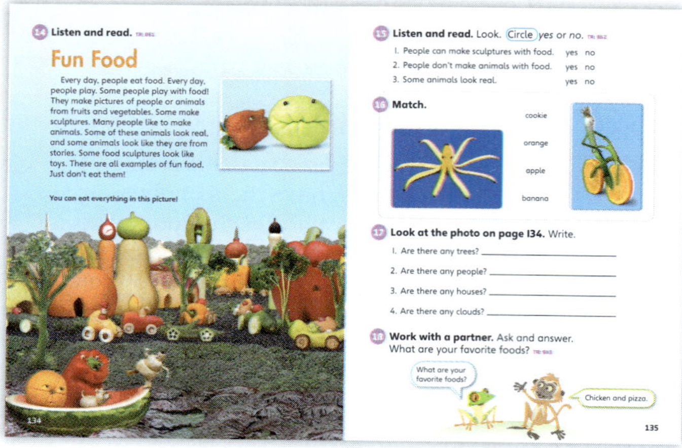


## Practice 15 16 17

- **15** Have students look at the top of p. 135. Point to Activity 15. Say *It's time to listen and read. Then we'll look and circle. Let's listen to* Fun Food *again. Then circle* yes *or* no. Play **TR: B62**. ✓ Have students point to parts of the photo on p. 134 that help them answer the questions.

- **16** Say *It's time to match. Look at the photos. Then draw a line to the words that name the food.* Allow time for students to study the photos. Then call on students to read the words aloud. Point to the banana octopus and ask *What food is this?* (a banana) Say *Find the word* banana. *Now draw a line from the word* banana *to the photo.* Have students match words to the two photos. Walk around the room to be sure they understand the task and, specifically, the instruction to draw a line.

- **17** Say *Now let's talk about the photo on page 134. Let's do one together.* Point to item 1 and say *Are there any trees?* **Think Aloud** Say *I look at the photo on page 134. I see trees.* Point to the broccoli trees. Say, as you write on the board, *I write* Yes, there are trees. *You write that, too.* When students have written the answer to item 1, have them finish the rest of the activity on their own. Finally, review the answers as a class.

## Wrap Up

- Draw or display another object created with food. The picture should include foods that students can identify, such as an egg person with a face, arms, hands, legs, and feet. Ask students to say what food or foods are in the picture and what the picture shows.

## Recap

- Say *We read about fun food. What did we learn?* On the board, write *FOOD SCULPTURE* as the start of a word cross. Write the word *ORANGE* vertically as a first example, using the second *O* in the word *FOOD*. Have students add other words they know. As they do, supply context, such as *Yes, we saw houses in the food sculpture.*

| | | | | | | | | | | | | | |
|---|---|---|---|---|---|---|---|---|---|---|---|---|---|
| | | | | | | | H | | A | | | C | |
| | | | | | | | O | | P | | | A | |
| F | O | O | D | | S | C | U | L | P | T | U | R | E |
| | | R | | | | | S | | L | | | S | |
| | | A | | | | | E | | E | | | | |
| | | N | | | | | S | | | | | | |
| | | G | | | | | | | | | | | |
| | | E | | | | | | | | | | | |

## Apply 18

- **18** Have students look at the bottom of p. 135. Point to the animal mascots and say *There they are again. It's Freddy the frog and Mia the monkey! Let's hear what they're saying.* Read the model dialogue. Then say *Listen* and play **TR: B63**.

- Form pairs. Say *Now you ask and answer with your partner. Take turns.* When both students have had a turn, call on students to share their answers with the class. Have them say both the question and their answer aloud.

## Extend

- Have students look back at the photo on p. 134. Ask *What food sculpture do you like best?* Have students write about it. You might provide these frames: *I like* ________ *best. It has* ________*. It's* ________. For additional support, provide a writing model and read it aloud. For example, *I like the red house best. It has a green top. It's big. It's fun.*

## Wrap Up

- Say *We read about fun food today. What are some things we learned about fun food?* Accept all reasonable answers and encourage the use of new vocabulary.

## Be the Expert

### Reading Strategy

**Summarize** Summarizing what they read is an important way for students to learn and explain new information. You can help students practice summarizing by asking them to come up with a single sentence that tells the writer's main idea. First, they should think about the topic. The topic is what the text is mostly about. Often, the title is a good clue to the topic. Repeated words, such as *fun*, in this case, are also good clues. Lead students in developing a sentence that sums up *Fun Food*. (Possible response: Some people make fun sculptures from food.)

### Formative Assessment

Can students

- summarize text?

  Revisit the reading on p. 134. Read only the title and the first three sentences. Have students tell you what they learned.

- talk about food sculptures?

  Show the picture of the bicycle sculpture on p. 135. Ask *What is it? What does it have? Is it fun? Do you like it?*

# Writing

**Writing** Write about favorite foods.

**Objectives**

Students will

- view and use a writing model.
- draw and write about favorite foods.

**Content Vocabulary** *lunchtime, lunch, dinner*

**Resources** Workbook p. 102; Classroom Presentation Tool: Writing; Teacher's Resource CD-ROM: Graphic Organizers (Three-column chart)

## Formative Assessment

Can students

- draw and write about favorite foods?

  Have students point to a favorite food in their drawings and then read the words that tell about it.

I eat my favorite foods at lunchtime and at night. For lunch, I like soup, a cheese sandwich, or a chicken sandwich. For dinner, I like salad, fish, and rice. I like to drink water or lemonade.

**19 Draw and write about your favorite foods.**

My favorite foods are ______________________________

______________________________

______________________________.

**20 Work in a group.** Talk about your picture.

136

## Present

- **Build background** Say *I eat lunch at lunchtime. I eat lunch at school. I eat dinner at night. I eat dinner at home.* Write the two meals on the board. Read them again and have students repeat.
- **Activate prior knowledge** Draw a three-column chart like the one below:

| | Food | Drink |
|---|---|---|
| Lunch | sandwich<br>banana | orange juice |
| Dinner | chicken<br>rice | lemonade |

- Work with students to list foods they like to eat at lunch and dinner.

## Write 19

- Have students open their books to p. 136. Read aloud the model as students follow along. Read the first sentence aloud again. *When does he eat his favorite foods?* (at lunchtime and at night)
- **19** Read the directions for Activity 19 aloud. Say *Draw your favorite foods here. Then write about them. Tell about a favorite drink, too.* To prompt students, write and say the following questions:

> What do you like for lunch?
> What do you like for dinner?
> What do you like to drink?

NATIONAL GEOGRAPHIC

# Our World

## Eat good food.

**21 Look and read.**

Eat fruits and vegetables.
Drink water and juice.

Cedar waxwing eating berries

**22 Read and copy.**

I eat fruits and vegetables. I drink water and juice.

_______________________________________

_______________________________________

137

## Value

**Value** Eat good food.

**Objectives**

Students will

- read about food values.
- read and copy two sentences.

**Resources** Values Poster

## Be the Expert

### Teaching Tip

The best way to teach values is to model them. Talk about some of the nutritious foods you like to eat, such as bananas or fish. Avoid reinforcing foods and drinks that may be unhealthy. Be a positive role model for students—remember that they're learning from your actions as well as your words.

## Share 20

- 20 Form groups. Point to Activity 20 at the bottom of p. 136. Say *Talk about your pictures. Use your sentences.* ✓ Walk around and ask questions, prompting students to describe their pictures.

## Value 21 22

- Say *Good food helps you grow strong.* Act out having strong muscles in your arms.
- Have students look at the picture on p. 137. Ask *What do you see?* (a bird) *What is the bird doing?* (The bird is eating.) Point to the title and read it aloud. Point to the berries in the photo. Say *The bird is eating good food.*
- 21 Say *Let's read. I'll read first. Then you read with me.* Read aloud and then have students choral read with you.
- 22 Point to Activity 22. Say *Now it's time to read and copy.* Read the two sentences aloud and say *Now you write.* Make sure students begin each sentence with a capital letter and end with a period.

## Project

**Objectives**

Students will

- talk about food.
- make a placemat.
- complete the Unit 8 Quiz.

**Resources** Assessment: Unit 8 Quiz; Picture Cards 129–145; Teacher's Resource CD-ROM: Activity Worksheet 8.4

**Materials** heavy construction paper or poster board; markers, crayons, or finger paint; scissors; glue

**23 Make a placemat.**

Cut out the pictures on page 173.

Glue the pictures.

Decorate and draw.

Write your name.

138

## Prepare

- Review the unit vocabulary words by holding up each of the Picture Cards in order and asking *What's this?* or *What are these?* After students name each item, have them use the word in a sentence or question, such as *I like soup* or *Do you like soup?*
- Use unit vocabulary and other familiar words to help explain the idea of a placemat. Act out the following actions on a classroom tabletop or desk as you say *First, I put down a placemat. Then I put down my lunch. I put it on a placemat. The placemat helps keep the table clean.*
- Have students open their books to pp. 138–139. Point to the finished placemat on p. 139. Say *We use placemats on tables. We put food on placemats. Today, you're going to make a placemat.* Ask *What's on this placemat?* (pictures of food)
- Help students read the first step on p. 138 aloud. Say *Cut out the pictures on page 173.* Help students locate the pictures in the back of their books. Model cutting one picture along the lines. Then read step 2. Act out gluing pictures to the placemat. Read step 3 aloud; show markers, crayons, or finger paint; and pretend to decorate and draw the placemat. Read step 4 aloud, pretending to write your name on the placemat.
- Hand out the materials that students need to make their placemats. Say *Now make your placemat. Use the steps on page 138 to help you.*

- Make sure students understand the steps before they begin. Answer any questions they have. Walk around the room and visit students as they work. If necessary, help them cut out and glue pictures and write their names.
- **Modify** If less time is available, pairs or small groups can work together to create one placemat.

## Share

- Have students form small groups and ask one another questions about their placemats. Suggest questions such as the following: *What food is that? What are those? Do you like ______?* Then have students come forward and model interviewing one another about their placemats.

## Be the Expert

### Teaching Tip

The development of eye-hand coordination can vary among young students. Although a neat final product is ideal, students who correctly follow directions and complete a project successfully also deserve praise and positive reinforcement, even if it is messy. Make a point of complimenting each student for his or her efforts in working with the materials to develop a finished product.

### Project Rubric

✓ Did students cut out and glue the correct pictures?
✓ Did students decorate their placemats?
✓ Did students sign their names?
✓ Did students ask good questions and give good answers about their placemats?

### Now I Can

Ask questions such as the following:

- *What foods did you eat today?*
- *Do you like bananas? Do you like soup? Do you like fish?*
- *What is your favorite food? What is your favorite drink?*

**Review Worksheet** For additional practice, direct students to Activity Worksheet 8.4.

### Unit Assessment

Give the Unit 8 Quiz. Hand out the quiz and go over the instructions with students. The quiz should take 15–20 minutes.

## Video

**Vocabulary 1a** *an apple, an orange, a banana, a sandwich, soup, a cookie*

**Vocabulary 1b** *chicken, an egg, fish, cheese pizza, a salad*

**Vocabulary 2** *milk, orange juice, tea, water, lemonade*

**Grammar 1** use *like* in the simple present (first and second person singular)

**Grammar 2** use the indefinite articles *a* and *an*

**Song** *Yes, Please!*

**Viewing** foods and drinks

**Story Time** *Little Red Hen Is Cooking*

**Resources** Student Book pp. 124–133

## Before You Watch

- Play Scene 1. Pause the video after Anna pulls out the apple but before Freddy identifies it. Ask *What does Anna have?* (an apple) Then press *Play* so students can hear the answer. Sum up by saying *Apples and oranges are good foods!*

## While You Watch

- Have students write all of the vocabulary words in a list. Say *Look and listen. Put a check next to the words Freddy says.*

- Pause the video as necessary to allow students to check off each item on their lists.

## After You Watch

- Group students and have them compare checklists. Ask *What words did you check?* Students should have checked every word except for *rice* and *cheese*; these two words are not in the video.

## Zoom In

### Vocabulary

- Have students raise their hands when they know a word before Freddy says it. Pause the video when students raise their hands and ask *What's the word?* Have a student say the word and others repeat. Then continue playing the video and see if students were right.

### Grammar

- Replay Scene 7, which begins with a dancing apple. Ask *What's dancing?* (an apple) Repeat with the running orange, skating banana, falling egg, turning cookie, and dropping sandwich. Be sure students include the word *a* or *an* in each identification.

### Song

- Use Scene 9 to review words for foods and drinks. Form groups and challenge them to write a new verse with a different food or drink. Model the first line of the verse. Have groups read or sing their new verses.

### Viewing

- Form pairs. Replay Scene 10, which shows animals eating and drinking. For all but the giraffe, have students ask and answer questions similar to the ones that Anna asks about the giraffe. Model an example for the monkey. Say *Is he eating pizza? Your partner answers, "No, he isn't. He isn't eating pizza."*

### Story Time

- View Scene 11. Ask *What is* Little Red Hen Is Cooking *about?* Ask questions to help students connect the story to their personal experiences. For example: *When has someone helped you? How did it make you feel?*

## Little Red Hen Is Cooking

Little Red Hen is making delicious food. Cat is watching, but he isn't helping. Will Little Red Hen share her food with Cat anyway?

## Before You Read

- **Activate prior knowledge** Act out cooking food. Pretend to put on an apron, take food out from cabinets, wash it, chop it, put it into a pot, and stir it on the stove. Ask *Is cooking hard work?* Allow time for responses, and then say *Yes, it is hard work.*

- **Introduce the strategy** Have students turn to the first page of the Reader. Work with them to complete an **I Read/I See/I Know** chart like the one below:

| I Read/I See | I Know |
| --- | --- |
| (I read/I see) Hen is cooking soup.<br>(I see) vegetables and things to make soup.<br>(I read) Cat is not cooking. Cat is asking about the soup. | Hen has to use a lot of vegetables. |

- Say *When you read, think about what you already know.* Ask *Does someone you know make soup or other food for you? Is it a lot of work?*

## While You Read

- Read the book aloud to students. Stop every few pages to ask questions that require students to connect to personal experience.

  p. 3: Ask *Does Cat like soup? Do you like soup? Who makes soup for you?*
  p. 6: Ask *Does Cat like cookies? Do you like cookies?*
  p. 7: Ask *Does Cat help Hen? Do you help people? Tell me how.*

## After You Read

- Ask *What was the story about? Do you know someone like Hen? Do you know someone like Cat? Tell me about them.*

- Say *Let's tell a new story.* Open the book again. Read the first spread. Turn to p. 4 and say *Here is where the new story begins. Cat says "Yes, I can help you!" What happens next?* Guide students to predict that Cat will also help on p. 7 and that Hen and Cat will share the food at the end of the story.

## Unit 8 Reader

**Text Type** folktale

**Vocabulary** *soup, cookie, egg, chicken, milk, orange, orange juice, banana*

**Grammar** use *like* in the simple present (first and second person singular)

**Reading Strategy** Connect Text to Personal Experience

**Resources** Picture Cards 129–145; Classroom Presentation Tool: Story Time; Video: Sc. 11—Story Time

## Be the Expert

### Reading Strategy

**Connect Text to Personal Experience** Strong personal connections enhance understanding. You can help students connect to personal experience by asking them to think of how characters remind them of people they know.

Ask students how actions remind them of things they've done or seen in real life. Even if students haven't done or seen what they read about, you can help them make personal connections by asking how they might feel or act in a similar situation.

### Text Background

Although this story is based on a folktale, it's not a typical folktale because it teaches a very clear lesson, something folktales don't usually do. This type of folktale is often brief, and even though it has characters, they are not developed. Instead, the stories teach a lesson in a straightforward, to-the-point way.

## Student Book

**TR: B48** **1** **Listen and say.**

| | |
|---|---|
| a banana | I want a banana. |
| cheese pizza | I want cheese pizza. |
| a salad | I want a salad. |
| an orange | I want an orange. |
| an apple | I want an apple. |
| rice | I want rice. |
| a sandwich | I want a sandwich. |
| a cookie | I want a cookie. |
| soup | I want soup. |
| chicken | I want chicken. |
| an egg | I want an egg. |
| fish | I want fish. |

**TR: B49** **2** **Listen. Point and say.**

a cookie, soup, banana, a salad, rice, a sandwich, an apple, chicken, cheese pizza, an egg, an orange, fish

**TR: B50** **3** **Work with a partner. Point. Ask and answer.**

What is it? It's an orange.

**TR: B51** **4** **Listen. Read and sing.**

Note: Lyrics for the song *Yes, Please!* are on pp. 248–249.

**TR: B52** **Grammar**

Note: Grammar 1, 1st chart, is on p. 250.

**TR: B53** **6** **What do they like? Listen and find. Circle and write.**

1. Do you like bananas? No, I don't like bananas.
   Do you like oranges? Yes, I like oranges.
2. Do you like sandwiches? No, I don't like sandwiches.
   Do you like cookies? Yes, I like cookies.
3. Do you like rice? No, I don't like rice.
   Do you like apples? Yes, I like apples.

**TR: B54** **Grammar**

Note: Grammar 1, 2nd chart, is on p. 251.

**TR: B55** **7** **What do they like? Listen and find. Circle and write.**

1. Do you like soup?
   No, I don't like soup.
   Do you like pizza?
   Yes, I like pizza.
2. Do you like salad?
   No, I don't like salad.
   Do you like fish?
   Yes, I like fish.
3. Do you like eggs?
   No, I don't like eggs.
   Do you like chicken?

**TR: B56** **8** **Listen and say.**

| | |
|---|---|
| tea | I like tea. |
| orange juice | I like orange juice. |
| water | I like water. |
| lemonade | I like lemonade. |
| milk | I like milk. |

**TR: B57** **10** **Look. Listen and read. Circle yes or no.**

1. Do you like orange juice?
   No, I don't like orange juice. I like lemonade.
2. Do you like tea?
   No, I don't like tea. I like water.

**TR: B58** **11** **Work with a partner. Say and stick.**

Number one. I like water.
I don't like water. I like tea. Number two.

**TR: B59** **Grammar**

Note: Grammar 2 is on p. 256.

**TR: B60** **12** **Play a game. Play with a partner. Find and say. Draw lines.**

Look! It's an apple. That is an apple, too.

**TR: B61** **14** **Listen and read.**

Note: Reading *Fun Food* is on p. 258.

**TR: B62** **15** **Listen and read. Look. Circle yes or no.**

Every day, people eat food. Every day, people play. Some people play with food! They make pictures of people or animals from fruits and vegetables. Some make sculptures. Many people like to make animals. Some of these animals look real, and some animals look like they are from stories. Some food sculptures look like toys. These are all examples of fun food. Just don't eat them!

1. People can make sculptures with food.
2. People don't make animals with food.
3. Some animals look real.

**TR: B63** **18** **Work with a partner. Ask and answer. What are your favorite foods?**

What are your favorite foods? Chicken and pizza.

## Workbook

**TR: 63** **3** **Listen to the song. Read. Draw lines to match.**

Note: Lyrics for the song *Yes, Please!* are on pp. 248–249.

**TR: 64** **4** **Listen to the song. Write. Use words from the box.**

Do you want a cookie? Do you want some cheese? Do you want a banana? Yes, please!

**TR: 65** **6** **Listen. Write.**

1. Do you like salad? No, I don't. I don't like salad.
2. Does she like fish? Yes, she does. She likes fish.
3. Do you like oranges? Yes, I do. I like oranges.
4. Does he like bananas? No, he doesn't. He doesn't like bananas.
5. Do you like sandwiches? No, I don't. I don't like sandwiches.

**TR: 66** **7** **Listen. Write.**

See script for **TR: 65** above.

**TR: 67** **13** **Listen. Write.**

1. Do you have a crayon?
2. I have an old pen.
3. Does a fish have an ear?
4. Does the puppet have a mouth?

**TR: 68** **16** **Play a game. Start at A. Listen. Go through the maze to the house.**

Do you like eggs?
I do. I like eggs. I have an egg.
Is there a sandwich?
Yes, there is a sandwich.
Is there chicken? I like chicken.
There is chicken.
I'm thirsty! Where is the milk?
There's the milk.
Where is my house?
There it is!

**TR: 69** **18** **Listen and read.**

Note: Reading *Fruit* is on p. 327.

**TR: 70** **26** **Listen. Circle.**

1. Do you like milk? No, I don't. I like orange juice.
2. Do you like water? Yes, I do. I like water.
3. Do you like lemonade? Yes, I do. I like lemonade.

# Answer Key

## Student Book

**Unit Opener** SB p. 124

flowers, fruit

**6** SB p. 130

1. circle oranges; oranges 2. circle cookies; cookies
3. circle apples; apples

**7** SB p. 131

1. circle pizza; pizza 2. circle fish; fish
3. circle chicken; chicken

**10** SB p. 132

1. no, 2. yes

**13** SB p. 133

1. No, there isn't a frog. 2. Yes, there is an orange.
3. Yes, there is a sandwich. 4. No, there isn't an eraser.

**15** SB p. 135

1. yes, 2. no, 3. yes

**16** SB p. 135

line from orange to orange slices
line from banana peel to banana

**17** SB p. 135

1. Yes, there are. 2. Yes, there are.
3. Yes, there are. 4. No, there aren't.

## Workbook

Go to pp. 325–328 for the Workbook Answer Key for this unit.

# In This Unit

**Theme** This unit is about animals and things animals do.

**Content Objective**

Students will

- identify animals and describe their actions.

**Language Objectives**

Students will

- name animals.
- talk about what animals can do.
- describe a favorite animal.

**Vocabulary**

**Vocabulary 1** *a cat, a chicken, a cow, a dog, a donkey, a duck, a frog, a goat, a horse, a rabbit, a sheep, a turtle*

**Vocabulary 2** *climb, crawl, fly, see, swim*

**Grammar**

**Grammar 1** use present progressive (third person plural)

**Grammar 2** use *want* + infinitive (first, second, and third person singular)

**Pacing Guides** LIU9

**Writing** Write about your favorite animal.

**Value** Be good to animals.

**Project** Make a class book about animals.

## Unit Opener

**Objectives**

Students will

- identify parts of a photo.
- check accuracy of statements.

**Academic Language** *check, false, true*

**Content Vocabulary** *bird, monkey*

**Resources** Video: Sc. 1—Introduction; Classroom Presentation Tool: Unit Opener; Teacher's Resource CD-ROM: Graphic Organizers (Word web); Home-School Connection Letter; Unit Opener Poster; Picture Cards 146, 149

**Materials** photo of dog or cat (*optional*)

Unit 9

# Animal Friends

In this unit, I will . . .
- name animals.
- talk about what animals can do.
- describe a favorite animal.

**Check T for *True* and F for *False*.**

1. There's a monkey and a cat. (T) (F)
2. The monkey likes the bird. (T) (F)
3. The bird is green. (T) (F)
4. The monkey is a baby. (T) (F)

140

## Introduce

- **Build background** Say *Today, we're going to learn about animal friends. Many people have animal friends.* Hold up Picture Cards 146 (a cat) and 149 (a dog) and say *These animals are our friends.* Ask *Do you have an animal friend? Raise your hand.* Model raising your hand. Ask *What animal friends do you have?*

- Hold up a photo of a dog or draw and color a picture of one on the board. Begin a word web with **dog** in the center circle. Point to the photo or picture of the dog. Say *This is a dog. What color is it?* Point to its legs. *How many legs?* Write answers in the word web. Ask students more questions to fill in the word web.

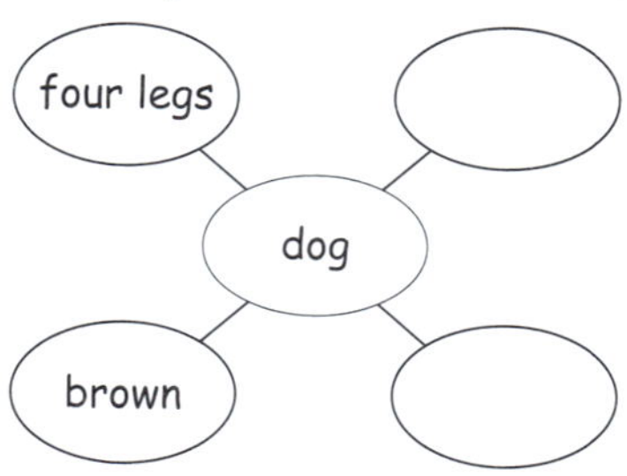

Macaque monkey and dove,
Neilingding Island, China

141

- Direct students' attention to the photo on pp. 140–141. Say *Look at the photo.* Point to each animal and say *This is a bird. This is a monkey.* Point to the bird and ask *What color is the bird?* (white, pink, orange) Point to the monkey and ask *What color is the monkey?* (brown, pink)
- Say *Animals can be our friends.* Point to the photo again. Say *Animals can be friends with other animals, too! The monkey and the bird are friends.*
- Have students look at the activity on p. 140. Say *Let's read and then check. Think about the sentence. Is it true or false?* If necessary, review *true* and *false*, using real-life examples. Read item 1 aloud and ask *Where is the monkey?* Students should point to the monkey. Ask *Where's the cat?* Pause and say *There's no cat. This sentence is not true. I check F for false.* Have students work together to complete the other three items. Review the answers as a class.

## Be the Expert

### About the Photo

This photo shows a baby macaque monkey on Neilingding Island, near Hong Kong in southern China. Show students China on a map.

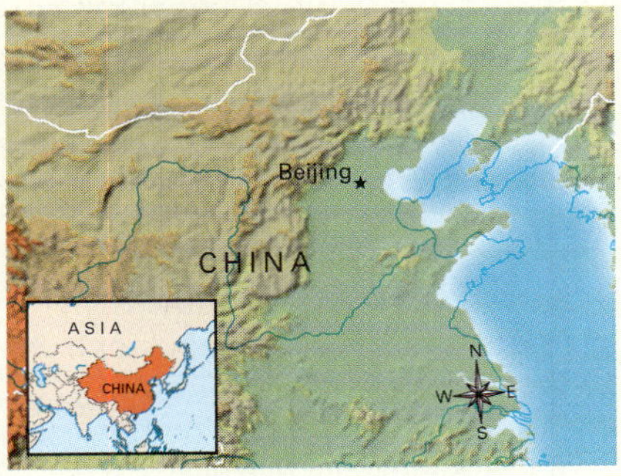


The monkey is just three months old in the photograph. Soon after it was born, it lost its mother, and animal rescue workers took care of it. In the animal-care shelter, the monkey bonded with the bird in the photo.

The real event here is not friendship, but imprinting. In the earliest days of its life, an animal learns from its mother or another guide—regardless of whether the guide is its biological mother or even from the same species. This helps explain why it's possible to domesticate animals.

### Teaching Tip

Word webs and other types of brainstorming activities are a good way to activate prior knowledge, introduce new content, and help students use any unit vocabulary they may have acquired. Encourage students to contribute during brainstorming sessions, and give as many students as possible a chance to share their ideas.

### Related Vocabulary

*hug*

## Vocabulary 1

**Objective**

Students will

- identify and use words that name animals.

**Vocabulary** *a dog, a goat, a rabbit, a duck, a horse, a turtle, a cat, a chicken, a donkey, a cow, a frog, a sheep*

**Resources** Workbook pp. 104–105; Audio CD TR: B64–66; Video: Sc. 2— Vocabulary 1a; Sc. 3—Vocabulary 1b; Classroom Presentation Tool: Vocabulary 1; Teacher's Resource CD-ROM: Graphic Organizers (KWL chart, Two-column chart), Activity Worksheet 9.1; Picture Cards 146–157

**Materials** poster board

## Warm Up

- Draw the following KWL chart organizer on a large piece of paper or poster board. Include the headings **Know**, **Want to Know**, and **Learned**. Write **Animal Friends** above the chart.

| Animal Friends | | |
|---|---|---|
| Know | Want to Know | Learned |
| | | |

- Ask *What animals can you name?* If students need prompting, hold up Picture Cards 146–157 one at a time. For each card, ask *What is it?* Post the cards that most students can name in the **Know** column. Post the others in the **Want to Know** column. When all of the cards are posted, point to and say each animal name aloud.
- Make a note to remember which animals were in which column. You will revisit this KWL chart at the end of the lesson.

**3 Work with a partner.**
Point. Ask and answer.

143

## Present

- **Give examples** Say *A dog is an animal. A cat is an animal. Let's learn more animals.* Point to the frog on p. 142. Say *A frog. A frog is an animal, too.* Ask *What color is the frog?* (green and orange) Say *Tell me more about the frog.* (It has big eyes and a big mouth. It has four legs.)
- Have students look at the photos on pp. 142–143. Point to each photo, say the name of the animal, and give a context sentence for each. Examples include the following:

  *A dog has four legs. Dogs like to run.*
  *Ducks are small. They like to swim.*
  *A horse is big and strong.*

- Encourage students to tell what they know about each animal or describe the photo in the book. Practice the pronunciation of each animal's name.

## Be the Expert

### Vocabulary Strategy

**Using a Dictionary** Make sure students understand that a dictionary is a list of words and their meanings. The words are in alphabetical, or ABC, order. Provide multiple opportunities for students to use a dictionary and practice finding words. Create lists of words beginning with different letters, name two, and have students tell which one would come first in a dictionary.

Using a dictionary (either in print or online) routinely helps students not only remember new vocabulary but also become more actively engaged in reading and writing activities.

### Related Vocabulary

*animals, farm, pets*

## Practice 1 2

- 1 Have students open their books to p. 142. Say *It's time to listen and say.* Say *Say each word and sentence you hear.* Model a turtle. Say *A turtle. A turtle is walking.* Motion for students to repeat the word and sentence. Ask *Are you ready?* Play **TR: B64**.
- 2 Say *Now it's time to listen, point, and say.* Play **TR: B65** and pause the track after the first word (*a dog*). Point to the photo of the dog and say *a dog.* Then play **TR: B65** from the beginning for students to point and say. Show Picture Card 150 and ask *What is it?* (a donkey) If students have difficulty naming and pointing to it, play **TR: B65** again.
- Say *Now I point and you say.* Point to various photos on pp. 142–143 and have students identify them. Form pairs and have students do the same with each other.

## Wrap Up

- Say *We learned words for animals.* Ask *What are they?* Have students name as many animals as they can. Say *I'm an animal. I start with d. What am I?* (dog, duck, donkey) Repeat with other letters or clues.

## Recap

- Say *We learned the names of many animals. What small animals did we learn about?* (turtle, frog, duck, cat, rabbit) *What big animals did we learn about?* (dog, horse, goat, cow, sheep, donkey)
- Put students in three groups. Give each group three Picture Cards. Choose from Cards 146–157. Have groups review the cards and identify the animals. Then have groups take turns standing up and showing one card to the class. Have the class say the animal's name. Continue until the class identifies all cards.

## Apply 3

- 3 Point to the model dialogue on the bottom of p. 143. Say *There are our friends, Freddy the frog and Eddie the elephant! They're talking. Let's listen.* Play **TR: B66**.
- Ask *What does Freddy the frog say?* (What is it?) Point to Freddy and ask *What's he doing?* (pointing to the donkey)
- Model with a student. Hold up your book as you point to the photo of a donkey. Ask *What is it?* Have the student answer *It's a donkey.* Have students form pairs. Say *Point to a photo. Ask "What is it?" Your partner answers. Take turns. Ask about different animals.* Walk around the room making sure that pairs are correctly naming all of the different animals. Point to an animal you don't hear either partner ask about, and ask *What is it?*

## Extend

- Say *Let's learn more about these animals.* Make a two-column chart with the headings **What It Is** and **What It Has.**

| What It Is | What It Has |
|---|---|
| turtle | a head, a body, four legs |
| frog | big eyes, a nose, a mouth, four legs |

- Point to the first column and ask *What is one animal we know about?* Write *turtle* in the first column. Say *Look at the photo of the turtle on page 142. What does it have?* Model the answer *It has a head. It has a body.* Ask *How many legs does it have?* (four) Write the answers in the second column.
- Put students in four groups and assign three animals from pp. 142–143 to each group. Hand out Picture Cards 146–157. Then have groups create a chart for their animals. Give students enough time to complete their charts.
- Have each group come to the front of the class and show the cards for their animals one at a time. As they show each card, have them use the chart to tell about the animal.

## Wrap Up

- Take out the KWL chart from the Warm Up activity. Review the animals that students "knew" and "wanted to know." Write the words for animals students knew in the first column. Post the appropriate picture cards in the second column. Ask *What animal names did we learn?* Write students' responses in the last column.

| Animal Friends | | |
|---|---|---|
| Know | Want to Know | Learned |
| cat, dog | | chicken, cow, donkey, duck, frog, goat, horse, rabbit, sheep, turtle |

## Be the Expert

### Teaching Tip

Try not to use a student's name when correcting errors. Rather than saying *John said, "The rabbits has four legs,"* say *I heard, "The rabbits has four legs."* Then ask students if they can identify and correct the error. Another option is to make mental notes of errors you hear and correct the student privately.

If you hear three or four errors within a short period of time, write them all on the board and ask students to identify and correct the errors. By presenting several errors at once, the focus is taken off of any one particular student.

### Formative Assessment

Can students

- identify and use words that name animals?

  Hand out Picture Cards 146–157 one by one and ask *What is it?*

**Review** For additional practice, direct students to Activity Worksheet 9.1.

## Song

**Vocabulary in the song**

**Vocabulary 1** *dog, cat, frog*

**Vocabulary 2** *see, climb*

**Grammar in the song**

**Grammar 1** use present progressive (third person plural)

**Resources** Workbook p. 106; Audio CD TR: B67; Video: Sc. 9—Song; Classroom Presentation Tool: Song

4 **Listen.** Read and sing. TR: B67

# Animals

*I see animals.*
*What are they doing?*
*I see animals.*
*Can you see them, too?*

*What do you see?*

*I see one dog.*
*Is it running?*
*Yes, it's running.*
*It's running in the sun.*

*What do you see?*

*I see two cats.*
*Are they climbing?*
*Yes, they're climbing.*
*They're climbing, and it's fun.*

*Running and climbing,*
*hopping and singing.*
*These are things we like to do.*

*Are you ready?*
*All together!*

*Run! Climb! Hop! Sing!*

144

## Use the Song 4

- **Activate prior knowledge** Say *Today we'll sing a song about animals. What animals do you know?* Write *dog* on the board. Have students come to the board and write their responses.
- **Build background** Point to *dog* and ask *What do dogs do?* (run, walk, jump) *What can cats do?* (run, walk, jump) *What can birds do?* (sing, walk, fly) *What can frogs do?* (jump, swim)
- Have students open their books to pp. 144–145. Say *Point to the title of the song.* Say *Tell me the title.* (*Animals*) Signal for students to respond together.
- Hold up your book and point to the pictures of the animals. Ask *What animals are in our song?* (a dog, cats, birds, frogs)
- Say *Look at the pictures.* Ask *What animal is running?* (dog) *What animals are singing?* (birds) *What animals are hopping?* (frogs)
- 4 Say *Our song tells what animals do.* Play **TR: B67**. Say *It's time to sing,* and ask students to listen and sing as they read along.

## Use It Again 5

- **Vocabulary 1** Put students in three groups. Assign each group *dog*, *cat*, or *frog*. Have students draw a picture of their animal and write the animal's name below their pictures. Then write the following on the board:

What do you see?

I see three frogs.
Are they hopping?
Yes, they're hopping.
They're hopping on a rock.

What do you see?

I see four birds.
Are they singing?
Yes, they're singing.
They're singing la, la, la!

La lalala!
La lala!

Running and climbing,
hopping and singing.
These are things we like to do.

Are you ready?
All together!
Run! Climb! Hop! Sing!

**5** **Sing again.** Hold up pictures.

145

## Be the Expert

### Teaching Tip

The first time students hear a song, encourage them to just listen. To help students recognize target vocabulary words, write them on the board and point to each when you hear it. The second time they hear the song, have students read the lyrics and point to target vocabulary words. After students can match the words they hear with the words they see, have them sing along.

I see one __________.
I see two __________.
I see three __________.

- Have students find the verse with their assigned animal. Sing *What do you see?* to each group. Have each group sing back the line from the appropriate verse (*I see one dog*; *I see two cats*; *I see three frogs.*)
- **5** Say *Now we all sing. Sing your part of the song. Show your pictures.* Play **TR: B67** and have students sing their parts while holding up their pictures.
- **Grammar 1** Have students count off by four. Say *Student 1, listen for the words* They're climbing. *Then show climbing.* Model using your hands to show climbing up something. Say *Student 2, listen for the words* They're hopping. *Show hopping.* Model hopping on one foot. Say *Student 3, listen for the words* It's running. *Show running.* Model running in place. Say *Student 4, listen for the words* They're singing. *You say* la la la *when you hear the words.* Play **TR: B67** again. Point to groups when it's their turn.
- **Grammar 2** Form four small groups. Have each group prepare and act out a question and an answer with *want to* for one of the animals in the song. Model. Say *You ask the dog "Do you want to run?" The dog says "Yes, I want to run."*

## Grammar 1

**Objective**

Students will
- ask and answer questions about actions.

**Grammar** use present progressive (third person plural)

**Resources** Workbook pp. 107–108, Audio CD TR: B68–71; Video: Sc. 6—Grammar 1; Classroom Presentation Tool: Grammar 1; Teacher's Resource CD-ROM: Graphic Organizers (Two-column chart); Picture Cards 13, 15, 18, 78

**GRAMMAR** TR: B68

What **are** the horses **doing?** They**'re running.**

**6 Listen and find.** Write. TR: B69

1. ______________ 2. ______________

3. ______________ 4. ______________

146

## Warm Up

- **Recycle** Draw two stick figures on the board. Add T-shirts, pants, and shoes. Give one figure long hair to show that it's a girl, and the other short hair to show that it's a boy. Alternatively, give them names to distinguish them. Point to the girl and ask *What's she wearing?* (She's wearing a T-shirt, pants, and shoes.) Point to the boy and ask *What's he wearing?* (He's wearing a T-shirt, pants, and shoes.) Circle both figures, point to them, and ask *What are they wearing?* (They're wearing T-shirts, pants, and shoes.) Say *They're wearing T-shirts, pants, and shoes. They're both wearing clothes.*

- **Preteach** Write the following on the board:

| | |
|---|---|
| He's wearing ______. | They're wearing ______. |
| She's wearing ______. | |

- Read the first column of sentences aloud. Point to the first sentence and ask *How many people?* (one) Point to the second sentence and ask *How many people?* (one) Say *Use is wearing to talk about one person.* Point to the sentence in the second column and read it aloud. Then ask *How many people?* (more than one) Say *Yes. Use are wearing to talk about more than one person.* If necessary, remind students how to form the appropriate contractions.

**GRAMMAR** TR: B70

| | |
|---|---|
| Are they **sleeping?** | No, they **aren't.** |
| Are they **eating?** | Yes, they **are.** |

**7 Listen and find. Circle.** TR: B71

1. sleeping walking
2. jumping eating
3. talking reading
4. sleeping jumping

147

## Be the Expert

### Our World in Context

Horses run fast, but they aren't the fastest land animals. The fastest racehorse might run 89 kilometers per hour (55 miles per hour) over a quarter-mile distance. Lions and antelopes are just as fast. Lions can run short distances at 80 kilometers (50 miles) per hour. Some kinds of antelope can also run 80 kilometers (50 miles) per hour. Cheetahs are even faster. They're the fastest land animals. They can run 114 kilometers (71 miles) per hour!

### Grammar in Depth

*They run* and *they're running* have different meanings. *They run* is in the simple present. The simple present is used to tell about actions in the present such as *Simon and Lee run.* It's also used to tell about facts, such as *They run fast*, or repeated actions, such as *They run every morning.*

*They're running* is in the present progressive tense. The present progressive is used to tell about actions happening now. It is also used to tell about actions that may happen over a long period of time, but not at the moment, such as *They're running in all the races this year.*

## Present

- Write the following on the board:

| | |
|---|---|
| What are the students doing? | They're walking. |

- Have two students walk from one side of the classroom to the other and back again. Point to the question on the board and ask *What are the students doing?* Model the answer. Point to the sentence on the board and say *They're walking.* Underline *They're* and say *There are two students. So we say They're.*

- Have students open their books to p. 146 and find the yellow grammar box at the top. Read the question and answer aloud or play **TR: B68**. Then have half of the class read the question aloud and have the other half read the answer.

- Show *sleeping* by closing your eyes, tilting your head, putting your hands together, palm against palm, and placing them at the side of your head. Ask two students to come forward and do the same. Ask and answer *What are they doing? They are sleeping. They're sleeping.* Point to a row or table of students. Say *Are they sleeping? No, they are not sleeping. They aren't sleeping.*

## Practice 6 7

- Have students open their books to p. 146. Say *Let's talk about this picture.* Ask *What's in the tree?* (birds) Ask *What are the birds doing?* (They are singing. They're singing.) *Where are the girls?* Pause long enough for students to point to the girls. *What are they doing?* (They are jumping rope. They're jumping rope.)

- 6 Direct students' attention to Activity 6. Say *Let's listen and find.* Hold up your book and point to the four lines at the bottom of the page. Play only the first item on **TR: B69**. Model *The question is* What are the birds doing? *I look for the birds in the picture. Here they are. They're singing.* Point to the line for number 1. *So I'll write* They're singing. *You write it, too.* Play the rest of **TR: B69** and have students finish the activity. When students are finished, review the answers as a class.

- Point to the yellow grammar box at the top of p. 147. Read the sentences aloud or play **TR: B70**. Ask *Who is this about?* Students should point to the children with the ice cream cones.

- Write the following on the board.

| | |
|---|---|
| Are they singing? | No, they aren't. |
| | Yes, they are. |

- Point to the picture of the cats on pp. 144–145. Read aloud the question on the board and model the answer *No, they aren't.* Then point to the picture of the birds and repeat the question. Guide students to say *Yes, they are.*

- 7 Say *Now you listen, find, and circle.* Play **TR: B71** and complete the first item with students. Then have pairs complete the activity. ✓ Point to the picture of the frogs. Ask *Are they eating?* (No, they aren't.) *Are they hopping?* (Yes, they are.)

- Review the answers to Activity 7 as a class. Play **TR: B71** again, if necessary.

## Wrap Up

- Say *I ask a question. You say the answer.* Model. Point to two students and ask *Are they eating?* Model the answer *No, they aren't.* Ask *What are they doing? They're sitting.*

- Point to two other students and ask *Are they sleeping?* (No, they aren't.) *What are they doing?* Continue pointing to different students and asking questions such as *Are they eating? Are they running? Are they jumping?*

## Recap

- Show Picture Card 13. Ask *What are they doing?* (They're reading.) Show Picture Card 15. Ask *What are the people doing?* (They're singing.) Show Picture Card 18. Ask *What are the people doing?* (They're walking.) Show Picture Card 78. Ask *What are they doing?* (They're cleaning.)

- Show Picture Card 13 again. Ask *Are they eating?* (No, they aren't). *Are they reading?* (Yes, they are.) Continue with the other picture cards.

## Apply

- Form small groups of three or four. Have each group look at another group and tell what the students in that group are and aren't doing. Have one group run in place. Say *They're running.* Provide one example of what they are not doing, such as *They're not sleeping.* Give groups enough time to prepare one or two sentences. Have the class repeat each sentence. Write the sentences on the board.

- **Expand** Look at the list. Read a sentence aloud and have students say another way to say the same thing by changing the contraction. For example, the sentence *They're not sleeping* can also be written *They aren't sleeping*. The sentence *They are talking* can be written *They're talking*.

## Extend

- Point to the following pictures in the Student Book and for each one, ask *What are they doing?* Then ask *What aren't they doing?* and have students come up with as many answers as possible.

  pp. 78–79: (They are/They're wearing clothes. They are/They're wearing shoes. They are/They're standing up.)
  p. 112: (They are/They're dancing. They are/They're jumping.)
  p. 145: (They are/They're singing. They are/They're sitting. They are/They're standing. They are/They're hopping.)

## Wrap Up

- Say *Draw a picture of two animals. Show them doing something. They can be running, walking, or jumping.* Give students a few minutes to draw their pictures.
- Put students in small groups. Have students show their pictures one at a time and ask *What are the animals doing?* The other group members look at the picture and answer *They're* ________. Have students take turns.
- Then have students show their pictures again and ask questions such as *Are they eating? Are they running?* Students in the group answer *Yes, they are* or *No, they aren't.*

## Be the Expert

### Teaching Tip

It's important to give all students an opportunity to speak in class. When you ask questions, don't always call on the most eager student. Call on as many students as possible, so that every student has an opportunity to speak.

### Formative Assessment

Can students

- ask and answer questions about actions?

  Draw two sitting cats. Ask *What are the cats doing?* Then say *Ask a question about the cats.*

# Vocabulary 2

**Objective**

Students will

- identify and use action words.

**Vocabulary** *see, climb, swim, fly, crawl*

**Resources** Workbook p. 109; Audio CD TR: B72–74; Video: Sc. 4—Vocabulary 2; Classroom Presentation Tool: Vocabulary 2; Teacher's Resource CD-ROM: Graphic Organizers (6-by-6 matrix), Activity Worksheet 9.2; Picture Cards 18, 125, 127, 158–162; Sound Card 20

**8 Listen and say.** TR: B72

see

climb

fly

swim

crawl

**9 Work with a partner.** Point and say.

**10 Look.** Listen and read. Circle *yes* or *no*. TR: B73

1. The birds are flying. yes no
2. The cat is swimming. yes no
3. The turtle is crawling. yes no

**11 Work with a partner.** Listen. Say and stick. TR: B74

1 2 3 4 5



## Warm Up

- **Activate prior knowledge** Say *We know some ways animals move.* Show Picture Card 18. Ask *What is this?* (walk) *Show me walk.* Have students act out walking. Show Picture Card 125. Ask *What is this?* (jump) Say *Show me jump* and have students act out jumping. Show Picture Card 127. Ask *What is this?* (run) Have students act out running in place.

## Present

- Say *Let's learn some more ways animals can move.* Have students open their books to p. 148. Point to *see*. Say *See.* Point to your eyes and say *I see with my eyes.* Point to *climb, fly, swim,* and *crawl.* As you point to each, say the word aloud and act it out. Have students repeat the word and action after you.

- **Give examples** Make a 6-by-6 matrix on the board. For each action word, ask *Can a (turtle) (see)?* For each positive answer, make a check mark in the chart.

| | turtle | duck | cat | horse | frog |
|---|---|---|---|---|---|
| see | ✓ | ✓ | ✓ | ✓ | ✓ |
| fly | | ✓ | | | |
| swim | ✓ | ✓ | | | ✓ |
| climb | | | ✓ | | ✓ |
| crawl | ✓ | | | | |

- Sum up each column of the chart for students like this: *A turtle can see, swim, and crawl.* Form pairs. Have each student choose one column of the chart and sum up the information for his or her partner.

✓ Point to the first cell of the column and ask *Can*

*a (turtle) see?* If students cannot answer, say *There is a check here. A turtle can see.*

## Practice 8 9 10

- 8 Have students open their books to p. 148. Say *Listen and say.* Say the first word and sentence on the audio: *See. The boy sees two birds in the sky.* Play **TR: B72**. Make sure students repeat the words and sentences correctly.
- 9 Form pairs. Say *Point to each picture. Tell your partner what it shows. Listen as your partner points and tells you.*
- 10 Have students keep the same partners. Say *Now look, listen, read, and circle.* Say *Let's do one together.* Play number 1 on **TR: B73**. Say *I listen. The birds are flying.* Point to the photo of the birds in Activity 8. Say *I look at the picture. I see the birds are flying.* Point to item 1 in Activity 10. Say *I circle yes. The birds are flying.* Have partners finish the activity. Play **TR: B73**.

## Apply 11

- 11 Say *Let's do a sticker activity.* Have pairs read the model dialogue aloud. Play **TR: B74**. Have a student help you demonstrate the steps as you say *I listen. I talk with my partner. We decide what sticker to use. I put it on number one. Then my partner listens, talks with me, and puts the sticker on number two.* Have pairs complete the activity. Walk around to monitor correct pronunciation and placement of stickers.

## Extend

- On the board, draw a park with a playground. Say *People are playing with friends. What are they doing? Use the words we learned.* Model sample responses, such as *Two boys are playing with a dog. They're crawling in the grass. They're swimming.*
- On the board, write *climb, crawl, fly, see,* and *swim.* Have students write sentences about the playground using as many of the words as they can. When they're done, have students form pairs and share their writing with their partners. Then have students share sentences with the class.

## Wrap Up

- Play a matching game. Have students match animals to the actions they might perform, and then make sentences using both the name of the animal and the action. Write the following words in two columns on the board, and have students make at least two matches: Column 1: *fly, climb, crawl, swim*; Column 2: *frog, turtle, sheep, duck.*

## Be the Expert

### Vocabulary Strategy

**Use a Dictionary** For practice with alphabetical order, have students tell which vocabulary words from this unit are found: after the word *run* and before *sit* (sheep, see); after the word *car* and before *circle* (cat, chicken); after the word *food* and before *fruit* (frog); and after the word *does* and before *draw* (dog, donkey).

### Sounds of English

**Single Sounds: /ŋ/**

The /ŋ/ sound (sleepi<u>ng</u>) may be difficult for learners of English.

To practice, have students pronounce the /iː/ sound (tr<u>ee</u>) for several seconds. While pronouncing the /iː/, have students point the tip of their tongue down and raise the back of their tongue to the top of the mouth. The /iː/ sound will change to the /ŋ/ sound.

Use Sound Card # 20 (swi<u>ng</u>). Have students put a hand in front of their faces. They should feel air coming out of their noses.

Example words: si<u>ng</u>, you<u>ng</u>, stro<u>ng</u>, cleani<u>ng</u>, cooki<u>ng</u>

### Formative Assessment

Can students

- identify and use action words?

  Show pictures of animals climbing, crawling, flying, seeing, and swimming. Ask *What is it doing?* or *What are they doing?*

**Review** For additional practice, direct students to Activity Worksheet 9.2.

# Grammar 2

**Objective**
Students will
- ask and answer questions with *want*.

**Grammar** use *want* + infinitive (first, second, and third person singular)

**Academic Language** *action word* (verb), *naming word* (noun)

**Content Vocabulary** *ride*

**Resources** Workbook p. 110; Audio CD TR: B75–77; Video: Sc. 7—Grammar 2; Classroom Presentation Tool: Grammar 2; Teacher's Resource CD-ROM: Activity Worksheet 9.3

**Materials** a photo of a person riding a horse; scissors

**GRAMMAR** TR: B75

| | |
|---|---|
| **Do** you **want to ride** the donkey? | No, I don't. |
| What **do** you **want to do?** | I **want to ride** the horse. |
| What **does** Anna **want to do?** | She **wants to see** the ducks. |

**12** **Look.** Listen and read. Write. TR: B76

1. Maria ______________________ the sheep.
2. Carlos ______________________ the frog.

**13** **Play a game.** Cut out the cards on page 175. Ask and answer. Play with a partner. TR: B77

## Warm Up

- **Activate prior knowledge** Offer a pencil to a student. Ask *Do you want a pencil?* Have the student answer in a complete sentence. For example: *Yes, I want a pencil.* Continue with other objects.

## Present

- Write the following on the board:

| | |
|---|---|
| want + naming word | want + to + action word |

- Point to the phrase on the left. Say *We can use want with naming words, such as pencil. I want a pencil.* Point to the phrase on the right. Say *We can use want to with action words, such as eat. Write the word want. Then write to. Then write the action word.* As you explain, write and say *I want to eat.*
- Have students open their books to p. 149. Point to the grammar box. Say *Listen.* Play **TR: B75**. Say *We learned a new action word, ride.* Show a photo of a person riding a horse. Say *You can ride a horse or a donkey.* Ask *What else can you ride?* (a bike)
- Write the following on the board:

| What do you want to do? | | |
|---|---|---|
| | to climb | a mountain? |
| Do you want | to swim | in the ocean? |
| | to ride | a horse? |

- Point to each sentence part in order as you say it aloud. Have students repeat. Model answering *Yes, I want (to climb) (a mountain)* or *No, I don't.*
✓ Ask *Do you want to ride a horse?* If students have difficulty answering correctly, review the word order on the board or replay **TR: B75**.

## Practice 12

- 12 Say *It's time to listen, read, and write.* Point to Activity 12. Play the first item on **TR: B76**. Model by saying *I listen to Maria. She says she doesn't want to ride the goat. She wants to ride the sheep.* Point to item 1 in the book and say *I write wants to ride on the line. Maria wants to ride the sheep.* Play the next item on the track and have students complete it on their own. Then review the answer as a class.

## Apply 13

- Ask *What do you want to do?* Accept any reasonable answers, restating them as *(Luc) wants to (eat lunch).* Ask *Do you want to play a game?*
- 13 Form pairs. Say *Now you will play a game.* Have students turn to p. 175 and cut out one set of cards each. Say and model *Put the cards face down in a pile.* Model with a student as you say *One partner picks up a card and asks about it. The other partner picks up a card and answers.*
- Read the model dialogue and play **TR: B77**. Have students read it aloud. Model playing the game with a student. Say *I pick up a card. The card shows ducks. I ask "Do you want to see the ducks?" What's on my partner's card? She has ducks, too. She says "I want to see the ducks." If she doesn't have ducks, she says "No, I don't."* Have students do the activity together, taking turns.

## Extend

- Have students think of a fun place to go, real or imaginary. Write the sentence frame *I want to go to* ________. You may need to help spell place names. Then ask *What do you want to do there?* Encourage students to say and write what they want to do, see, and play with while there. After students answer in the first person, help the class rephrase each sentence in the second or third person. Offer examples such as *You want to go to the moon* and *My brother wants to go to the ocean.*

## Wrap Up

- Write the following sentence endings on the board.

  ________ *to see the sheep?*
  ________ *to climb the mountain?*
  ________ *to ride the donkey?*

  Create three groups. Assign each group one of the sentence endings. Challenge groups to write as many complete sentences as they can that make sense and use *want + to*. Have students write their sentences on the board and read them aloud.

## Be the Expert

### Grammar in Depth

**Infinitives** The infinitive is a verb form that in English usually begins with *to* and is followed by the base form of the verb: *to run, to swim, to climb.* An infinitive, however, does not act as a verb. Infinitives can act as nouns, adjectives, adverbs, or direct objects.

Noun: I like to swim. (*to swim* is a noun, and also the direct object)

Adjective: Is there anywhere to climb? (*to climb* modifies *anywhere*)

Adverb: She runs to catch the train. (*to catch* modifies *runs*)

### Teaching Tip

Use gestures when teaching grammar. For example, point to yourself if you're the subject of the sentence, or point to students if they are the subject. In this way, you reinforce the correct placement of the subject in various grammar structures. For example, point to yourself if the word *I* appears between *do* and *want* in the question types taught in this lesson. Point to a student if *you* is used between *do* and *want*.

### Related Vocabulary

*carousel, merry-go-round, pond*

### Formative Assessment

Can students

- ask and answer questions with *want*?

  Ask *Do you want to see the cats?* Have students answer in a complete sentence. Then have students ask you a question using *want*.

**Review** For additional practice, direct students to Activity Worksheet 9.3.

## Reading

**Objectives**

Students will

- scan text for information.
- read and talk about animal babies.

**Reading Strategy** Scan Text for Information

**Content Vocabulary** *bunnies, calf, chicks, elephant, kittens, lambs, puppies*

**Resources** Workbook pp. 112–113; Audio CD TR: B78–80; Classroom Presentation Tool: Reading

**Materials** twelve note cards; Picture Cards 146–147, 149, 155–156

**14 Listen and read.** TR: B78

# Animal Babies

Who loves babies? Everyone! Let's learn about some animals and their babies. Some animals have big families. Cats have many baby cats, called kittens. Baby dogs are called puppies. Baby chickens are called chicks. Baby rabbits are called bunnies. Some animals, like sheep and elephants, have small families. Baby sheep are called lambs. A baby elephant is called a calf. Everyone loves animal babies!

Baby Asian elephant

150

## Warm Up

- **Activate prior knowledge** Say *Today we're going to read about animal babies.* On the board, draw a big cat and a small—"baby"—cat. Use simple drawings such as a small circle for the head, larger oval for the body, triangles for ears, small circle for a mouth, dots for eyes, and a curl for the tail.

  The baby can look like the adult, but smaller. Say *This is a cat.* Point to the small cat and say *This is a kitten.* Under the cat, write *cat*. Under the kitten, write *kitten*. Explain that a kitten is a baby cat.

## Present 14

- Have students count off by six. Say *Ones, you're cats; Twos, you're dogs; Threes, you're chickens; Fours, you're rabbits; Fives, you're sheep; Sixes, you're elephants.* Point to each group in turn and say *Cats, dogs, chickens, rabbits, sheep, elephants.* Say *Draw your animal. Draw a mother and a baby.* Make drawings on the board to help groups get started. Say *Make the mother big. Make the baby small.* Encourage students to label their drawings. When groups are done, have students hold up their pictures and name the animals. Model to help groups name the animals: *There's the mother (sheep). There's the baby (lamb).*

**15** **Listen and read.** Circle *yes* or *no*. TR: B79

1. A baby rabbit is called a bunny. yes no
2. A baby sheep is called a chick. yes no
3. A baby elephant is called a calf. yes no

**16** **Read and write.**

**Animal Families**

| cat | dog | chicken | rabbit | sheep | elephant |
|---|---|---|---|---|---|
| ↓ | ↓ | ↓ | ↓ | ↓ | ↓ |
| | | | | | |

**17** **Look and write.**

1. How many kittens? ____________
2. Are there any puppies? ________
3. How many bunnies? __________
4. Are there any chicks? ________

**18** **Work with a partner.** Ask and answer. What are your favorite animals? TR: B80

151

## Be the Expert

### About the Photo

This photo shows a baby Asian elephant. There are two main types of elephants—African and Asian. Asian elephants usually have smaller ears than African elephants. African elephants live in hotter climates, so they need bigger ears to help release body heat.

### Our World in Context

Rabbits live on every continent except Antarctica. Although most people know baby rabbits as bunnies, a baby rabbit can also be called a kit.

### Teaching Tip

When possible, have students make visual representations to show new vocabulary or to aid them in acquiring new concepts. By drawing or cutting out pictures, students become more actively involved in learning. Kinesthetic learners are also accommodated. If you have students use this option more than once, ask them to keep a vocabulary portfolio that includes their drawings and cutouts.

- **14** **Read together** Say *Now we're going to read about baby animals.* Have students open their books to p. 150. Play **TR: B78** and have students listen. Ask students to hold up their drawings when they hear their animals named. Play the track a second time and ask students to read with you.
- **Think Aloud** Model scanning the text for information. Say *I want to find the name of a baby rabbit.* Model scanning a page of text. Say *I move my eyes over the reading fast. I don't read everything again. I don't have to read every word. I'm looking for the word rabbit. Here it is.* Hold up your book and point to the sentence about rabbits. Say *I look for the word that names baby rabbits. Here it is. They're called bunnies.*
- Play **TR: B78** a third time and have students read along silently. Pause at the end of the following sentences. Ask questions such as:

  **Sentence 5:** *Do cats have big families?* (Yes, they do. They have many kittens.)
  **Sentence 7:** *What are baby chickens called?* (chicks)
  **Sentence 9:** *What animals have small families?* (sheep and elephants) *What is a baby elephant called?* (a calf)

14 Listen and read.

Animal Babies

Who loves babies? Everyone! Let's learn about some animals and their babies. Some animals have big families. Cats have many baby cats, called kittens. Baby dogs are called puppies. Baby chickens are called chicks. Baby rabbits are called bunnies. Some animals, like sheep and elephants, have small families. Baby sheep are called lambs. A baby elephant is called a calf. Everyone loves animal babies!

150

15 Listen and read. Circle yes or no.

1. A baby rabbit is called a bunny. yes no
2. A baby sheep is called a chick. yes no
3. A baby elephant is called a calf. yes no

16 Read and write.

Animal Families

cat dog chicken rabbit sheep elephant

17 Look and write.

1. How many kittens? ________
2. Are there any puppies? ________
3. How many bunnies? ________
4. Are there any chicks? ________

18 Work with a partner. Ask and answer. What are your favorite animals?

What are your favorite animals?

I like dogs and turtles.

151

## Practice 15 16 17

- Provide practice with the names of animal babies. Say *I'm a mother elephant. I have one baby. What is its name?* (a calf) Repeat with chicken/chick, dog/puppy, cat/kitten, sheep/lamb, and rabbit/bunny. You can vary the questions and add context by saying, for example, for the rabbit, *I have many babies.* (bunnies)
- 15 Have students open their books to p. 151. Point to Activity 15. Say *It's time to listen, read, look, and circle. Read these sentences. Listen and then circle yes or no.* Play **TR: B79**. ✔ Ask *Is a baby elephant called a calf?* If students say *no*, model scanning the text on p. 150 to find the answer.
- 16 Say *Now you read and write.* Point to the diagram in Activity 16 and say *Let's do one together.* Point to the box with *cat* and ask *What does it say?* (cat) Ask *What's a baby cat called?* (kitten) Follow the red arrow down and say *Let's write* kitten *here.* Have students complete the rest of the items on their own. Walk around the room to be sure students are on task. If students do not know what word to write, model scanning the text on p. 150 to find the answer.
- 17 Say *It's time to tell about the photos. Let's do one together.* Model by saying *I read number one. How many kittens? I find the photo of kittens. I count the kittens. One, two, three, four kittens. I write* four. Say *Now you try it.* When students are finished, review the answers as a class.

## Wrap Up

- Say and write the following sentence frames: *A mother ________ has ________. She does not have ________.* Model completing the frames. Say *A mother (rabbit) has (bunnies). She does not have (a calf).* Then ask students to complete the frames two or three different ways on their own.

## Recap

- Draw two or three animal families on the board. For example: a mother sheep with one lamb or a mother chicken with five chicks. Have students tell about each family, and ask questions such as *How many chicks does the chicken have?* For more practice, add other animals.

## Apply 18

- Draw a cat on the board. Say *A cat is my favorite animal.* Draw a duck next to the cat. Say *I like ducks, too. My favorite animals are cats and ducks.* Draw a horse next to the cat. Say *I like horses, too. My favorite animals are cats, ducks, and horses.* Ask *What's your favorite animal?* As students name their favorite animals, ask *Do you like (horses)?* Say *You like (dogs) and (horses).*
- 18 Have students look at the model dialogue on the bottom of p. 151. Say *Let's hear what Polly the parrot and Eddie the elephant are talking about today.* Read the model dialogue aloud. Then say *Listen* and play **TR: B80**.
- Form pairs. Say *Ask and answer with a partner. Take turns. You can name an animal or an animal baby.* When students are done, have them share their dialogues with the class.

## Extend

- Form pairs. Have pairs role play being animal mothers or fathers. They and their families meet another animal family. Each mother or father introduces herself or himself and the babies. Model this way, playing both parts and changing your voice, and perhaps also the angle at which you face the class when you change your role. Add hand gestures, too, both for greeting and for pointing out the babies. In one voice say *Hello Father Chicken. I'm Mother Dog. These are my five puppies. That's Peter the Puppy, and those are his brothers and sisters, Paula, Pablo, Pat, and Priya.* In another voice, say *Hello Mother Dog. I'm Father Chicken. This is my chick. He's Charlie the Chick.*

## Wrap Up

- Play a matching game. Form twelve pairs or groups. On twelve note cards, write the following: *dogs, cats, chickens, rabbits, sheep, elephants; puppies, kittens, chicks, bunnies, lambs, calf.* Hand out cards and have "families" find and greet one another. Model for students: *I'm Mother Cat. I'm a kitten. Hello, Mother Cat! Hello, Kitten!*

## Be the Expert

### Reading Strategy

**Scan Text for Information** When you scan a text, you look for specific information. Sometimes scanning is confused with previewing, which helps a reader get an overview of a text by looking at the title, subheads, and other graphic elements. Scanning is also different from skimming, which is quick reading, mainly focused on finding the main ideas and topic sentences. Unlike previewing and skimming, scanning is often done after reading to recall or find a single detail.

### Formative Assessment

Can students

- scan text for information?

  Have students quickly find information in the text on p. 150 that tells which animals have small and large families.

- read and talk about animal babies?

  Hold up photos of or picture cards for a sheep, chicken, cat, dog, and rabbit. Have students name each animal and its baby.

## Writing

**Writing** Write about your favorite animal.

**Objectives**

Students will

- view a writing model.
- draw and write about favorite animals.

**Content Vocabulary** *cute*

**Resources** Workbook p. 114; Classroom Presentation Tool: Writing; Teacher's Resource CD-ROM: Graphic Organizers (Word web)

### Formative Assessment

Can students

- draw and write about favorite animals?

  Have students read aloud one sentence they wrote about their pictures.

My favorite animal is my cat. Her name is Missy. She is white, brown, and gray. Missy has two kittens. They are so cute! Boots is black with two white feet. Snowy is all white. I love them all.

**19** **Draw and write about your favorite animal.**

My favorite animal is ______________________

______________________

______________________

**20** **Work in a small group.** Talk about your picture.



## Present

- Have students open their books to p. 152 and look at the writing model. Say *Let's read this writing model.* Read the model aloud. Read it a second time and have students read it with you.
- Ask *What does the writer tell about?* (the cat's name and color, the cat's kittens and their colors) As students respond, list their answers on the board.

## Write 19

- **19** Point to the empty space on p. 152. Say *Draw a picture of your favorite animal here.*
- **Think Aloud** Make a word web on the board. Write *cow* inside. Say *I'm going to write about a cow. What can I say about a cow? I can say the cow's name. Her name is Flower. I can also tell about her color. Flower is brown. I can tell how she looks, too! She has four legs.* Add these details to your web. Review what the web shows: your favorite animal, its name, its color, and what it looks like.
- Say *Now you make a web. Write information about your favorite animal.*
- Point to the blank lines and say *Write about your favorite animal here. Use your web to help you write sentences.*

NATIONAL GEOGRAPHIC

# Our World

## Be good to animals.

**21 Look and read.**



A hiker and her dog, the Himalayas

**22 Read and copy.**

I am good to animals.

153

## Value

**Value** Be good to animals.

**Objectives**

Students will

- read about animal-related values and activities.
- read and copy a full sentence.

**Resources** Values Poster

## Be the Expert

### Teaching Tip

**Classroom Management**

Students may be eager to talk about and share more examples from their own lives. Talking should be encouraged, but sometimes too much off-topic talk can move a lesson off course. For example, many students don't have pets, and they may not be interested in hearing accounts of having pets. Make the best of a student's enthusiasm for the topic by suggesting that he or she talk to you about it later or write about it in a journal.

## Share 20

- 20 Form small groups. Point to Activity 20 at the bottom of p. 152. Have students take turns talking about their pictures.
- Ask each group member to say one thing about each person's writing. Write possible responses on the board: *My favorite animals are (rabbits and puppies), too. I like your writing.* Model these (and other) ways to be helpful: *(An elephant) is one favorite animal. Do you have another favorite animal?*

## Value 21 22

- Write *Pets* on the board. Say *Pets are animals that we usually keep in our homes.* Give examples of pets, such as dogs, cats, and rabbits.
- Point to the photo on p. 153. Ask *What do you see?* (a person, a dog, a mountain) Say *We give pets water. We give them food, too.* Point to the title and say *Be good to animals. We are good to animals by giving them food and water.*
- 21 Say *Let's read now. I'll read first.* Read aloud slowly the first time. Read again at a more natural pace and then have students read with you.
- 22 Point to Activity 22. Read the sentence aloud. Then say *You write it.* Walk around to be sure students begin the sentence with a capital letter and end it with a period. ✓ Ask *What goes at the end?* Remind students to place the period at the end of the sentence.

## Project

**Objectives**

Students will

- talk about animals.
- make a class book about animals.
- complete the Unit 9 Quiz.

**Resources** Assessment: Unit 9 Quiz; Picture Cards 146–162; Teacher's Resource CD-ROM: Activity Worksheet 9.4

**Materials** drawing materials; old magazines with images of animals; large note cards or pre-cut paper; poster board; yarn or string

**23 Make a class book about animals.**

1 Choose an animal.

2 Glue your picture.

3 Write about your animal.

4 Write your name.



## Prepare

- Hold up Picture Cards 146–162 one by one. Ask *What's that?* or *What are they?* After students name each animal or action, have them use the word in a complete sentence, such as *A goat can climb a mountain.* Ask follow-up questions, such as *Yes, that's a horse. Does it have long legs? Does it run fast?*
- Have students open their books to pp. 154–155. Hold up the book and point to the model class book on p. 155. Say *This is a page for a class book. The class book is about animals.*
- Give out the materials students will need. Read the first step on p. 154, and then say *Choose an animal to (draw, cut out) and write about.* Walk around the room and ask students to say their animal's name aloud. Then ask students to say one thing about the animal.
- Read step 2. Model gluing your picture and the note card or paper to the poster board. Leave space to write your name. Have students do the same.
- Have students write about their animals and sign their names. Provide assistance as necessary.

**Now I can . . .**

- ◯ name animals.
- ◯ talk about what animals can do.
- ◯ describe a favorite animal.

155

## Be the Expert

### Teaching Tip

Allowing students to make choices about their learning and learning products is important. When students have a say in classroom decisions, such as how to arrange the class book, they tend to be more motivated and stay on task. For young children, limited choices are appropriate. As children get older, more open-ended choices can be introduced.

### Project Rubric

✓ Did students include a picture on their pages?

✓ Did students write clearly about their animals?

✓ Did students sign their names?

✓ Did all students help organize and create the book?

## Share

- Go around the room and have each student stand up, show his page, say the animal name, read what he wrote, and sit down. Then ask the class *How should we put our book together?* Lead the class to the following possibilities, or others like them: alphabetical order by animal names, alphabetical order by students' names, or order by animal size—largest to smallest or smallest to largest. Have the class vote on a way to put the book together. Then have students work together to assemble the class book.
- Ask *What should the book title be? What should the cover look like?* Put students in groups and assign each a different part of the process, such as writing a neat and colorful title, making the cover picture, numbering the pages, and tying the book together with yarn or string.
- **Modify** If less time is available, pairs or small groups can work together to create one page per two or three students.

### Now I Can

Ask questions such as the following:

- Hold up Picture Cards of animals and ask *What is this?*
- *What can a horse do? What can a frog do? What can a duck do?*
- *What is your favorite animal? What does it have? What can it do?*

**Review** For additional practice, direct students to Activity Worksheet 9.4.

### Unit Assessment

Give the Unit 9 Quiz. Hand out the quiz and go over the instructions with students. The quiz should take 15–20 minutes.

# Video

**Vocabulary 1a** *a cat, a dog, a rabbit, a turtle, a frog*

**Vocabulary 1b** *a chicken, a cow, a horse, a duck, a goat*

**Vocabulary 2** *fly, swim, climb, crawl, see*

**Grammar 1** use present progressive (third person plural)

**Grammar 2** use *want* + infinitive (first, second, and third person singular)

**Song** *Animals*

**Viewing** animals and their actions

**Story Time** *Too Many Animals*

**Resources** Student Book, pp. 140–149

## Before You Watch

- Say *We're going to see a video about animals and how they move.*

## While You Watch

- Write *climbing, flying, crawling,* and *swimming* on the board. Pause the video as necessary and have students write sentences using these words, such as *The birds are flying.*

## After You Watch

- Have students share their sentences. Play the video again, pausing to show animals climbing, flying, crawling, or swimming. Have students read their sentences to describe the action on screen.

## Zoom In

### Vocabulary

- Pause the video after each animal. Make some of the animal sounds. For example, say *I say, "Meow!" What am I?* (a cat) *I say, "Quack." What am I?* (a duck)

### Grammar

- During Scene 6: Grammar I, pause and ask *What are the ducks doing?* Have students write three things the ducks are doing. (*They're flying. They're climbing. They're swimming.*)

### Song

- Play Scene 9: Song: *Animals*. Form groups. Say *Put some new animals in the song.* Model *The song says that the dog is running. A horse can run, too. I want to change the song. I sing "I see one horse. Is it running? Yes, it's running. It's running in the sun."* Have groups make their changes. Encourage students to sing their new verses aloud, mimicking the actions from the video.

### Viewing

- Before students watch Scene 10, write animal names and actions in two columns. Column I includes *dogs, cows, frogs, goats, ducks,* and *cats*. Column 2 includes (in scrambled order) *flying, drinking, sleeping, running,* and *climbing*. Have students match each animal with its action and then form sentences, such as *The (cows) are* ________ or *They are* ________.

### Story Time

- View Scene 11: Story Time. Ask *What animals are very small?* (the butterfly, the frog) *What animals are very big?* (the goats, the horse, the cow)

- View *Too Many Animals* a second time. Ask *Who can go in the shed?* (the small animals) *Who cannot go in the shed?* (the cow, the big animals) *How are the animals the same?* (They are all running, climbing, or swimming in from the rain.) *How are they different?* (Some are small. Some are big.)

***Too Many Animals***

When it starts to rain, a butterfly flies into a shed. One by one, more animals join the butterfly. How many animals go into the shed? And will they all fit?

## Before You Read

- Hold up Picture Cards 35, 36, 148, and 151–154 and have students identify them. Write *shed* on the board. Write and say *Shed. A shed is a small house for things or animals.*
- **Predict** Line up the cards and say *In this story, it's raining. Where can the animals go?* (in the shed)
- **Introduce the strategy** Model a cause-and-effect relationship. Draw a person standing next to a house. Then draw a rain cloud and rain drops. Say *It's raining. He doesn't like to be in the rain.* Draw an arrow to show the person going into the house. *He goes in his house when it's raining.* Say *An effect is something that happens. A cause makes something happen. The rain makes him go in the house. The rain is the cause. He goes in the house. That's the effect.*
- Give students a T-chart organizer and label the columns **Cause** and **Effect**. Say *Let's read a story called* Too Many Animals. *We can talk about causes and effects.*

## While You Read

- Read the book aloud. Stop every few pages to ask questions, have students identify cause-and-effect patterns, and write answers in the chart.

  p. 3: *It's raining. What does the rain make the animals do?* (go into the shed)

  p. 6: *Two goats climb in. How many animals are in the shed?* (eight animals)

  p. 11: *A cow walks in the shed. Are there too many animals now?* (yes)

## After You Read

- Check comprehension by asking questions. Ask *Why do the animals go into the shed?* (It's raining.) *What two animals go into the shed first?* (the butterfly and the frog) Say *The butterfly and frog fit in the shed. That does not cause a problem. Other animals go in. What happens?* (There are too many animals.) Ask *What happens when the cow goes in?* (The shed breaks.) Hold up a small stick and break it to demonstrate the meaning of *break*.

## Unit 9 Reader

**Text Type** folktale

**Vocabulary** *fly, frog, duck, swim, goat, climb, horse, cow*

**Grammar** use present progressive (third person plural)

**Reading Strategy** Identify Cause and Effect

**Resources** Classroom Presentation Tool: Story Time; Video: Sc. 11—Story Time; Picture Cards 35, 36, 148, 151–154; Teacher's Resource CD-ROM: Graphic Organizers (T-chart)

**Materials** a small stick

## Be the Expert

### Reading Strategy

**Identify Cause and Effect** To recognize cause and effect in stories, readers need to ask *What happened?* The answer is the effect. Then they need to ask *Why did that happen?* The answer is the cause.

Help students recognize causes and effects by providing organizers that make the relationships clear. In this story, for example, one cause—rain—has an important effect: it makes the animals enter the shed. Another cause-and-effect event involves the number of animals and the shed: because too many animals entered it, the shed broke apart.

Having students organize causes and effects into different columns as they read helps them see the important events of a story and understand why those events happen.

### Text Background

*Too Many Animals* is a folktale from Ukraine, a country in Eastern Europe. Folktales are stories that one generation passes down to the next generation. Many folktales offer a lesson about how people should act or behave. Like other folktales, *Too Many Animals* happens in a real-world setting but includes unrealistic events.

## Student Book

**TR: B64** ① **Listen and say.**

| | |
|---|---|
| a turtle | The turtle is walking |
| a frog | The frog is jumping. |
| a dog | The dog is running. |
| a cat | The cat is sleeping. |
| a duck | The duck is walking. |
| a horse | The horse is running. |
| a chicken | The chicken is eating. |
| a donkey | The donkey is walking. |
| a goat | The goat is eating. |
| a rabbit | The rabbit is sleeping. |
| a cow | The cow is walking. |
| a sheep | The sheep is eating. |

**TR: B65** ② **Listen. Point and say.**

a dog, a goat, a rabbit, a duck, a horse, a turtle, a cat, a chicken, a donkey, a cow, a frog, a sheep

**TR: B66** ③ **Work with a partner. Point. Ask and answer.**

What is it? It's a donkey.

**TR: B67** ④ **Listen. Read and sing.**

Note: Lyrics for the song *Animals* are on pp. 276–277.

**TR: B68 Grammar**

Note: Grammar I, Ist chart, is on p. 278.

**TR: B69** ⑥ **Listen and find. Write.**

I. What are the birds doing? They're singing.
2. What are the ducks doing? They're walking.
3. What are the cats doing? They're sleeping.
4. What are the horses doing? They're running.

**TR: B70 Grammar**

Note: Grammar I, 2nd chart, is on p. 279.

**TR: B71** ⑦ **Listen and find. Circle.**

I. Are the boys walking?
Yes, they are.
What are they doing?

2. Are the girls eating?
No, they aren't.
What are they doing?

3. Are the mothers reading?
Yes, they are.
What are they doing?

4. Are the frogs sleeping?
No, they aren't.

**TR: B72** ⑧ **Listen and say.**

| | |
|---|---|
| see | The boy sees two birds in the sky. |
| climb | A cat is climbing a tree. |
| swim | The turtle is swimming. |
| fly | Two birds are flying in the sky. |
| crawl | A turtle is crawling on a rock. |

**TR: B73** ⑩ **Look. Listen and read. Circle yes or no.**

I. The birds are flying
2. The cat is swimming.
3. The turtle is crawling.

**TR: B74** ⑪ **Work with a partner. Listen. Say and stick.**

Number I. The dogs are sleeping.
OK. Number 2.

**TR: B75 Grammar**

Note: Grammar 2 is on p. 284.

**TR: B76** ⑫ **Look. Listen and read. Write.**

I. Maria, do you want to ride the goat?
No, I don't. I want to ride the sheep.

2. Carlos, do you want to see the ducks?
No, I don't. I want to see the frog.

**TR: B77** ⑬ **Play a game. Cut out the cards on page 175. Ask and answer. Play with a partner.**

Do you want to see the goats?
No, I don't. I want to see the cows.

**TR: B78** ⑭ **Listen and read.**

Note: Reading *Animal Babies* is on p. 286.

**TR: B79** ⑮ **Listen and read. Look. Circle yes or no.**

Who loves babies? Everyone! Let's learn about some animals and their babies. Some animals have big families. Cats have many baby cats, called kittens. Baby dogs are called puppies. Baby chickens are called chicks. Baby rabbits are called bunnies. Some animals, like sheep and elephants, have small families. Baby sheep are called lambs. A baby elephant is called a calf. Everyone loves animal babies!

I. A baby rabbit is called a bunny.
2. A baby sheep is called a chick.
3. A baby elephant is called a calf.

**TR: B80** (18) **Work with a partner. Ask and answer. What are your favorite animals?**

What are your favorite animals?
I like dogs and turtles.

## Workbook

**TR: 71** (3) **Listen to the song. Write. Read. Draw lines to match.**

Note: Lyrics for the song *Animals* are on pp. 276–277.

**TR: 72** (5) **Listen. Write.**

1. What are the cats doing? They're running.
2. What are the horses doing? They're jumping.
3. What are the goats doing? They're eating.
4. What are the cows doing? They're walking.
5. What are the sheep doing? They're sleeping.

**TR: 73** (6) **Listen. Write.**

See script for **TR: 72** above.

**TR: 74** (11) **Listen. Read. Write.**

1. I see two turtles.
2. The turtles are crawling.
3. The chicken is flying.
4. A girl is climbing.

**TR: 75** (12) **Listen. Write.**

1. Do you want to ride a horse?
   No, I don't.
2. What do you want to do?
   I want to see the goats.
3. Does Lena want to see the goats?
   No, she doesn't.
4. What does she want to do?
   She wants to ride the donkey.
5. Do you want to see the chickens?
   No, I don't.

**TR: 76** (13) **Listen. Circle.**

See script for **TR: 75** above.

**TR: 77** (16) **Listen and read.**

Note: Reading *More Baby Animals* is on p. 330.

# Answer Key

## Student Book

**Unit Opener** SB p. 140

1. F, 2. T, 3. F, 4. T

(6) SB p. 146

1. The birds are singing. 2. The ducks are walking. 3. The cats are sleeping. 4. The horses are running.

(7) SB p. 147

1. walking, 2. jumping, 3. reading, 4. jumping

(10) SB p. 148

1. yes, 2. no, 3. yes

(12) SB p. 149

1. wants to ride 2. wants to see

(15) SB p. 151

1. yes, 2. no, 3. yes

(16) SB p. 151

| | | | | | |
|---|---|---|---|---|---|
| cat | dog | chicken | rabbit | sheep | elephant |
| kitten | puppy | chick | bunny | lamb | calf |

(17) SB p. 151

1. four, 2. yes, 3. one, 4. yes

## Workbook

Go to pp. 328–331 for the Workbook Answer Key for this unit.

# Review: Units 7-9

**Vocabulary** U7–U9

**Grammar** U7–U9

**Academic Language** *heads, tails*

**Resources** Workbook pp. 116–117

**Materials** coins, playing pieces (buttons, tokens, or other small, flat objects)

- **Play the game** Say *Let's play a fun game! Open your books to pages 156 and 157. Look at all the photos.* Give students a few moments to scan the photos. Then ask *What's one part of the body you see?* Call on several students to respond. (eyes, nose, arms, mouth, hand) Ask *What's one animal you see?* Call on several students to respond. (duck, cow, goat, cat, rabbit, dog, horse)
- Point to the pizza photo on p. 157 and ask a student *(Mari), do you like cheese pizza?* (Yes, I do. I like cheese pizza.) Repeat the question, asking different students about other pictured foods.
- Hold up a coin. Point to the "heads" side and say *This is heads. You move one space for heads.* Use a playing piece to demonstrate moving forward one space in the game. Count aloud as you move. Then point to the "tails" side. Say *This is tails. Move two spaces for tails.* Demonstrate moving forward two spaces, counting aloud as you move.
- Model playing the game. Have a student come to the front of the room to be your partner. Put a playing piece on *Start*. Flip a coin and show *heads*. Say *This is heads.* Move one space and ask your partner *What color are her eyes?* Prompt the student to answer. (Her eyes are brown.) Then have your partner flip the coin. For *tails*, have the student move two spaces. Have the student ask *What is the duck doing?* Say *The duck is standing*. For *heads*, have the student move one space. Ask *Do you like bananas?* (Yes, I do.)
- Point to the model dialogue on p. 157 and have two students read it aloud. Then put students in pairs.

## Be the Expert

### Teaching Tip

**Classroom Management** Keeping order in the classroom can be especially challenging when students play games or participate in other collaborative activities. To maintain order, review with students the classroom rules right before beginning a game. You may want to consider displaying the written rules somewhere in the classroom where students can easily refer to them. Make sure to word rules in a positive way. For example, instead of saying *Don't cheat*, say *Play fairly*.

Give a coin and a playing piece to each pair. Say *Play the game. Look. Ask questions and answer. Take turns.*

- **Sentence frames** If students need help thinking of questions and answers, write examples on the board:

| | |
|---|---|
| What color is ______? | I don't like ______. |
| Her hair is ______. | What's the ______ doing? |
| What color are ______? | It's ______. |
| Her eyes are ______. | What are ______ doing? |
| Do you like ______? | They're ______. |
| Yes, I do. | Do you want to ______? |
| No, I don't. | Can the ______ ______? |
| I like ______. | Yes, it can ______. |

- **Modify** If class time is limited, have students play the game in small groups. Another option is to play the game as a class. If you choose the second option, make sure each student gets the chance to flip the coin, move the playing piece, and ask and answer questions.
- Provide an extra challenge during the game by having students act out the questions and answers as they say them. For example, a student who asks *Can the rabbit jump?* could jump as he asks the question. The student who answers could then mimic the action.

## Student Book (Unit Zero)

**TR: A2 1 Welcome to Our World!**

Eddie the elephant    Mia the monkey
Polly the parrot    Freddy the frog

**Activity I. Look and listen. Say.**

SI: Hello. I'm Eddie. What's your name?
S2: Hi. My name's Mia.

S3: How old are you, Freddy?
S4: I'm five. How old are you, Polly?
S3: I'm seven. It's my birthday!
S4: Happy Birthday!

**TR: A3 2 Look and listen. Say.**

red    orange
purple    white
yellow    black
blue    green

**TR: A4 3 Listen. Point and say.**

black    white
blue    green
yellow    purple
red    orange

**TR: A5 4 Work with a partner. Point. Ask and answer.**

Example
SI: What color is it?
S2: It's red!

**TR: A6 5 Look and listen. Say.**

A, B, C, D, E, F, G, H, I, J, K, L, M, N, O, P, Q, R, S, T, U, V, W, X, Y, Z

**TR: A7 6**

**Look and listen. Say.**

a square    a rectangle
a triangle    a star
a circle

**TR: A8 7 Listen. Point and say.**

a rectangle    a circle
a star    a triangle
a square

**TR: A9 8 Look and listen. Say.**

one, two, three, four, five, six, seven, eight, nine, ten

**TR: A10 9 Listen. Point and say.**

three    five
eight    ten
four    six
two    one
seven    nine

**TR: A11 10 Ask and answer.**

SI: How many blue squares?
S2: Three.

**TR: A12 11 Look and listen. Say.**

draw    sing
listen    sit down
point    stand up
read    walk
say    write

**TR: A13 12 Listen. Point and say.**

stand up    listen
draw    sing
sit down    write
read    point
say    walk

**TR: A14 13 Listen and do.**

draw    sing
listen    sit down
point    stand up
read    walk
say    write

## Workbook (Unit Zero)

**TR: 02 1 Listen. Read. Write. Use words from the box.**

SI: Hello. I'm Eddie. What's your name?
S2: Hi. My name's Polly.

S2: I'm seven. How old are you, Eddie?
SI: I'm six. It's my birthday!

**TR: 03 3 Look. Listen and circle.**

five    four
one    ten
nine    seven

**TR: 04** **4** **Listen and read. Look. Draw a line to match.**

1. a star
2. a square
3. a rectangle
4. a triangle
5. a circle

## Workbook (Review: Units 1-3)

**TR: 32** **1** **Look. Listen and circle.**

1. S1: Is it a clock?
   S2: Yes, it is. It's a clock.
2. S1: What is it?
   S2: It's a butterfly.
3. S1: What are they?
   S2: They're crayons.
4. S1: Who's she?
   S2: She's my grandmother.
5. S1: How many brothers do you have?
   S2: I have two brothers.

**TR: 33** **3** **Listen and read. Circle.**

1. How many sisters do you have?
2. I don't have any sisters.
3. Who's he?
4. He's my baby brother.
5. He's young.
6. I have a big family.

## Workbook (Review: Units 4-6)

**TR: 54** **1** **Listen and read. Circle.**

1. Where's your brother?
   He's in the bathroom.
2. What are you wearing?
   I'm wearing a pink skirt.
3. What's that?
   That's my brown truck.
4. What are those?
   Those are my dolls.
5. Do you want a puzzle?
   No, I don't.
6. Does your brother want a bike?
   Yes, he does.

**TR: 55** **2** **Listen and write.**

1. Is this your hat?
   No, it isn't. It's my mother's hat.
2. Are these your pants?
   No, they aren't. They're my brother's pants.
3. What's that?
   That's my robot.
4. What are those?
   Those are my socks.

**TR: 56** **3** **Listen. Look at the picture. Color.**

Color the lamp brown.
Color the sofa purple.
Color the puppet yellow.
Color the gloves pink.
Color the shoes red.
Color the train blue.
Color the board game orange.
Color the skirt black.

## Workbook (Review: Units 7-9)

**TR: 78** **1** **Listen. Circle.**

1. Do you like sheep?
2. Yes, I do. I like sheep.
3. Does she like lemonade?
   No, she doesn't. She likes milk.
4. Can you climb?
   I can climb. I have strong arms.
5. Can the chicken fly?
   The chicken can fly.
6. What do you want to do?
   I want to ride a donkey.

## Workbook

Go to pp. 303, 312, 313, 322, 331, and 332 for the Workbook Answer Key for the Unit Zero and Review pages.

Unit 0

# Welcome to Our World!

**1 Listen.** Read. Write. Use words from the box. TR: 2

Hi name seven six

1. Hello. I'm Eddie. What's your __name__?
2. __Hi__. My name's Polly.
3. I'm __seven__. How old are you, Eddie?
4. I'm __six__. It's my birthday!

**2 Read.** Write.

A _B_ C D _E_ F G _H_
I _J_ K L M _N_ O _P_
Q R S _T_ U V W _X_ Y _Z_

1

**3 Look.** Listen and (circle). TR: 3

3 (5) (10) 6 2 8 (7) (9) (4) (1)

**4 Listen and read.** Look. Draw a line to match. TR: 4

1. a star — orange
2. a square — purple
3. a rectangle — white
4. a triangle — green
5. a circle — red

**5 Read.** Look at Activity 4. Color.

1. Color the square purple.
2. Color the circle red.
3. Color the rectangle white.
4. Color the triangle green.
5. Color the star orange.

2

**6 Read and draw.**

1. Draw three yellow stars.
2. Draw two black circles.
3. Draw one blue square.

**7 Look and match.** Write the number.

[10] sing
[1] write
[3] walk
[5] draw
[8] stand up
[6] read
[2] listen
[9] point
[4] say
[7] sit down

3

Unit 1

# My Classroom

**1 Listen.** Look and match. Draw lines. TR: 5

1. a board 2. a classroom 3. a clock 4. a computer 5. a crayon

4

**2 Work with a partner.** Point. Ask and answer. Are your answers the same?

6. a map 7. paper 8. a pen 9. a pencil 10. a table

5

**3 Listen to the song.** Circle. TR: 6

I have my

and I have my

**4 Listen.** Write. TR: 7

We can count from one to ten.

1 2 3 4 5 6 7 8 9 10

**5 Listen.** Color. TR: 8

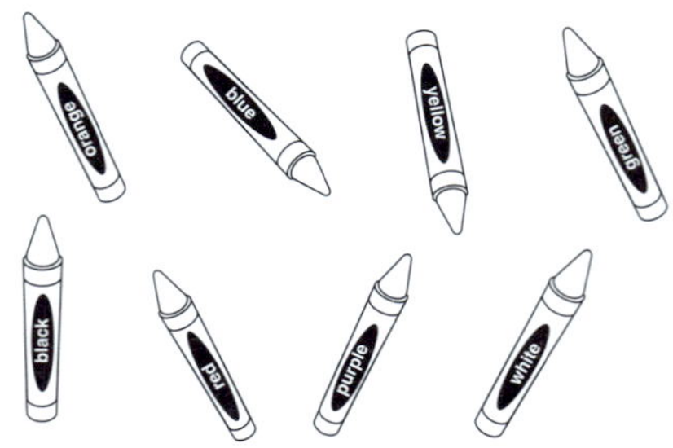


6

**GRAMMAR**

| | | |
|---|---|---|
| **Is it** a table? **Is it** a map? | Yes, **it is. It's** a table. No, it **isn't. It's** paper. | **It's** = It is **isn't** = is not |

**6 Listen.** Circle. TR: 9

1. Yes, it is. No, it isn't.
2. Yes, it is. No, it isn't.
3. Yes, it is. No, it isn't.
4. Yes, it is. No, it isn't.
5. Yes, it is. No, it isn't.

**7 Circle one object in the list.** Draw and color it. Work with a partner. Ask and answer.

crayon
paper
pen
table

7

8

**8 Look and draw lines.** Write.

a clock a computer a crayon a map a pen

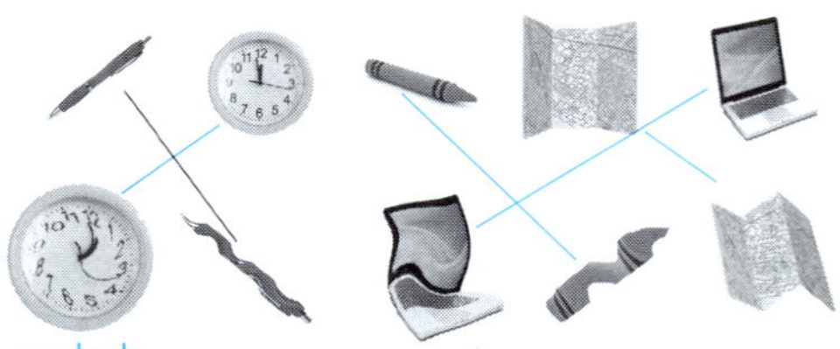

a clock a pen a computer a crayon a map

**9 Listen.** Look and read. Write. TR: 10

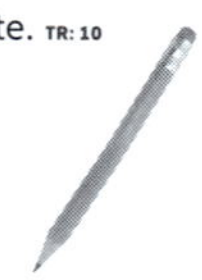

1. Is it a pencil?

Yes, it is.

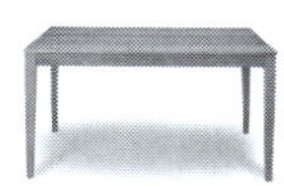

2. Is it a table?

Yes, it is.

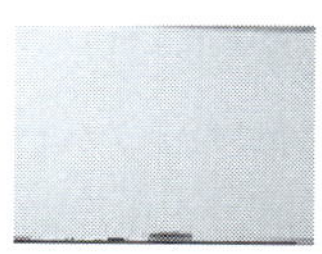

3. Is it a map?

No, it isn't.

**10 Read and match.** Write the numbers.

1 2 5 3 4

1. an eraser 2. a book 3. a desk 4. a picture 5. a chair

**11 Listen and find.** Color. Write. TR: 11

1. picture
2. book
3. eraser
4. chair
5. table

9

**GRAMMAR**

| | |
|---|---|
| **What** is it? | It's an eraser. |
| **What color** is it? | It's orange. |
| **How many** erasers? | Three. |

**12 Listen and write.** Draw lines. TR: 12

1. What is it?
2. What color is the clock?
3. How many pencils?
4. What is it?
5. How many books?

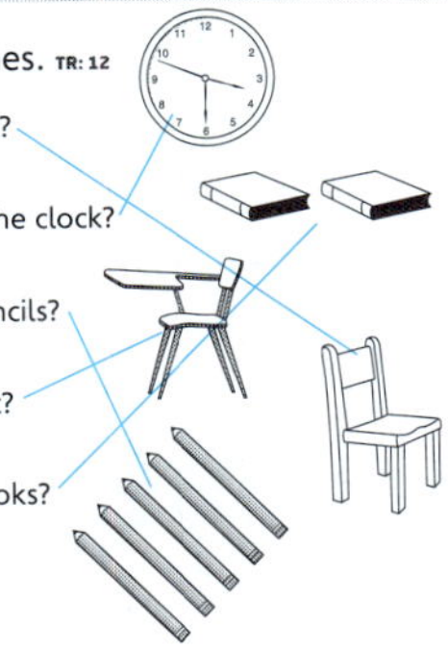

**13 Look and write.**

1. Look at page 9. It's gray. What is it? a picture
2. Look at page 9. It's orange. What is it? a desk
3. Look at page 6. How many crayons? eight
4. Look at page 9. It's green. What is it? an eraser
5. Look at page 8. How many boards? one
6. Look at page 9. It's yellow. What is it? a chair

10

**14 Listen and draw a line.** TR: 13

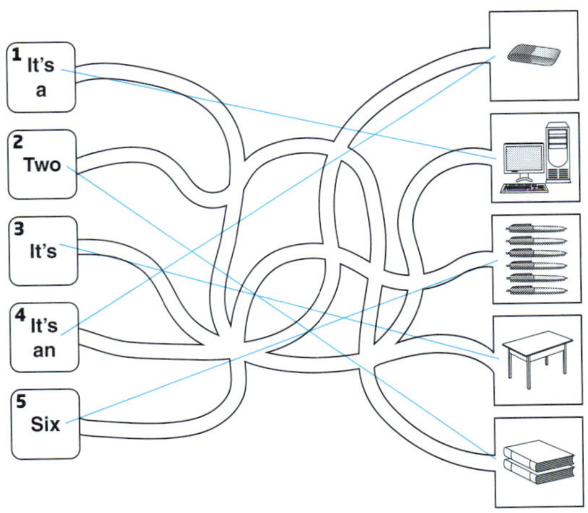


**15 Cut out the letters on page 119.** Work with a partner. Make words.

How many words? ______

11

**16 Listen and read.** TR: 14

# The English Alphabet

In the past

A B C D E F G H I K L M
N O P Q R S T V X Y Z

23 letters

Now

A B C D E F G H I **J** K L M N
O P Q R S T **U** V **W** X Y Z

26 letters

**17 Read.** Circle *yes* or *no*.

1. Now the English alphabet has 20 letters. yes (no)
2. Letters represent sounds. (yes) no

**18 Read and write.**

1. In the past: How many letters? 23
2. Now: How many letters? 26

12

**19** **Read and write.**

| The English Alphabet | |
|---|---|
| In the past | A B C D E F G H I K L M N O P Q R S T V X Y Z |
| Now | A B C D E F G H I J K L M N O P Q R S T U V W X Y Z |

**20** **Listen and find.** Color. TR: 15

13

**21** **Write.**

I'm    is    name    What's    your

Hello. My name is Sonia. What's your name?

Hi. I'm Mark.

**22** **Look and write.**

| | | |
|---|---|---|
| ? | Is it a pencil?<br>What is it? | What color is it?<br>What's your name? |
| . | No, it's a map.<br>It's a computer. | It's yellow.<br>I'm Freddy. |

1. Is it a clock ?
2. What is it ?
3. It's an eraser .
4. What's your name ?
5. It's blue .
6. How many desks ?

14

**23** **Listen and circle. Color.** TR: 16

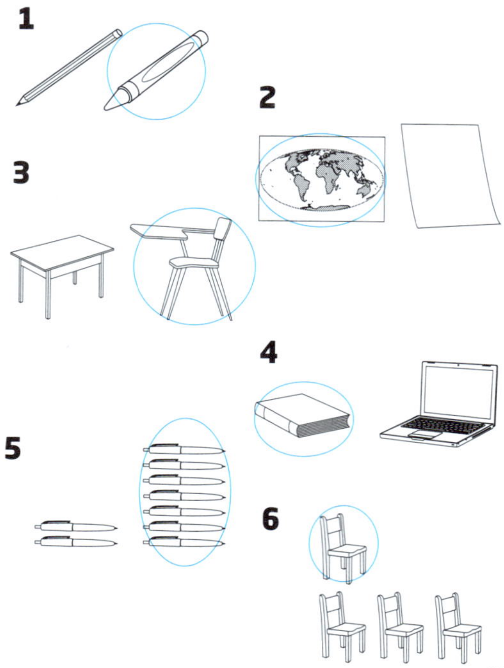


15

Unit 2

# My World

**1** **Listen.** Look and match. Write the number. TR: 17

6 a river    3 grass    9 the sun    1 a bird

4 a mountain    8 the sky    5 the ocean

10 a tree    7 a rock    2 a butterfly

16

**3 Listen to the song.** Circle. TR: 18

1. Where are the birds?
   Where are the sun and the moon?
   They're in the ______.
2. Where are the fish?
   Where are the waves?
   They're in the ______.
3. Where are the trees?
   Where are the rocks?
   They're in the ______.

**4 Listen.** Write. TR: 19

mountains ocean sky

The rainbows and the mountains
and the ocean and the sky,
they are part of our world, part of our world.
Our beautiful world!

18

**GRAMMAR**

| | | |
|---|---|---|
| What **is** it? | It**'s** a tree. | **'s** = **is** |
| What **are** they? | They**'re** trees. | **'re** = **are** |

**5 Write.**

1. What are they?
2. What is it?
3. What are they?
4. What is it?
5. What is it?
6. What are they?

**6 Write.**

1. They're trees.
2. It's a river.
3. They're birds.
4. It's grass.
5. It's a mountain.
6. They're butterflies.

19

**7 Look and draw lines.** Write.

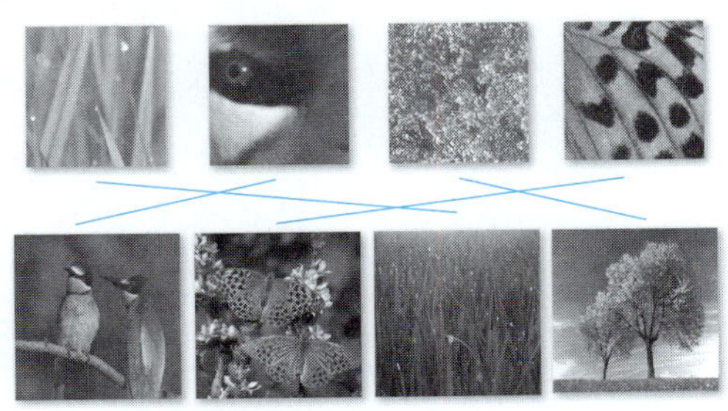

birds butterflies grass trees

**8 Listen and look.** Write. TR: 20

1. What are they?
   They're rocks.
2. What is it?
   It's a river.
3. What are they?
   They're mountains.

20

**9** **Read and match.** Write the numbers.

1 | 3 | 5 | 4 | 2

1. the moon 2. a star 3. a cloud 4. a bush 5. a flower

**10** **Color.** Work with a partner. Ask and answer.

What are they? They're ______.

What is it? It's ______.

21

GRAMMAR

**Where** is the moon? It's **in** the sky.
**Where** are the birds? They're **on** the big rock.

**11** **Draw lines.**

1. The butterfly is on the grass.
2. The clouds are in the sky.
3. The birds are in the tree.
4. The frog is in the river.
5. The flowers are on the bush.

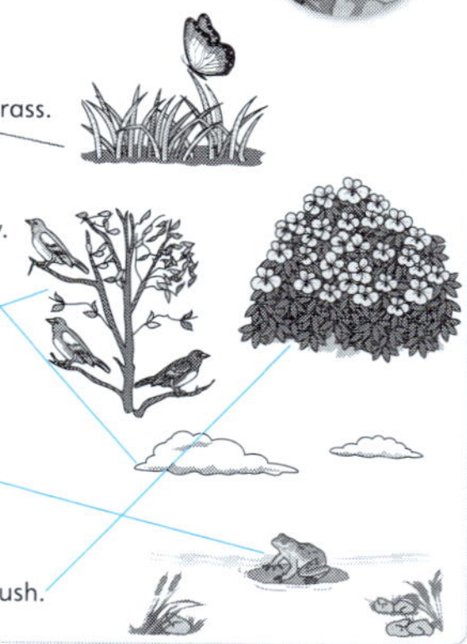

**12** **Look at the pictures.** Write.

1. Where is the butterfly?
2. Where are the clouds?
3. Where are the birds?
4. Where is the frog?
5. Where are the flowers?

22

**13** **Look at the pictures.** Circle the words.

| | | | | | | | | | | |
|---|---|---|---|---|---|---|---|---|---|---|
| m | i | f | s | a | n | p | u | o | n | c |
| o | m | x | o | d | n | f | a | s | s | l |
| u | o | b | i | r | d | s | o | t | r | o |
| n | o | w | y | o | l | m | n | a | z | u |
| t | n | i | c | c | g | s | w | r | q | d |
| a | s | c | r | k | z | k | s | y | j | s |
| i | b | c | k | b | t | a | c | l | h | f |
| n | t | s | u | d | r | i | v | e | r | l |
| s | v | b | u | s | h | j | r | w | o | k |
| f | l | o | w | e | r | s | u | i | f | s |

**14** **Work with a partner.** Ask and find. Color.

bird butterfly star flower

23

**15** **Listen and read.** TR: 21

# The Northern Lights

Like rainbows, the Northern Lights show colors in the sky. You see their colors at night.

**16** **Read.** Circle *yes* or *no*.

1. You see Northern Lights in the day. yes no
2. Northern Lights are black and white. yes no

**17** **Read and circle.**

1. A rainbow is in the sky. The ______ is in the sky.
   a. moon b. sun
2. Northern Lights are in the sky. The ______ is in the sky.
   a. moon b. sun

24

**18 Read and check.**

| | Northern Lights | Rainbows |
|---|---|---|
| in the sky | ✓ | ✓ |
| many colors | ✓ | ✓ |
| in the day | | ✓ |
| at night | ✓ | |

**19 Color the picture.**

25

**20 Write.** Look at your picture on page 25. Describe it.

1. The trees are ____________________.
2. The mountains are ____________________.
3. The stars are ____________________.
4. The sky is ____________________.
5. The Northern Lights are ____________________.

**21 Look and write.**

| | | |
|---|---|---|
| Big letter: **W I H F** | **W**hat is it?<br>**W**hat color is it?<br>**H**ow many trees? | **I**t's a tree.<br>**I**t's green.<br>**F**our trees. |
| Small letter: **w i h f** | W**hat is it**?<br>W**hat color is it**?<br>H**ow many trees**? | I**t's a tree.**<br>I**t's green.**<br>F**our trees.** |

W w  H h  I i  T t  M m

1. W hat's your name?
2. H ow many pencils?
3. I s it a butterfly?
4. T he bird is in the tree.
5. M ountains are big.

26

**22 Listen and circle. Color.** TR: 22

27

Unit 3

# My Family

**1 Listen.** Look and match. TR: 23

10 family  6 brother  8 baby  2 father
5 grandmother  3 mother  1 parents  7 sister
9 a photo  4 grandfather

28

**2 Work with a partner.** Ask and answer. Are your answers the same?

29

30

**3 Listen to the song.** Check. TR: 24

| | Family in the song | Your family |
|---|---|---|
| big | ✓ | |
| small | | |
| big brother | ✓ | |
| big sister | | |
| little brother | | |
| little sister | | |
| baby brother | | |
| baby sister | | |
| 2 boys | ✓ | |
| 2 girls | ✓ | |

**4 Listen.** Write. TR: 25

all
big
short
tall

Some are short,
and some are tall.
I have a big family,
and I love them all!

**GRAMMAR**

| | | |
|---|---|---|
| **Do** you **have** any brothers or sisters? | Yes, I do. | |
| How many sisters **do** you **have**? | I **have** one sister. | **don't** = |
| How many brothers **do** you **have**? | I **don't have** any brothers. | **do not** |

**5 Listen.** Circle. TR: 26

1. I have two brothers. — I have two sisters. (circled)
2. I don't have any sisters. — I don't have any brothers. (circled)
3. One. I have a baby brother. — One. I have a baby sister. (circled)
4. I don't have a big sister. (circled) — I don't have a big brother.

**6 Look and listen.** Write. TR: 27

baby big brother family sister

Lisa

Hi, I'm Lisa. I have a big family.

I have a big brother.

I have a little brother.

I have a big sister.

And I have a baby sister, too!

31

32

**7 Look at Miguel's family.** Write.

Juana—mother
Ana—grandmother
Angel—father
Paco—grandfather
Pablo—brother
Rosa—sister
Luis—brother
Lola—baby sister

1. Is Miguel's family big or small? big
2. How many brothers? two
3. How many sisters? two

**8 What about your family?** Draw and write.

1. How many sisters do you have?

   I ________.

2. How many brothers do you have?

   I ________.

**9 Look and read.** Circle.

1. tall short
2. tall short
3. young old

4. young old
5. small big
6. small big

**10 Read.** Draw and color.

a big book

an old grandmother

a tall tree

a small book

a young boy

a short tree

33

**GRAMMAR**

| | | |
|---|---|---|
| **Who**'s he?<br>**Who**'s she? | He's my baby brother.<br>She's my sister Ana. | Who's = Who is |

**11 Listen.** Write the number. TR: 28

5 3 4

2 6 1

**12 Look at the photos.** Write.

1. She's my sister.
2. He's my father.
3. She's my grandmother.
4. She's my mother, and he's my baby brother.
5. He's my grandfather.
6. He's my brother.

34

**13 Listen.**
Draw a line. TR: 29

**14 What is the secret message?**
Look at the letters and numbers.
Write the letters.

| | | | | | | |
|---|---|---|---|---|---|---|
| A 1 | B 2 | C 3 | D 4 | E 5 | F 6 | |
| G 7 | H 8 | I 9 | J 10 | K 11 | L 12 | |
| M 13 | N 14 | O 15 | P 16 | Q 17 | R 18 | S 19 |
| T 20 | U 21 | V 22 | W 23 | X 24 | Y 25 | Z 26 |

9 12 15 22 5 13 25 6 1 13 9 12 25

I love my family.

35

**15 Listen and read.** TR: 30

# Families Around the World

Families are different. They are big or small. Families live in different places, too.

a family in China

a family in Australia

This small family lives in China. And this small family lives in Australia. This big family lives in Ethiopia.

a family in Ethiopia

36

**16 Read.** Circle *yes* or *no*.

1. The small families live in China and Ethiopia. yes (no) — circled: no
2. The big family lives in Ethiopia. (yes) no — circled: yes
3. Families are different. (yes) no — circled: yes

**17 Look at the chart.** Read. Check.

| Family | Big | Small |
|---|---|---|
| in China | | ✓ |
| in Australia | | ✓ |
| in Ethiopia | ✓ | |
| your family | | |

**18 Read.** Look at the photos on page 36. Write.

1. The family in China is small.
2. The family in Australia is small.
3. The family in Ethiopia is big.
4. The family in China has one baby.
5. The family in China has two parents.
6. The family in Australia has one baby.
7. The family in Ethiopia has four babies.

37

**19 Look at the picture.** Pretend you are the person in the middle. Write about "your" family.

1. Hi. My name is Names will vary.
2. In this picture, you see my family.
3. I have a big family.
4. My father is tall, and my mother is short.
5. I have two brothers and two sisters.

**20 Look and write.**

| | | |
|---|---|---|
| Who? | I | have one brother. |
| | My father | is tall. |
| | You | have five crayons. |
| What? | The flower | is yellow. |
| | The tree | is tall. |
| | The map | is on the table. |

1. ____________ have three sisters.
2. ____________ is short.
3. ____________ is green.
4. ____________ is on the desk.

38

**21 Listen and circle.** TR: 31

1

brother (sister)

2

(grandfather) grandmother

3

father (mother)

4

old (young)

5

(small) big

6

tall (short)

39

## Review

**1 Look.** Listen and circle. TR: 32

1.
2.
3.
4.
5.

40

**2 Look and write.**

1. What color is the rock? It's black.
2. What color are the clouds? They're white.
3. How many flowers? Five flowers.
4. Where is the sun? It's in the sky.
5. Where are the birds? They're on the rock.

**3 Listen and read. Circle.** TR: 33

| | |
|---|---|
| 1. How many brothers do you have? | How many sisters do you have? |
| 2. I don't have any sisters. | I have four sisters. |
| 3. Who's he? | Who's she? |
| 4. She's my baby sister. | He's my baby brother. |
| 5. He's young. | He's old. |
| 6. I have a small family. | I have a big family. |

41

Unit 4

# My House

**1 Look and match.** Write the number.

42

| | | | |
|---|---|---|---|
| 1 a bathroom | 6 a TV | 10 a lamp | |
| 7 a kitchen | 8 a dining room | 3 a mirror | |
| 9 a bed | 2 a bedroom | 5 a sofa | 4 a living room |

**2 Work with a partner.** Point. Ask and answer.

43

**3 Listen to the song. Circle.** TR: 34

1. Where do you sleep?

   I sleep in the ____.

   Is there a ____?

   Yes, there is.

2. Where do you eat?

   I eat in the ____.

   Is there a spoon?

   Yes, there is.

**4 Write a new verse for the song.**

Use some words from the boxes.

| | | |
|---|---|---|
| read<br>sit down | dining room<br>living room<br>kitchen<br>bedroom | chair<br>sofa<br>bed |

Where do you ____________?

I ____________ in the ____________.

Is there a ____________?

Yes, there is.

44

**GRAMMAR**

| | | |
|---|---|---|
| Is there a lamp in the bedroom? | Yes, **there is**. | **isn't** = is not |
| Is there a TV in the bedroom? | No, **there isn't**. | |

**5 Listen.** Circle. TR: 35

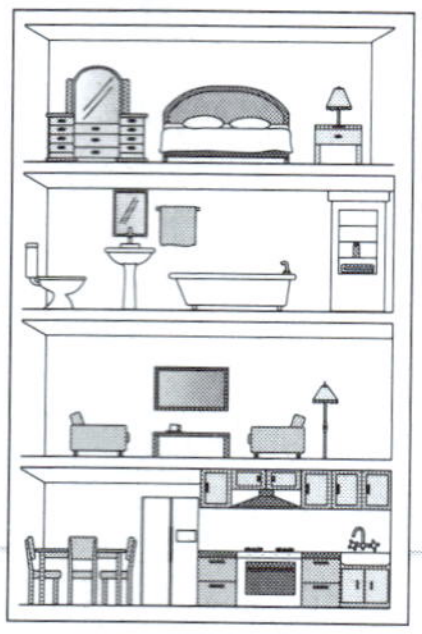

1. **Yes, there is.** No, there isn't.
2. Yes, there is. **No, there isn't.**
3. Yes, there is. **No, there isn't.**
4. **Yes, there is.** No, there isn't.
5. Yes, there is. **No, there isn't.**
6. **Yes, there is.** No, there isn't.
7. Yes, there is. **No, there isn't.**
8. Yes, there is. **No, there isn't.**

**6 Look and listen.** Write. TR: 36

1. Is there a TV in the living room?
   Yes, there is.
2. Is there a bed in the kitchen?
   No, there isn't.
3. Is there a lamp in the bathroom?
   No, there isn't.
4. Is there a lamp in the living room?
   Yes, there is.

45

**7 Circle one room in the list.** Draw it.

dining room
bedroom
living room
kitchen

**8 Write about your picture.**

1. What is your picture?
   It's a ____________.
2. Is there a table in your picture?
   ____________
3. Is there a sofa in your picture?
   ____________
4. Is there a mirror in your picture?
   ____________
5. Is there a lamp in your picture?
   ____________

46

**9 Look.** Read. Match. Draw lines.

a. Who's cooking?
b. Who's watching TV?
c. Who's cleaning?
d. Who's sleeping?
e. Who's eating?
f. Who's taking a bath?

1. 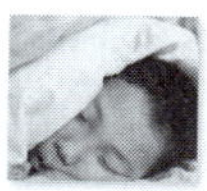
2. 
3. 
4. 
5. 
6. 

**10 Work with a partner.** Say. Find and answer.

1. She's watching TV. 6
2. He's cleaning. 2

47

**GRAMMAR**

| | | |
|---|---|---|
| Where's your father? | He's in the kitchen. He**'s cooking**. | 's cooking = is cooking |
| Where's your sister? | She's in the kitchen. She**'s eating**. | 's eating = is eating |

**11 Listen.** Circle. TR: 37

1. **She's cleaning.** She's cooking.
2. **He's sleeping.** He's cleaning.
3. **She's watching TV.** She's taking a bath.
4. He's taking a bath. **He's eating.**

**12 Look at the pictures.** Write.

1. Where's the baby?
   She's in the bedroom. She's sleeping.

2. Where's the brother?
   He's in the bathroom. He's taking a bath.

3. Where's the grandmother?
   She's in the kitchen. She's cooking.

4. Where's the father?
   He's in the living room. He's cleaning.

48

**13 Work with a partner.** Ask and find. Color. Write.

lamp mirror sofa
TV girl boy

**14 Look at the picture.** Read. Write.

1. Where's the girl?

 She's in the living room. She's watching TV.

2. Where's the boy?

 He's in the living room. He's reading.

49

**15 Listen and read.** TR: 38

# A House in the Trees

This house is in the trees. It is a tree house! A tree house can have a living room, a kitchen, and a bedroom.

**16 Read.** Circle *yes* or *no*.

| | | |
|---|---|---|
| 1. A tree house is in the sky. | yes | (no) |
| 2. There is a bedroom in the tree house. | (yes) | no |

50

**17 Look at the chart.** Read. Write.

Where is it? in the trees ← tree house → What rooms can it have? a living room, a kitchen, a bedroom

**18 Read and write.**

1. Where is a tree house?

 A tree house is in the trees.

2. What can a tree house have?

 A tree house can have a living room, a kitchen, and a bedroom.

**19 Draw a tree house.** Write.

What rooms does your tree house have?

__________

__________

51

**20 Look at the picture.** You are on the sofa. Color the sofa green. Color the lamp yellow. Color the TV black. Write about your living room.

1. Hi, I'm Names will vary.
2. In this picture, I am on the green sofa.
3. I am in the living room.
4. There is a yellow lamp.
5. There is a black TV.
6. I am watching TV.

**21 Look and write.**

| | | |
|---|---|---|
| Big letter: W I | **W**here's your father? **I**s he in the kitchen? | **?** |
| Big letter: Y T H | **Y**es, he's in the kitchen. **T**his is my father. **H**e's cooking. | **.** |

1. Where's your sister?
2. Is she in the dining room?
3. Yes, she's in the dining room.
4. She's eating.

52

**22 Look.** Read and circle.

1. Is there a frog in the kitchen?
   (Yes, there is.) No, there isn't.
2. Is there a lamp in the dining room?
   Yes, there is. (No, there isn't.)
3. Where's the sofa?
   It's in the dining room. (It's in the living room.)
4. Where's the bird?
   She's in the dining room. (She's in the living room.)

**23 Circle and draw.**

There is a **frog / monkey** in the **bedroom / living room**.
It's **cleaning / sleeping**.

53

Unit 5

# Cool Clothes

**1 Look and match.** Write the number.

54

| | | | | |
|---|---|---|---|---|
| 5 a dress | 10 a hat | 8 socks | 6 shoes | 4 a jacket |
| 7 gloves | 1 a T-shirt | 9 pants | 2 a skirt | 3 a shirt |

**2 Work with a partner.** Point. Ask and answer.

55

**3 Listen to the song.** Write. Read. Draw lines to match. Color. TR: 39

1. I'm wearing my brown shoes, and I really like them.
2. I'm wearing my purple pants, and I really like them.
3. I'm wearing my orange shirt, and I really like it.
4. I'm wearing my pink skirt, and I really like it.

**4 Write a new verse for the song!** Use some words from the box.

dress gloves hat jacket
shoes skirt socks T-shirt

I like my ________! I like my ________!
I like my ________! I like my ________!

56

GRAMMAR

| | | |
|---|---|---|
| What **are** you **wearing**? | **I'm wearing** white shoes. | **'m wearing** = am wearing |
| You're wearing white shoes. | | **'re wearing** = are wearing |
| What **is** he **wearing**? | My brother**'s wearing** a hat. | **'s wearing** = is wearing |

**5 Listen.** Write. TR: 40

1. What __are__ you wearing?
   I'm wearing a skirt.
2. What are you wearing?
   __I'm__ __wearing__ a jacket.
3. What are you __wearing__?
   I'm wearing a T-shirt.
4. What is your brother wearing?
   My __brother's__ wearing pants.

**6 Listen.** Look at the chart. Read. Check. TR: 41

| | Mother | Father |
|---|---|---|
| skirt | ✓ | |
| dress | | |
| pants | | ✓ |
| socks | | ✓ |
| shoes | ✓ | ✓ |
| shirt | ✓ | ✓ |

57

**7 Work with a partner.** Draw your partner. What is your partner wearing? Ask and answer.

**8 Write about your picture.**

1. What is __Name will vary.__ wearing?
2. ______ wearing ______

58

**9 Look at the picture.** Write. Use words from the box.

closet
shelf
skirt
gloves

__closet__
__shelf__
__gloves__
__skirt__

**10 Listen.** Look at the picture. Color. TR: 42

**11 Look at the picture.** Read and write.

1. Where is the shelf?
   __The shelf is in the closet.__
2. Where are the gloves? __The gloves are on the shelf. or The gloves are in the closet.__
3. What color is the hat?
   __The hat is purple.__
4. What color are the shoes?
   __The shoes are brown.__
5. What color is the skirt?
   __The skirt is pink.__

59

GRAMMAR

| | | |
|---|---|---|
| What**'s that**? | **That's** my pink hat. | **'s that** = is that |
| What **are those**? | **Those are** my brown pants. | **That's** = That is |

**12 Listen.** Write the number. TR: 43

**13 Listen and write.** Listen again to the audio in Activity 12.

1. __What's that__?
   __That's__ my dress.
2. What __are those__?
   Those are my socks.
3. What are those?
   __Those are__ my gloves.
4. __What's__ that?
   __That's__ my jacket.
5. What's __that__?
   That's my shirt.
6. What __are those__?
   Those are my shoes.

60

**14** **Play a game.** Cut out the cards and the closet on page 121. Color the cards. Put them in the closet and on the shelf. Play with a partner. Point. Ask and answer.

**15** **Listen and draw a line.** TR: 44

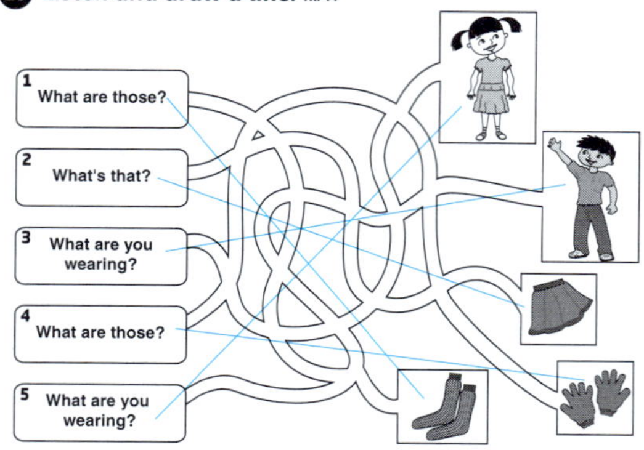


61

**16** **Listen and read.** TR: 45

# Clothes for Work

People all over the world wear special clothes to work. Some people wear gloves and hats to work.

A chef wears special clothes for cooking.

a doctor

a builder

a police officer

**17** **Read.** Look. Circle *yes* or *no*.

1. The chef wears a tall hat to cook. (yes) no
2. The chef wears gloves. yes (no)

62

**18** **Look at Activity 16.** Check ✓ the clothes.

| | chef | doctor | builder | police officer |
|---|---|---|---|---|
| hat | ✓ | | ✓ | ✓ |
| gloves | | ✓ | | ✓ |
| shirt | | ✓ | | ✓ |
| T-shirt | | | ✓ | |
| pants | | ✓ | ✓ | ✓ |
| shoes | | ✓ | ✓ | ✓ |
| skirt | | | | |
| jacket | ✓ | | | |

**19** **Read and write.**

1. The chef is wearing a hat and a jacket.
2. The doctor is wearing gloves, a shirt, pants, and shoes.
3. The builder is wearing a hat, a T-shirt, pants, and shoes.
4. The police officer is wearing a hat, gloves, a shirt, pants, and shoes.

**20** **What do you wear to school?** Write. Ask a partner. Write.

I wear ______________________ to school.

______________ wears ______________________.

63

**21** **Look at the picture.** Write about the clothes.

1. The chef is wearing a tall white hat.
2. She is wearing a white jacket.
3. She is wearing black and white pants.
4. She is wearing two black shoes.

**22** **What's in your closet?** Write about the clothes in your closet. Use color words.

pink purple brown blue red green black white yellow

______________________

______________________

______________________

______________________

______________________

64

**23** **Color.** Read and write.

1. What's that?
   That's a hat.
2. What are those?
   Those are stars.
3. What is the boy wearing?
   He's wearing a hat, a jacket, pants, and shoes.
4. What is the girl wearing? She's wearing a hat, a shirt/ dress, a skirt, socks, and shoes.
5. What color is the skirt?
   Answers will vary.
6. What is in the closet?
   A dress is in the closet.

65

Unit 6

# My Toys

**1** **Look and match.**
Write the number.

| | | | |
|---|---|---|---|
| 8 | a kite | 1 | a top |
| 10 | a ball | 4 | a car |
| 6 | a drum | 7 | a puppet |
| 9 | a train | 5 | a game |
| 3 | a bike | 2 | a truck |

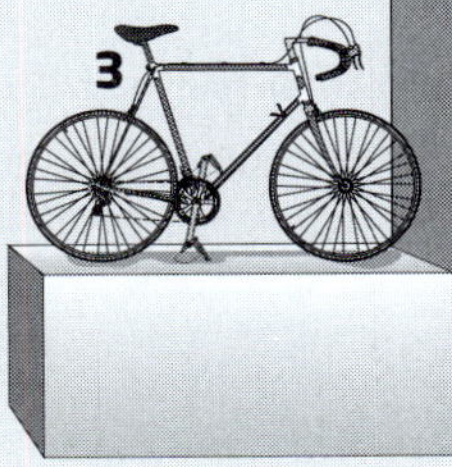

66

**2** **Work with a partner.**
Point. Ask and answer.

67

**3** **Listen to the song.** Check. TR: 46

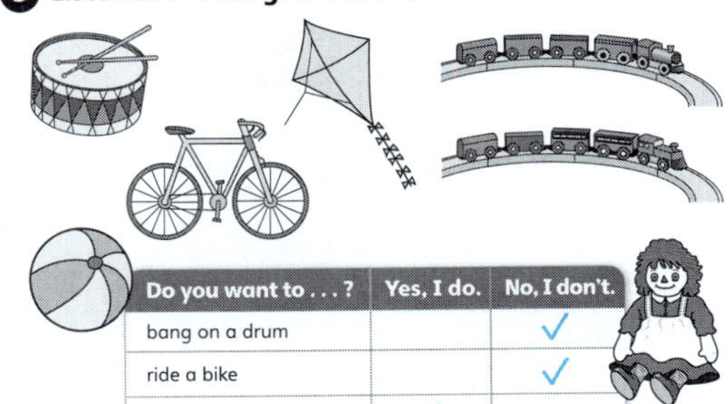

| Do you want to . . . ? | Yes, I do. | No, I don't. |
|---|---|---|
| bang on a drum | | ✓ |
| ride a bike | | ✓ |
| fly a kite | ✓ | |
| dress my doll | | ✓ |
| kick a ball | | ✓ |
| play with trains | ✓ | |

**4** **Listen.** Write. TR: 47

ball bike doll drum kite trains

1. Do you want to bang on a drum?
2. Do you want to ride a bike?
3. Do you want to fly a kite?
4. Do you want to dress my doll?
5. Do you want to kick a ball?
6. Do you want to play with trains?

68

**GRAMMAR**

| | | |
|---|---|---|
| **Do** you **want** a top? | No, I **don't**. | **don't** = do not |
| **Do** you **want** a car? | Yes, I **do**. | |
| **Does** he **want** a top? | Yes, he **does**. | |
| **Does** she **want** a top? | No, she **doesn't**. She wants a car. | **doesn't** = does not |

**5 Listen and read.** Circle. TR: 48

1. Yes, I do. — No, I don't. (circled)
2. Yes, I do. — No, I don't. (circled)
3. Yes, she does. (circled) — No, she doesn't.
4. Yes, he does. — No, he doesn't. (circled)
5. Yes, I do. (circled) — No, I don't.
6. Yes, she does. — No, she doesn't. (circled)

**6 Listen and read.** Draw a line. TR: 49

1. Do you want a car?
2. Does she want a drum?
3. Does he want a ball?
4. Do you want a train?

No, I don't. I want a bike.

Yes, I do. I want a car.

Yes, she does. She wants a drum.

No, he doesn't. He wants a kite.

69

**7 Listen.** Write. TR: 50

1. Do you want a ball?
   No, I don't.
2. Does she want a truck?
   No, she doesn't.
3. Does she want a train?
   Yes, she does.
4. Do you want a bike?
   Yes, I do.

**8 Look.** Read and write.

1. Does the boy want a truck? No, he doesn't.
2. Does the girl want a bike? No, she doesn't.
3. Does the boy want a ball? Yes, he does.
4. Does the boy want a drum? No, he doesn't.
5. Does the girl want a train? Yes, she does.

70

**9 Look at the picture.** Write.

board game doll puzzle robot teddy bear

doll

teddy bear

puzzle

robot

board game

**10 What about you?** Read. Check ✓. Then ask a partner. Check.

| | I want | I don't want | My partner wants | My partner doesn't want |
|---|---|---|---|---|
| a doll | | | | |
| a teddy bear | | | | |
| a board game | | | | |
| a robot | | | | |
| a puzzle | | | | |

71

**GRAMMAR**

| | | |
|---|---|---|
| **Is this** your puzzle? | No, **it** isn't. It's Marco's puzzle. | **isn't** = is not **It's** = It is |
| **Are these** your dolls? | No, **they** aren't. They're Anita's dolls. | **aren't** = are not **They're** = They are |

**11 Write.**

1. Is this your robot?
2. Are these your teddy bears?
3. Are these your puzzles?
4. Is this your board game?
5. Are these your robots?
6. Is this Mia's puppet?
7. Is this Anya's drum?
8. Are these Ivan's puzzles?

**12 Listen and write.** TR: 51

1. Yes, it is.
2. No, they aren't.
3. No, they aren't.
4. No, it isn't.
5. Yes, they are.
6. No, it isn't.
7. Yes, it is.
8. Yes, they are.

72

**13 Play a game.** Cut out the game board and cards on page 123. Take a card. Read the word. Match the word to the picture. Play with a partner. Take turns.

**14 Look at the pictures.** Circle the words.

| | | | | | | | | | |
|---|---|---|---|---|---|---|---|---|---|
| g | a | m | e | t | b | i | c | k | l |
| a | z | o | m | u | i | z | c | a | r |
| n | t | r | u | c | k | a | z | k | o |
| e | r | d | o | b | e | l | o | i | b |
| b | a | l | l | x | l | a | f | t | o |
| k | i | s | r | p | u | p | p | e | t |
| s | n | f | p | u | z | z | l | e | e |
| u | g | d | r | u | m | m | a | s | l |
| m | d | o | l | l | u | z | z | m | p |

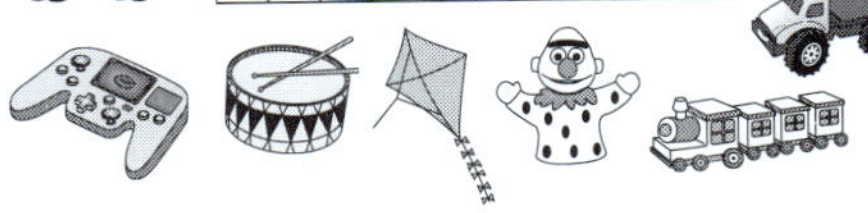

73

**15 Listen and read.** TR: 52

# We ♥ Kites

This kite looks like a fish.

These kites are in a kite museum in China.

People around the world love kites. People fly kites. There are even kite museums! This kite museum is in China. It has big kites and small kites. Some kites look like birds. Some kites look like butterflies. Some kites look like fish!

**16 Read. Look.** Circle *yes* or *no*.

1. There are kite museums. (yes) no
2. This museum is in China. (yes) no
3. There are robots and trains in the museum. yes (no)

74

**17 Look at the chart.** Read. Write.

Kite Museum

- Where: China
- What: big kites, small kites, fish kites, butterfly kites, bird kites

**18 Look and read.** Match. Write the number.

1. This kite is a bird.
2. A butterfly is on this kite.
3. This kite is a teddy bear.

75

**19 Look at the picture.** Write about the toys.

1. A doll, a car, and a train are on the shelf.
2. A puzzle and a board game are on the table.
3. There is a big robot.
4. The girl wants a puppet.
5. The boy wants a drum.

**20 What do you want?** Draw a toy you want. Write about it.

This is the toy I want.

What is it? It's a ________.

Is it big or small? It's ________.

What color is it? This ________ is ________.

76

**21** **Listen and circle.** TR: 53

(Yes, he does.)
No, he doesn't.

Yes, she does.
(No, she doesn't.)

(Is this your robot?)
Are these your robots?

No, it isn't.
It's Mateo's car.
(No, they aren't.
They're Mateo's cars.)

(No, I don't.
I want a car.)
Yes, I do.
I want a puppet.

(Do you want a truck?)
Do you want a train?

77

## Review

**1** **Listen and read. Circle.** TR: 54

1. (He's in the bathroom.) He's in the bedroom.
2. I'm wearing a pink shirt. (I'm wearing a pink skirt.)
3. (That's my brown truck.) Those are my brown tops.
4. (Those are my dolls.) Those are my balls.
5. (No, I don't.) Yes, I do.
6. No, he doesn't. (Yes, he does.)

**2** **Listen and write.** TR: 55

1. Is this your hat?
   No, it isn't. It's my mother's hat.

2. Are these your pants?
   No, they aren't. They're my brother's pants.

3. What's that?
   That's my robot.

4. What are those?
   Those are my socks.

78

**3** **Listen.** Look at the picture. Color. TR: 56

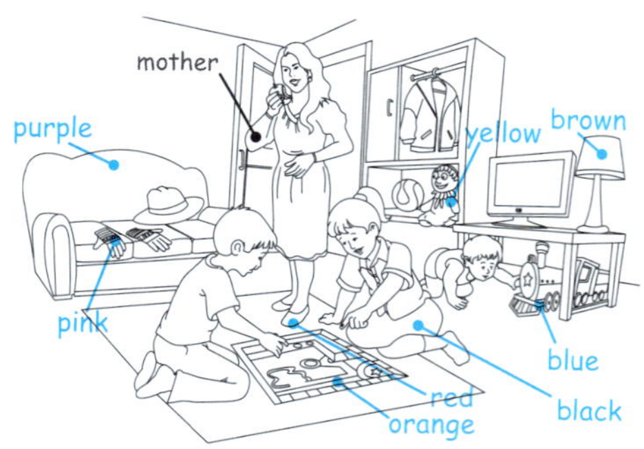


**4** **Look at the picture.** Write.

1. The mother is in the living room. She's eating.
2. A hat and gloves are on the sofa.
3. A jacket is in the closet.
4. Is there a teddy bear on the shelf?
   No, there isn't.
5. Is there a TV in the living room?
   Yes, there is.
6. What does the baby want?
   The baby wants a train.

79

Unit 7

# My Body

**1** **Look and write.**

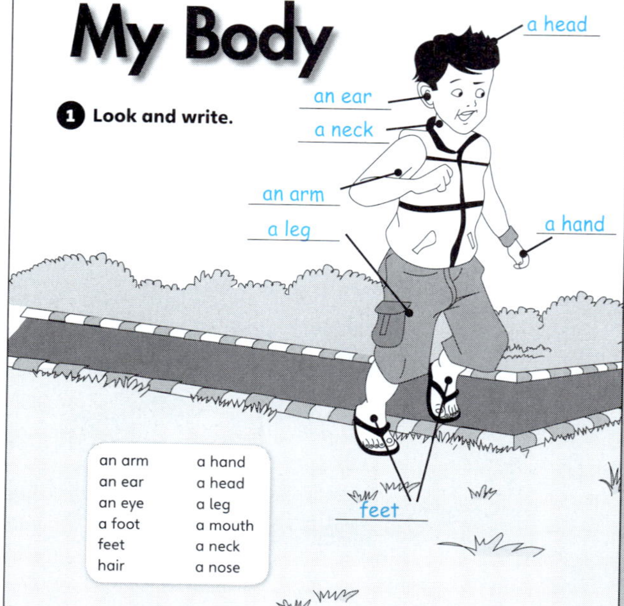


| | |
|---|---|
| an arm | a hand |
| an ear | a head |
| an eye | a leg |
| a foot | a mouth |
| feet | a neck |
| hair | a nose |

80

**2** **Work with a partner.** Point. Ask and answer. Take turns.

81

**3** **Listen to the song.** Use words from the box. Write. TR: 57

clap feet hands jump
legs mouth sing walk

1. Legs, legs. Move your __legs__.
Can you __walk__ with me?
2. Feet, feet. Move your __feet__.
Can you __jump__ with me?
3. Mouth, mouth. Move your __mouth__.
Can you __sing__ with me?
4. Hands, hands. Move your __hands__.
Can you __clap__ with me?

**4** **Listen and draw.** Add labels. Use words from the box. TR: 58

body
legs
feet
mouth
hands

Students should draw a person dancing, and label the body, legs, feet, mouth, and hands.

82

**GRAMMAR**

I have black hair. **My** hair is black.
You have black hair. **Your** hair is black.
Nico has black hair. **His** hair is black.
Rosa has black hair. **Her** hair is black.
You and I have black hair. **Our** hair is black.
You and Nico have black hair. **Your** hair is black.
Nico and Rosa have black hair. **Their** hair is black.

**5** **Listen and read.** Circle. TR: 59

| | |
|---|---|
| 1. **My nose is small.** | Your nose is small. |
| 2. My eyes are green. | **Her eyes are green.** |
| 3. **Your hands are small.** | His hands are small. |
| 4. Her mouth is red. | **His mouth is red.** |
| 5. **Our hands are small.** | Their hands are small. |

**6** **Listen and read.** Circle. TR: 60

| | | | | |
|---|---|---|---|---|
| 1. | | **Her** | His | feet are small. |
| 2. | | His | **My** | feet are big. |
| 3. | | Her | **His** | hands are big. |
| 4. | | His | **Her** | hands are small. |
| 5. | Is | **your** | my | nose small? |

83

**7** **Look.** Write about the girl and her grandfather. Use words from the box.

Her His

1. She is short.
__Her__ legs are short.
__Her__ arms are short.
2. He is tall.
__His__ feet are big.
__His__ hands are big.
3. Look at her head.
__Her__ hair is black.
__Her__ mouth is small.
__Her__ nose is small.
4. Look at his head.
__His__ hair is white.
__His__ mouth is big.
__His__ nose is big.

**8** **What about you?** Write about your head.

1. __My__ hair is ______________.
2. __My__ mouth is ______________.
3. __My__ nose is ______________.
4. __My__ eyes are ______________.

84

**9** **Look and read.** Circle.

1. walk run

2. run jump

3. walk run

4. strong legs small legs

5. short neck long neck

6. strong arms short arms

**10** **Work with a partner.** Read. Ask and answer. Check.

| | me | my partner |
|---|---|---|
| strong legs | | |
| long legs | | |
| jump | | |
| long hair | | |
| walk | | |
| strong hands | | |
| run | | |

85

GRAMMAR

I **can** jump. He **can** run. She **can** run.

**Can** you jump? Yes, I **can**.

**11** **Listen.** Write. TR: 61

1. No. He _can_ walk.
2. _Can_ his sister jump?
3. Yes, she _can_ run.
4. _Can_ the baby run?

**12** **Look at the photos.** Read. Write.

1. Can the father cook?
_Yes_, he _can or can cook_.

3. Can the baby sister cook?
_No_, she _can eat_.

2. Can the brother clean?
_Yes_, he _can or can clean_.

4. Can she watch TV?
_Yes_, she _can or can watch TV_.

86

**13** **Play a game.** Cut out the cards on page 119. Take a card. Read the question. Answer. Take turns.

**14** **Read and match.** Write fun sentences.

| | | |
|---|---|---|
| Can you | walk | on the grass? |
| Can a baby | run | in the ocean? |
| Can a mother | jump | on one foot? |
| Can he | cook | on two feet? |
| Can she | sleep | in a river? |
| Can I | eat | in a kitchen? |
| | | in a bedroom? |

1. _Can you cook in a kitchen?_
2. ______
3. ______
4. ______

**15** **Read the questions in Activity 14.** Write answers.

1. ______
2. ______
3. ______
4. ______

87

**16** **Listen and read.** TR: 62

# Polar Bears

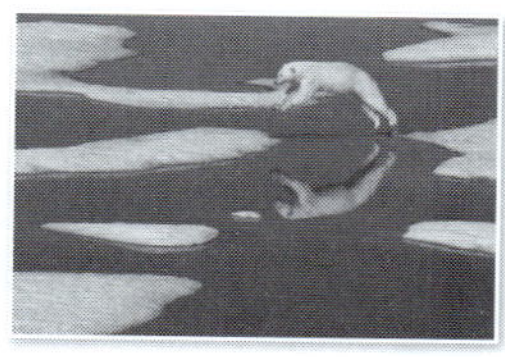

These bears are polar bears. The small polar bears are babies. Their legs are short. Their mother is big. She has a big body. Her head is small. Her eyes and ears are small. Polar bears can walk and jump. Their legs are strong. A polar bear can stand on two legs!

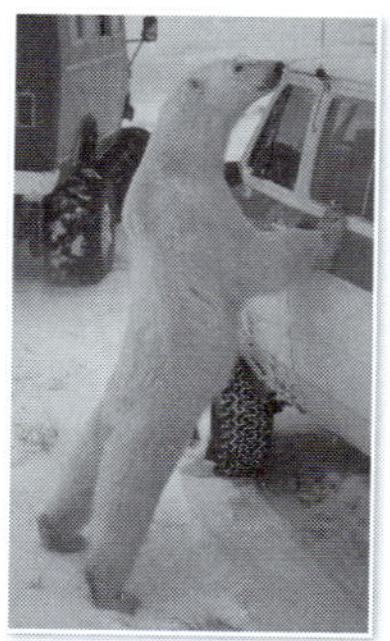

**17** **Read.** Circle.

1. A mother polar bear is **big.** **small.**
2. Baby polar bears are **big.** **small.**
3. Polar bears have strong **arms.** **legs.**
4. A mother polar bear has a **big** **small** head.
5. A mother polar bear has a **big** **small** body.
6. Baby polar bears have **short** **long** legs.

88

**18** **Look at the chart.** Read. Write.

Big Polar Bear

What does it have?
a big body
a small head
small eyes
small ears
strong legs

What can it do?
stand on two legs
walk
jump

**19** **Read and write.**

1. A big polar bear has a small head.
2. It has strong legs.
3. A big polar bear can stand on two legs.

**20** **What about you?** What do you have? What doesn't a polar bear have? Write.

I have ______.

A polar bear doesn't have ______.

89

**21** **Draw a picture of yourself.** Write about your body. Use words from the box.

| | | | | | |
|---|---|---|---|---|---|
| arms | ears | eyes | hair | hands | head |
| legs | mouth | neck | nose | foot | feet |

My name is ______.

I have ______.

I have ______.

My ______ is ______.

My ______ is ______.

I have ______.

**22** **Look and write.**

| Who? What? | has, have, is, are |
|---|---|
| She | has short hair. |
| I | have long hair. |
| My hair | is brown. |
| Her hair | is black. |
| Her eyes | are green. |

1. He has long legs.
2. Her legs are ______.
3. My eyes are ______.
4. His nose is ______.

90

**23** **Read.** Look at the picture. Circle.

1. He can jump.
2. His legs are long.
3. Its neck is long.
4. Its ears are long.
5. Her arms are strong.

**24** **Look at the picture.** Read. Write.

1. Who can run? She/The girl can run.
2. Who can eat? She/The mother can eat.
3. Who can sleep? The baby can sleep.
4. Who can jump? He/The boy can jump.

91

Unit 8

# Good Food

**1** **Look and write.**

| | | | | | |
|---|---|---|---|---|---|
| 10 | a salad | 6 | an egg | 2 | an apple |
| 9 | rice | 12 | soup | 7 | fish |
| 4 | chicken | 5 | a cookie | 1 | a banana |
| 3 | an orange | 11 | a sandwich | 8 | a cheese pizza |

92

**2** **Work with a partner.** Ask. Point and answer.

93

**3** **Listen to the song.** Read. Draw lines to match. TR: 63

1. Pizza?
I like pizza!

2. Apples?
I like apples!

3. Chicken?
I like chicken!

**4** **Listen to the song.** Write. Use words from the box. TR: 64

Do you want a cookie ?

Do you want some cheese ?

Do you want a banana ?

Yes, please!

banana cheese cookie

**5** **Write a new verse for the song!** Use some words from the box.

Do you want ________________?

Do you want ________________?

Do you want ________________?

Yes, please!

an apple
some chicken
an egg
some fish
an orange
some rice
a salad

94

**GRAMMAR**

| | |
|---|---|
| **Do** you **like** eggs? No, I **don't**. I **don't like** eggs. | don't = do not |
| **Do** you **like** soup? Yes, I **do**. I **like** soup. | |
| **Does** he **like** eggs? No, he **doesn't**. He **doesn't like** eggs. | doesn't = does not |
| **Does** he **like** soup? Yes, he **does**. He **likes** soup. | |

**6** **Listen.** Write. TR: 65

1. Do you like salad?
2. Does she like fish?
3. Do you like oranges?
4. Does he like bananas?
5. Do you like sandwiches?

**7** **Listen.** Write. TR: 66

1. No, I don't. I don't like salad.
2. Yes, she does. She likes fish.
3. Yes, I do. I like oranges.
4. No, he doesn't. He doesn't like bananas.
5. No, I don't. I don't like sandwiches.

95

**8** **Work with a partner.** Ask and answer. Look at the chart. Check ✓ the foods you like. Make an ✗ for the foods you don't like.

| | You like | You don't like | Your partner likes | Your partner doesn't like |
|---|---|---|---|---|
| bananas | | | | |
| soup | | | | |
| eggs | | | | |
| apples | | | | |
| rice | | | | |
| fish | | | | |

**9** **What about you?** Look at the chart. Write the foods you like ☺. Write the foods you don't like ☹.

☺ ________________________________

________________________________

☹ ________________________________

________________________________

96

**10 Look and read.** Color.

1. Color the lemonade yellow.
2. Color the tea brown.
3. Color the milk white.
4. Color the orange juice orange.
5. What does not have a color? water

**11 What do you like?** Read. Check ✓. Ask a partner. Do you like the same things?

| | I like | I don't like | My partner likes | My partner doesn't like |
|---|---|---|---|---|
| milk | | | | |
| water | | | | |
| orange juice | | | | |
| tea | | | | |
| lemonade | | | | |

**12 Look at the chart.** Write what you like.

I like ______________.

**GRAMMAR**

| | |
|---|---|
| **an** orange | **a** banana |
| **an** eraser | **a** pizza |
| **an** arm | **a** leg |

**13 Listen.** Write. TR: 67

1. Do you have __a__ crayon?
2. I have __an__ old pen.
3. Does a fish have __an__ ear?
4. Does the puppet have __a__ mouth?

**14 Read.** Write. Use *an* or *a*.

1. I am eating __an__ apple.
2. She has ______ orange.
3. Do you have __a__ banana?
4. No, I have __a__ salad.
5. He is eating __a__ cheese pizza.
6. I want __an__ egg.
7. Do you want __a__ cookie?
8. Does the fish have __an__ eye?
9. Does the puppet have __a__ neck?



**15 Look at the picture.** Read. Color.

1. Color the salad green.
2. Color the rice white.
3. Color the chicken yellow.
4. Color the cookies brown.
5. Color the apple red.
6. Color the oranges orange.

**16 Play a game.** Start at **A**. Listen. Go through the maze to the house. TR: 68

**17 Look at the maze.** What foods are there? Write.

an apple, a salad, a cookie, an orange, soup, a pizza, a fish, an egg, a sandwich, a chicken, milk



**18 Listen and read.** TR: 69

# Fruit

Every day, people eat fruit. Many people grow fruit. Some people grow fruit on farms. Some people grow fruit at home. Some people grow fruit trees. Apples, oranges, and lemons are fruits. They grow on trees. People can eat the fruit. They can make juice from the fruit. People can make lemonade from lemon juice and water.

Some people grow fruit on farms.

A family is growing a lemon tree at home.

**19 Read.** Circle *yes* or *no*.

1. Many people grow fruit. (yes) no
2. Some people grow on trees. yes (no)
3. Oranges grow on trees. (yes) no

**20** **Look at the chart.** Read. Write.

| Fruit | | |
|---|---|---|
| Where do people grow fruit? | What fruits grow on trees? | What can people do with fruit? |
| on farms | lemons | eat it |
| at home | apples | make juice |
| | oranges | |

**21** **Read and write.**

1. Where do people grow fruit?
   People grow fruit on farms and at home.
2. What fruits grow on trees?
   Lemons, apples, and oranges grow on trees.
3. What can people do with fruit?
   They can eat it and make juice.

**22** **Match.** Look. Read. Write the number.

1. 
2. 
3. 

[2] This is an apple tree.
[1] These are orange trees.
[3] This is a lemon tree.

101

**23** **Look at the picture.** Write what the family likes to eat and drink.

1. The father likes salad.
2. The mother likes lemonade.
3. The girl is eating a banana.
4. Her brother is eating an egg.

**24** **Read and write.**

| Who? | What? |
|---|---|
| I / You | like pizza. |
| The girl | likes milk. |
| The boy | likes orange juice. |

1. He ______.
2. She ______.
3. I ______.
4. You ______.

102

**25** **Look at the picture.** Read. Write.

1. What is the girl eating?
   She is eating fish, rice, and salad.
2. What does the boy have?
   He has an egg, a sandwich, water, and a banana.
3. What is the grandmother eating?
   The grandmother is eating an apple.
4. What does the grandfather like?
   The grandfather likes soup.
5. Who likes tea?
   The grandmother likes tea.

**26** **Listen.** Circle. TR: 70

| | |
|---|---|
| 1. Yes, I do. I like milk. | (No, I don't. I like orange juice.) |
| 2. (Yes, I do. I like water.) | No, I don't. I don't like water. |
| 3. (Yes, I do. I like lemonade.) | No, I don't. I like tea. |

103

Unit 9

# Animal Friends

**1** **Look and match.** Write the number.

| | |
|---|---|
| [3] a goat | [12] a cow |
| [11] a chicken | [6] a horse |
| [1] a cat | [10] a dog |
| [9] a duck | [8] a turtle |
| [2] a frog | [5] a sheep |
| [4] a rabbit | [7] a donkey |

104

**2** **Work with a partner.** Ask. Point and answer.

**3** **Listen to the song.** Write. Read. Draw lines to match. TR: 71

1. I see one dog.
   Is it running?
   Yes, it's running.
2. I see two cats.
   Are they climbing?
   Yes, they're climbing.
3. I see three frogs.
   Are they hopping?
   Yes, they're hopping.

**4** **Write a new verse for the song!** Use words from the boxes.

| | | |
|---|---|---|
| goats | eating | on the grass |
| rabbits | sleeping | in the sun |
| donkeys | walking | on a mountain |

I see five ________.

Are they ________?

Yes, they're ________.

They're ________ ________.



**GRAMMAR**

What **are** the goats **doing?** They**'re eating.**
**Are** they **running?** No, they **aren't.**
**Are** they **walking?** Yes, they **are.**

They're = They are
aren't = are not

**5** **Listen.** Write. TR: 72

1. What are the cats doing?
2. What are the horses doing?
3. What are the goats doing?
4. What are the cows doing?
5. What are the sheep doing?

**6** **Listen.** Write. TR: 73

1. They're running.
2. They're jumping.
3. They're eating.
4. They're walking.
5. They're sleeping.



**7** **Look.** Read. Write.

1. What are the frogs doing? They're jumping.
2. What are the ducks doing? They're eating.
3. What are the donkeys doing? They're walking.
4. What are they dogs doing? They're sleeping.

**8** **Look at the picture.** Read. Circle.

1. Are the rabbits jumping? Yes, they are. No, they aren't.
2. Are the chickens running? Yes, they are. No, they aren't.
3. Are the cats eating? Yes, they are. No, they aren't.

**9** **Work with a partner.**
Ask and answer.

**10 Look.** Read. Match. Write the numbers.

1. The goat is climbing.
2. The cat is crawling.
3. The sheep see a dog.
4. The ducks are swimming.
5. The ducks are flying.

3

5

4

1

2

**11 Listen.** Read. Write. TR: 74

1. I see two turtles.
2. The turtles are crawling.
3. The chicken is flying.
4. A girl is climbing.

109

**GRAMMAR**

| | | |
|---|---|---|
| **Do** you **want to see** the cow? | No, I don't. | don't = do not |
| **Does** he **want to see** the cow? | No, he doesn't. | doesn't = does not |
| What **do** you **want to do**? | I **want to see** the frog. | |
| What **does** Ivan **want to do**? | He **wants to ride** the horse. | |

**12 Listen.** Write. TR: 75

1. Do you want to ride a horse?
2. What do you want to do?
3. Does Lena want to see the goats?
4. What does she want to do?
5. Do you want to see the chickens?

**13 Listen.** Circle. TR: 76

1. No, I don't. (circled) No, she doesn't.
2. I want to see the goats. (circled)
   She wants to see the goats.
3. No, I don't. No, she doesn't. (circled)
4. I want to ride the donkey.
   She wants to ride the donkey. (circled)
5. No, I don't. (circled) No, she doesn't.

110

**14 Look at the picture.** What are the animals doing? Read. Check. ✓

| | birds | chickens | frogs | goats | rabbits |
|---|---|---|---|---|---|
| eating | | ✓ | | | |
| swimming | | | ✓ | | |
| flying | ✓ | | | | |
| sleeping | | | | | ✓ |
| climbing | | | | ✓ | |

**15 Write questions.** Ask a partner. Write the answers.

| | | |
|---|---|---|
| Do you<br>Does she<br>Does he<br>Does a turtle<br>Does a dog | want to see<br>want to ride | six donkeys?<br>two horses?<br>a bike?<br>a goat?<br>three sheep? |

1. Do you want to see a goat? Yes, I do.
2. ______________________ ______________
3. ______________________ ______________
4. ______________________ ______________

111

**16 Listen and read.** TR: 77

# More Baby Animals

A baby turtle comes from an egg. Do you see the egg?

You know about some baby animals. Let's learn about more baby animals. A baby cow is called a calf. Baby horses and baby donkeys are called foals. Baby goats are called kids. Some animals come from eggs. Ducks and turtles come from eggs. Baby ducks are called ducklings. Baby turtles are called hatchlings. There are many baby animals!

112

**17 Read.** Circle *yes* or *no*.

1. Ducks come from eggs. (yes) no
2. Baby cows are called kids. yes (no)
3. Hatchlings are baby turtles. (yes) no

**18 Read and write.**

| Animal | Baby animal |
|---|---|
| duck | duckling |
| turtle | hatchling |
| cow | calf |
| horse | foal |
| donkey | foal |
| goat | kid |

**19 Read and write.**

1. What is a baby duck called? a duckling
2. How many animals have babies called foals? two
3. What is a baby cow called? a calf

113

**20 Look at the picture.** The boy's name is Ivan. He has ducks. Color the ducks. Write about them.

1. How many ducks does Ivan have?
   Ivan has three ducks.
2. What are their names?
   Their names are ______.
3. What colors are the ducks?
   They're ______.
4. What are the ducks doing?
   Sample answer: They're eating, flying, and swimming.

**21 Circle the animal you want.** Color it.
Write about it.
What color is it?
What is it doing?

I want ______

114

**22 Look.** Read. Write.

1. What does the girl want to do?
   She wants to see the cats.
2. Does the boy want to see the sheep? No, he doesn't.
3. What does the boy want to do?
   He wants to climb the tree.
4. What do the sheep want to do? They want to eat.

**23 Play a game.** Cut out the cards on page 125. Play with a partner. Ask and answer.

115

## Review

**1 Listen.** Circle. TR: 78

1. (Do you like sheep?) Does he like sheep?
2. (Yes, I do. I like sheep.) No, I don't. I don't like sheep.
3. Yes, she does. She likes lemonade. (No, she doesn't. She likes milk.)
4. (I can climb. I have strong arms.) He can climb. He has strong arms.
5. The chicken can swim. (The chicken can fly.)
6. (I want to ride a donkey.) She wants to ride a donkey.

**2 Write and match.**

1. I see a cow.
2. I want to eat an egg.
3. Does a rabbit have long ears?
4. I want to eat an apple.
5. Does he want to eat an orange?

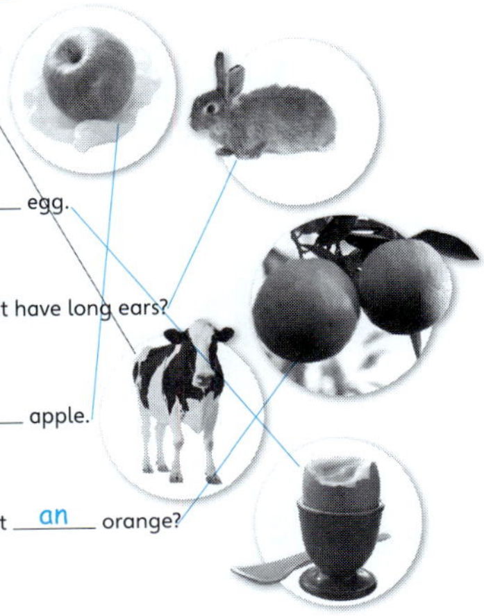

116

**3** **Read.** Look at the picture. Circle.

1. The turtle has a long neck.
2. The goat likes sandwiches.
3. She likes salad.
4. Her hair is long. She has a sandwich.
5. His hand is on his ear. His foot is on the rock.

**4** **Look at the picture.** Read. Circle.

1. What are the horses doing?
   They're walking. They're running.
2. What is the frog doing?
   It's swimming. It's jumping.
3. Are the goats sleeping?
   Yes, they are. They're sleeping. No, they aren't. They're eating.
4. Are the ducks swimming?
   Yes, they are. They're swimming. No, they aren't. They're flying.

117

**Unit 1** Use with Activity 15 on page 11.

| | | | | | |
|---|---|---|---|---|---|
| t | p | r | e | o | l |
| m | a | c | i | p | b |
| d | o | i | e | l | n |
| s | r | c | h | k | y |

**Unit 7** Use with Activity 13 on page 87.

| | | | | |
|---|---|---|---|---|
| Can you jump? | Can you run on the grass? | Can you walk on the moon? | Can you cook? | Can you watch TV? |
| Can you clean your bedroom? | Can you eat a cloud? | Can you sing? | Can you walk? | |

119

**Unit 5** Use with Activity 14 on page 61.

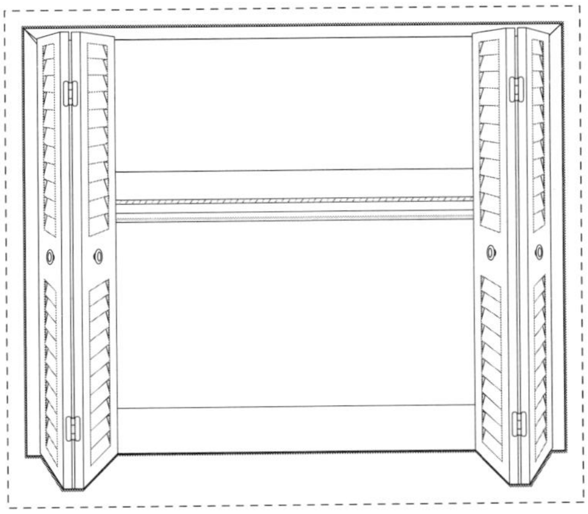



**Unit 6** Use with Activity 13 on page 73.

| | | | |
|---|---|---|---|
| a robot | a puppet | a drum | a truck |
| a ball | a drum | a bike | a puzzle |
| a puppet | a kite | a doll | a train |

**Unit 9** Use with Activity 23 on page 115.

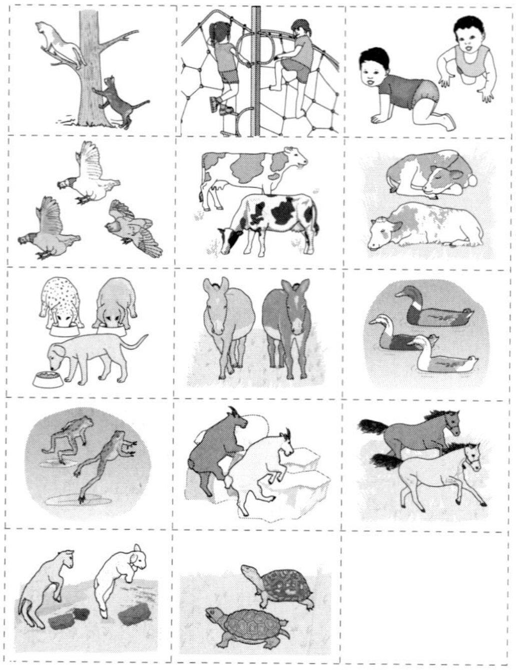

125